The Sports Tourists' Guide to the English Premier League

2018-19 Edition

ISBN: 978-1-54395-860-7

Silver Way Publishing Inc.
1123 MD Rte 3 N Suite 207
Gambrills, MD, 21054
www.silverwaypublishing.com

Printed in the United States of America

To our wonderful wives, Victoria and Megan, without whose encouragement, support and grace this book would've never happened.

Table of Contents

Introduction

Thank you very much for your purchase of The Sports Tourists Guide to the English Premier League, the 2018-19 edition.

If this is your first time reading our Premier League primer, congratulations. We hope what you hold in your hand is the best resource you could possibly have in terms of Premier League history, club history, current events, ticketing and travel tips, and more. To help you understand exactly what's inside, we've reprinted the introduction to the our original book from a year ago, below.

If you bought our book previously and are back for the second edition, we thank you from the bottom of our hearts. Your continued support and kind words are what led us to do this again.

Last time we had nine weeks... this time, just three (and our day jobs barely gave us that!) But we pulled off the organizational feat of seeing 20 games in 22 days over late September and early October of this season.

We've updated all of the team histories, tips, numbers and tables – including in the promotion/relegation and cup chapters. We've added full histories of the newly-promoted teams – Cardiff City, Fulham and Wolves.

We've also written a brand-new essay for every team. Remember, the essays were written at a certain moment and time of the season, and are based on our individual experience. Everyone will have a different point of view and that's what makes it fun.

Again, take a look at last year's introduction for a reminder of exactly what's inside the book. Or, just skip to the chapter for your favorite team and start poking around.

The first time I walked into Slainté, just off the cobblestone streets of Fells Point in Baltimore, I felt like I was walking into a secret club.

It was a bright, sunny, fall Saturday before the world was awake sometime in 2001, I believe. The only sound to break the morning stillness was the occasional crash of last night's glass against the dumpster behind one of the bars. Just hours before, this block was packed with people.

But at 7:30 a.m., the only bar open for business was Slainté. Inside, there were about six middle-aged, mostly English men and a cranky Irish bartender.

My brother Ryan and I had come here to see soccer – or as we were constantly corrected – football, the English version.

We bellied up to the bar, ordered steak and eggs and a Guinness, and immersed ourselves in the satellite broadcast on TV. They only got one, maybe two games a week. And if your team wasn't playing, so be it. Anything involving Arsenal, Manchester United, Liverpool, Chelsea – or even Leeds and Newcastle at that time – would dominate the broadcasts.

That's why most veteran Premier League fans in America root for one of those teams. They were all we knew, minus an occasional glimpse of a lesser opponent.

We were in awe at the sounds of the stadium that crackled over the bar's speakers; the raucous, non-stop singing, the way the crowd reacted with cheers or jeers at every small detail of the game. We didn't talk much during those games, we just listened and observed, picking up what we could from the old Englishmen through osmosis.

Once we saw Steven Gerrard score against Manchester United, we found our new hero and confirmed our favorite club.

Nowadays, when I'm in town, we go watch games together at Smalltimore, a specifically Liverpool bar in the Canton neighborhood of Baltimore. Before a recent Liverpool-Arsenal game, we showed up 40 minutes early. There wasn't a seat left and barely anywhere to stand. And this happens all across the country every weekend.

The English Premier League isn't a secret club in America any more.

From one bar with five people in it, to bars packed with Premier League fans, the English game has come a long way in the United States in a very short period of time.

A lot of that is thanks to NBC Sports, the heroes of American Premier League fans. Before NBC Sports there was Fox Soccer Channel, which eventually started showing three or four games a weekend by the mid-2000s. But the channel wasn't on every cable package and it didn't get widespread attention. ESPN made a half-hearted foray into the Premier League, but it was NBC Sports that put every team – not to mention everyone's English crush, Rebecca Lowe – in our living rooms every weekend.

In August 2015, NBC Sports ponied up $1 billion for the exclusive rights to show the Premier League in the US for six years, until 2021-22. *The New York Times* quoted Mark Lazarus, chairman of the NBC Sports group after:

"We have always believed in this sport; this particular league, the finest in the world, had a growth trajectory. We think that there's still plenty of headroom for this property to grow from an audience point of view, both on television and digital."

For the 2017-18 season, NBC started a new NBC Gold service for $49 a year that gives you access to every team's games and replays. For the first time as an American, if you want to be a Burnley fan, you can be one – and see every game as if you were a Seattle Mariners fan living in LA.

In 2016-17, NBC's affiliate networks averaged 420,000 viewers per Saturday 10 a.m. timeslot, meaning across all games. In the league's final year on ESPN and Fox Sports, that number was just 220,000.

It's worth noting that 2016-17 viewership was down 18% from 514,000 average viewers in 2015-16. However, the NFL, America's most watched sport saw it's viewership drop by 17% over the same season, coinciding with the presidential election.

Certainly, the TV experience is a big reason for the growth in the game and the amount of jerseys you see around America these days, even on little kids. But there's something else to this, something more anecdotal than scientific.

We believe more and more American sports fans are looking for something different, an alternative to the bloated prices and sterile environment of many American stadiums. There's the constant distraction of the Jumbotron and the loud MC ruining the beauty and natural buzz of a baseball game or the "three snaps and a Viagra commercial" TV format of NFL and college football. Or the 25 minutes of timeouts that squeeze the life out of the last two minutes of every basketball game.

We're not here to argue about which sport is better. We love football, baseball, basketball, hockey… all of the American sports. But we cannot deny the attraction of English football.

Americans want to feel passionate about their sports teams again. And they can see others displaying that passion on TV every week, beamed in straight from England. The singing, the standing, the emotions riding on every play… the same noise I heard over the crackle of Slainté's sound system is what's drawing hundreds of thousands of people to the game.

Major League Soccer and its fans have done a great job creating that atmosphere in a lot of their stadiums. The runs of FC Cincinnati and amateur side Christos FC in the 2017 Lamar Hunt US Open Cup show how widespread the popularity of soccer is in the US.

We're huge fans of MLS, though we wish they'd adopt promotion and relegation. But we, like most soccer/football fans, know the best product is the English Premier League.

And that's why we wrote this book.

More and more casual fans are tuning in to the Premier League. They're watching on TV, they're showing up at the pub on Saturday mornings and they're starting to plan their vacations around a trip to England.

My brother Ryan took me to my first game at Anfield on a hospitality ticket. We ate dinner in the Boot Room, chatted with former player Jimmy Case, and saw Fernando Torres bag two goals right in front of us in a win over Chelsea in 2010.

Everything about it was incredible, including the walk back downtown after the game, the cementing of my brother and I's soccer and Liverpool bond. It was one of the best sporting experiences of my life.

This time, I got to go to Anfield – and every other Premier League stadium – with my best friend and my new fiancée.

What we've created together is a Premier League resource written from an American perspective. There are already some wonderful books on the Premier League, written by English people. But we wanted to help "translate" that information to outsiders, both in America and all over the world.

We want this book to be accessible to beginners, people just starting to follow the Premier League – like some of our good friends. But we also want it to be informative and entertaining for the veteran Premier League fan – the people like us, who've been following the league for years.

If you're thinking about traveling to England to see a Premier League game – we've put resources in this book to help you.

We didn't contact any of the clubs before we went. We didn't attempt to get press passes or freebies. We wanted to go through the same process as everyone else. And we wanted to share our opinions without influence.

We attempted to buy tickets the same way you would, so we could spot any tricks or glitches in the process. Buying tickets in England is a lot different than here in the US. Inside the book, we'll share the best way to get tickets for all 20 current Premier League teams, individually.

And that's not all. We also put together the pertinent facts about all 20 clubs, including their history, past and present, in easy-to-understand bits. We'll tell you who each club's biggest rival is and how many trophies they've won.

We hope if you read this book, you'll walk into any stadium in the Premier League – confident that you know your stuff and you're ready to rub shoulders with local fans.

We walked the towns, went to the pubs and talked to the locals. And we brought back some special, in-depth tips for every club.

Even if you don't plan to travel to England, we hope our longer essays on each team help you live vicariously through us, and gain deeper knowledge of these clubs, their town, and their fans.

One thing to remember: These are just snapshots of each club on one day and at one moment in its history. Our experience is just that – our experience. It reflects the opinions we heard at that time. But we hope we've connected the dots between what we saw – and the club and town's larger place in the Premier League universe.

That doesn't mean your experience will be like ours. For instance, we really hope Everton fans find Goodison in a more rowdy mood than we did.

But what was most important to us was giving an honest and fair assessment of each club, its stadium and fans.

Yes, we happen to be Liverpool fans. But we approached every club like we were fans (even Manchester United). We learned the history, we sang the songs, and we tried to understand the climate before we went. (I've been watching almost every team's game, every weekend, for the last 5-10 years through one online plan or another.)

In every situation, no matter how much we knew going in, there was always something unique we picked up. There's just something about being there and among the local fans that gives you a much fuller understanding of the team at that moment in time. You can't get that on TV.

We also want to make it clear that we're not affiliated with the Premier League in any way, shape or form. The opinions expressed in this book are our own. We're not compensated by the league in any way nor are we attempting to present ourselves as such. This is very much the "unofficial" guide to the Premier League, the street level version without all the glossy stuff they show you in the brochure.

We ended up going to 27 stadiums, including Wembley and a handful of playoff contenders in the Championship. We attended as many games as we could together so it wasn't just one man's observation forming our opinions.

The only place we didn't get into was Bournemouth, but that's a story unto itself, as you'll see in that chapter.

It's been a whirlwind experience, but I do think we went to England at the right time. English football is at a crossroads. Foreign money – including from some less-than-stellar American owners – is washing over the league. 100-year old stadiums that were cauldrons of sound and passion are being torn down to build larger, American-style stadiums with sterile environments and loads of fans sitting on their hands.

The soul of English football is up for grabs...

We've already seen this movie in the US and we don't like it. A lot of the people we talked to in England thought American tourists would prefer those kinds of new stadiums.

But that's a common misunderstanding in England about American fans. We hear the exact opposite from our acquaintances here in the US. They want the tight quarters, the standing-room only sections of singing and chanting, not the same experience you get here in the US.

That's what makes the league attractive to outsiders. It's different.

So we hope the new White Hart Lane is as loud as the old. We hope Everton's new stadium on the docks is as intimate as Goodison Park. We hope further expansions of Anfield don't change the current atmosphere. And we hope, at least once in your life, you get to experience a European night at Old Trafford, no matter who you root for.

We sincerely hope you enjoy *The Sports Tourists' Guide to the English Premier League* and we hope it gives you a greater understanding of your club and the English Premier League in general.

Most of all, we hope this book leads you to fun, whether it's enjoying our stories or taking a once-in-a-lifetime trip to see your club play at their home ground, singing shoulder to shoulder with your fellow supporters.

If this book plays a small part in that moment, all of our efforts will have been worth it.

~ Blair Morse

Promotion and Relegation: Changing the Way Americans Think About Sports

On Saturday, May 26, 2018, Tom Cairney scored in the 23rd minute as his Fulham side defeated Aston Villa, 1-0, in the EFL Championship playoff final in front of more than 85,000 at Wembley Stadium.

Two weeks earlier, as the Premier League season had come to an end, Swansea City, Stoke City and bottom of the table West Bromwich Albion were headed for relegation.

What does all that mean?

For Americans, sports seasons end with playoffs, not the regular season. Whether it's baseball, basketball, hockey, American football or even Major League Soccer, a playoff system exists to determine a champion. And it does not matter if your team won the Super Bowl or went 1-15, the same teams will be back in the same league the following season (although, maybe not in the same location --- sorry San Diego Chargers, Oakland Raiders, Montreal Expos and Atlanta Flames fans).

European football is considerably different in its league makeup, as well as how it handles champions and poor performing clubs. The English football league system is affected each year by promotion and relegation, which influences the ensuing season's make-up. We will explain the concept of promotion and relegation shortly, but first, let's talk about the structure of the Premier League, the Football League and…everything else.

Back in 1863, English Football's governing body, the Football Association, was established, primarily to formalize the game of soccer itself, especially the rules. The Football Association allowed its clubs to turn professional as early as 1885, but organization, especially when it came to scheduling matches, was sorely lacking.

The English Football League was founded in April 1888 at the Royal Hotel in Manchester. League founder William McGregor was the club secretary of Aston Villa at the time, and he sent a letter to many of the prestigious clubs earlier in the year detailing the need for an organized league to emerge, with home and away contests against each of the other clubs in the league. Several clubs met a few weeks later and minutes from that meeting stated that "a strong feeling was evinced that something should be done to improve the present unsatisfactory state of club fixtures and to render them more certain in their fulfillment and interesting in character."

Twelve clubs, six from Lancashire (Accrington, Blackburn, Bolton, Burnley, Everton, Preston North End), and six from the Midlands (Aston Villa, Derby County, Notts County, Stoke, West Bromwich Albion, Wolverhampton) created the first national football league in the world.

The league represented the climate of the times, as it was composed entirely of working-class northern teams. Teams from London and the south normally were comprised of schoolboys and gentlemen, whereas the northern sides were made up of factory workers and other professional occupations. Immigrants flocked to the contests to develop community in their new home. The first season kicked off in the fall of 1888, with Preston North End winning the inaugural league crown.

More than 125 years later, over 7,000 teams compete in 24 levels of English football. Explaining the overall structure is equivalent to describing the numerous levels of Minor League baseball, with its short season rookie leagues, high and low A ball, Double and Triple-A divisions and everything else. Except, add roughly 18-20 more levels to it. This is all very complex, so we will simply focus on the top four flights of English football.

In a move that sounds eerily like what the Big Five power conferences have hinted at for years in American college football and basketball, the 'Big Five' of English football --- Arsenal, Everton, Liverpool, Manchester United, and Tottenham Hotspur --- pushed for its own league in the early 1990s, where top clubs that spent the most money could continue to attract the world's top talent by spending and making more.

Formerly known as the First Division, the Premier League separated from the Football League prior to the 1992-93 season. Everton has competed in the top flight the most, having now spent 116 of 120 seasons at this level. Arsenal, meanwhile, has competed in the top flight for 92 straight seasons, 28 years longer than the next closest team, Everton.

A 1991 court ruling in favor of the separation pushed things forward, and BSkyB, led by Rupert Murdoch, whom American fans know as the owner of Fox, put forth a monstrous bid, more than 300 million pounds over five years, to televise the Premier League games over a five-year period.

A juggernaut was born. At that time, the league featured 22 teams, but dropped down to 20 prior to the 1995-96 campaign as part of an earlier agreement to limit the number of clubs and slightly shorten the season to preserve top talent. Currently, these 20 squads constitute the elite of English football. Only 49 clubs have made it to the Premier League in 25 years, including newly promoted Huddersfield and Brighton.

The Premier League is the one you see all the time from August through the following May on NBC Sports. In addition to those internationally famous clubs, which now also include Chelsea and Manchester City, it also currently includes lesser known ones (at least outside of England) like Bournemouth, Burnley, Huddersfield and Watford.

Each year, the teams in the Premier League play a total of 38 league matches, one home and one away against each of the other clubs in the league. This does not count FA Cup, League Cup and any European matches played by those squads (see next chapter). At the end of the regular season, the side with the most points (wins = 3 points, draws = 1 point, losses = manager on the hot seat) is named champion. Man City comfortably won the 2017-18 season with 100 points (32 wins, 4 draws and 2 losses), finishing a league-record 19 points ahead of second-place Manchester United. No playoffs took place. If two teams finished tied for first in points, goal differential is the first tie-breaker.

During the Premier League's existence, goal differential has determined the champion only once, and that was Manchester City's thrilling title triumph over Manchester United during the 2011-2012 season. Both sides finished with 89 points, but Man City's goal differential was eight points higher (64-56). When Eden Dzeko and Sergio Aguero scored in extra time in the second half to give Man City a 3-2 win over Queens Park Rangers in the regular season finale, it represented English football drama at its best.

While the champion tends to be determined long before the season's final day, there's also drama at the bottom of the table too, thanks to the existence of promotion and relegation.

What that means, simply, is that every year the three worst teams in the Premier League are demoted to the next level, the Championship. And, the three best teams in the Championship are promoted to the Premier League. This process happens at every level of English football.

That's 92 teams spread out over four leagues, playing more than 2,000 matches each season to win a couple of titles and move a few teams up and down the leagues. Most clubs have been relegated and promoted at least once.

It's a unique concept meant to keep the league's competition in balance and make more matches meaningful toward the end of the season.

Think about it from the perspective of the wild card in the National Football League and Major League Baseball. The NFL introduced a wild card playoff game in the late 1970s, and has since moved to two wild card teams in both the American and National Football Conference, which results in two wild card games against the lowest division winners of each conference the first week in the playoffs.

MLB brought about the wild card in 1995, when it moved to three divisions in each conference. In 2012, it added the one-off playoff game between two wild card teams, with the winner advancing to the divisional round.

Why did the NFL and MLB add these wild cards? Simple. Revenue. More teams in the playoffs means more teams still in contention to get into those playoffs late in the season which, in-turn, means larger crowds at home games of those borderline postseason teams. It makes the season more interesting for everyone involved, and more money is spent and accrued across the board.

Promotion and relegation, in English football, helps produce drama at the end of the season for teams facing relegation, and in the lower leagues, creates added excitement for the four clubs competing in the respective playoffs.

So, how did promotion and relegation come about? It was brought into play in English football at the end of the 19th century. After the Football League formed in 1888 with 12 teams, it quickly expanded to 14 and then 16 teams by 1892, and added a second division from teams that were in the former Football Alliance, including Nottingham Forest, The Wednesday (later Sheffield Wednesday) and Newton Heath (later Manchester

United). By 1898, the concept of promotion and relegation was introduced to offer a way of balancing divisions competitively as much as possible.

Let me show you how it looks in practice.

2017-18 Premier League Table

Place	Team	Points
1	Manchester City	100
2	Manchester United	81
3	Tottenham Hotspur	77
4	Liverpool	75
5	Chelsea	70
6	Arsenal	63
7	Burnley	54
8	Everton	49
9	Leicester City	47
10	Newcastle United	44
11	Crystal Palace	44
12	Bournemouth	44
13	West Ham United	42
14	Watford	41
15	Brighton & Hove Albion	40
16	Huddersfield Town	37
17	Southampton	36
18	Swansea City	33
19	Stoke City	33
20	West Bromwich Albion	31

The Premier League is now a separate entity from the Football League, although promotion and relegation keep the two connected. While Manchester City was celebrating its record-breaking title-winning performance Stoke City, Swansea City and West Bromwich Albion were readying for a new season one flight down. This next level is the Championship, which used to be known as the Second Division, and then the First Division after the creation of the Premier League in 1992.

2017-18 Championship Table

Place	Team	Points
1	Wolverhampton Wanderers	99
2	Cardiff City	90
3	Fulham	88
4	Aston Villa	83
5	Middlesbrough	76
6	Derby County	75
7	Preston North End	73
8	Millwall	72
9	Brentford	69
10	Sheffield United	69
11	Bristol City	67
12	Ipswich Town	60
13	Leeds United	60
14	Norwich City	60
15	Sheffield Wednesday	57
16	Queens Park Rangers	56
17	Nottingham Forest	53
18	Hull City	49
19	Birmingham City	46
20	Reading	44
21	Bolton Wanderers	43
22	Barnsley	41
23	Burton Albion	41
24	Sunderland	37

This league has 24 teams. Each year, three teams are relegated down from the Premier League and three clubs come up from League One, which is the next level down. The Championship also sends three teams up to the Premier League. Two teams earn automatic promotion: that year's league champ, which was Wolverhampton in 2017-18 (30 wins, 9 draws, 7 losses) and the second-place team, Cardiff City.

2017-18 Championship Play-offs

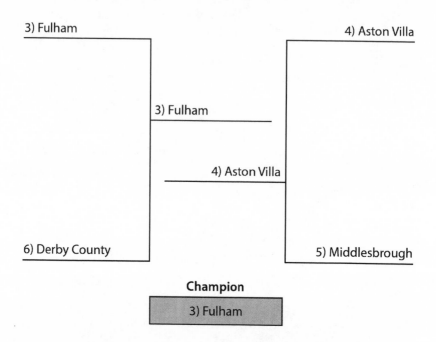

3) Fulham

4) Aston Villa

3) Fulham

4) Aston Villa

6) Derby County

5) Middlesbrough

Champion

3) Fulham

A third club emerges from a mini-playoff system that provides some of the most exciting drama around. Teams that finish third through sixth square off in a semifinal round (3 vs. 6, 4 vs. 5) that features a home-and-home set-up. Teams advance based on the combined aggregate total of those two matches.

The third seed, Fulham, advanced over No. 6 seed Derby County by an aggregate score of 2-1. Aston Villa, the No. 4 seed, defeated No. 5 Middlesbrough, 1-0. The final is played at Wembley Stadium and is a nationally celebrated affair. Fulham advanced on Cairney's goal and headed back up to the Premier League for the first time since 2013-14.

What that means is that, with three clubs coming down from the Premier League, and three teams coming up from League One, and three teams promoted or relegated to those same two leagues, 25 percent of the clubs competing in the Championship change from season to season. What would the NBA look like next season without the Sixers, Nets, Kings, Timberwolves, Knicks and Hawks and with teams like the Austin Spurs, Maine Red Claws and Iowa Energy from the Development League in it?

While Fulham celebrated its playoff triumph, Barnsley, Burton Albion and Sunderland were relegated down to League One, the third-tier league that features 24 clubs as well. Sunderland has had an especially rough couple of years, getting relegated from the Premier League and the EFL Championship in back-to-back seasons.

2017-18 League One Table

Place	Team	Points
1	Wigan Athletic	98
2	Blackburn Rovers	96
3	Shrewsbury Town	87
4	Rotherham United	79
5	Scunthorpe United	74
6	Charlton Athletic	71
7	Plymouth Argyle	68
8	Portsmouth	66
9	Peterborough United	64
10	Southend United	63
11	Bradford City	63
12	Blackpool	60
13	Bristol Rovers	59
14	Fleetwood Town	57
15	Doncaster Rovers	56
16	Oxford United	56
17	Gillingham	56
18	AFC Wimbledon	53
19	Walsall	52
20	Rochdale	51
21	Oldham Athletic	50
22	Northampton Town	47
23	Milton Keynes Dons	45
24	Bury	36

While those three clubs were going down, League One champion Wigan Athletic (29 wins, 11 draws, 6 losses) and runner-up Blackburn Rovers, both former Premier League sides, moved back into the Championship. With the same playoff setup, Shrewsbury Town defeated Charlton Athletic and Rotterham United defeated Scunthorpe United to set up another final at Wembley Stadium. Defender Richard Wood scored twice, including the winning goal in the 103rd minute, as Rotterham earned the promotion with a 2-1 victory.

2017-18 League One Play-offs

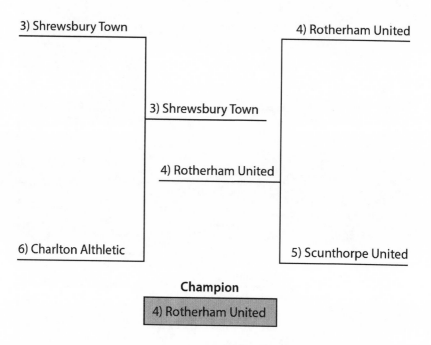

While Wood and his teammates celebrated, four League One sides were in despair. League One relegates four clubs down to League Two, the lowest of the three tiers of the Football League and the fourth tier of English football overall. Oldham Athletic, Northampton Town, MK Dons and Bury were sent packing after the 2017-18 season.

2017-18 League Two Table

Place	Team	Points
1	Accrington Stanley	93
2	Luton Town	88
3	Wycombe Wanderers	84
4	Exeter City	80
5	Notts County	77
6	Coventry City	75
7	Lincoln City	75
8	Mansfield Town	72
9	Swindon Town	68
10	Carlisle United	67
11	Newport County	64
12	Cambridge United	64
13	Colchester United	62
14	Crawley Town	59
15	Crewe Alexandra	56
16	Stevenage	55
17	Cheltenham Town	51
18	Grimsby Town	51
19	Yeovil Town	48
20	Port Vale	47
21	Forest Green Rovers	47
22	Morecambe	46
23	Barnet	46
24	Chesterfield	38

League Two, which also features 24 clubs, sent four up. This included league champion Accrington Stanley, followed by second-place Luton Town and third-place Wycombe Wanderers.

A similar playoff setup, now featuring teams that finished 4-through-7, takes place at this level. Coventry City, the sixth-place team, defeated No. 5 seed Notts County, while Exeter City, the fourth-place side, knocked off Lincoln City. Jordan Willis, Jordan Shipley and Jack Grimmer all scored in the second half to give Coventry City a 3-1 victory over Exeter City in front of more than

50,000 at Wembley. It was the second consecutive season Exeter City dropped the final.

2017-18 League Two Play-offs

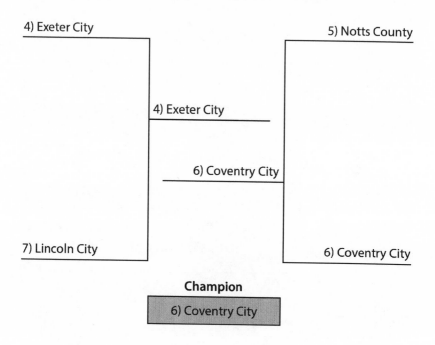

And this leads to the scariest relegation possible. Two clubs from League Two are relegated out of the Football League and into the National League. This is dubbed non-League football and, although several teams come right back to the Football League within a couple of years, many have disappeared into the black hole altogether, never to be seen again.

2017-18 National League Table

Place	Team	Points
1	Macclesfield Town	92
2	Tranmere Rovers	82
3	Sutton United	79
4	Boreham Wood	75
5	Aldershot Town	75
6	Ebbsfleet United	74
7	Fylde	73
8	Dover Athletic	73
9	Bromley	70
10	Wrexham	70
11	Dagenham & Redbridge	68
12	Maidenhead United	64
13	Leyton Orient	60
14	Eastleigh	56
15	Hartlepool United	56
16	Halifax Town	55
17	Gateshead	54
18	Solihull Moors	54
19	Maidstone United	54
20	Barrow	49
21	Woking	48
22	Torquay United	42
23	Chester	37
24	Guiseley	33

This year, Barnet and Chesterfield shared that dubious honor. Non-league sides Macclesfield Town and Tranmere Rovers moved up from the National League. Macclesfield Town (27 wins, 11 draws, 8 losses) won the league, while Tranmere Rovers defeated Ebbsfleet United and Boreham Wood, 2-1, at Wembley, to earn its own place back in the Football League after a three-year absence.

With the advent of the Premier League, the finances now thrown around are simply ridiculous. Let's look at what it means, financially, to currently spend a year in today's top flight, from the bottom up.

2017-18 Premier League Prize Money

Team	Equal Share	Merit Based	Facility Fee	Total
Manchester City	£84.4m	£38.4m	£33.2m	£156m
Manchester United	£84.4m	£36.5m	£38.1m	£159m
Liverpool	£84.4m	£34.6m	£30.7m	£149.7m
Tottenham	£84.4m	£32.6m	£30.7m	£147.7m
Chelsea	£84.4m	£30.7m	£33.2m	£148.3m
Arsenal	£84.4m	£28.8m	£33.2m	£146.4m
Burnley	£84.4m	£26.9m	£12.3m	£123.6m
Leicester City	£84.4m	£25m	£19.6m	£129m
Everton	£84.4m	£23.1m	£22.1m	£129.6m
Watford	£84.4m	£21.1m	£16m	£121.5m
Bournemouth	£84.4m	£19.2m	£16m	£119.6m
Brighton & Hove	£84.4m	£17.3m	£12.3m	£114m
West Ham	£84.4m	£15.4m	£18.4m	£118.2m
Huddersfield Town	£84.4m	£13.4m	£12.3m	£110.1m
Newcastle United	£84.4m	£11.5m	£19.6m	£115.5m
Southampton	£84.4m	£9.6m	£18.4m	£112.4m
Crystal Palace	£84.4m	£7.7m	£17.2m	£109.3m
Swansea City	£84.4m	£5.8m	£12.3m	£102.5m
Stoke City	£84.4m	£3.8m	£12.3m	£100.5m
West Brom	£84.4m	£1.9m	£13.5m	£99.8m

src: http://www.totalsportek.com/money/premier-league-prize-money

West Brom finished dead last in the Premier League in 2017-18, ending an eight-year run in the top flight. Still, thanks mostly to the largesse provided from television contracts, the Baggies brought in 94.7 million pounds.

All 17 clubs that remain in the Premier League made at least 100 million pounds.

So, with West Brom now down in the Championship, it gets no more money, right? Especially since the three leagues below the Premier League combined receive just 90 million pounds a year for the broadcast rights to all league and cup competitions.

Wrong.

So-called parachute payments now play a direct vital role in the Premier League/Championship relationship. *GazetteLive*'s

Anthony Vickers explains that the payments, first introduced in 2005, were initiated because "having spent heavily on transfers and wages to compete in the top flight, relegation spelt disaster for the likes of Bradford, Southampton, Crystal Palace, Leeds, Norwich and Charlton, all who went into administration after relegation."

What are parachute payments? Daniel Geey, who publishes the blog *The Final Score on Football Law* explains that they are "funds provided by the Premier League to clubs relegated from the Premier League to the Football League Championship. They are primarily to provide a financial cushion for the relegated clubs to adjust to life outside the lucrative Premier League competition."

Vickers continues to state these payments "have two aims. Firstly to let relegated clubs manage the tricky transition to the Championship, mainly paying the wage bill in the first season while they either geared up for a swift return or looked to sell players and run contracts down.

The second aim was to ensure the league stayed competitive by encouraging newly promoted sides to feel they could strengthen their squad without risking financial ruin."

The payments are broken into three years, as long as the club has been in the Premier League for more than one season. If up for only a year, as in Hull's and Middlesbrough's case in 2016-17, the parachute payments are only for two years. These payments are front-loaded to handle the initial shock of going down. Stoke, Swansea and West Brom will receive 40 million pounds this season, 35 million in 2018-19 and 15 million in 2019-20.

That provides some financial support to relegated teams, but that does not make everything better. Relegation sucks. It does not matter that you were competing in arguably the most competitive league in the world, if you were relegated, you were one of the three worst teams in that league. If your team finishes 1-15 in the NFL, you don't stand there with your chest out saying, 'Yeah, but we are one of the 32 best football teams out there.' Your team is just not good enough against the competition it is currently facing, and that is a fact.

"That was the lowest point of my career…no, in fact it's the lowest point of my life," Middlesbrough's Ben Gibson told *The Guardian* after his club clinched relegation after a loss to Chelsea in 2017. "It means so much. We've got to put it right."

Since the Premier League's inception, a total of 20 clubs have come right back up a year after being relegated down, including

Hull City ahead of 2016-17, and Newcastle ahead of 2017-18. But, that is less than one team a year, and seven of those 20 squads only lasted a year when they came back up.

The clubs going down face numerous changes, from players who feel they are still Premier League-talent signing elsewhere, to dealing with wage bills that aren't as economically feasible at the lower levels. Also, keep in mind that the 40 million-pound parachute payment is half what the club would have received from just the 80.4 million-pound equal share distribution in the Premier League alone.

These defiant, angry and hopeless feelings felt by the clubs and their supporters are contrasted directly against the euphoric feelings of Huddersfield and Brighton fans, who saw their clubs move up to the Premier League for the first time after the 2017-18 season. For them, the raw emotions of witnessing their clubs make that leap, either through placing second in its season-long performance, as in Brighton's case, or with that dramatic win at Wembley for Huddersfield, will probably never be matched. You don't forget your first time. Heck, even new Premier League tenants Cardiff City, Fulham and Wolves should be excited, even though those clubs have all been up at least once before. At least for the time being.

In addition to those emotional highs are the pragmatic financial pluses of reaching the Premier League. Let's look at it from that perspective, as the *Los Angeles Times'* Kevin Baxter did after the 2015-16 Championship season had concluded with Middlesbrough's promotion. Regarding then 'Boro manager Aitor Karanka:

"In a 90-minute span last weekend Karanka made $246 million for his company...by coaching Middlesbrough to a 1-1 draw with Brighton in the final game of the League Championship's regular season, Karanka assured the club promotion to the English Premier League and won it a share of the EPL's new $12-billion TV deal."

According to Baxter, "analysts at Deloitte UK say the revenue difference between teams in the EPL and teams in the second-tier Championship will be $140 million next season...

Compare that to the $35 million Germany got from FIFA for winning the 2014 World Cup or the $69 million Barcelona got from UEFA for winning the last Champions League."

According to ESPN, Fulham's Wembley triumph was worth "170.3 million pounds.

"That playoff match has become the football equivalent of the 725,000-pound-per-square-inch pressure that forms diamonds, concentrating all the weight of a 46-game season into a single 90 minutes that bear the greatest riches of any game in sport."

Because of this annual survival contest, clubs have celebrated reaching safety in one league as much as another celebrates promotion. Leicester City, the upstart Premier League champions from the 2015-16 season, faced relegation the previous year. Sitting in the relegation zone at the start of April, seven points from safety, the Foxes won seven and lost only one in its final nine matches to stay in the league and set up their title run the next season.

Sunderland was in an even more precarious position in the 2013-14 season, sitting seven points from safety in the relegation zone in mid-April. The Black Cats survived a tough closing schedule by winning on the road at Chelsea and Man United and drawing with Man City, surviving the cut by the time the season ended.

Fulham (2007-08), West Ham (2006-07) and Wigan (2011-12) all overcome seemingly insurmountable odds to stay in the Premier League by escaping relegation late in the season, but the term Great Escape was coined, appropriately so, during West Brom's famous last-day survival in 2004-05. As we will discuss in that team's chapter, no club had clinched relegation going into the final match day of the season, and the Baggies sweated out a 2-1 win and had to wait for another result to secure safety. When was the last time you saw a team finish 17th overall and have players carried off the field? Because that is what happened that day at The Hawthorns.

On the flip side, when was the last time you frequented your local pub, only to have one of the local side's stars in there with some champagne chanting 'Let's go fucking mental!' after getting promoted? That's what happened with Watford's Troy Deeney, who celebrated with some of his teammates and others in a nearby pub after Watford was promoted from the Championship following the 2014-15 season.

Brighton's promotion sparked a seemingly endless celebration. Huddersfield's playoff penalty win over Reading set off a great party in Wembley that stretched back to West Yorkshire. Heck, Portsmouth went nuts after winning the League Two title and getting promoted to League One.

Swansea City in 2011, Queens Park Rangers in 2014, Huddersfield in 2017. These are just a handful of the squads whose playoff victories and subsequent promotion to the Premier League ignited city-wide celebrations.

Getting promoted is glorious. Getting relegated has the feeling of a funeral. That's football in England and Europe. Unfortunately, that is not the case in the States. Major League Soccer has survived and grown for over 20 years, since its formation in 1995 following the success of the 1994 World Cup in America.

League play began in 1996 and there are currently 223 teams competing after the addition of expansion team LAFC ahead of the 2018 season. Cincinnati, Miami and Nashville are the next clubs to join over the next few years.

It is also a league that does not partake in promotion and relegation, meaning two leagues sanctioned by the U.S. Soccer Federation, the North American Soccer League (NASL) and the United Soccer League (USL), could not potentially send teams up, and MLS teams would not come down. According to ESPN FC, MLS rejected a "$4 billion global media rights deal…which would have quadrupled the annual rate of MLS' current deal." It "would have run for 10 years starting in 2023."

However, the proposal came with the contingency that promotion and relegation become standard in the league's operation. It originated from an owner of a Miami club in the NASL not approved for expansion, and MLS had many valid reasons to not accept the bid. Promotion and Relegation is a foreign concept on American soil – it is not utilized in any of the sports leagues.

Until that time comes, if it ever does, Americans will continue enjoying the emotions -- the highs and lows -- of its adopted English clubs competing for survival or fighting for promotion.

A Basic Guide to England and Europe's Other Trophies

A Premier League team's season is not limited to the 38 games they play on the league schedule. All 20 Premier League teams are automatically entered in two other domestic tournaments: the FA Cup and the League Cup – currently called the Carabao Cup due to sponsorship.

Teams that finish in the top four of the Premier League are rewarded the next season with a berth in Europe's elite competition, the Champions League. Typically, the next two or three teams in the standings earn a berth in the lesser Europa League.

These competitions add more fixtures to the list and give you another chance to see your team in action.

Here's some more information about these unique tournaments:

The FA Cup is the granddaddy of them all, the oldest football tournament in England and by most accounts, the world. The first FA Cup was contested at the end of the 1871-72 season.

It's a single elimination tournament that serves as England's version of the NCAA basketball tournament – except its run intermittently over nine different weekends throughout the year.

The best thing about the FA Cup is that potentially any Sunday League team in England can enter – and theoretically end up playing at Old Trafford, Anfield or eventually the final in Wembley Stadium.

In reality, only the biggest, richest clubs win the competition because it is still the second-most prestigious trophy in England – and to teams outside the Premier League, the most prestigious.

The history of the FA Cup is the history of football. The creation of the FA Cup brought structure to the system of local leagues and different rules that plagued the growth of football.

The idea came from Charles Alcock, the secretary of the FA, who wanted to create a competition between the industrial "company" teams of the North and the "old boy" teams of the South, made up of alumni from schools like Eton College, Oxford and Charterhouse School. Thanks to train lines now dotting the English landscape, a national tournament of this type was possible for the first time.

At the time, the English Football Association, or FA, was only seven years old. And most teams stuck to local friendlies or small competitions. The FA needed a marquee event to bring together these clubs scattered throughout the country.

Alcock proposed a nationwide challenge cup, open to all 50 teams then part of the FA. Only 15 entered the first season, with the first round taking place on Nov. 11, 1871. The final was played at the Kennington Oval in London on March 16, 1872, with Wanderers FC – a team of London public school alumni – beating the Royal Engineers. Alcock himself started for the winning team!

By 1885, professional football was legalized, and the paid teams of the industrial North began a decades-long period of dominance in England's preeminent competition.

In fact, starting in 1883 with Blackburn Olympic, teams from the Midlands and farther north won 18 straight FA Cups, and 38 of the next 40, broken up by two lonely wins for Tottenham Hotspur, in 1901 and 1921. Tottenham's victory in 1901 still stands as the only victory for a non-league team since the Football League was created.

In all, the North won 60 titles between 1883 and 1960, when Tottenham won the first of back-to-back titles… the first two in a row to southern clubs during that span.

Aston Villa led the way with seven of those titles, Blackburn Rovers and Newcastle won six each, and West Bromwich Albion had five.

The Football League was formed out of the growing interest in the FA Cup – yet still the Cup took a romantic hold on the English consciousness. And in 1923, Wembley Stadium, then called the Empire Stadium at Wembley, was built specifically to host the FA Cup final.

The paint was still drying on the seats when Wembley opened its door for the first time to host the 1923 FA Cup Final between Bolton Wanderers and West Ham United, only four days after construction finished. The announced crowd of 126,047 was estimated to be only half the actual number of people inside Wembley, easily making it one of the largest attended games in sports history.

The crowd was so large they spilled out onto the playing field, like an old-time baseball game of the same era. The 1923 final – won by Bolton 2-0 – is known as the "White Horse Final" and is commemorated with the White Horse Bridge at the new Wembley Stadium. The "white horse", a gray mare named Billie, and its handler, policeman George Scorey, were credited with singlehandedly clearing the field of thousands of people so play could resume.

By 1938, the final was broadcast on live TV to the whole nation, beginning a tradition that lasts to this day, with the exception of the war years between 1940-45, when no FA Cup was contested.

All of England gets together on that Saturday in May, throws back a few pints and gathers around the television to watch England's sporting crown jewel, the FA Cup final. In America, Memorial Day weekend kicks off the summer. In England, it's Cup final weekend.

The reason the FA Cup became such a tradition is that for many years, the FA Cup final – and some of the other rounds – were the only live games shown on TV, thanks to the British Broadcasting Corporation (BBC) ownership of the rights, which continues to this day.

Sometimes – rarely for the small clubs – your team gets the ultimate English prize: a day out at Wembley for the FA Cup final.

The 2018 FA Cup final was the third matchup between Chelsea and Manchester United in the tournament's history and the rubber match. United defeated the Blues 4-0 in 1994, but Chelsea took the 2007 title 1-0 in extra time.

Chelsea's manager that day was Manchester United's manager for the present-day matchup, Jose Mourinho. Chelsea had lost the 2017 final to Arsenal, but Antonio Conte had his men ready for this matchup. The Blues choked up United in the midfield and a 22nd minute penalty by Eden Hazard was enough for the 1-0 Chelsea victory.

The win was Chelsea's eighth FA Cup, tying them with Tottenham for third all-time. United could've won its 13th FA Cup, which would've put them in a tie with Arsenal for the most ever. For Conte, he went out on a good note as he was fired less than two months later. Apparently, the FA Cup isn't as worth as much to some foreign owners.

But it's not just the FA Cup final that captures England's attention. We mentioned the FA Cup was like England's version of the NCAA basketball tournament. And that's because the real attraction of the FA Cup to the neutral fan is the upsets.

All teams in the top 10 tiers of English football are eligible to enter the FA Cup. The four highest levels – the Football League – are automatically entered. Levels 5-10 qualify so long as they have a sufficient stadium and meet some clear eligibility requirements.

But that means that a team from Level 10, playing in a league like the Southwestern Peninsula League or the Eastern Counties League, could end up playing – or hosting – a big club like Manchester United, Chelsea, Manchester City, Liverpool or Arsenal. That's what makes the romance of the FA Cup.

No time was better for upsets than the 1970s, right as the FA Cup was gaining a larger audience on TV. The iconic moment is Ronnie Radford's smashing goal from 30 yards that drew his non-league Hereford United side level with Newcastle in the third round of the 1972 FA Cup. A late goal by Ricky George sealed the win for Hereford, the first in the modern era for a non-league team against a First Division opponent – and a harbinger of Newcastle's fortunes in the Cup over the next 40 plus years. To put that upset in perspective, imagine a 15-seed upsetting a two-seed in the NCAA basketball tournament.

The very next year, 1973, Second Division Sunderland became the first non First-Division team to win an FA Cup in the modern era, beating Don Revie's Leeds – a team thought to be the best in Europe – 1-0. The moment is immortalized outside the Stadium of Light in Sunderland with a statue of coach Bob Stokoe, arms outstretched, running onto the field with the belt of his trench coat flapping in the wind to celebrate.

Second-division Southampton pulled off the same feat in 1976, beating Manchester United, and then West Ham did the same thing in 1980, fending off Arsenal in the final. Brighton and Hove Albion nearly knocked off Manchester United in the 1983 final, drawing the Red Devils 2-2 and forcing a replay that United won 4-0, just days after Brighton were relegated from the First Division. The 2017-18 season is the Seagulls' first in the top division since then.

Nowadays there are still replays for FA Cup games that end in a draw, but not in the final. Finals go to 30 minutes of extra time and eventually penalty kicks if the game is still tied.

Part of the competitiveness of the FA Cup is due to the schedule, with games played mostly on weekends, and the English leagues adjusting their schedule to give the FA Cup the spotlight.

The League Cup is viewed and often referred to as the FA Cup's "little brother." But its possible England's lesser-known competition may have packed even more drama into its relatively short history.

Then Football League secretary Alan Hardaker created the League Cup in 1960 because of his anger at English teams' increased interest in European competitions at the expense of domestic. Hardaker hoped the League Cup – open only to teams in the Football League, England's top four divisions – and it's prize money would entice England's powers to stay at home.

"Hardaker's Folly" as the tournament is sometimes called, did not have the desired effect, as clubs like Manchester United and Liverpool didn't even enter the tournament in the early years, according to *The Guardian.*

Hardaker kept working to force the League Cup down club's throats, getting the final a spot at Wembley Stadium. In 1967, he hit upon a way to get teams' attention. Ironically, he offered up a berth in one of the European competitions he hoped to destroy.

First, the League Cup winner went to the Inter Cities Cup, which became the UEFA Cup and later merged with the Cup Winners Cup to become what we now know as the Europa League – more on the Europa League in a moment.

Interestingly enough, the winner of that 1967 final didn't get to go to Europe. Rodney Marsh, now a soccer pundit on SiriusXM Radio in the US, famously led Third Division Queens Park Rangers to a 3-2 come-from-behind victory over West Brom, from the First Division. QPR's Third Division status actually made them ineligible for European competition.

Partly because of the lack of interest in the early days, clubs from outside the First Division made an early impact on the competition. Norwich City, then in the Second Division, won the second-ever League Cup in 1962, by a 4-0 aggregate score over Rochdale, from the Fourth Division.

QPR got its famous win in 1967 and two years later, Third Division Swindon Town got a goal and an assist from Don Rogers in extra time to break a 1-1 tie with Arsenal and claim the Cup.

After the addition of the automatic European spot, the higher profile teams started to pay more attention to the League Cup – or at least, they did in the later rounds. The Cup has always been played with squads full of backups and young players in the early rounds, a problem that persists to this day.

In the old days, the problem was made worse by the number of fixtures, created by Hardaker's two legs per round format, home and away. Unlike the FA Cup, the leagues do not alter their schedules to fit the League Cup and games are played during the week, usually smack in the middle of the European group stages, all but forcing the big clubs to play weakened teams.

Now, only the semifinals are two legs, but the League Cup heats up just before the draining Christmas time fixture list, and the semifinals come just after it. Often the quality, like this past season, isn't great.

But the finals have produced loads of drama – with some whispers that the League Cup final is better entertainment value than the FA Cup.

It also brings a Cup final to the dog days of February and March, before the league games start getting dramatic. It's a great way for fans visiting England to see a game for cheap, as tickets are easier to acquire.

Unlikely Bristol City made it to the semifinals in 2017-18 before falling to Manchester City over two legs. Oft-injured City defender Vincent Kompany got to have his moment in the sun in the final at Wembley Stadium against Arsenal.

Kompany scored the second of three goals in a Manchester City rout, 3-0. Kompany was named man of the match. Sergio Aguero and David Silva added the other goals. The League Cup was the fifth in City's history and its third in the last five years.

The League Cup is officially known as the Carabao Cup after its current sponsor, a Thai energy drink company. In the past, through various sponsorships, its been known by different names, the Milk, Littlewoods, Rumbelows, Coca-Cola, Worthington, Carling and Capital One Cups.

Manchester United, along with Aston Villa and Chelsea, have won the Cup five times – tied for second best. Liverpool are the

League Cup masters, however, with eight victories – and they've played in 12 finals. From 1981-84, Liverpool won four straight League Cups.

Sixteen of the 66 Cup finals have gone to a replay (in the old days), extra time or a penalty shootout. And since the final went to a one-game format in 1967, only nine Cup finals have been won by two or more goals. Little brother or not, the League Cup finals have entertained over the years.

Hardaker never got his wish. The League Cup was never able to dull the luster of European competition. And the tournament that's been the source of exhilaration and anguish for English football is the most glamorous competition in the world: **The Champions League.**

Originally known as the European Cup when it began in 1955, the Champions League is the richest competition in the world and features the best teams from leagues all across Europe, including Russia, Israel, Ukraine and Turkey.

Thanks to Fox Sports, the Champions League has been on TV in America as long as the Premier League, on Tuesdays and Wednesdays at 2:45 or 3:45 p.m. throughout the fall and winter. Even casual fans can hum the over-the-top orchestral theme song.

This season, however, the Champions League has moved to a hodgepodge lineup of websites and channels, including Telemundo and Bleacher Report Live.

This is the tournament most fans dream about winning. And for neutrals, this is the chance to settle the arguments – England vs. Spain vs. Germany vs. Italy? Barcelona or Manchester United? Real Madrid or Bayern Munich?

The Champions League is the most important competition in all of club football. And second only to the World Cup for prestige – though many would say it's a higher quality competition.

Over 380 million people from 200-plus countries watched the 2015 Champions League final – over three times more viewers than the Super Bowl. In the US, over 3 million people watched the Champions League final last year – more than in England!

TV and ticket sales helped the Champions League generate around 2.09 billion euros in revenue in 2017-18.

And last year's winner, Real Madrid, defeated Liverpool in the final, 3-1. The club won 102 million euros in prize money and every player on the team got a 2.66 million euro bonus.

Teams from every country in Europe are entered in the tournament. How many teams from each league is determined by a complicated formula that rates each league and feeds it into a mathematical equation known as the "coefficient."

Currently, the top three leagues – as determined by the coefficient – are Spain, Germany and England. They each get four teams in the Champions League.

The next three rated leagues, Italy, France and Russia, get three teams each.

After that, the seventh through 15th rated countries get two teams each (Portugal, Belgium, Ukraine, Turkey, Netherlands, Greece, Austria, Czech Republic, Switzerland). Every one else sends just its domestic champion; including the bottom three rated countries, Kosovo, San Marino and Andorra.

Like we mentioned, typically England gets four places in the Champions League, and it's a tense race to secure those places – or else meet the ire of owners and fans. Supporters of the big clubs are constantly talking about how important it is to finish in the top four and qualify for the Champions League.

Part of it is the prestige of the Champions League. Another part is the money involved. A berth in the group stage is worth a minimum of 12.7 million euros and potentially more for each group stage win (1.5 million euros), and draw (500,000 euros). Make it to the round of 16, you get another 6 million euros, and so on and so forth.

For example, a team that won three group stage games and drew one, then made it to the semifinals, would bag a total of 37.7 million euros. Even for the smaller countries, just making it to the playoff round can mean a critical three million euro payday.

In 2017-18, English qualification was secured relatively early with Manchester City winning the league by 19 points. United finished second, followed by Tottenham and Liverpool in third and fourth. Arsene Wenger retired after Arsenal failed to qualify for a second straight year.

Most of the larger teams that enter the tournament go directly to the group stage, as all four English teams did this year. Sometimes the fourth-place English team must contest a two-leg, home-and-away playoff to qualify for the group stage.

But even before that, the so-called "minnows," the smaller clubs in Europe, play two preliminary rounds just to get to the final group stage qualifier. These games start in July and the final is played in early June, making the Champions League a truly "year-round" competition.

Ultimately, the tournament is narrowed down to 32 teams, in eight groups of four, just like the World Cup. In this case, every club plays the others in its group twice, one at home and one away. The top two teams in each group advance to the knockout round, and the third-place teams drop down to the Europa League knockout round.

The knockout rounds are two legs, home and away, determined by aggregate goals. In the case of a tie, away goals carry more weight. The final is one game with extra time and penalty kicks, played at a neutral site. This year's final is June 1, 2019 at Wanda Metropolitano in Madrid, Spain.

The European Cup was established in 1955, a joint effort between the board of UEFA – the Union of European Football Associations – and the editors of *L'Equipe*, the sports magazine in France. *L'Equipe* and its editor Gabriel Hanot had been calling for a European-wide competition between the champions of all of Europe's leagues, to determine who was the best.

In the midst of trying to organize the tournament themselves, *L'Equipe* was joined by a supportive UEFA board, which quickly signed on most member countries and organized a tournament starting in the fall of 1955 and culminating in the June 13, 1956 final, held at the Parc de Princes in Paris.

Real Madrid won that first European Cup, and indeed the first five, led by Argentinian Alfredo Di Stefano and Hungarian Ferenc Puskas, considered by many to be the two best players of the era.

English teams did not compete in the first European Cup, with Chelsea reluctantly withdrawing under pressure from the misguided Hardaker and the Football League. Manchester United's manager, Matt Busby, wouldn't be cowed and entered United in the Cup in 1956-57, against Hardaker's wishes.

United were knocked out in the semifinals by Real Madrid, but suffered a terrible tragedy during the next season's competition in 1958 when its plane crashed on takeoff in Munich, killing 23 people, including eight of United's starting 11 – one being 21-year old Duncan Edwards, who many considered the greatest of his generation.

Busby survived the crash, as did future England World Cup champion and knight, Sir Bobby Charlton. United rebuilt and in

1968, rose like a phoenix to win an emotional European Cup final over Benfica, 4-1, at Wembley Stadium. Charlton scored the first and last goals for United, who netted three times in extra time to break the tie.

It was the first title for an English team and the first held in England. But it wasn't the first for a British team, nor was it the first final contested on British soil. Hampden Park in Glasgow hosted the 1960 final, a 7-3 shellacking of Eintracht Frankfurt at the hands of Real Madrid.

And it was Celtic of Glasgow's famous "Lisbon Lions" who were the first British team to win the European Cup, just a year before United in 1967.

Celtic's attack unlocked Internazionale's (Milan) notoriously suffocating defense. Inter went up 1-0 early in the game and then set its defensive trap. But Celtic kept coming; taking 42 shots to Inter's five and eventually scoring two goals for the famous win at the Estadio Nacional in Lisbon. Remarkably, all 11 players in Celtic's lineup grew up within 27 miles of Parkhead, the Glasgow club's home stadium.

Celtic's win was the beginning of an era of Northern European dominance of the competition. The first 11 European Cups, before Celtic's win, all came from Spain, Italy or Portugal. Of the next 18 finals, 17 of the winners hailed from Northern Europe, including a run of six straight and seven of eight titles from England.

Dutch teams won four straight Cups from 1970-73, the last three all coming from Amsterdam's Ajax. That was followed by three straight wins for Bayern Munich, including a 2-0 Cup final victory over Don Revie's Leeds United in 1975.

Then it was England's turn to dominate when Liverpool won the first two of its five European Cups, the most in England, back-to-back in 1977 and 78.

The Reds' run of dominance was broken up, not by a European power, but by Brian Clough's unlikely Nottingham Forest squad – the biggest underdog story in European Cup history. Forest won two straight European Cups, over Sweden's Malmo and Hamburg of Germany. Before the 1980 semifinal against Ajax, Clough and his players had drinks in an Amsterdam bar. At the time, the English were so dominant, they could afford to get drunk and still beat Europe's best!

Liverpool added another title in 1981 over Real Madrid, and Aston Villa won the 1982 European Cup over Bayern Munich. Notably, during England's dominant run, six straight games ended in 1-0 scores, an indication of the style of play at the time.

After Hamburg interrupted the English dominance for a year, Liverpool added its fourth title in 1984, beating Rome in its home stadium, the Stadio Olimpico, on penalty kicks. A year later, things took a dark turn for English teams – and Liverpool fans were at the center of it.

This was during the height of hooliganism in English football – and wherever its teams traveled, violence and destruction followed. Europe had been wary, and there were clashes with police and Liverpool fans in Rome the year before.

The 1985 final, between Liverpool and Italy's Juventus, was held at the Heysel Stadium in Brussels. Juventus fans were sold tickets on the day of the game that seated them right in the middle of the Liverpool section. Violence broke out and Liverpool fans attacked the Juventus fans, forcing them to retreat over a decaying wall that collapsed. The crushing weight of people and wall killed 39 people, mostly Juventus fans.

The game went on, as authorities feared calling it off would lead to more fan violence. Juventus won on a questionable Michel Platini penalty, 1-0.

Arrests and extraditions would be made in the coming months – and Liverpool hooligans were deemed to be the guiltiest party. Europe had seen enough of English hooliganism mucking up their games. So had the English authorities.

On May 31, just two days after the disaster, FA president Bert Millchap, with then-Prime Minister Margaret Thatcher's support, announced an indefinite ban on English teams competing in Europe from outside 10 Downing Street, the Prime Minister's home. Two days later, UEFA made it official – with Liverpool getting an extra year beyond the overall English ban.

The ban would not be lifted until 1990. And no other English team would win the title until Manchester United in 1999. During that period, Italy's AC Milan won three titles and lesser European lights like Portugal's FC Porto, France's Marseille, Holland's PSV Eindhoven, Yugoslavia's Red Star Belgrade and Romania's Steaua Bucharest would all win European Cups.

Starting with the 1992-93 season, the European Cup, strictly a knockout competition, became the UEFA Champions League with the addition of a 32-team group stage, in the style of the World Cup.

Eventually, Liverpool completed its own move from tragedy to triumph, from villain to darlings, in the 2005 final in Istanbul. Despite finishing fifth in England, they reached the Champions League final under coach Rafael Benitez against heavily favored AC Milan and it's star-studded lineup, led by Brazil's Kaka.

Milan romped to a 3-0 lead in the first half and all looked lost. Then the so-called "Miracle of Istanbul" happened, with Steven Gerrard netting the first Liverpool goal and Xabi Alonso putting away a missed penalty to tie it 3-3.

The game eventually went to penalties where Liverpool's Polish goalie Jerzy Dudek continued his heroics and Liverpool eked it out, winning it's fifth European title – the most in England, as Reds' fans remind every one, every weekend.

Arsenal lost the 2006 final to Barcelona before Milan exacted revenge on Liverpool in the 2007 final.

Chelsea lost to Manchester United in the first all-English final in 2008 at the Luzhniki Stadium in Moscow, punctuated by an ill-timed John Terry slip on a penalty. United then lost two finals to Barcelona in 2009 and 2011. Chelsea returned to the final in 2012 and this time, the Blues defeated Bayern Munich on penalties with Terry missing out on the final through red card suspension.

Liverpool were the first English team to reach the final in six years when the Reds took on Real Madrid last year in the final in Kiev, losing 3-1 after star Mohammed Salah was forced off with an injury in the first half.

Real Madrid are the all-time leaders with 13 European Cup/Champions League victories. AC Milan is next with seven. Bayern Munich and Barcelona join Liverpool with five.

So if the Champions League is the tournament for the best teams in Europe, why the need for the **Europa League**, Europe's number two competition?

It's a combination of two ideas really: First, the desire to have certain cities host other European clubs every year, no matter where they finished in their league, because of the promise of larger crowds and larger gate receipts in those cities.

This is why the Inter Cities Fairs Cup was created at the same time as the European Cup. This was for cities like Amsterdam, London, Manchester, Barcelona, Napoli, etc – port cities with yearly trade fairs the games could be scheduled around.

The second reason is that domestic soccer is a lot like college basketball in America. There is a conference champion and a conference tournament champion – and they're not always the same team.

For many years, the National Invitational Tournament (NIT) was as competitive or more so than the NCAA tournament because the NCAA only accepted conference tournament champions. The NIT would then invite jilted regular season champions who didn't win their tournament.

In Europe, the European Cup invited the regular season champs, so the first Cup Winners Cup was held in 1960-61 to reward the winners of domestic cups across Europe who did not win their league.

In 1971-72, the Inter Cities Fairs Cup became known as the UEFA Cup because the tournament had expanded beyond just trade fair cities. In 1998, the Cup Winners Cup merged into the UEFA Cup and in 2004-05, a group stage was added to the competition for the first time. In 2009-10, the group stage was expanded to 48 teams and renamed the UEFA Europa League.

Qualification is complicated and digs deep into Europe's talent pool. In England, the fifth and sixth-place teams in the previous season's Premier League standings qualify for the Europa League, along with the League Cup winners.

If the League Cup winner is one of the top six teams, then the seventh-place team gets an invite to the Europa League. In 2016-17, in a rare exception, Man United won the League Cup and finished sixth in the Premier League. But since they won the Europa League, they gained automatic qualification to the 2017-18 Champions League.

The losers of the Champions League qualifying round, like the 2017-18 champion Atletico Madrid drop into the Europa League group stage. That stage is made up of 48 teams in 12 groups of four.

Like the Champions League, each team plays each other twice, home and away. The top two teams in each group advance to the knockout rounds, where they are joined by the eight third-place teams from the Champions League group stage.

These 32 teams play a series of two-leg knockout rounds until the one-game final, held at the Parc Olympique Lyonnais in 2017-18. The 2018-19 final is on May 29, 2019 at the Olympic Stadium in Baku, Azerbaijan.

For the soccer fanatic, the Europa League is a smorgasbord of unheard-of clubs, and deep dives into Spain, Italy and Germany. As we mentioned, Sevilla has won the most UEFA Cup and Europa League titles with five. Juventus, Inter Milan and Liverpool all have three titles. Tottenham has two; Chelsea and Man United have one title each.

Spurs also have a Cup Winners Cup (1963) and Chelsea have two Cup Winners Cups (1971 and 1998). Arsenal (1994), West Ham United (1965), Manchester City (1970) and Everton (1985) have all won Cup Winners Cups.

But because of the League Cup qualification route, some other smaller English clubs have made their mark in the UEFA Cup and Europa League. Ipswich Town won the 1981 UEFA Cup final. Middlesbrough went all the way to the final in 2006 before getting routed by Sevilla, 4-0.

Fulham reached the 2010 final after beating Juventus in the Round of 16, in part thanks to a goal from American Clint Dempsey. They lost, 2-1, in the final against Atletico Madrid, were relegated in 2014 and haven't returned to the Premier League since.

Europa League games are played on Thursday nights in Europe, and are shown on the same channels as the Champions League in the US with either 1 p.m. and/or 3 p.m. start times. This year Arsenal and Everton both made the group stage. Arsenal and Chelsea have already advanced to the knockout rounds of this year's Europa League. Burnley were eliminated after three rounds of playoff qualifying, falling to Olympiacos just one round short of the group stage.

Because of its proximity to the weekend games, the Europa League is often a place to play younger or second-team players. As a result, tickets can be easier to get and indeed, we were able to attend Chelsea and Arsenal Europa league group stage matches this season for nearly half the price of a league game.

Just goes to show, when you're planning a trip to England, don't overlook the Cup competitions, even the lesser ones. You can get more bang for your buck because there's just something about an elimination game and a European night that brings out the best in English fans.

9 Tips For Getting the Most Out of Your Premier League Experience

1) Become an Official Member of Your Favorite Club

This can easily be done online and will cost you anywhere from $25 to $60 a year depending on the team. But if you're even thinking about going to a game in the next couple of years, you need a membership. Most teams require it to buy tickets. Some teams don't even use paper tickets; they put them right on your membership card, which then slides through a scanner at the turnstile.

If you join your local supporters club (see #9), having an official membership will help your local club get official recognition from the football club – which can mean discounted tickets.

The longer you're a member – and the more tickets you buy – the more points you'll accrue with the club. For the clubs where it's difficult to get tickets – which is most of them – you'll need those points if you want to make this a regular trip, see European or Cup games, or attend an away game in your club's supporters section.

Even better, you'll get free goodies. Most clubs will send out a care package to their international members. You'll get a membership card and various club-branded trinkets from scarves to key chains to USB sticks. And you'll get some kind of booklet filled with club history and interviews. You'll feel a bit special the day you get it in the mail.

2) Don't Bring Your Beer Into the Stands

This is a major no-no in England and in most cases, will get you kicked out of the stadium immediately.

There is no alcohol allowed in the seating areas beyond the concourse level or "within view of the field" by rule. Signs are posted everywhere, but in case you miss them like we did the first time, the ushers will definitely stop you. And they're not all as nice as the Watford usher was to us. You could immediately get kicked out before the game's even started. Those are the rules.

Before the game and at halftime, the concourse area will be packed with people, double and triple fisting their beers and chugging to finish before play starts again. Be prepared for long lines. If you really want to get drunk, go to the pub early before the game. It's impossible or unhealthy to try to do so in the stadium – and still watch the match.

3) Walk as Much as You Can

Almost every stadium we went to is walkable from the city center or a train station. Seek out the proper route, get an umbrella or some rain gear, and prepare to walk a mile or two to the stadium.

Yes, it'll be good exercise, but we also found it to be the absolute best way to soak up the atmosphere and see the real England while mingling with fans. England's towns are mostly all designed to be walkable, and in lots of places there are canal ways with paths that take you totally off the street.

If you head out early, you'll see the local crowds moving towards the stadium and usually get a tip on which pub was best for that day's pregame activities.

4) Make Sure You Have Your Ticket Before You Go to the Pub

You're dressed and ready to go to the match. First stop: the pub.

But before you go, you'll want to make sure you have your game tickets or your membership card. Most of the home supporters' only pubs will have a big, scary guy outside to check your info and make sure you're not an away supporter there to cause trouble.

If you're picking up your ticket at will call, then you'll need to allow for time to go get your ticket first, then head to the pub.

5) Do NOT Wear Away Colors in Home Seats

Don't be a wise guy. Play by their rules. If you're the kind of person who turns up at games in Philly with New York gear on to make a statement, don't try it over there. The reaction will be even worse, if you can imagine that.

At best, you'll get kicked out by the stewards – the fine print on the tickets clearly states they have the right to do so. And it's for your own protection, because if they don't get you first, it's likely someone else will. And you will be outnumbered.

Yes, we didn't see as much fighting in England as there used to be and certain home fans were extremely tame. But, best not to push it. See your team at home, get official away tickets, or if you must get regular tickets at an away venue – wear neutral colors and don't sing along with the away fans or you'll be outed.

6) If You Can't Get a Ticket, Don't Expect to Watch the Game at the Pub

For various reasons, mostly misplaced protectionism, the Premier League TV product is really bad in England. On a number of occasions, one of us went to the game and one to the pub. But on 3 p.m. Saturday (10 a.m. US Eastern Time) starts, the game isn't on anywhere. A couple of the special timed games will be on at 5:30 p.m. Saturday and Sunday.

But in the main 3 p.m. Saturday BST slot, we got an old guy on TV reading out the reports from the multitude of games going on from a teleprompter. No highlights, no in-game updates. Nothing you're used to from an NFL Sunday, or channels like the MLB and NFL networks.

Basically, it's like watching sports in the 1980s, but with less highlights. And in fact, a lot of people we talked to in England stream NBC Sports' US broadcasts through a VPN to watch their local game on TV. The concept of a Saturday afternoon at the bar with games on multiple screens and people partying like they were at the stadium is foreign there.

7) Give the Championship a Chance

Some of the most fun we had in England came at Championship stadiums watching an exciting game in the playoff race. It's far easier (and cheaper) to get tickets to Championship games and you get more of the old school English football environment.

There's some really good talent and creative young coaches in the Championship, and it's an "any given Sunday" kind of league, no matter who you're playing you're never safe. We particularly enjoyed our time at Elland Road in Leeds, the Stadium of Light in Sunderland and the Liberty Stadium in Swansea.

8) Join a Supporters Club in the US and Watch Games with a Crow

Maybe it's not that easy for you to get to England, or you're worried you won't know anybody. That's a reason to join a supporters club here in the US.

Participation in stateside supporters clubs is soaring. And with NBC Sports' outstanding coverage on TV, more bars and restaurants are opening up early to give supporters' clubs a place to watch games.

This is a great way to meet other fans of your club and find likeminded people here in the US. Many of them will likely have connections to the English city of your club as well.

I love my club – the Liverpool Supporters Club of the Palm Beaches – and our pub, Brogues Downunder Bar. As soon as we told the guys – many of them Liverpool transplants – that we were headed to England, we immediately had scores of dinner recommendations, places to go, etc.

A lot of times, supporters groups will also get group rates on tickets and hotel reservations. These special tours can be an easy way to see a game without all the planning.

You can find your local supporters club on Facebook or Twitter and inquire with the page administrator as to how to join and where they watch games. You can also go to most team's official website and browse the list of officially recognized supporters clubs.

9) Use Air BnB in Most Places

You'll notice that we haven't recommended any hotels in the book and that's for a reason. We needed two rooms almost everywhere we went and for that, AirBnB is far more convenient and affordable.

We consistently found great places in cool parts of town, sometimes just a week or two ahead of time. The website is extremely easy to use and there are price options of all sorts, from cheap, bare minimum to luxury apartments in the ritzy part of town.

Make sure you pay attention to the reviews, which is the lifeblood of AirBnB. Check out the host's reviews carefully for any red flags. Make sure you leave honest feedback on the public reviews – if something is wrong, say it.

Most importantly, it means follow the rules and keep the place clean so you ensure you get good review. We got a couple hard-to-get places because our reviews were so good.

One other thing to note… most apartments in England only have a washer, most drying is done the old-fashioned way, on a drying rack. A few of the places we stayed had washer/dryer combinations, where it's all in one machine. But be aware you're not going to have a standard dryer to dry your clothes. Depending on the size of the city, there are a few sporadic laundromats with traditional, separate dryers.

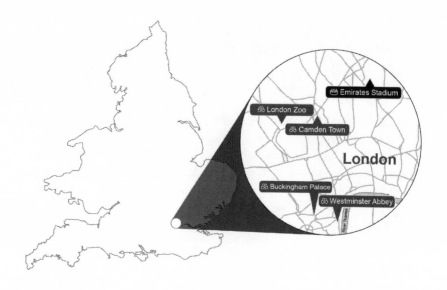

Arsenal Football Club

Year Founded: 1886

Colors: Red and White

Nickname: The Gunners

Stadium: Emirates Stadium

Address: Hornsey Road, London N7 7AJ, UK

Capacity: 60,260, 3rd in Premier League

2017-18 Average Attendance: 59,323, 3rd in Premier League

Trophies

Premier League/First Division (13): 1930-31; 1932-33; 1933-34; 1934-35; 1937-38; 1947-48; 1952-53; 1970-71; 1988-89; 1990-91; 1997-98; 2001-02; 2003-04

FA Cup (13): 1929-30; 1935-36; 1949-50; 1970-71; 1978-79; 1992-93; 1997-98; 2001-02; 2002-03; 2004-05; 2013-14; 2014-15; 2016-17

League Cup (2): 1986-87; 1992-93

European Cup Winners Cup (1): 1993-94

Current Ownership: Stan Kroenke, Kroenke Sports & Entertainment

Current Manager: Unai Emery (1st season)

2017-18 Finish: 6th in Premier League, 19W, 13L, 6D

Europa League: Lost in semifinals to Atletico Madrid, 2-1 aggregate.

FA Cup: Lost in third round at Nottingham Forest, 4-2

League Cup: Lost in final to Manchester City, 3-0

The Sports Tourists' Tips for Arsenal:

It's a Big Stadium – Look for Poor Matchups

An Arsenal membership (34 pounds for a Red Lite membership) is required to purchase tickets for games at the Emirates Stadium, but you'll find tickets more readily available here than at most other big clubs. Perhaps it's the dip in form or the size of the stadium or both, but good seats in the Clock End and throughout the stadium are available, particularly for midweek matchups, or games against lesser lights from outside of London. We had no problem getting tickets for a group stage Europa League math against FC Vorskla Poltava. And the tickets were nearly half the price of Premier League tickets.

Go on the Weekend If You Can

Not only is the stadium more boisterous and the crowd more excited on a Saturday evening or Sunday afternoon, but also the surrounding neighborhoods around the Emirates Stadium shut down quickly on weeknights. After the game we found it hard to find a bite to eat or more than a drink or two at most of the pubs down Holloway Road and Upper Street, a bustling area just hours before the game.

Three Tube Stops to Choose From

The most common place to disembark from the London Underground for the Emirates is the Holloway Road station, directly across from the stadium. But, as you can imagine, this station can be a zoo on game day/night. Less than a half-mile away is the Highbury and Islington station. You come right out, make a left on Holloway Road and you'll have a chance to walk past all of the pubs and eateries on the way to Arsenal. And if you're even more ambitious, you can choose to get off at Angel station and walk north on Upper Street, until you make a left on Holloway Road at the Highbury and Islington stop. Again, this longer walk (about 1.1 miles) opens up even more food and beverage options on your way, and passes our favorite spot in London to sit and read or relax, the Islington Green.

Tollington Arms Pub

The Gunners Pub is another popular pre-game watering hole just a couple blocks from the Emirates, but we enjoyed the Tollington Arms even more. Unlike a lot of pregame pubs, it doesn't feel the need to look as rundown as possible. Instead it's kept clean and looks like a bar you would go to even if it wasn't game day (something we can't say for a lot of others around England). There's great outdoor seating in front of the pub on game days, so you can watch people stream in to the Emirates. And it's spacious inside, with enough room to get a beer, but crowded enough to start a conversation with a fellow fan. Keep in mind, Arsenal supporters only are allowed in this pub before and after the games, and you'll need your membership card or ticket to prove it.

Camden Town

London's legendary counter culture, rock and roll neighborhood, Camden is home to lots of live music and funky people. It's located just off Regent's Park and the London Zoo, so it's a great place to end a day of walking with some people watching and beer.

The Old Queen's Head

Just north of the Angel Station up Essex Road (adjacent to Upper Street), from the outside the Old Queen's Head pub looks like it could barely fit 15 people. But with a giant upstairs dance floor and excellent bar service, it can fill up and still be fun. This is a great place to start your game day before moving on to the more crowded pubs right next to the Emirates. But it's also a great place to go on a night you're not watching a game, too.

Planet Organic

One thing that's often hard to find on a road trip, especially on the other side of the world, is healthy food options. Planet Organic in Islington (Essex Road) was our savior. They have real, healthy smoothies and lunch options at the back counter. And for once, the smoothies weren't filled with sherbet or ice cream or some other unhealthy nonsense, just good, natural fruit and veggies. The organic chocolate isn't bad either, if you're into that kind of thing.

Our Arsenal Experience

Only two matches into the new era, Arsenal fans could be forgiven if they had already started asking themselves, "Has anything changed?"

Stalwart gaffer Arsène Wenger stepped aside after 22 years, three Premier League titles and seven FA Cups following the conclusion of the 2017-18 season. Unai Emery arrived to fill his vacant seat at the end of May.

The Spaniard won three straight Europa League titles with Sevilla and led Paris Saint-Germain to 87 wins and one Ligue 1 title in two seasons before taking over in north London.

At his unveiling press conference, Emery described the opportunity with Arsenal as a "dream come true." He added that his long-term intention was to turn Arsenal into "the best team in the Premier League and also the world."

No less than former Gunners great Alan Smith said that it will be a "long road back" for Arsenal.

"I think success would be a top four finish," Smith added. "That would be a fantastic achievement... it's more about being a more substantial team with more substance, a bit more steel and a team which won't roll over... It's about changing that reputation back to Arsenal being tough to beat."

So, with supporters providing a spark of nervous energy, Emery emerged at the Emirates ahead of his team's 2018-19 season opener with champions Man City calm, cool and collected. A picture of him was posted in the stadium next to the phrase, "To the Next Chapter."

However, the hosts dropped a 2-0 result to Pep Guardiola's club. Six days later, they traveled to southwest London and dropped a 3-2 decision to Chelsea.

In light of this start, it was fair to ask, are Emery's new Gunners just like Wenger's old ones?

Were Arsenal fans going to see the same movie with a different lead actor?

That question must have laid in the subconscious of Arsenal's squad, because the club's response was a resounding "NO!"

Emery's new look group went on an 11-match win streak that encompassed seven Premier League tilts, three Europa League group stage games and a League Cup win over Brentford. A 2-2 draw with Palace brought the streak to an end, close enough to the club's record 14-match win streak to inspire newfound faith and joy.

And it all started at the top.

"Our success is first down to treating every match with the same importance," Emery said. "We need to have the same level of excitement for each match, so that we can make the Europa League games have the same excitement as the Premier League. Every title for us is very important... I want to play for every title going forward."

The streak put Emery in the same room as Arsenal legends Herbert Chapman (1925-34), George Graham (1986-95) and Wenger as Arsenal managers with win streaks of 11 or better.

During the club's run, contributions came from everywhere:

Goals from Nacho Monreal and Danny Welbeck in a 3-1 win over West Ham, the first match in the streak...

Scores from Shkodran Mustafi, Pierre-Emerick Aubameyang and Alexandre Lacazette in a 3-2 win over recently promoted Cardiff...

Debut tallies for Sokratis Papastathopoulos, Matteo Guendouzi and Emile Smith-Rowe in a 3-0 Europa League win over Qarabag in Azerbaijan.

It goes on and on. NBC's Robbie Earl described Arsenal as "robust" in his reviews of Arsenal's 1-1 draw versus Liverpool in early November.

With those two draws and another League Cup win, this time 2-1 over Blackpool, Arsenal extended its unbeaten run to 14.

Smith said he was looking for a bit of steel to propel Arsenal into the future. He found it in Lucas Torreira.

The Uruguayan, who played five games for his country in the World Cup in Russia, signed for 26 million pounds from Sampdoria over the summer.

Generously listed at 5-foot-5, Torreira is all grit. *The Guardian* sportswriter Barney Ronay noted Torreira's persistence in the Liverpool game, crediting him, along with Granit Xhaka, with forming a "Pulis-style cage in front of the defense."

Two-thirds of the way through the first half, he took down Liverpool's Sadio Mane.

"In front of the press box two home fans stood up and spontaneously hugged," Ronay added. "Vigor, energy, persistence, grit. What a change to see all of these things."

Maybe the most telling stat of the Gunners' newfound tenacity is their scoring lines when broken up by half. In the club's first 11 matches of the 2018-19 Premier League campaign, Arsenal had scored six goals in the first half, while conceding eight.

However, in the second half, Arsenal scored 19 goals and allowed just six. The Gunners have scored seven goals in the first 15 minutes of the second half while allowing none, indicating a readiness coming back out from the locker room. The credit would seem to go to the coaching staff.

We saw this first-hand as the Arsenal received a booming strike from Granit Xhaka in the 49th minute and a Mesut Ozil winner in the 58th of a 2-1 victory over Newcastle at St. James' Park in September.

And, they are closing games strong. They outscored opponents 7-3 in the game's final 15 minutes during the 11-game win streak.

It was this new-and-improved Arsenal side we expected to see on display at the Emirates for the Gunners' Europa League group stage opener against Vorskla Portava, from Ukraine.

We weren't sure what we would get on a Thursday night in the club's second consecutive year of Europa League play after that 19-year-long string of Champions League nights, but it ended up being one of the most pleasant experiences we had on this trip.

Europa League games are a fantastic opportunity to see Premier League clubs, as tickets are normally readily available. And they are usually offered at a much cheaper price. Our seats in the Clock End were just 17 pounds apiece – half what a Premier League ticket would cost.

It also allows supporters to see little-known squads like Vorskla, named after the river that runs through the city of Poltava, located almost 200 miles to the east of Kiev, which was playing Arsenal for the first time.

Vorskla plays in the Premier Liha in Ukraine. The club finished third last year behind stalwarts Dynamo Kiev and Shakhtar Donetsk, which have won 26 of the 27 Premier Liha titles between them. The club was 26 points behind Donetsk, but Vorskla's third-place finish was tied for its best ever.

The club has only existed in its current form since 1984, although the team history goes back as far as 1955. The Ukrainian squad's full value is 11 million pounds, or roughly one-fifth the transfer fee for Aubameyang, who came over from Borussia Dortmund in January.

Meanwhile, this was Arsenal's 34th season in European competition. The club has won two European honors – the 1969-70 Inter-Cities Fairs Cup and 1993-94 UEFA Cup Winner's Cup – and reached six finals.

Brief History of the Emirates Stadium

Arsenal FC have made two strategic moves in its history, first from the far reaches of the East End in Woolwich to the Highbury neighborhood of North London, where the Gunners played for 93 years at Arsenal Stadium, also known as Highbury.

In 1998, after Highbury residents rejected any further expansion to Arsenal Stadium, the club decided to fund it's own stadium nearby. Construction began in 2002 and in 2006, Arsenal moved from Highbury into a brand-new, state-of-the-art facility called the Emirates Stadium, due to a long-term sponsorship agreement with Emirates Airlines.

"The Emirates" added 26,000 more seats than Highbury, to a capacity around 61,000. It resembles a modern NFL stadium more than a traditional English football stadium. But, in the long term, the Arsenal board hopes it will keep them amongst the top clubs in Europe because of the revenue it generates, and not just because there's 25,000 more seats.

Already, the game day revenue just from executive boxes and club seats is equal to the whole game day revenue at Arsenal Stadium.

Like all big, new stadiums we saw, the quiet, spacy atmosphere of the Emirates has been criticized, although many rival fans were calling the smaller confines of HIghbury the "Library" for years, so perhaps it's not the stadium at fault. On our trip, we also found the wait to get through the turnstiles at the Emirates unnecessarily longer than anywhere else in England, something you wouldn't expect from a brand-new stadium.

Yes, the Gunners were favored.

The Emirates was extremely inviting. Fans were talking and bouncing around and supporters came from all over. Arsenal does an excellent job of recognizing its worldwide network of fans, allowing banners up throughout the stadium to display supporter allegiance from Australia to Alabama.

It was night-and-day compared to the experience we had in Manchester the night before for City's Champions League match with Lyon. We had a terrible time there, as you will see in that chapter.

These midweek matches normally offer a drastic change in the starting lineups, and Arsenal gave Bernd Leno his first start. The goalkeeper signed from Bayer Leverkusen over the summer and is expected to supplant Peter Cech sooner rather than later.

In front of nearly 60,000, Arsenal took the lead in the 38th minute on a goal from Aubameyang. The Gabonese striker was essentially a 1-for-1 replacement for Olivier Giroud, who was sold to Chelsea. Since his Premier League debut in February, and through the Vorskla match, Aubameyang was second only to Liverpool's Mo Salah in goals scored in Premier League play.

Aubameyang and Alexandre Lacazette, who transferred from Lyon prior to the 2017-18 season, have quickly turned into an indomitable duo for the Gunners. They scored a combined 12 league goals in an eight-game stretch through the Liverpool draw.

After the break, Welbeck scored in the 48th and Aubameyang scored again in the 56th as the Gunners stayed true to their second-half quick strike capabilities. Ozil, the highest scoring German ever in the Premier League as of October 2018, added a fourth goal for the Gunners in the 76th minute.

Arsenal did surrender two goals late in the 4-2 triumph, and the crowd did groan and moan a bit, but everyone left the Emirates in a good mood.

Arsenal is in a unique situation. As a club, it probably does not want to be in the Europa League. But under Emery, a man who is proud of his consecutive titles run with Sevilla, the Gunners have just the leader to engage them in another run.

In league play, the Liverpool match served as a litmus test for Emery's squad, which admittedly had built its streak up against lower caliber opponents. Despite going down in the second half on a James Milner goal, Arsenal recovered to earn the point at home on a beauty from Lacazette, who put himself in position to score through perseverance and determination.

The Guardian's David Hytner asked, "Would the team of the later Arsène Wenger years have fought back to equalize in the closing stages? Would they have continued to believe against opposition as streetwise as Jürgen Klopp's Liverpool?"

The answer is no. On that evening, Emery, who constantly tells reporters, players and anyone who will listen that he "wants to write a new history" at Arsenal was able to watch his squad's unyielding resolve in the face of a seemingly overwhelming opponent.

At the same time, Emery is not giving in to supporters who already feel Arsenal is ready for a title run. He remembers those results in August against City and Chelsea. He knows the path back to the top of the table is longer than anyone is willing to admit.

His players are working…

Hard.

Hytner noted that, under Wenger, the players "would finish training and sometimes feel they could do it all again. Modern professionals are supposed to need sleep after training. Wenger's usually did not."

In the same piece, Hytner goes on to state that "It is a different story now. Under Unai Emery the players know they have worked, and they certainly sleep. It is one example of the shifting sands at the club but, when the broader picture is laid out, it adds up to revolution… The only things left standing from the Wenger era are the walls."

The results and the process reflect Emery's career in the lower Spanish tiers at Llorca.

"I was a second division B player and I've had to work very hard," Emery said. "I tell the players: 'The moment we stop working hard on this, as soon as we stop dedicating hours to this, we'll fail.'"

While Emery stays focused on the process, supporters cannot contain their delight. Fans can be heard chanting "We've got our Arsenal back" at the Emirates. We heard it once or twice on the Vorskla evening.

Momentum is building back in north London.

"Arsenal… ARSENAL… ARSENAL!!!"

~ Brian Burden

North London Derby vs. Tottenham

The North London Derby matches two teams whose grounds are approximately 4.5 miles apart, both located at the top of the map of London, just above the downtown Tube grid. While it doesn't have the same luster as other nationwide derbies, or the veracity of other London derbies, this game means everything to both sets of fans.

Arsenal weren't always located in North London, but when they moved to Highbury in 1913, the derby was born. In 1919, after World War I, the league was expanded and a vote was held to decide which of six teams would fill the final, new spot in the First Division. Tottenham finished 20th the year before and expected to get the spot, but Arsenal won the vote – thanks to bribery, Spurs' fans would say.

The rivalry has some high-water marks, usually in favor of Arsenal. In 1971, the Gunners claimed the league title over Leeds with a win at White Hart Lane on Ray Kennedy's header three minutes from time. The famous Invincible team claimed the title with a draw at White Hart Lane, celebrating on the field with an inflatable trophy after the Premier League chose not to present the trophy in a hostile environment.

Arsenal finished ahead of Tottenham in the Premier League for 22 straight years, leading to a tongue-in-cheek holiday called "St. Totteringham's Day" – the day Arsenal clinch a spot ahead of Spurs in the standings; and an infamous chant, "It happened again… Tottenham Hotspur, it happened again."

There was no "St. Totteringham's Day" in 2016-17 or 2017-18, however, as Tottenham finished ahead of Arsenal both years.

Arsenal also considers all London clubs rivals, mostly Chelsea at the moment. The Blues owner Roman Abramovich and former coach Jose Mourinho were determined to take Arsenal's crown as the dominant London team in the early 2000s, and they've been largely successful. Arsenal earned some revenge in the 2017 FA Cup final, beating league champion Chelsea, 2-1, in a thriller.

Brief History of Arsenal Football Club

Arsenal Football Club was founded in 1886 far from its current North London location. A group of workers at the Royal Arsenal Factory in Woolwich, then Kent, but now part of greater East London, started the team. They called themselves Dial Square for the sundial on top of the factory.

Soon they were called Royal Arsenal and then Woolwich Arsenal, and in the early days of professionalism, were joined by a group of players who had been champions at Nottingham Forest. The Forest connection led to the team's red and white colors.

Without enough of a crowd out in the eastern marshes, in 1913 Woolwich Arsenal moved to Highbury in North London, dropping the Woolwich to become Arsenal FC. The cannons on their crest and nickname, the Gunners, continue to represent the club's origins.

Arsenal didn't enter the national conscious until they hired Herbert Chapman away from Huddersfield Town in 1925. Chapman was coming off back-to-back First Division titles and an FA Cup with Huddersfield. In his first season, he took an
Arsenal team that had flirted with relegation to second-place in the First Division – behind his old club.

The Gunners finally broke through in the 1930 FA Cup, beating Huddersfield and sparking a run of trophies, including four of the next five First Division crowns and another FA Cup in 1936. During the 1934-35 title run, Ted Drake scored a club record 44 goals and would go on to be Arsenal's all-time scorer in the pre-World War II era. Sadly, Chapman died of pneumonia in January 1934, right as the team he put together rose to glory. Arsenal added one more title before World War II put everything on hold.

In the first decade after the war, Arsenal, now established as one of the most famous teams in England, grabbed three more league titles and an FA Cup. Then the Gunners embarked on an 18-season trophy drought, which was ended in dramatic fashion with a trophy double in 1970-71.

After winning the Inter Cities Fairs Cup the season before, the young, talented squad was primed for a run at the title. On the final day of the season, it was in the Gunners' sights. A win or a goalless draw would clinch the trophy – any other result would mean Leeds were champions. Ray Kennedy's late header beat rivals Tottenham, 1-0, on the road at White Hart Lane to earn the victory. Five days later, Arsenal had to come from behind against another talented young club, Liverpool, to win the FA Cup and do the double for the first of three times in the club's history.

Arsenal went another 18 years after that without a league title – winning just the 1979 FA Cup, before former player and Millwall coach George Graham took over in 1986. Building around a disciplined defensive approach epitomized by defender Tony Adams – England and club captain – the famous song of "One-nil to the Arsenal" struck fear in opponents hearts. Graham won a League Cup in his first year, and then added two more league titles, powered by the goal scoring exploits of Alan Smith and Ian Wright.

Arsenal then won both the FA and League Cups in 1993, and earned its first (and only) major European trophy the very next year, winning the Cup Winners Cup, 1-0, over Parma, the last trophy of the Graham era. And that leads to the Arsene Wenger era, arguably the most glorious in this great club's history because of one particularly brilliant team.

Wenger, an unknown French manager at the time, was hired in the fall of 1996 and in his second season, took Arsenal to the double – Premier League and FA Cup titles – playing with a vastly more open passing and attacking style compared to Graham. In 1999, he signed young French striker Thierry Henry – the greatest player in the club, and perhaps the Premier League's, history. Henry is Arsenal's all-time leading scorer with 228 goals. With the skill and speed of Henry, combined with the playmaking ability of Dutchman Dennis Bergkamp and Spaniard Robert Pires, and the midfield stewardship of captain Patrick Vieira, the Gunners won the double again in 2002, and back-to-back FA Cups in 2003. Then in 2003-04, the impossible happened.

A superb season from Henry and defensive reinforcements Kolo Toure and Sol Campbell took Arsenal to another level when the Gunners became the first – and only – team in modern history to finish the season unbeaten, winning 26 games and drawing 12 while outscoring opponents, 73-26. The team known as "The Invincibles" are considered not just the best in Arsenal history, but arguably the best in English league history.

Wenger also gets credit for helping design and build the team's first-class training facility at Colney and for steering the team through a tight financial squeeze brought on by the building of the Emirates Stadium and their 2006 move from Highbury.

Unfortunately, like most of its history, Arsenal was never able to turn that domestic dominance into victory in Europe, reaching the Champions League finals just once before losing to Barcelona, 1-0, in the 2006 final. And since "The Invincibles" season, Wenger has failed to win another league title – with the drought now reaching 13 seasons. In 2016-17, the Gunners streak of 22 consecutive seasons in the top four of the Premier League, and 19 in the Champions League, came to a halt with a fifth-place finish. It was followed by a sixth-place finish in 2017-18. Wenger's final year at the helm.

2017-18 Season Review

Arsène Wenger's 22nd and final season with Arsenal went out with more of a whimper than a bang. The club finished out of the Top 4 for the second consecutive season, totaling 63 points to place sixth in the Premier League table, the lowest finish and points total in the Wenger era.

The points total was the club's worst since 1995-96, and their place in the table was the lowest since a 12th-place finish in 1994-95. They surrendered 51 goals, the most in league play since 1983-84, when the club allowed 60 goals in a 42-game season.

The finish means the Gunners failed to qualify for the Champions League for a second straight season. A run to the Europa League semifinals, where Wenger's squad lost to eventual champ Atletico Madrid, did nothing to soften the blow. It was the first time since 1997-98 that Arsenal was not in the Champions League.

Although Arsenal was still strong at Emirates (15-2-2) Stadium, the Gunners managed just four wins away from north London, going 4-11-4 on the road. In fact, Arsenal's season-ending victory at Huddersfield represented the club's only away win in 2018, and the team managed just 16 points on the road.

The FA Cup had been a source of pride for Wenger and the Arsenal faithful, with the Gunners winning three of the last four cups, including a record 13th in 2016-17. However, Arsenal fell to Nottingham Forest in the club's opening match, negating even the possibility of temporary happiness.

Arsenal made a much deeper run in the League Cup, knocking off Chelsea in the semifinals before falling to Manchester City, 3-0, in the final.

The club made a few moves, trading Alexis Sanchez to Manchester United for Henrikh Mkhitaryan in January and bringing Pierre-Emerick Aubameyang over from Borussia Dortmund on a club-record transfer. He proceeded to score 10 goals in 13 league games, providing a spark for the future. Aubameyang scored twice to lead the Gunners in an emotional 5-0 victory over Burnley in Wenger's last match at the Emirates.

In addition, Alexandre Lacazette led the club with 14 goals and Aaron Ramsey had seven goals and eight assists in somewhat of a rebound year.

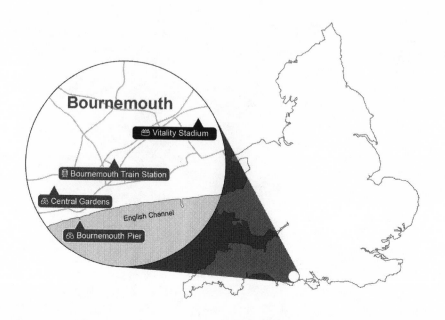

AFC Bournemouth

Year Founded: 1890

Colors: Red and Black Vertical Stripes

Nickname: The Cherries

Stadium: Vitality Stadium

Address: King's Park Drive, Bournemouth BH7 7AF

Capacity: 11,329, 20th in Premier League

2017-18 Average Attendance: 11,105, 20th in Premier League

Trophies

None

Current Ownership: Maxim Demin

Current Manager: Eddie Howe (10th season, 167W, 123L, 79D)

2017-18 Finish: 12th in Premier League, 11W, 16L, 11D

FA Cup: Lost in third round replay at Wigan, 3-0 (tied 2-2 in first game)

League Cup: Lost in fifth round at Chelsea, 2-1

The Sports Tourists' Tips for Bournemouth

Relegation May Be Your Only Hope for Tickets

Obviously, if you're a Bournemouth fan, you wouldn't hope for them to get relegated. But the truth is, tickets to see Bournemouth are pretty much unavailable right now because of the size of the stadium. But when a team falls down the standings some of the fans stop going. And that may be the opening you need to see tickets reach a general sale. If not, just keep watching and waiting.

Go to King's Park on a Gameday

Even if you can't get tickets, King's Park on a fall or spring day is a treat. There are big fields, places for kids to play and an ice cream stand. On top of that, you can hang out near the Vitality Stadium and get involved in the pregame atmosphere. During the game, you can listen for the swings of the crowd to tell you what's happened.

Best Town on the South Coast?

There are beautiful towns strung across the South Coast, but Bournemouth may take the cake. The narrow streets are loaded with shops, restaurants and pubs. The city's Gardens are extensive with winding paths that go through the center of town.

Bournemouth's beach is the most scenic we saw in England, with beautiful sand – unlike the rocks in Brighton and docks in Southampton – tucked into the cliffs running along the road. The Bournemouth Pavilion and Pier are picturesque.

Seek Out the Four Horsemen in the Triangle

The Triangle area is a confusing confluence of curving roads, but its also where most of the highly –rated pubs in Bournemouth are located. The Four Horseman isn't necessarily a "gameday" pub, but it's got everything you want for a non-gameday. The Four Horseman has an extensive beer menu, high-quality food and live music more often than not. We only got to visit three different Bournemouth pubs, but this was the best atmosphere of the bunch.

Come Down From London

If you're living or staying in London for an extended period, Bournemouth is perfect for a weekend road trip. It's easy to reach by train – the ride is around two hours. And the relaxed setting will help you unwind from the big city for a couple days. Maybe if you're lucky, you can get into the Vitality Stadium to see a game.

Our Bournemouth Experience

There have been legendary quests in history...

Those to find the Holy Grail...

Others to locate the Fountain of Youth...

But for us, our biggest quest was to discover vitality...

Two seats in the Vitality that is!

Arguments can be made about the toughest sports venues to get into, but few present as unique a challenge as Bournemouth's Vitality Stadium. With a current capacity of 11,329 and supporters delighting in the club's first stay in the top tier, attaining tickets to the Premier League's smallest cathedral has been a challenge, to say the least.

In fact, it was the only home ground we were unable to get into during our first trip through the league. We tried and tried to no avail. For us, Vitality remained a great secret...

A forbidden city...

A lost treasure...

And it left us feeling a bit incomplete. So, when we made our second trek to the UK, we were determined to get the golden ticket to Eddie Howe's football factory.

The Cherries are one of the Premier League's greatest success stories, having almost been out of the English Football League as recently as 2008-09.

That season, the club was deducted 17 points before a ball was ever kicked for failing to get out of administration ("legal procedure that allows a business in financial trouble to keep operating without being forced to sell off assets to pay debts," according to BBC Sport) and remaining insolvent, finishing 21st in League Two.

Howe, a defender for both Bournemouth's youth and senior clubs, came on board as manager during that disastrous campaign, and oversaw a rebuilding of his club, resulting in a promotion to League One immediately after finishing second in 2009-10.

After a failed dalliance with Burnley, Howe came back in October 2012 and again made an immediate impact, leading his Cherries to another promotion, this time to the EFL Championship.

Just two years later, Bournemouth won that division and made its first appearance in England's top tier in club history. The team survived the first season, finishing 16th. It improved on that with a ninth-place finish in 2016-17 and stayed reasonably close a year later, finishing 12th with 44 points.

The seaside resort town in southern England was buzzing at a fever pitch for the Cherries, and we wanted to experience the fervor. This year, we were getting into that stadium.

It took some work, but we secured hospitality seats for Bournemouth's league match with Crystal Palace in early October. After enjoying some quality time strolling some of the seven miles of beaches the city is known for, we traveled over to Vitality.

It wasn't a Cup final 0r a promotion final at Wembley. It wasn't even a match with Premier League title implications. But we were as giddy as if we were attending any one of the above. We were finally getting in!

After arriving outside the stadium, we took a walk around the periphery. Like many clubs in England, Bournemouth does a great job chronicling the best parts of its club history via photographs. The great teams, the beloved squads, the winners.

Eddie Howe showed up in a lot of those pictures, along with top assistant Jason Tindall.

Those two have been nearly inseparable the past 20 years. Tindall was born two weeks before Howe in November 1977. Howe is a Bournemouth lifer, starting with the club in 1994. Tindall joined Howe, who made his senior team debut in 1995, at Bournemouth in 1998.

The two played together in Bournemouth's central defense for four years before Howe moved on to Portsmouth. They came back together in January 2009, with Tindall serving as an assistant at Bournemouth and Howe appointed as caretaker manager once Jimmy Quinn was sacked on New Year's Eve. They have been together ever since, sandwiching two coaching stints with the Cherries around an 86-match stint with Burnley between 2011-2012.

When Howe and Tindall took over as the youngest managerial pair in all of English football that January, Bournemouth was 91st out of 92 teams and on its way out of the Football League.

By early November 2018, the Cherries were sixth in the Premier League, mentioned in the same breath as the traditional top six teams, and visions of future European play dancing in supporters' minds for the first time.

Brief History of Vitality Stadium

Bournemouth began playing in its current location – originally a wasteland on the edge of King's Park – in 1910. The land was leased to the club – then called Boscombe FC – by JE Cooper-Dean, a local businessman and land owner. The long term lease had one stipulation, all renovations had to be approved by the Cooper-Dean estate.

The original stadium for this small club was called Dean Court, in honor of its benefactor. 107 years later, it's called Vitality Stadium thanks to sponsorship and it's still the home of Bournemouth, albeit on the massive stage of the Premier League.

Because of its small footprint off to one side of King's Park, Vitality Stadium only holds 11,360 people – making it the smallest stadium in the Premier League, just over half the size of Watford's Vicarage Road. Tickets are extremely hard to come by and limited to the hard-core locals. There are none of the modern-day cash cows, like club boxes or hospitality seating.

In 2005, facing financial troubles, Bournemouth sold the stadium to Structadene for 3.5 million pounds, and leased it back for 300,000 pounds a year.

Any attempts to expand beyond its current configuration have been hampered by Structadene's insistence that AFC Bournemouth pay for the renovations completely and the Bournemouth Borough Council's rejection of a larger stadium in King's Park because of pressure from the locals.

As of late 2016, Bournemouth was looking for new locations in the area to hold a more modern, expanded stadium fitting of a Premier League team. Until then, the Cherries hope to stay in the Premier League long enough to justify the step up in ground quality.

"Who knows what we can achieve? If we had this conversation six years ago, we'd have been in dreamland to think we'd be where we are," Tindall told Stuart James in October 2018. "We don't want to put any kind of limits on it, saying we're never going to do this or that; each year we're striving to be better."

The two share an office and often share the technical area. If you watch Bournemouth games, those two are often right next to each other, probably more so than any manager and assistant manager in the league.

"We're constantly talking to each other – it's the way we've always been," Tindall said.

In fact, when Howe was being courted by multiple clubs, including Burnley, in January 2011, it was Tindall that served as his getaway driver to avoid the press.

While discussing the success of that duo, we made our way into Vitality for the start of our VIP experience. This is often the best way to see a club when regular tickets are not available. Although pricier, the clubs normally make it worth your time and your dime. Bournemouth would be no different.

We were escorted into a large dining area that overlooked the field and enjoyed a quaint dinner with a couple and a group of men we thought were passionate Cherries supporters, but who turned out to be Man U backers.

Dinner was served, a trivia contest took place and so much more. Again, you can have similar experiences at virtually all the clubs in the top tier if you are willing to pay up. The differences you will find are in the service and some of the quirky perks that come with clubs' offerings. Thanks to the great meal, good drink and a festive atmosphere, Bournemouth's ranks as one of the best.

After the meal, we headed out to our seats on the right side of the West Stand, directly across from the Palace supporters. This was tough for us. We root for Bournemouth, the little engine that could that powers onward with an exciting brand of soccer.

But, we also root hard for Palace, especially because their supporters are some of the consistently loudest we have come upon.

This was a big match for Bournemouth. It was the club's first time on television in the UK all season. Additionally, it had never won on a Monday night in the Premier League. It was the only match that evening, a marquee contest under the lights that added an extra flair to the experience.

Howe and Tindall weren't happy with the way the Cherries started the 2017-18 season with four losses, spending the first half of the season just trying to escape the drop zone. The two made sure their squad would be fitter and better prepared for the new campaign, through a fiercer training regimen and additional pre-season contests.

2017-18 Season Review

Bournemouth finished 12th in 2017-18 and secured a fourth consecutive season in the Premier League. The Cherries started the season with four straight losses and spent the bulk of the first half either in or just above the drop zone.

They did take advantage of clubs either just promoted (Brighton, Huddersfield, Newcastle) or soon to be relegated (Stoke, Swansea, West Brom) finishing 7-2-3 against them.

Despite winning just four games on the road, Bournemouth had the ninth best record away in the league, better than Arsenal and Everton.

More importantly, Eddie Howe's club defeated Arsenal and Chelsea during a stretch where the Cherries won five and drew seven in 14 games, losing just twice between Boxing Day and the middle of April.

That stretch of play boosted Bournemouth from 18th to a spot in the top half of the table. Three straight losses – Liverpool, Man U and Southampton – brought the club back to Earth. Wins over Swansea and Burnley closed the season on a high note.

Overall, despite adding the likes of Nathan Ake and Jemain Defoe, Bournemouth never won more than two straight games and could not improve on its 9th-place finish in 2016-17.

Callum Wilson and Josh King each led the club with eight goals while Junior Stanislas, Lewis Cook, Ryan Fraser and David Brooks offered healthy glimpses of potential for the future.

Bournemouth went out early in the FA Cup, losing at League One side Wigan on a replay, 3-0. The Cherries reached the quarterfinals of the League Cup, losing at Chelsea, 2-1.

The Cherries made Howe and Tindall look like geniuses in the opening portion of the season, pulling three wins and 10 points from the first six matches. They looked even better in the opening minutes of our game, overwhelming Palace in an exciting start. Josh King, Callum Wilson, Ryan Fraser and Lewis Cook all had an extra gear to begin with.

But it was David Brooks, an 11.5 million-pound Sheffield United transfer who shined the most early on. The 21-year-old represented both Wales and England at the youth level before

New Forest Derby v. Southampton

AFC Bournemouth has never really had a true derby, at least not until two seasons ago when the Cherries were put in the same division as Southampton, the closest club to Bournemouth's Dorset location.

Just 27 miles apart, the train ride between Southampton and Bournemouth's South coast locations goes through a national park called The New Forest. Some publications have started calling the rivalry, the "New Forest Derby", but the name hasn't really caught on. Bournemouth was always seen as Southampton's little brother. When the Cherries had financial problems, Southampton held charity matches to raise money for them. Loads of Bournemouth academy players, like Adam Lallana, have made the move to the big city, Southampton.

The same goes for local fans. With Bournemouth mired at the lower levels of the Football League and Southampton in the top division, many locals adopted Southampton as their club. On top of that, because it's such a vacation destination, many Bournemouth locals aren't originally from there.

The teams had never met regularly until Southampton had financial troubles of its own and dropped into League One in 2010-11, the same league as Bournemouth. The Saints won both matchups that year and were promoted to the Championship, then up to the Premier League the very next season.

Bournemouth took a little longer, but the two teams have played four times in the past two Premier League seasons, with Bournemouth earning a 2-0 home win in 2015-16, the first competitive victory for the Cherries over Southampton since a 1987 League Cup game. Last season, Bournemouth lost at Southampton and drew at home.

Southampton's hated rivals will always be Portsmouth. Southampton fans are more amused and annoyed then passionate about a rivalry with Bournemouth. For Bournemouth fans, years of playing the little brother has built up the rivalry. Will it catch on? That depends on Bournemouth's Premier League staying power.

deciding on Wales for his senior career. And he scored the opener here in the fifth minute, taking a pass from Wilson before finishing for his first Bournemouth score.

The score elicited an eruption from the fans that sounded intimidating in the compact complex. Vitality is a single tier complex all around, so every sound was contained, promoting each cheer to mass effect.

The Cherries are intoxicating to watch in real-time. You get the sense that every sequence is played out with the urgency that normally comes with the last few minutes of matches, even just seconds into the competition. The youngsters moved at a dizzying pace early.

The visitors equalized early in the second half on a controversial non-call. Patrick Van Aanholt slipped behind Simon Francis and received a pass from Wilfried Zaha, Palace's talisman. Despite being clearly offside, no flag went up and Van Aanholt blasted a right-footed shot into the goal in the 55th minute.

Yet, with no Christian Benteke up top, Palace's over reliance on Zaha made the Eagles fairly toothless in attack most of the evening. Still, Bournemouth could not take the lead and, as the clock moved closer to the 90th minute, Palace's supporters got louder and louder.

But, that may have been to compensate for a Palace side that was slipping toward the end of regulation. Bournemouth wasted no time taking advantage. A late sequence from Bournemouth into Palace's end resulted in a free kick. Those who follow soccer know that, since the World Cup, referees have been instructed to pay closer attention to the physicality that takes place between opposing players on set pieces.

That attention paid huge dividends for Bournemouth and cost Palace dearly.

Palace's Mamadou Sakho scuffled with Bournemouth's Jefferson Lerma, pushing him away to the extent the referee blew his whistle and issued a warning specifically to Sakho about his actions.

As play started back up and Fraser took the kick, Sakho threw his arm up and made significant contact with the Colombian as the whistle blew. The referee pointed to the spot and a bewildered Sakho and Palace looked on as Junior Stanislas gave the Cherries the lead in the 87th minute.

The goal elicited yet another deafening roar from the Cherries' supporters. Three more points were in hand.

Bournemouth held on and Palace was denied its 100th Premier League win and 200th overall victory in the top flight. Zaha was denied in his bid to become the first Palace player to score in four straight away matches since Mark Bright accomplished the feat in the fall of 1991.

The match ended with an air of WWE to it. Palace players sniped and griped at one another as well as with Bournemouth and the two sides came close to fisticuffs at the close of affairs. It was just what you might expect from a Monday night full of entertainment.

Offensively, the Cherries are finding the back of the net with more regularity. Their two goals in the win over Palace were followed by four in a shutout victory over Watford five days after we visited Vitality.

These six goals helped give Bournemouth reach 16 goals in its first eight league games, a number the club did not reach until Boxing Day last year.

For the first quarter of the season, Howe and Tindall's preparations have worked, especially on the offensive end. Observers rightfully praise Howe for not playing 10 men behind the ball when he goes up against the giants. His side is aggressive and brings the game to its opponent, whomever that might be.

In short order, Howe's club has emerged as one of the favorites to have a season similar to Burnley's in 2017-18, possibly qualifying for European play for the first time by finishing a few more notches up the table.

Not bad for a club that was 91st a decade ago. And it has all been done in this little stadium built in 1910. And we were finally there to witness a game. Quest complete! Our 28th stadium was in the books.

We have now been to all 20 home grounds currently in the Premier League, as well as the homes of Hull, Leeds, Reading, Sheffield Wednesday, Stoke City, Sunderland, Swansea City and West Brom, not to mention Wembley Stadium on multiple occasions.

Where will we go to next?

~ BB

Brief History of AFC Bournemouth

For over 100 years, AFC Bournemouth was a mostly forgotten about club in a beautiful place – the sandy cliffs of the South Coast in Dorset. The original seeds of the club were planted by the Boscombe St. John's Institute Football Club, which started play in 1890. Boscombe is a nearby town to Bournemouth.

That club folded in 1899 and Boscombe FC was formed out of what was left. In 1902, Boscombe FC moved to King's Park, right next to where the Vitality Stadium stands today. In 1910, JE Cooper-Dean gave the club a long lease on a patch of wasteland on the edge of King's Park. The new location was called Dean Court, after the man who gave them the ground.

It's thought the team's nickname, "the Cherries", came from this same period as Cooper-Dean also kept a number of cherry trees on his nearby property. Boscombe's jerseys were also black and red vertical stripes, like Bournemouth's today.

The Cherries didn't play in a fully professional league until they joined the Southern League in 1920. Before that, the club competed in the semi-professional Hampshire League and did not enter the FA Cup until 1913-14. In 1923, its first year in the new Third Division South, the club changed its name to Bournemouth and Boscombe Athletic.

The Cherries remained in the Third or Fourth Division for the next 64 years, changing its name to AFC Bournemouth in 1971, allegedly so the club would be at the top of alphabetical lists of Football League teams.

Cherries' fans have long riffed off Millwall's song, singing "Nobody knows us and we don't care." Truly, AFC Bournemouth made very little noise besides a run to the FA Cup quarterfinals in 1957.

Things changed when one of England's most well-known coaches, Harry Redknapp, set up camp at Bournemouth and made his first mark as a coach at the South Coast club. Redknapp played 101 games in four years with Bournemouth in the 1970s, before moving to the US to play for and eventually serve as assistant coach with the Seattle Sounders. In 1982, he returned to Bournemouth as assistant manager and in 1984 he took over the head job.

It was that season when Redknapp and the Cherries made a name for themselves in the FA Cup. In the third round, Bournemouth drew a home game with Manchester United, the defending Cup champions. United would also go on to win the Cup in 1985 as well. Milton Graham scored the first goal, followed up quickly by an Ian Thompson goal to make it 2-nil, a scoreline that held.

"The only person that thought we could win was Harry – at least that's what he said to us," Thompson said. "Then when it was still scoreless at halftime, we began to believe in ourselves."

Later that season, Bournemouth won the Football League trophy, a tournament contested between Third and Fourth division teams, and then won the Third Division in 1986-87, moving up to the Second Division for three years.

In 1990 Redknapp and four others, including Redknapp's good fried Brian Tiler, Bournemouth's managing director, were traveling in a mini-bus in Italy during the World Cup. A car hit them at full speed and flipped the bus over. Tiler was killed, as was the bus driver and the two Italians in the other car. Redknapp, doused in gasoline, had to be dragged away from the accident and was thought dead. The accident left Redknapp with his now famous facial tic. After a long recovery, Redknapp's heart wasn't into football and he quit Bournemouth in 1991-92. (Though he ended up in charge of West Ham months later.)

The Cherries sunk back into football oblivion – and nearly beyond. With the club's finances in disarray, Bournemouth were docked 10 points and relegated from League One in 2007-08, dropping to the bottom of the Football League. The next year, the Cherries were docked 17 points to start the season as punishment for financial administration. They lingered at the bottom of English professional football all season, trying to make up the gap. Former defender Eddie Howe, then 31 years old, was named head coach.

Slowly, Bournemouth chipped away at the gap and got in position to reach safety with a win on the final day of the season. Club legend Steve Fletcher banged in a goal to beat Grimsby Town, clinching safety in the so-called Great Escape. The very next season, 2009-10, Bournemouth was promoted to League One. The Cherries won another promotion, to the Championship, in 2012-13 and two years later, they won the 2014-15 Championship title, led by 20 goals from Callum Wilson – still a regular in the current lineup.

It was the first time Bournemouth made it to the top division of English football. Instead of going right back down, the Cherries – buoyed by back to back wins at Chelsea and home against Manchester United – hung onto 16th place and safety, despite losing four of their last five games.

In 2016-17, Bournemouth soared to new heights, moving into the top 10 of the most competitive league in the world, with an impressive ninth-place finish.

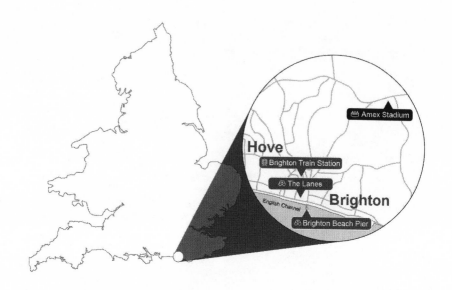

Brighton and Hove Albion Football Club

Year Founded: 1901

Colors: Blue and White

Nickname: The Seagulls; The Albion

Stadium: American Express Community Stadium

Address: Village Way, Brighton BN1 9BL, UK

Capacity: 30,666, 14th in Premier League

2017-18 Average Attendance: 30,397, 12th in the Premier League

Trophies:

None

Current Ownership: Tony Bloom

Current Coach: Chris Hughton (5th season, 76W, 48L, 46D)

2017-18 Finish: 15th in Premier League, 9W, 16L, 13D

FA Cup: Lost in quarterfinals at Manchester United, 2-0

League Cup: Lost in third round at Bournemouth, 1-0 (AET)

The Sports Tourists' Tips for Brighton and Hove Albion

Tickets are Easy to Get

Brighton is a popular ticket, but still an easy one to get. You will have to register with the club for free, but a membership is not required to buy tickets, though it will give you priority for the bigger games. Tickets should be available on general sale for less glamorous opponents.

Take the Bus to the Game – It's Free

The reason it was so hard to find a place to build the Amex is because there is no available space near the center of town. The Amex is nearly four miles up a hill from Brighton city center. It's best to take public transport. You can take the train directly from Brighton train station to the Falmer stop. You are also eligible for a free bus ride from downtown to the Amex and back with your ticket purchase.

Enjoy an Evening Out on the Lanes

Brighton is a fun town and the best place to go for hustle and bustle are the Lanes, a series of snaking brick-lined alleys packed with coffee shops, restaurants, and pubs. This is of the coolest neighborhoods in all of England. Our favorite stop on the lanes (amongst many) was Dos Sombreros, a funky Mexican place on Ship Street – not far from where Brighton and Hove Albion was founded.

Spend a Day Out at Brighton Beach Pier

So Brighton has a huge waterfront area, looking out at the English Channel. Unfortunately, it's made of rocks, not sand. But built over top of those rocks is Brighton Beach Pier, perhaps the best beach pier we've ever been to. There's everything there, junk food, video games, carnival rides, a roller coaster. And smack in the middle, a pub called The Victoria, where we watched Tottenham end its curse against Arsenal and made some new friends. Highly recommended.

Dance For God's Sake

This place isn't the home of Fatboy Slim for nothing. On most nights you can find somewhere to dance and someone very talented on the turntables. Brighton stays up late and sleeps in, it's England's party getaway town. Keep an eye out for flyers and tune into 1 Brighton FM for information on shows. We especially recommend our boy Steve KIW, and Michael Hosie's Whiskey Preachin Radio Show. Great guys with a great ear for music.

The Black Dove Pub

There isn't really a pub atmosphere near the stadium; instead people drink in pubs downtown before heading to the Amex on the bus or train. The Black Dove wasn't the most packed bar before a game, but the St. James' Street establishment had the best service both on a lazy early afternoon and later when the bar was packed. Lots of different beers, quality cocktails and more cider options than the average English pub as well. Staff was friendly, this was one of the best pubs we went to in England.

VIP Pizza

This may be the best pizza we had in England. Located on Old Steine, this is authentic Italian pizza (Very Italian Pizza is what the VIP stands for) with incredible dough. It's a tight squeeze inside, but in the convivial Brighton atmosphere, it made things fun.

Our Brighton and Hove Experience

Once you make it to the Premier League, how do you stay up?

Do you spend ungodly sums of money on new players to replace the ones that got you promoted?

Do you go all out in an aggressive attack and, if you lose 6-3 as a result, so be it?

Do you play 10 men behind the ball against most of the big boys and hope for lower goal differentials, then try to steal points against some middle of the pack and lower table sides?

Clubs have tried all of these options. One club that seems to have a good handle on how best to stay in the Premier League is Brighton.

The day we arrived at what is fondly known as Sussex by the Sea, the Seagulls made a big announcement. Towering center back duo Lewis Dunk and Shane Duffy had each signed five-year contract extensions, through 2023.

Watch a Brighton game and the pair are hard to miss. Dunk, an English national and Duffy, an Irish national who hails from the tumultuous border town of Derry, are both 6-foot-4 and tower over most of the opposition.

Dunk is a Brighton native who has made more than 200 appearances for the Seagulls as they progressed from League One to the Premier League for the first time. He has paired with Duffy since the latter moved from Blackburn Rovers in 2016.

The two were born six weeks apart and represent the defensive mindset of the club.

"I am delighted for Lewis and Shane," said Brighton boss Chris Hughton after the extension announcement. "They have been terrific players for the club, helping us win promotion and establish ourselves in the Premier League last season… They have formed a very good central defensive partnership, and have played a really important role in what we've achieved."

Brighton finished 15th with 40 points in its inaugural Premier League season. The Albion won just nine games and dropped 16. Those are not flashy numbers, but keep in mind the club scored just 34 league goals. It allowed 54, which was good for ninth best in the league.

The defense posted 10 clean sheets. That is largely because of Dunk and Duffy.

"He's got it all. He wins headers and tackles, he's a good blocker of the ball but also his range of passing is second to none," former Brighton defender Adam Hinselwood said of Dunk. "The amount of blocks he makes to stop chances and the goals he sets up with his playing out is excellent too."

Duffy came out of Everton's academy. While there, he faced life-threatening surgery on a ruptured liver after a violent collision on the field, and he has had to fight tooth and nail his whole career to get to the top flight.

The pair are the heart of the Seagulls, and were perhaps the main reason they stayed up in 2017-18, the club's first year in the Premier League. Now, the club can begin thinking about a long-term foundation for continued success.

More players have been brought in, including Iranian Alireza Jahanbakhsh, signed from AZ Alkmaar in the Dutch Eredivisie for a club-record 17 million pounds before the season.

Brighton is also extending players it feels should continue to serve as the club's foundation, like Duffy, Dunk and Israeli Beram Kayal, who has been with the Seagulls since January 2015, making more than 100 appearances.

Kayal would go on to score a 29th-minute winner in a 1-0 victory over Newcastle two weeks after our match.

As notable as all these signings and extensions may be, the biggest recent move made by the club will probably go unnoticed by most followers.

After roughly two years planning for and developing the position, Brighton recently appointed Dan Ashworth as the club's new technical director. He is currently The Football Association's Technical Director and will officially join the Seagulls in the spring.

"Dan's CV speaks for itself, and while his work alongside Gareth Southgate, with England's senior men's team, was well documented last summer during the World Cup, it's also worth highlighting his excellent work and successes across all the England men's, women's and junior teams," Brighton chairman Tony Bloom said.

Ashworth will essentially oversee everything involving football development – from the academies to all medical evaluations. He has worked with other clubs, like Norwich and West Brom, but it has been his recent success with the Three Lions that has earned him more notoriety.

Brief History of the American Express Community Stadium

After years of stadium instability, Brighton and Hove Albion now have one of the spiffiest new stadiums in the Premier League. Originally called Falmer Stadium, the ground is currently known as the American Express Community Stadium, thanks to a sponsorship deal with the city's biggest employer.

The stadium opened for the 2011-12 season, but the site was identified as far back as 1997, around the time the club's previous owners sold the Goldstone Ground, Brighton's historic home. After two years on the road at Gillingham, the Albion moved into Withdean Stadium, a glorified track and field complex. At that point, the goal was to build a new stadium by the mid-2000s at the site near the University of Sussex.

Because of its location, partly in Brighton and Hove, and partly in Lewes, the club had to go through a prolonged period of objections and appeals before finally gaining full approval to build. New owner Tony Bloom, who made his fortune on internet gambling and property development, loaned 80 million pounds of his own money to complete the 93-million pound project.

Construction finally began in 2008 and the stadium was opened for play in 2011. The first home game was played against Doncaster, the same team who Brighton played in the last game at the Goldstone Ground.

The Amex, as its called, has a capacity of 30,666 people and is a blue and white sight to behold, during the day or when lit up at night. In 2012, the Amex won an international stadium award for Best New Venue.

He is the man credited with creating England's DNA program, which impacts both the men's and women's teams from U-17 through the senior clubs. According to its website, EnglandDNA.com, it is a "resource…to help clubs and coaches at all levels of the game learn more about the vision for future England teams…to ensure consistency and connection between all our age-group teams."

Think of a high school football team and how a junior varsity is meant to run the same offense and defense as the varsity, and how the feeder system teams are often taught the same, so that by the time kids are playing varsity, they have had thousands of reps within the same system.

Recent World Cup wins at the U-17 and U-20 levels for the men, combined with the senior women's side qualifying for the 2019 Women's World Cup, serve as testaments to Ashworth's comprehensive abilities.

And now, he's turned his attention to the Albion.

"Ashworth… is another important step in consolidating our place in the Premier League and to strengthen our foundations for the club's future," Brighton chief executive Paul Barber said. "We are thrilled to have attracted someone of Dan's caliber to our club, and we are delighted with the widespread acclaim that has greeted news of his appointment."

It is the kind of move that can make the difference for years down the road.

However, that move is for the club's future. Presently, the Seagulls were struggling. Coming into October of the 2018-19 campaign, Brighton had just one win in its first seven league games. More alarmingly, the defense had already conceded 14 goals.

Their opponent for our early October match was West Ham, a club the Albion recently had success with, including two wins in 2017-18. Glenn Murray had a brace in Brighton's 3-0 win in London, and added another goal in a 3-1 win at the AMEX later in the season.

In addition to excitement over Ashworth's hiring and the Dunk and Duffy extensions, there was a buzz heading into the stadium over the recent return of Brighton favorite Jose Izquierdo. The Colombian, who also scored in both wins against West Ham, hurt his knee early in his first World Cup match against Japan and had missed the start of the season.

He returned for the waning minutes of the club's previous match, a 2-0 setback at Man City. Although Izquierdo would not start against the Hammers, every time he got up and worked his way to the North Stand to stretch and warm up, the home crowd shouted in delight.

"I've been here for three-and-a-half years now and have been part of something unbelievable by getting this club to the Premier League," Izquierdo said. "I am one of the old boys in the dressing room now, and I am happy to continue here at the club."

As the clubs came out, the fans sang Sussex By the Sea, its long-time anthem that concluded with:

Good Ol' Sussex by the sea
Good Ol' Sussex by the sea

Oh we're going up
To win the cup
For Sussex by the sea

Over 30,500 were cheering, but one man stood stoically on the touchline, his eyes darting around the field, strategically moving his Brighton chess pieces.

Manager Chris Hughton made more than 400 appearances and won two FA Cups and a UEFA Cup with Spurs and also played in the 1988 Euros and 1990 World Cup with Ireland. He has led the Seagulls since being appointed in the middle of the 2014-15 season to save a club struggling toward the bottom of the Championship.

Hughton previously managed Norwich and Newcastle during Premier League stints. He brought Duffy in and Glenn Murray back, and added exciting French winger Anthony Knockaert during his time. He knows how to lead clubs fighting to stay in the Premier League.

Kayal arrived at the AMEX a month after Hughton was hired. He knew the club was trending upward from his first conversation with the gaffer.

"I knew from the first day that the manager wanted to build something," Kayal said. "In the first few minutes I spoke with him, he said that he's looking to take the club into the Premier League. Obviously if you look at the facilities it was ready to go, and this is why we're going step by step to the next level. Everyone here at the club from the chairman to the kit man is pulling together to achieve this."

The game began and West Ham took control early. A consistent theme ran throughout the match – unfulfilled West Ham opportunities. Although the Hammers held an overall 13-5 shot advantage, both sides only had four go on goal.

To be fair, Duffy and Dunk tallied their usual number of blocked shots in the contest as well. When both are in the game, it's kind of like trying to shoot over the big wood obstacle in the *FIFA* soccer game training exercises.

It was Murray, the veteran in his second stint with the Seagulls, who again did damage to West Ham, scoring in the 25th minute.

The crowd saluted Murray's result with one of their favorite chants:

There's only one Glenn Murray
One Glenn Muuuurrrrraaaayyyy
Walking along

Singing a song
Walking in a Murray Wonderland

Murray is beloved in Sussex, although that was not always the case. He is not quite a character actor, not quite the big star. His is a story that represents most soccer players.

Born in Maryport in 1983, the striker started with such obscure clubs as non-league Workington Reds and United Soccer League side Wilmington Hammerheads before going through places like Barrow, Carlisle United and Rochdale until finally reaching Brighton when the club was in League One in 2008.

He spent three seasons there before leaving for the Seagulls' rivals Crystal Palace, whom he helped lead to promotion to the Premier League, at Brighton's expense.

However, the prodigal son returned, first on loan from Bournemouth ahead of the 2016-17 season. He scored 15 goals before his loan became permanent midway through the season. He added eight more goals, including one in Brighton's 2-1 win over Wigan that secured the club's first promotion to the Premier League in April 2017.

Murray just keeps chugging along. He led Brighton with 14 goals in 2017-18, including a winner against Palace in the FA Cup, and started the 2018-19 season strong. He scored in a 3-2 loss to Man U, then added braces in consecutive 2-2 draws with Fulham and Southampton. His West Ham tally was his 99th for the club. His longevity and production, at an advanced soccer age, is impressive.

"Glenn has always had the knack for being in the right place at the right time – he's a player who has looked after himself really well and that enables him not only to get the goals but to have an impact in the game," Hughton said afterward.

Other than Murray's goal, and Izquierdo's late-game appearance, the only scene more delightful than Brighton's first clean sheet of the season was the joy on Knockaert's face. He scored in a recent 2-1 loss to Spurs and was involved in four of the club's last five goals, notching three assists for his efforts.

It looked more like the Knockaert who darted up and down the field, creating havoc on the wings during Brighton's promotion season. It was not the case last year, and it took a long time for supporters to understand why.

Knockaert recently revealed he was suffering from depression that kicked in last season with the combination of his father's passing and the breakdown of his marriage that occurred immediately after. He needed help, and he made the decision to reach out.

"I received a lot of messages of support and I really appreciated it," Knockaert told the Brighton matchday magazine. "I also got a lot of messages from people who are going through the same thing and I think in life we can all help each other. That's what I was trying to do.

"I'm enjoying football again," adds the Frenchman. "I feel so much better than I did last year and I want to keep the form that I've been showing since the start of the season…It's been a really good start for me and hopefully I can keep it going that way."

Recently, professional athletes such as DeMar DeRozan and Kevin Love have revealed that they, too, suffer from depression. The importance here is that it doesn't matter if you make $20,000 or $25 million a year, anyone can suffer from the same issues.

"I just want to leave a message to footballers and people in general, that as soon as they go through this, it's really important to talk to someone and not be scared… It's nothing to be ashamed of, you have to talk to someone because you never know what can happen in your life… Depression is a really bad thing and you don't really take it seriously until it happens to you."

In the same interview, Knockaert touched on the progress he has seen Brighton make as a club since he has been there.

"We have already moved forward a lot – we have seen that these past two or three years. The owners have spent a lot of money for a club that was in the Championship two years ago but what hasn't changed is the fact that it's still a family club, where everyone loves each other. Longer term, the dream would be to play in Europe with this club but we have to be realistic at this stage with the aim of maintaining our Premier League position this season."

The shutout over West Ham started a three-game win streak, the club's longest in the top flight since 1981.

Three weeks after the West Ham game, Brighton was home again against Wolves. Murray scored in the 48th minute as the Seagulls won, 1-0 in front of an AMEX-record 30,654. It was his 100th goal for the Seagulls. He is the club's leading post-World War II scorer and now trails just Tommy Cook (123) in career goals.

With that little streak, Brighton sat 12th in the table. Just where it should be.

~ BB

Brief History of Brighton and Hove Albion

Brighton and Hove Albion may be reaching the peak of its history – just 20 years after its nadir. As outlined in further detail in this chapter, the Albion were nearly relegated out of the Football League and professional football in 1997.

On top of that, the club was in administration as a result of heavy debts sustained in the 80's and early 90's. Even worse, the club's owners sold the Goldstone Ground, home for over 90 years, and had no alternative stadium nearby.

Somehow the team on the field fought off relegation, led by coach Steve Gritt. And the fans in the stands – many of whom repeatedly protested by storming the field – helped save the club from financial ruin and poor ownership. Brighton hung on to its spot in the Third Division – and the Football League – in 1996-97 and 97-98, got a new, local owner in Dick Knight, and stayed afloat while playing games 70 miles away in Gillingham for two years before coming back to play at the Withdean Stadium, a local track and field complex.

Now, Brighton and Hove are in the Premier League for the first time – and the top division of English football for the first time since 1983. But the history of Brighton and Hove Albion goes beyond the last 20 years and it's push for promotion to the top after falling to the bottom.

The club was formed on June 24, 1901 at the Seven Stars Pub on Ship Street after two other Brighton-based clubs had failed. The new team was originally called Brighton and Hove United, but changed its name to Brighton and Hove Albion after complaints from Hove FC. Hove and Brighton are sister cities, like Minneapolis and St. Paul, and are now combined as one city. No one is sure where the Albion came from in the name, though West Bromwich Albion was one of the top clubs in England at the time.

In its second season, Brighton and Hove actually moved in with Hove FC, sharing the Goldstone Ground. Two years later, Hove left and Albion had the ground to themselves until it was sold in 1997.

Albion played in the First Division of the Southern League, then a competitor of the Football League. In 1909-10, Brighton and Hove won the Southern League title, earning a place in the FA Charity Shield, now called the Community Shield, against Football League champions Aston Villa. Albion won, 1-0, at Stamford Bridge on Charlie Webb's goal and were considered the best team in England.

Fans began singing "Sussex by the Sea" during that season. This is the team's adopted song, as well as the unofficial anthem of Sussex, the South Coast county where Brighton and Hove is located.

In 1920 the Southern League became the Third Division of the Football League and Brighton and Hove remained there, doing not much of anything until 1957-58 when Albion won the Third Division and were promoted to the Second Division. The promotion was short-lived as Albion were relegated in 1961-62 and were relegated again the next year from the Third Division. Two years later, in 1964-65, Brighton won the Fourth Division and did not return to the depths of the Football League until that fateful 1996-97 season.

In 1974, Brighton and Hove hired legendary manager Brian Clough, who won the First Division title with lowly Derby County before being fired in acrimonious circumstances. He only stayed at Brighton for eight months before taking a job with his hated rivals, Leeds United for just 44 days, a much-written about part of English football history. But, Clough left behind his assistant Peter Taylor, who was expected to take Brighton to promotion by ambitious owner Mike Bamber. Taylor got the Albion to fourth place in 1975-76, but left to join Clough at Nottingham Forest, where they would eventually win two European Cups.

But Taylor's recruitment set the tone for the Albion's most glorious period until now. He picked up 19-year old Peter Ward from Burton Albion and signed Brian Horton from Port Vale, making him club captain. Alan Mullery took over as coach and the very next season after Taylor left, 1976-77, Brighton won promotion to the Second Division behind 36 goals from Ward.

It was during that season when five contentious games with Crystal Palace – including two FA Cup replays – created a nasty rivalry between the two teams, despite their being 50 miles apart. During a 2-0 League win in February at the Goldstone, Brighton fans began chanting "Sea Gulls" in response to Palace's "Eagles" chant. The nickname stuck and Brighton and Hove Albion now wear the Seagull on its crest. Both teams won promotion to the Second Division together in 1977 and Palace pipped Brighton for the 1978-79 Second Division crown, though both teams were again promoted together to the First Division.

The Albion hung on until 1983 when they were relegated, but just days later nearly became the first team in history to win an FA Cup the same season it was relegated. Midfielder Jimmy Case led the team to famous wins over Manchester City and his old club, Liverpool, before facing Manchester United in the final. Gordon Smith scored early, but United took a 2-1 lead until Gary Stevens equalized in the dying moments to force extra time.

Smith was handed a 1-on-1 with the keeper, what should have been the crowning moment for Albion. BBC radio announcer Peter Jones famously says, "And Smith must score…" But he didn't. His hard and low shot was stopped by United keeper Gary Bailey, and the tie game went to a replay five days later. Brighton was easily beaten by United, 4-0. Never before or since have the Seagulls advanced past the sixth round of the FA Cup.

After the debacle of 1997-98, and the move back to Brighton at the Withdean Stadium, the Albion won two straight promotions, fired by the goals of the club's greatest ever player, according to a recent poll, Bobby Zamora. Zamora would later play for England and take Fulham to the UEFA Cup final, but he started his career banging in 82 goals in 119 appearances from 2000-03. Brighton bounced between the Championship and League One before winning League One in 2010-11 behind 22 goals from Glenn Murray.

Frustratingly, Brighton and Hove made the Championship playoffs three times in four years, losing in the semifinals all three times. To make matters worse, in 2013 it was Crystal Palace who beat them on its way to the Premier League. Now, after finishing second in the Championship in 2016-17, Brighton is back at the top. The Sea Gulls surprised many pundits by staying up in in their first season, finishing 15th.

M23 Derby v. Crystal Palace

This is one of the most unexpected derbies in England and it will restart after a four-year hiatus this Premier League season. Brighton and Hove and Crystal Palace's rivalry has been dubbed the "M23 Derby" for the highway that links the 50 miles between Selhurst Park in South London and Brighton's American Express Community Stadium.

Neither team is loaded with trophies – so why are two teams from so far apart such rivals? The rivalry goes back to the 30s, 40s and 50s – Brighton fans still sing about a famous Boxing Day (Dec. 26) "when Brighton fought until the end and Palace fans ran away forever more," likely referring to a 1951 Christmas Day and Boxing Day back-to-back between the two teams. Brighton won 2-1 at Selhurst Park on Christmas and then 4-3 at the Goldstone Ground on Boxing Day. The interesting thing is that Brighton fans will sing this song even when they're not playing Palarse, as Albion fans call them.

But things got really heated between the two teams in 1976 when former Tottenham teammates and rivals, Alan Mullery and Terry Venables got the head jobs of Brighton and Palace, respectively. The two clubs had geared up for a promotion push out of the Third Division – one that was ultimately successful for both teams, though neither would win the league.

It was outside the league where the rivalry boiled over during a three-game FA Cup dogfight over two weeks in November and December 1976. Somewhat overmatched, Palace battled for a 2-2 draw at the Goldstone Ground, then held on for a 1-1 draw in the subsequent replay at Selhurst Park. A third replay was scheduled for neutral ground at Stamford Bridge.

Down 1-0, Brighton had a goal called off for handball, after an admitted shove by the Palace keeper. Then in the 78th minute, Brighton was awarded a penalty. Captain Brian Horton tucked it away to tie the game – except the goal was called back because other players had encroached in the penalty box before the kick was taken. According to *The Guardian's* account, the encroaching players were from Palace, not Brighton.

Horton's retaken kick was saved, knocking Brighton out of the FA cup. To add insult to injury, a seething Mullery had coffee poured on him by Palace fans, leading to indecent gestures from Mullery – and a rivalry was kicked off. After that season, Brighton changed its nickname from the Dolphins to the Seagulls, a direct response to Palace's bird mascot, the Eagle.

More recently, in 2013, Brighton were knocked out of the Championship playoff semifinals by Crystal Palace, losing the second leg 2-0 at home on a Wilfred Zaha brace. Before the game, the Palace team arrived at their locker rooms in Falmer Stadium (now the Amex) to find shit smeared all over the doors and toilets, no doubt a greeting from Brighton supporters.

Heading into the 2018-19 season, the M23 Derby is the most even derby in all of England. Both teams have 38 wins while Palace has scored 143 goals to Brighton's 135.

The clubs met three times in Brighton's first season in the Premier League, playing to a scoreless draw at Brighton in November. Palace won at home in April, 3-2. In between, the Seagulls won a third-round FA Cup tilt at home in January, 2-1.

2017-18 Season Review

In Brighton's first season in the Premier League, and first in the top-flight since 1982-83, it took them four games to both score a goal and earn a win. However, the Seagulls overcame many doubters who picked them to go right back down, finishing 15th to earn a second season in the top tier.

A five-match unbeaten streak early in the season had Brighton in the top half of the table heading into December. A five-match winless streak, punctuated by a 4-0 loss at home to Chelsea in mid-January had the Seagulls in 16th and facing a battle for relegation.

Chris Hughton's squad responded immediately, earning 11 points in its next five matches, including three wins, highlighted by a 2-1 victory over Arsenal in early March that featured goals by Lewis Dunk and Glenn Murray and pushed the team into 10th place. The veteran Murray led the club with 12 league goals and 14 overall.

The Seagulls would only win one of its final nine matches, but it was a significant victory. German Pascal Groß scored in the 57th minute and Brighton blanked Manchester United, 1-0, in front of 30,611 at the AMEX to ensure safety.

Gross had seven goals and eight assists after signing for just three million pounds from German side Ingolstadt. He scored the club's first goal of the season and added a converted penalty in a draw against top four side Spurs as well.

The club was fairly even at home, winning seven times and dropping eight, but struggled away from the AMEX, winning just twice. The Seagulls performed admirably on defense with stalwarts Dunk and Shane Duffy in the middle and Australian Mat Ryan in goal. The team posted 10 clean sheets and only surrendered 54 goals, best in the bottom half of the table and ninth overall.

On the flip side, their 34 goals scored was fourth worst in the league. The Seagulls reached the sixth round of the FA Cup for the first time since 1982-83, defeating rival Crystal Palace, Middlesbrough and Coventry City to reach the quarterfinals, where they lost to Manchester United, 2-0.

The club's stay in the League Cup was much shorter. Brighton defeated Barnet in the second round, but lost to Bournemouth in extra time in the third round, 1-0.

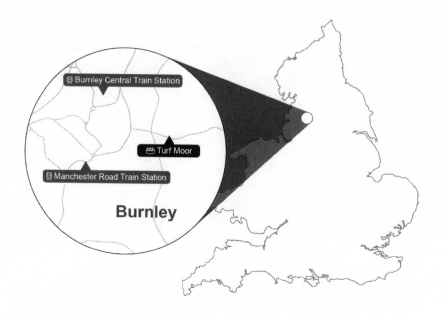

Burnley Football Club

Year Founded: 1882

Colors: Claret and Blue

Nickname: The Clarets

Stadium: Turf Moor

Address: Harry Potts Way, Burnley BB10 4BX, UK

Capacity: 21,944, 18th largest in Premier League

2017-18 Average Attendance: 20,692, 17th in Premier League

Trophies:

EPL/First Division (2): 1920-21; 1959-60

FA Cup (1): 1913-14

Current Ownership: Mike Garlick

Current Coach: Sean Dyche (7th season, 103W, 80L, 73D)

2017-18 Finish: 17th in Premier League, 14W, 12L, 12D

FA Cup: Lost in third round at Manchester City, 4-1

League Cup: Lost in third round to Leeds United, 2-2 (5-3 on penalties)

The Sports Tourists' Special Tips for Burnley

Best Value in England

Burnley FC do not require a membership to purchase tickets and we were able to snag two seats just a few rows behind the goalie in the David Fishwick End for just 30 pounds each. When you consider you pay more just for a membership at most clubs, let alone the ticket, Burnley might be worth your time whether you're a fan or not. Our tickets were to see Huddersfield on a beautiful Saturday afternoon.

Go to the Burnley Cricket Club

This is a must for out-of-towners and away fans, but even Burnley fans will enjoy the atmosphere at the Cricket Club before the game. The Club is just off the back of Turf Moor and has parking available for a reasonable fee. There's a bar inside and plenty of TVs and bartenders. Away fans make up most of the crowd, but there are Burnley supporters in there too and it remains a very civilized atmosphere. We definitely recommend making this your watering hole before and after the game.

Take a Drive Through the East Lancashire Countryside

To the north of Burnley is what's known as Pendle Hill. It's about a 25 minute drive outside of Burnley, but what you get are old (and narrow English roads) with lots of small, brick lined pubs, restaurants and shops. It's a very pleasant drive through some of the best scenery Lancashire has to offer.

Have a Curry at Aroma on Your Walk Out

Aroma, on Church Street, is an easy walk from Turf Moor and on the way to Burnley Central train station. It's a beautiful restaurant and not too crowded after the game. The curry is excellent and the staff are very friendly. You can sit down or grab carryout. If you're in Burnley on Sunday, lots of restaurants/stores close early or altogether. Aroma is open.

Our Burnley Experience

Burnley FC's 2018-19 campaign started like something out of a dream. After an incredible, grinding performance the season before and some poor showings from bigger clubs like Everton, Newcastle and West Ham, the Clarets finished an unlikely seventh place in the Premier League.

This is considered the best of the rest, the first team to finish behind the so-called Big Six of Manchester City, Manchester United, Liverpool, Tottenham, Chelsea and Arsenal.

And the spot comes with a seemingly shiny reward: a place in Europe. Specifically, Burnley earned passage into the early qualifying rounds of the Europa League, the secondary European competition behind the Champions League. It was only the Clarets third time in European competition and the first in 42 years.

Burnley's European adventure took a while to reach its climax. The Clarets were forced to start their season on July 26, only 11 days after the World Cup ended. Most clubs were just arriving at training camp after the long summer.

And the reward for all of Burnley's endeavor the previous season? To what exotic location would their supporters get to travel?

One of the funniest YouTube videos of the season is a Burnley fan's sarcastic reaction to being drawn with Scotland's Aberdeen in the first two-leg qualifier.

"Of all the places we could've gone in Europe – and we get f**king Aberdeen."

Burnley did what they do under no-nonsense coach Sean Dyche and ground out a win over two legs. But there was still more to come. In fact, Burnley had to make it through three two-leg qualifiers just to reach the group stage. The first three matches came before the Premier League season had even kicked off.

The Clarets got through the second round against Turkish side Basaksehir before hitting their first road block in the final qualifying round, a 3-1 loss at Olympiacos. It's no surprise that loss was sandwiched around bad performances in the Premier League as well, a home loss to Watford and a drubbing on the road at newly promoted Fulham.

You see, Burnley does not have a squad built for multiple competitions. Last season, Dyche only used about 17 or 18 players for any significant time. The familiarity was a big part of the club's consistency and ability to churn out results.

Once the Clarets added six matches, including two in Turkey and Greece, to the first four weeks of the season, consistency went out the window. And the lack of depth on the roster showed.

As a seventh-place finisher, Burnley made over 119 million pounds in 2017-18, including 27 million pounds worth of Premier League prize money based on the final position in the table. That's three times more than they made for finishing 16th in 2016-17. And because of their lack of spending, Burnley had the fifth highest net revenue in *all of Europe,* according to a UEFA report released in 2017.

But while fans were excited about the prestige of Europe, trips to Aberdeen and three rounds of qualifiers not withstanding, the club itself had a long-term mission. And a spending orgy to buy extra players for one five-week period seemed irresponsible.

Instead the club spent money on a new academy facility, opened in 2017, at a cost of 10.6 million pounds. The idea is to help develop more first-team players in house. As a result, the academy was upgraded from a Category 3 to a Category 2 designation. And they hope to achieve rare Category 1 status within a couple years. With each improvement, the club is able to recruit a higher caliber youth player.

Dyche told the *Training Ground Guru:*

"At the very first board meeting I attended, I asked where the Premier League money had gone from that season [2009-10]. They said: 'What do you mean?' I told them I had played at Turf Moor loads of times and the changing rooms were still the same. They didn't have a training ground, really. Yet the money had been spent. I told them: 'You can't do that again.' There had to be a bigger picture, a bigger future than that."

In the long term, this seems like a sensible plan to keep Burnley competitive and in the Premier League for as long as possible. Then maybe all that money would be spent to compete with the big boys. After all, just 26 years ago Burnley was as low as the Fourth Division, fighting for its football lives.

Attendance at Turf Moor in those days was dreadful with barely 5,000 a match compared to nearly 21,000 now. And the match day revenue could've only been a fraction of what its like at Turf Moor in these, the halcyon days of the club.

But of course, the sensible approach did not add any sexiness to this year's European dream. Back home and needing at least two goals to move on, the Clarets looked exhausted and it was only August. The heavy-legged players spurned chance after chance with the match ending in a 1-1 draw and Burnley's European dream was over before it ever really amounted to anything.

Even worse, the Clarets returned focus to the Premier League to find themselves in an early relegation scrap with only one point from their first five matches. Dyche didn't want to talk about a European hangover.

"It's a story that started five months ago," Dyche said after losing to Watford. "It's here, it's real and we have to get on with it."

But the fact of the matter is, it's happened to a few clubs who reached for the glory and didn't have a roster deep enough to compete on both fronts. Just two seasons ago, West Ham made the Europa League, flamed out and never recovered, fighting relegation all season before finishing 11th with 45 points, closer to relegation than Europe.

Would that same fate befall Burnley?

Upon our arrival in East Lancashire, the question seemed to have been answered completely. Burnley stormed back from the much-needed two-week international break by jumping a hot Bournemouth team, 4-nil. Then the Clarets came from behind to beat Cardiff in Wales, 2-1, in another early-season relegation six-pointer.

As fictional Cleveland Indians manager Lou Brown said, "That's called a winning streak."

Now, Burnley was facing the other relegation favorite, tiny Huddersfield, who implausibly stayed up the previous season. Huddersfield was promoted after scoring just one goal in three playoff games.

It didn't get much better in the Premier League as Huddersfield finished with just 28 goals in 38 games, tied with Swansea for worst in the division. Now, the Terriers came to Turf Moor with just one goal in the previous three games. Nevertheless, the away crowd was buoyant, arriving early to hang out in the bleachers of the Burnley Cricket Club, adjacent to Turf Moor.

The club is one of the more unique pregame locations in the Premier League. And in fact, Turf Moor was originally built for cricket in 1833. Only 50 years later did they add a football club.

2017-18 Season Review

Staying in the Premier League was the main goal for Burnley in 2017-18, but a flying start made the fans dream bigger. On opening day Burnley jumped defending champion Chelsea with three first-half goals, including a brace from Sam Vokes.

Two weeks later, Chris Wood scored in stoppage time to earn a draw at Tottenham and the Clarets followed with a road draw at Anfield and a win on the other side of Stanley Park, at Everton. In fact, Burnley didn't pick up its second home win until October 30. But still the Clarets found themselves in seventh place – a European position – because of their solid away form.

The home win over Newcastle sparked a run of six wins in eight matches, four of them 1-0 grinders. Unfortunately, during that run, influential Irish winger Robbie Brady went down with a knee injury. One of Burnley's strengths was the fact that 11 of the players started 20 games or more. That lineup consistency also cloaked a lack of depth. Brady's injury just before the crowded December fixture schedule put the team on the back foot.

The Clarets failed to win a game from December 16 through the end of February. Luckily, the rest of the teams around them were just as bad and Burnley held onto seventh place. With three road games in the next five, the impossible dream of Europe seemed to be slipping. But coach Sean Dyche picked up the pieces and strikers Wood and Ashley Barnes found their form.

Burnley reeled off five straight wins, getting all three points away at West Ham, West Brom and Watford. The Clarets scored seven goals after the 60th minute on that run, including four late goals by Wood. The winning streak sewed up seventh place and Burnley was back in Europe for the first time since 1967-68.

Wood finished as the club's leading scorer with 11 goals. Goalkeeper Nick Pope, a backup before a season-ending injury to Tom Heaton, became a contender for the England job and won the Clarets' Player of the Year award.

The cricket field serves as a parking lot and tailgate area catering mostly to away fans, thought plenty of Burnley fans mingled with the Huddersfield crowd. This isn't a typical tailgate where you hang out by your car with your own beer. Instead, you go inside the club or buy a beer from their outdoor tap, then you go sit in the bleachers or hang around on the cricket field chatting.

This rivalry, between East Lancashire's Burnley and Yorkshire's Huddersfield is billed as a "War of the Roses", red vs. white. The reason is the historical origin of the War of the Roses, the war for the right to the English throne, fought intermittently from 1455-1487 between the Houses of Lancaster and York.

Despite that fact that neither of these houses truly represents these regions and in fact, the House of Lancaster held lands in Yorkshire, it has become legend. Each county is represented by a different colored rose, based on Shakespeare's interpretation in Henry VI. Supposedly, members of the nobility chose a red or a white rose to show their allegiance. The House of Lancaster chose red; York, white. Historical evidence doesn't back this up, but the legend lives on as Lancashire is still represented by the red rose and Yorkshire, the white.

Eventually, the War of the Roses became a bit of a stalemate with both sets of nobles depleted from killing each other. The crown was handed to a third party, the Tudor family, who ruled through Queen Elizabeth I's death in 1603. They presided over the early expansion of Great Britain's kingdom.

Despite that contentious history, the atmosphere at the Burnley Cricket Club was playful. Burnley, after all, saves its vitriol for its own Lancashire neighbors, Blackburn. There's even a book in the team store simply chronicling Burnley's greatest victories over Blackburn.

This game had a similar vibe to the War of the Roses. Lots of attrition for not much end result. Burnley started the better of the two teams, taking the initiative to a clearly nervous Huddersfield side most in the Burnley crowd described as "absolute shit" before the game. But that wasn't completely true. The Terriers certainly lacked end product. But they'd held Tottenham in check the week before, save for three bad minutes.

The good news for Burnley was the return of defender James Tarkowski, who left the previous week's game with a shoulder injury. He immediately showed his value with a powerful headed clearance before coming to the rescue a couple of minutes later when Laurent Depoitre found himself wide open.

Tark or "Tarkie" as the fans called him, swooped in to block the shot with his body and preserve the early nil-nil score.

Tarkie's block proved important because 20 minutes into the half, Burnley scored a goal against the run of play. Strike Sam Vokes headed one straight at the keeper just minutes earlier. On his second opportunity, he opted for placement instead of power and nodded the cross low and to the far post to give Burnley the 1-0 lead.

Vokes had been a one-man wrecking crew, winning everything that came near him in the air for the first half hour. Fresh off scoring the winning goal at Cardiff the week before, Vokes seemed inspired. But the rest of the Burnley team was lethargic. And Huddersfield continued to dominate the ball and push forward.

Tarkowski nearly caused a disaster in the 37th minute when he scuffed a clearance, perhaps because he lost it in the bright sunshine. Depoitre missed the easy deflection anyway.

It's often amusing to watch the crowd in England at sunny games like this. Yours truly was the only one wearing sunglasses. And the others were clearly bothered by the lack of shades. Everyone covered their eyes with their programs and squinted into the distance for much of the game until an occasional cloud spelled relief for their retinas.

Maybe some day sunglasses will catch on in England. Hopefully, around the same time as dryers, unlimited Wi-Fi and healthy eating. We'll see.

The Burnley fans were squinting when they watched Christopher Schindler's game-tying goal in the 66th minute. He ducked his head in for a clever header and a goal that had been coming for the Yorkshiremen.

Schindler became the game's controversial figure – unfairly – just a few minutes later. After the goal the Clarets finally woke from their slumber and pushed forward. While trying to win a header, Schindler took an elbow to the head from Vokes. Then Ashley Westwood ripped two shots that were both blocked, the second one by Schindler's head.

The big German staggered and then dropped to the pitch as blood streamed from his forehead. Having won the ball, Huddersfield went all the way up the pitch. Only when they were thwarted just outside the penalty area did the referee blow the whistle dead to rush on medical help for Schindler. Burnley, having just gotten possession back, was rightfully incensed.

But the chants of "Let him die" and "Cheat" at Schindler didn't cover the Burnley fans in glory. One fellow quickly annoyed everyone else in the section during the seven-minute injury stoppage by repeating himself over and over about how terrible the call was and how Schindler was clearly faking.

For his part, Schindler lay motionless for the majority of the time before eventually sitting up with blood caked on his face and jersey. As anyone who's ever taken an elbow or a ball to the head at close range, let alone both, in a 10-second span can attest… it doesn't feel good.

All around the world, including the English Premier League, people are more educated about head injuries. And admittedly, the pest in the stands was shouted down by those around and ended up leaving the game early.

But there is still some confusion about the rules for head injuries in England. While the league and the English FA have a policy of "If in doubt, sit them out," the decision ultimately rests with club staff. The doctors of Premier League clubs have called for a 10-minute concussion break that would allow an independent doctor to assess the player and determine if they have a concussion. A temporary substitute would be used. And there's even been talk of adding a fourth substitute for unexpected head injuries late in the game, especially to goalkeepers.

But that was only a proposal. And in the end, if the team and the player have to make the decision – they will always ignore safety to return to the pitch. So after a long delay, you can imagine the crowd's reaction when Schindler came back onto the field after two minutes on the sidelines. He was clearly not well, bending over at the waist when not involved with the play and generally shaking off the cobwebs.

It seemed like a clear-cut case for a head injury. Huddersfield had one sub left. To be honest, it was a bit perverse to watch Schindler stumble around for the last 10 minutes of the game, like blood sport.

In the end, he helped Huddersfield keep its precious point. Burnley had drawn at home with a team at the bottom of the table – and looked utterly bad doing it. Just weeks ago the Clarets were marching through Europe. Now it looks like they're trudging into a brutal winter fight against relegation.

~ Blair Morse

Brief History of Turf Moor

Turf Moor is the second-oldest football ground in the Premier League, behind Chelsea's Stamford Bridge – but Burnley's modest home has a history that goes all the way back to 1833, when it was built for cricket. Before that, it was a large grassy field with a coal pit used during the Industrial Revolution.

A year after Burnley FC was formed in 1882, the Burnley Cricket Club offered them a chance to share Turf Moor for just 65 pounds. Burnley's directors agreed and the Clarets – then referred to as the Turfites or the Moorites in honor of their home stadium – began playing at Turf Moor in 1883 and have never left. In fact, they still share the facility with the Burnley Cricket Club, who have a field around the back – and who also have the best pre-game party on match day.

Turf Moor hosted games in the very first year of the Football League, as Burnley was one of the founding members. In 1886, Turf Moor hosted Prince Albert, the first member of the royal family to attend a football match. After opening the Victoria Hospital in Burnley, he took in the first half of Burnley-Bolton.

The highest ever attendance came during the days of standing room only, when 54,755 people attended a February 24, 1924 FA Cup game against Huddersfield, then the best team in the country. Eventually, the famous Longside Stand and Bee End were replaced and modernized. And roofs were added over all four stands.

Former owner Bob Lord had grandiose plans for Turf Moor, hoping to buy the cricket field and build a hotel and nightclub. He was never able to acquire the cricket club however and ended up with a parking lot for his efforts. Though in 1974, he paid to relay the pitch, add new drainage systems and remove a slight slope the field had throughout its history.

Turf Moor's current capacity is 21,994 – making it the fourth smallest in the Premier League. Various improvements and expansions have been proposed in the last 15 years, but Burnley's up and down fortunes on the field have kept the plans on hold until the club can put away more money by staying in the Premier League on a more permanent basis. The 2018-19 season marks the club's third straight season at the top level.

~ BM

The East Lancashire Derby vs. Blackburn Rovers

Burnley contest the East Lancashire Derby – also called the Cotton Mills Derby – with Blackburn Rovers, located just eight miles to the west. There are other clubs close to Burnley, like Preston North End and Accrington Stanley, but the Yorkshire border is just east, and the Pennine Hills are to the north – so it seems the rivalry grew with the more accessible Blackburn to the west.

The rivalry is one of the fiercest in English football and almost completely overlooked by the English media. Violence in the crowd is a regular here and the fans have long memories. In fact, this is one of only three derbies – and the only one contested by two English clubs – where its against the law for visiting fans to travel to the game on anything but a police-escorted bus convoy.

Mark Hughes, now manager of Stoke City, played and coached Blackburn and told *The Independent:*

"It was a big derby long before I played in it. I had no idea what kind of emotions the game generated in both cases – two towns less than a dozen miles apart. It is up there with any game in the Premier League in terms of sheer intensity. There is a lot of talk about people overstepping the mark when Blackburn and Burnley meet, but I really enjoyed the atmosphere, there was a real crackle in the air."

Blackburn's Simon Garner is the most hated man in Burnley. Rovers' all-time leading scorer bagged plenty of goals at Turf Moor. One time he had bricks thrown at him while he was taking a penalty, and another time escaped a Burnley fan that asked him if he was Simon Garner, who the fan said he intended to stab. Garner was jailed for four weeks in a contempt of court from divorce proceedings. Placed in an East Lancashire jail, he had to be protected by Blackburn inmates from the Burnley inmates calling for his head.

Many Burnley fans believe Garner was behind the plane that flew over Turf Moor in 1991 as Burnley trailed Torquay United 2-0 during the Fourth Division playoffs. The plane was pulling a banner that said, "U R stayin down 4ever, luv Rovers – ha, ha, ha."

The joke is on Blackburn now; as Rovers were only promoted back to the Championship last season – and Burnley has won the last four matches, including a League Cup win in August 2017. Burnley won easy, 2-0, on the road at Ewood Park and now has 48 wins to Blackburn's 45 in 113 meetings.

Brief History of Burnley Football Club

Burnley FC are proud to be one of the founding members of the original Football League, one of only four current Premier League teams to make that claim. Everton, Stoke and West Brom are the others. And in fact, Burnley's history goes even further back than that. The team was actually founded six years before the Football League, in 1882, after switching codes from rugby to football.

In 1883, Burnley moved into Turf Moor, sharing the site with the local cricket club whose fields are around the back, an arrangement that continues to this day. In fact, Turf Moor is the second-oldest continuously used stadium in the Premier League, behind Stamford Bridge.

Burnley spent 11 of its first 12 years in the First Division, but failed to win a major trophy. After spending the first 13 seasons in the 20th century in the Second Division, Burnley picked up steam with promotion in 1912-13, and won the club's first trophy in 1914 – it's only FA Cup win, 1-0 over Liverpool. The next season the Clarets climbed to fourth in the league, but World War I stopped the club's momentum in its tracks.

After the war, Burnley took second in 1919-20 and then won the First Division crown for the first time in 1920-21. The season started poorly as Burnley fell to the bottom of the league in the first week of September after opening with three straight losses, two to Bradford City and one to Huddersfield. In the very next match, the Clarets reversed their fortunes in a big way, beating Huddersfield, 3-0. More importantly, the victory set off a run of league dominance not seen again until Arsenal's "Invincibles" of 2003-04.

The Huddersfield win was the first of 30 straight games without a loss, a streak that lasted until March. Burnley won 21 of its 30 games in that stretch and cruised to the title with six games to play. After a third-place finish the next season, it made fans wonder what could've happened if Burnley's golden era had included the four seasons lost to World War I.

By 1930, Burnley dropped out of the top flight and didn't return until the 1947-48 season. In 1952-53, the Clarets established themselves as a key First Division club, going on a run of 12 straight top-10 finishes, part of a run of 16 of 19 seasons in the top half of England's highest league.

The high watermark was the team's last major trophy, the 1959-60 First Division title, put together by two of the club's most important figures: the coach, Harry Potts, whose name adorns the road outside Turf Moor; and crafty Northern Irishman Jimmy McIlroy, whose name is on one of the main stands at Turf Moor.

Potts was an innovator, playing a straight 4-4-2 long before it was fashionable. He also had the advantage of having played for Burnley for 13 seasons. He was the Clarets' leading scorer in 1946-47, which ended with promotion back to the First Division. And it was his header that went off the crossbar as Burnley lost the FA Cup final to Charlton in extra time that same season.

In 1959-60, his team was built around the creativity of McIlroy, wing Jimmy Anderson and leading scorer Ray Pointer. They battled for the title with Wolverhampton until the very end. Trailing by one point to Wolves and tied with Tottenham, Burnley had one last make-up game at Manchester City to win the title. Brian Pilkington's header gave the Clarets the lead four minutes in, but City equalized in the 12th minute. Tiny 20-year old Trevor Meredith volleyed the winner in the 30th minute and Burnley held on to win the crown.

The Clarets made it to the European Cup quarterfinals the next season and finished runner up in the league and FA Cup in 1961-62. After that, the club's glory years waned with relegation to the Second Division in 1971-72, and eventually all the way down to the Fourth Division in 1985-86, where they would remain for nine years, before bouncing up and down at higher levels. But Burnley never returned to the top division until current coach Sean Dyche led his team of hard-working misfits to playoff promotion in 2009.

Burnley's time at the top lasted just one season, but the Clarets returned again in 2014-15, again only for one season. The next year, led by Danny Ings and Andre Gray's goal scoring, Burnley won the Championship title and moved back up to the Premier League. Last season, Burnley finished an astonishing seventh place, the best team not considered to be a part of the "Big Six." The seventh place finish earned a Burnley a return to Europe for the first time in 42 years with a spot in the Europa League qualifying knockout round.

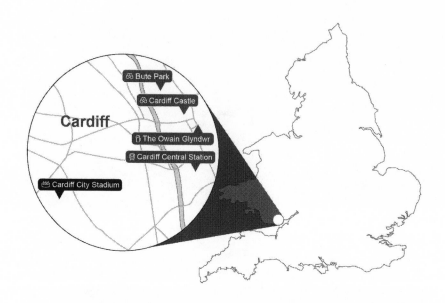

Cardiff Football Club

Year Founded: 1899

Colors: Blue

Nickname: The Bluebirds

Stadium: Cardiff City Stadium

Address: Leckwith Rd., Cardiff CF11 8AZ, UK

Capacity: 33,316, 10th largest stadium in Premier League

2017-18 Average League Attendance: 20,164, 13th in Premier League

Trophies:

FA Cup (1): 1926-27

Current Ownership: Vincent Tan

Current Manager: Neil Warnock (3rd Season, 44W, 24L, 19D)

2017-18 Finish: 2nd in English Football League Championship, 27W, 10L, 9D

FA Cup: Lost in fourth round vs. Manchester City, 2-0

League Cup: Lost in second round vs. Burton Albion, 2-1

The Sports Tourists' Tips for Cardiff

Cardiff City is an easy Premier League Ticket

If you don't have specific allegiances in the Premier League, consider Cardiff as a location to see any opponent, including major clubs like Arsenal, Chelsea and Liverpool. You will still need to get a membership card as soon as possible and plan ahead, but tickets are readily available, especially since the Bluebirds have historically been in the relegation zone during their stints in the Premier League.

If Cardiff drops back down to the English Football League Championship, keep them in mind for those matches as well. That league is non-stop fun, and the table as a whole is considerably more competitive. The crowd atmosphere at Cardiff City Stadium, particularly in the Canton Stand End, is impressive and exciting. You could see Cardiff lose 5-nil and still have a great experience.

Work Your Way Down to the Pierhead

On a bright, sunny day in Cardiff, one of the best things to do is make your way down to Cardiff Bay. Around in some fashion for more than 120 years, The Pierhead at Cardiff Bay features restaurants, pubs and docks full of boats offering sightseeing opportunities in the bay.

A major focus of the area is on conservation efforts and signs detailing the improvements are plentiful. We recommend you walk the Pierhead, grab an ice cream cone and read about the Bay and what is being done to improve the area. As a plus, it is also a great outing for kids. There are numerous activities for them throughout the area.

The Pierhead also hosts special events. On the day we went, there was a huge firefighter competition and demonstration, bringing firefighters from all around the region. It created a high energy atmosphere, despite being somewhat out of place.

Make a Historical Stop at Cardiff Castle

We stayed in downtown Cardiff and, on our way to pick up tickets at Cardiff City Stadium on our first day, came upon Cardiff Castle, located, obviously, on Castle Street. The old

Roman wall is visible from the street, which surrounds the castle. Walk through it to the main entrance for a couple nice photos of the Norman Keep as well as other grounds areas, without spending a dime.

For 13 pounds, you can get a comprehensive tour, and there are additional opportunities (a house tour in particular) that we did not do and cost extra. There is also a beautiful trebuchet replica present on the grounds.

If you are around on the weekend, you can take a tour of the Clock Tower, one of the more recognizable sites in all of Cardiff. Altogether, you can spend the day exploring around 2,000 years of history.

Mosey around Bute Park and see Cardiff City's First Ground

Adjacent to Cardiff Castle, and just off the banks of the River Taff, you will find the quaint grounds of Bute Park. Here lies more than 100 acres that were once part of Cardiff Castle.

As you walk through the park, you can grab a hot chocolate or ice cream cone at Summerhouse Café, open year-round. Enjoy the views of the onsite arboretum, as well as the recreation grounds, which were hosting a circus when we were there.

Within Bute Park, cross one of multiple footbridges to get to the other side of the river, and you will find Sophia Gardens. This is where Cardiff City, originally known as Riverside FC, played its matches from its inaugural season in 1899 through 1910.

Bute Park is perfect for a leisurely stroll before you make your way a mile down the road to Cardiff City Stadium and the next big match.

Tour the "Other" Stadium in Cardiff – Principality

Previously known as Millennium Stadium, Principality is the national stadium of Wales. Originally built to host the 1999 Rugby World Cup, the stadium is still home to the Welsh national rugby team, as well as the country's national soccer team.

It has hosted six FA Cup finals and the 2017 Champions League final, the Speedway Grand Prix of Great Britain and multiple concerts. Located a mile and a half from Cardiff City Stadium, and near Cardiff Castle, the stadium is the second largest in the world that features a retractable roof.

You can learn these fascinating tidbits, visit the Dragon's Lair, where the Welsh National team dresses, and more when taking a stadium tour. Available daily (with the exception of some holidays and match days), the cost is 12.50 (pounds) per adult and 38 for a family of four.

We recommend taking stadium tours in general because of all the cool, behind-the-scenes tidbits you get, but this is one stadium you will not experience a Premier League match at, so do yourself a favor and take the tour.

Watch a Match and Have a Pint at the Owain

There are several of your typically stuffy, smoke-filled pubs with closer proximity to Cardiff City Stadium. However, for our money and comfortability, we recommend the Owain Glyndwr (10 St. John St.) in the City Centre.

The Owain is big, has a solid menu for eats, and most importantly, numerous screens for all the matches you can watch before and after the Bluebirds play.

The pub has two floors, several rooms and features live music as well. On nice days, you can even venture outside to their picnic area and enjoy a pint while people watching.

The pub's location also puts you near several food-truck style offerings nearby. There is a mall and several recognizable franchises, but we recommend getting some grub from the more local offerings. We had curry noodles twice and they were both phenomenal and quite affordable.

Our Cardiff Experience

Visitors can be forgiven if, upon their entrance into Cardiff City Stadium, they immediately feel lost.

You may think you are in Cardiff, Wales, but virtually every billboard, video ad and flyer – even Cardiff City's kit – is telling you to go somewhere else.

Visit Malaysia…

Visit the Philippines…

Visit Vietnam…

You are even encouraged to visit Langkawe, an archipelago of 99 islands in the Adaman Sea, some 30 kilometers off the coast of northwestern Malaysia. Apparently, Cardiff City's advertising is geared toward sending you virtually anywhere in Southeast Asia, far away from the only current Welsh Premier League grounds as you can get.

It makes sense, given the club's current ownership. Vincent Tan – Tan Sri Vincent Tan Chee Yioun – is a Malaysian businessman and investor who made a fortune introducing McDonald's to his home country. He purchased the Bluebirds in 2010 and his eight-year reign in Cardiff has been a whirlwind of both successful and controversial activity.

Cardiff City has earned promotion to the Premier League twice since 2013. In 2012-13 the Bluebirds finished eight points clear of Hull City to win the English League Championship, earning the club's first promotion to the top flight in 53 years.

After one dismal seven-win, 30-point season, Cardiff was relegated back to the Championship. The club stayed in the top half of the table its first three years back but failed to reach the playoffs. However, under the watchful eye of manager Neill Warnock, Cardiff finished second behind Wolves in 2017-18 and earned another automatic promotion to the Premier League.

However, it hasn't been all roses and dandelions for Tan. *USA Today* pointed out Tan's drawbacks in December 2013. "Cardiff City fans do not like Vincent Tan…for the usual reasons fans don't like an owner – an unwillingness to spend money to improve the team, tension between ownership and the team's management, etc.

"They also don't like Vincent Tan because Tan seems to be using the club much like a 12-year-old in "owner mode" on the FIFA 14 video game."

Fans can abide by plenty. You can raise prices. You can make transportation difficult. You can lose. You can make curious personnel decisions. There are a lot of things you can do as an owner that won't cause your fan base to stay away.

What you cannot do is mess with a team's history. In soccer, one of the biggest ways of doing that is by changing a team's colors, something Tan did.

Cardiff has a powerful blue as its base color, something that has been in place since 1910, 11 years after the club was originally formed. But blue wouldn't do for Tan. He changed the team's primary color to red? Why? Because Tan is from Asia, and he knows red will sell well there.

Tan also considered changing Cardiff City's nickname. He did not like Bluebirds. He did like Dragons, a mythical creature with historical connections to Wales (it's on the Welsh flag) that has appeared on previous Cardiff City crests.

Oh yeah, dragons are also popular in Asia.

Tan also made some questionable personnel decisions, even bringing in a player behind then-manager Malky Mackay's back.

Tan is an owner, so he can do what he pleases within legal means. He does run the risk of alienating the club's supporters, however, when large changes are made as *USA Today* noted in 2013:

"In England...most fans view owners more as stewards of the club, while the team is 'really' owned by the supporters. For now, the fans have had enough. Change the colors, fine. Undermine the manager, OK. But with Tan's latest move to rename the club, it might be a bridge too far. An owner only owns a soccer team so much."

Tan relented in 2015, returning the club to its original colors with Bluebirds firmly in place as the nickname. These may not be important things from a worldly perspective, but from the viewpoint of the supporters who live and die with their club, restoring the history was crucial.

Making sure the club did not drop out of the Premier League again was the top order of business when we arrived in Wales at the end of September. The Bluebirds were winless in their first seven league matches, having secured just two points from scoreless draws with fellow relegation contenders Huddersfield and Newcastle.

To put that start into perspective, the Bluebirds won twice and totaled eight points in its first seven matches of their previously failed Premier League season in 2013-14.

Going into our match, Cardiff City had been outscored 14-3. The Bluebirds surrendered 12 goals in three straight losses, and had been shut out four times already. In the previous two weeks, they were blasted by Chelsea, 4-1, and at Cardiff City Stadium by Man City, 5-nil.

Brief History of Cardiff City Stadium

In 2009, Cardiff City Stadium became just the third home ground in the then 110-year history of the Bluebirds. Cardiff City played at Sophia Gardens from 1899-1910 and Ninian Park from 1911-2008. The new stadium is located half a mile from Sloper Road, where Ninian was located.

Cardiff City Stadium is built on the site of the former Cardiff Athletics Stadium and is part of the larger Leckwith development, which also features a large retail park and some fast-food restaurants. The stadium had an original capacity of 27,000, but with expansion projects, especially the construction of two additional tiers in the Ninian Stand, the official capacity heading into the 2018-19 season is 33,316.

In addition to Cardiff City, the stadium was also home to the Cardiff Blues rugby team for a brief period of time. Above each main end is a large digital screen. The outside of Cardiff City Stadium has two notable historical items. First, the club brought some of its history to the new stadium by bringing the Ninian Park entrance gates and placed them outside Cardiff City Stadium for the same purpose.

The other is the statue of Fred Keenor, the captain of the 1927 FA Cup-winning Bluebirds side. The statue is one of our favorites as it depicts Keenor while holding the FA Cup and waving his left arm to the cheers of Cardiff's supporters.

Things were already looking bleak as the club looked to be a one-and-done Premier League squad yet again, what the pundits call a "top-flight tourist."

The club's poor start was already wearing on Warnock.

"If we don't get results, no doubt it will become someone else's problem," Warnock told BBC Sport. "There is no doubt. Every manager is under pressure…You can only do your job really, what will be will be. The worst thing used to be when the manager to be would come and watch the game! The following manager is there watching before you've had the sack! That's happened to me a couple of times."

Warnock is a grizzled old gaffer who took over Cardiff City when it sat near the bottom of the Championship table in mid-October 2016. When the Bluebirds were promoted following their second-place finish in the Championship in 2017-18, it was a record-eighth time Warnock's clubs had achieved that feat.

His run of promotions began in 1986-87, when he led Scarborough up in to the Football League. He has guided Notts County up a tier twice and Huddersfield and Plymouth up once each. He led Queens Park Rangers, Sheffield United and, now, Cardiff, to the Premier League.

He is not the most well-liked manager in social circles, but he gets results. The Bluebirds were promoted against heavier spending clubs like Aston Villa, Middlesbrough and Sheffield Wednesday. But if his club did not start getting some points soon, beginning with the match we were attending against Burnley, Cardiff would be right back down competing against those same clubs – most likely without Warnock.

We entered the Grandstand section wanting to see a Cardiff City squad fighting to stay up. We wanted to see a hardscrabble, knock-down affair that was potentially a relegation six-pointer, despite Burnley's recent form.

The Guardian's Jacob Steinberg highlighted the match's importance for Cardiff City. "This is the kind of fixture that Cardiff City have to circle in red ink in the calendar," Steinberg said. "If Cardiff are going to stay in the Premier League, then they really need to take three points when teams like Burnley pay them a visit."

Early on in the match, the standout was Cardiff City's Josh Murphy. The 11 million-pound Norwich City transfer was electric on the wing, with the speed necessary to get around the Clarets' defenders and create havoc in the defensive third.

In the 17th minute, he worked a give-and-go with another new signee, Greg Cunningham from Preston, and went directly at Burnley keeper Joe Hart. Murphy's shot caromed off the near post and Cunningham's follow-up attempt wasn't even on goal. The Bluebirds were humming early though.

And the crowd loved it. Warnock applauded Cardiff's faithful in that same BBC Sport interview discussing his managerial future.

"Any manager will tell you, there are times you think 'is it worth it'? But then I see 30,000 Cardiff fans singing against Burnley and I think 'yes it is'."

Perhaps the most pleasant experience of a pleasant weekend in Cardiff was the constant singing and chanting in the Canton Stand to our left.

It started before the game, with the supporters loudly singing Cardiff's anthem, "Men of Harlech."

Tongues of fire on Idris flaring,
News of foe-men near declaring,
To heroic deeds of daring,
Call you Harlech men!

There are more lyrics to this military march that has ties to the 15th century siege of Harlech Castle in northwest Wales. The song famously appeared in the 1964 film, *Zulu*, and it got the crowd in form against the Clarets.

The Bluebirds got a helping hand when Burnley defender's James Tarkowski left with an injured shoulder in the 27th minute. Tarkie is one of the Clarets' most consistent performers.

Hart came up big for Burnley eight minutes later. Victor Camarasa, a recent Real Betis signing, threaded a pass into Keneth Zohore, who tried to sneak a first touch past the former England No. 1. Hart was up to the task and sent it out for a corner.

Cardiff had the better of the run in the first half. The home side's direct style troubled Burnley throughout, particularly from set pieces, leading to one disallowed goal by Murphy and a clearance off the line before halftime.

Unfortunately, an attack described often as toothless again held true to form, as the Bluebirds failed several times to find the back of the net.

Again, that did not fail to stymie the Canton End crowd, who added their recent Allez Allez Allez rendition:

We're the famous Cardiff City
We come from Sloper Road
When they talk about the Welsh Cup
We've won it fucking loads
We beat Real Madrid
We won the FA Cup
But still you don't believe us
The fuckin Blues are going up!
Allez Allez Allez

2017-18 Season Review

Cardiff City had a record-breaking season to remember, earning a place back in the Premier League by winning 27 matches and finishing second in the EFL Championship. In doing so, the Bluebirds posted 90 points, the most in the club's 119-year history.

Manager Neil Warnock's club opened the season with five wins and spent a good portion of the season in second place. They only lost two or more games in a row twice the whole year. In fact, from mid-February on, the Bluebirds sat outside second place for just one week, and the club pipped Fulham to the second automatic promotion position by two points.

Over the past 30 years, since 1986-87, Warnock has earned a record eight promotions for his clubs. He is also the first manager to get four different clubs promoted to the top flight (Notts County, Sheffield United, Queens Park Rangers and Cardiff). Warnock took over the club when it was in the Championship's drop zone in October 2016 and had his team headed to the Premier League just more than a year and a half later.

Defender Sean Morrison was the standout on a club that tied with Wolves for the fewest goals conceded during the season with 39. He also contributed offensively with seven goals. Junior Hoilett had 11 goals and 11 assists.

Cardiff's run in the domestic cup competitions was short-lived. The club lost in the second round of the League Cup to Burton Albion and to Manchester City in the fourth round of the FA Cup.

Evoking past history – the club's 1927 FA Cup win, its 99-year stay at Ninian Park (on Sloper Road) and its historic victory over giants Real Madrid at home in the first leg of a 1971 European Cup Winners' Cup quarterfinal – the supporters were equally nostalgic and sarcastic, and it played great with the game.

Burnley took the lead early in the second half when Johann Berg Gudmondsson headed in a flailing cross past Neil Etheridge, who could not get down low enough to keep it out. There was a lack of concentration from Cardiff's defense – just seconds – that would be replicated later.

Murphy's form held true throughout and he evened the contest nine minutes after Gudmondsson's opener. Gabonese defender Bruno Ecuele Manga took possession on the right side of the penalty box and sent in a crisp, low pass that Murphy one-timed into the upper right-hand corner past Hart to open his Cardiff account.

Hart kept the game even with a fantastic one-handed tip of another Murphy scorcher over the bar in the 67th minute. The Canton Stand faithful poked and prodded at Hart in the second half, chanting 'England's No. 4' to which the 31-year-old could only grin.

Another Murphy attempt went wide in the 69th minute, evoking the first negative response near us in the Grand Stand. "Our technical ability is absolute rubbish," an older man said two rows back. "We haven't Premier League forwards, have we."

It wasn't a question.

The locals may have been politely perturbed in the 69th minute. They were downright pissed off in the 70th.

The ensuing goal kick after Murphy's miss worked its way up to Gudmondsson on the left side of the penalty box. He sent a short but firm cross over to Welshman Sam Vokes, who directed his powerful header into the far-right corner of the net.

Etheridge was disgusted. He kicked the ball back into the net as Vokes celebrated with his Burnley teammates.

Two shots on goal. Two goals. That is all it would take for Burnley, who were outshot by Cardiff, 19-3. The win pushed the Clarets, which started off slow thanks to a Europa League qualifying-hangover, toward midtable.

For Cardiff, which lost a week later at Spurs, the eight-match winless streak is its worst start to a season since 1964-65. The Bluebirds joined Huddersfield and Newcastle in the winless club, the first time in Premier League history three clubs were without a victory after eight games.

However, Warnock's side did respond with two wins in its next four contests, over Brighton and Fulham. Either way, the local supporters were happy. There was an understanding that the club would probably go back down right away, and that is okay.

"We love coming here, and we like seeing the big clubs from the Premier League, but playing in the Championship is where we are best suited," said an older lady sitting next to us who has attended Cardiff games since the late 1970s.

"That competition is more our level, and the games tend to be better and closer throughout the entire season. It is great to go up, but it is not the worst thing in the world to go back down."

And in between, you can go to Malaysia.

~BB

Brief History of Cardiff City Football Club

What is known now as Cardiff City FC began as Riverside FC in 1899 as a place for the local Riverside Cricket Club players to do something over the winter offseason. The Bluebirds originally played at Sophia Gardens, adjacent to Cardiff Castle. The team changed its name in 1909, soon after Cardiff achieved city designation. This was two years before it began play at Ninian Park, where the club would stay for 99 years, until 2008.

With no Welsh football league at the time, Cardiff joined the English Football League system in 1910, playing in the Southern Football League before joining the Football League in 1920.

Cardiff's golden period was during that time, in the 1920s, when it reached two FA Cup finals and finished second in the First Division. The club joined the Football League in 1920 and brought in several expensive players, including Jimmy Gill, and immediately earned promotion to the First Division.

Len Davies was a major reason for the team's success during that decade. He is the club's all-time leading scorer with 181 total goals, and recorded Cardiff's first hat trick in January 1922.

The Bluebirds lost the 1925 FA Cup final to Sheffield United, 1-0, and then defeated Arsenal in the 1927 final by the same score. The Keenor statue outside Cardiff City Stadium depicts that winning moment. Hughie Ferguson scored the winning goal in the 74th minute. Ferguson scored 32 goals for Cardiff that season, a record that would stand for more than 75 years.

Cardiff City remains the only club outside of England to have ever won it. Current Cardiff supporters even mention this title, the club's only major trophy, in their version of *Allez Allez Allez*.

Cardiff City spent the most time in the top flight in club history during this time period. They competed at that level for eight consecutive seasons to be exact, from 1921-22 through 1928-29, including a second-place finish in 1923-24, the club's best. In fact, that season featured the closest finish in history, as Huddersfield won on the basis of goal ratio.

Both teams had 57 points and a goal differential of 27. The Terriers won the title based off a .024 goal average difference (Cardiff scored one more goal, but allowed one more goal as well). Davies missed a penalty kick in a scoreless draw on the final day of the season against Birmingham that would have made the difference.

After the Bluebirds were relegated following the 1928-29 season, they did not appear again in the top flight until 1952-53, earning promotion after defeating Leeds, 3-1, in front of more than 52,000 fans at Ninian Park. Cardiff stayed up for five years. Since going down in 1956-57, Cardiff made a brief appearance back to the top in 1960-61 and 1961-62, and then not again until they first showed up in the Premier League in 2013-14.

That's not to say that the club did not experience other successes. Cardiff has won the Welsh Cup 22 times, second only to Wrexham. The cup has been the top Welsh domestic competition since 1877-78. The Bluebirds first won their first title in 1911-12 and last won in 1992-93.

A new rule was instituted in 1995 preventing any Welsh clubs currently competing in the English Football League (Cardiff City, Colwyn Bay, Merthyr Town, Newport County, Swansea City, Wrexham) from competing in the Welsh Cup. This is why the Bluebirds have no titles to their name since 1993.

Winning Welsh Cups allowed Cardiff to access European play by competing in the European Cup Winners' Cup several times. The club reached the semifinals in 1967-68, losing to SV Hamburg by an aggregate score of 4-3.

Over the years, Cardiff defeated such European clubs as Sporting Lisbon (the cup holders at the time), FC Porto and, most notably, Real Madrid. A Nigel Rees cross was headed in by Brian Clark as the Bluebirds defeated Madrid in the first leg of the 1970-71 quarterfinals. Although they fell by aggregate after a second-leg defeat in Spain, Cardiff and its fans would never forget that monumental victory. Hometown legend John Toshack made his debut for the club in November 1965 and scored more than 100 goals before departing for Liverpool in 1970.

Other than a handful of Welsh Cup titles and a Third Division championship in 1992-93, the Bluebirds were quiet for the rest of the 20th century. They did win a big third-round FA Cup match in 2002, with Scott Young scoring the winner over then Premier League leaders Leeds United.

Robert Earnshaw, a Welshman born in Zambia, joined the club in 1998 and scored more than 100 goals through 2004. Earnshaw set single season scoring record with 35 goals in all competitions in 2002-03, surpassing Hughson's 1926-27 mark. He was sold to West Brom due to club financial difficulties in 2004.

That same year, the Bluebirds were promoted back to the second tier for the first time in 18 years, defeating Queens Park Rangers in a playoff final at Millennium Stadium on an Andy Campbell goal in the 114th minute.

Cardiff signed former Liverpool standout Robbie Fowler and former Chelsea standout Jimmy Floyd Hasselbaink ahead of the 2007-08 season. The moves did not pay off in league play, but the club reached the FA Cup final for the first time in 81 years, losing to Portsmouth, 1-0, in front of nearly 90,000 at Wembley.

In May 2010, Malaysian businessman Vincent Tan took over the club, which he still leads today.

The Bluebirds competed in England's second tier for 10 straight seasons, from 2003-04 through 2012-13, and came close to promotion to the Premier League three straight years.

In 2009-10, Cardiff lost to Blackpool in the playoff final. The club lost to Reading in the playoff semifinals in 2011 and in the same round to West Ham in 2012. Cardiff did reach the 2012 League Cup final where it played Liverpool to a 2-2 draw before losing on penalty kicks. Cardiff left nothing to chance in 2012-13, winning the English Football League Championship with 87 points, besting second-place Hull by eight points. This was the first time the club was back in the top flight in 51 years. Unfortunately, Cardiff's first foray into the Premier League was a short one, with a club-record low 30 total points in the 2013-14 season.

Cardiff went back down to the Championship for four years, earning automatic promotion back to the Premier League with a club-record 90 points in a second-place Championship finish in 2017-18.

South Wales Derby vs. Swansea City

We almost had it. We were four points away from crossing one of our ultimate soccer bucket list items off the list. Swansea City vs. Cardiff City. The battle of the Welsh. Cardiff City was coming back up to the Premier League after four years in the EFL Championship, finishing second in 2017-18 behind Wolves.

Swansea City battled to stay in the Premier League, but in the end, was not able to claw its way out of relegation in 2017-18. Swansea finished 18th, three points behind 17th-place Southampton, and were relegated after seven straight years in the Premier League.

What is often recognized as one of the fiercest rivalries in all of soccer was not going to happen in 2018-19, unless the two sides drew each other in one of the domestic cup competitions. In fact, the last time Cardiff and Swansea played each other was February 2014, Cardiff's one previous season in the Premier League.

As we previously described in our Swansea chapter, this is the type of rivalry where away fans are guided through to a specific location at the opposing stadium, for everyone's safety.

On November 2013, 2,200 Swansea City supporters traveling on 47 coaches, made the 40-mile trip east to Cardiff City, for the first-ever Premier League match between the two rivals.

The Guardian's Stuart James described the setting at Cardiff, a logistical feat that went off without a hitch.

"Match tickets will be issued on board and after stopping off at a designated holding point not too from the ground, a handful of coaches at a time will complete the final stage of the journey to Cardiff City Stadium. The whole operation is organized with military precision and, assuming everything goes to plan, the two sets of supporters will not get anywhere near each other."

Swansea holds a 44-35 advantage, with 27 draws, in the rivalry. This updated record includes matched played against each other in the Welsh Cup (Cardiff leads, 21 wins to seven, with eight draws). Cardiff defeated Swansea in the 1955-56 and 1968-69 Welsh Cup final. The Swans bested Cardiff in the 1981-82 final. Cardiff is second to Wrexham in total Welsh Cups won with 22. Swansea is third with 10.

"This poisonous rivalry transcends football...The enmity is deep-rooted and strays into all sorts of grievances, right down to why Cardiff, the capital city, got the Senedd (Welsh Assembly) and Swansea, the poor relation, ended up with a new swimming pool," James said.

In fact, in April 2018, *The Telegraph* ranked it as the fiercest rivalry in all of English football.

"For some years away fans were banned from this fixture, which gives you an idea of how bad it got... It's the perfect rivalry: heartfelt, meaningful and completely off its head."

Perhaps the most famous encounter between the supporters occurred in 1988. Supporters from both sides went at each other after a match at Swansea. According to the *South Wales Evening Post*, "50 Swansea fans chased 30 Cardiff supporters on the beach near County Hall and into the sea."

One eyewitness noted that "they were up to their chests in water... It was quite comical to watch. Eventually the police managed to get the Swans fans away and the Cardiff fans out of the sea looking like drowned rats." Swansea still refers to it when the clubs meet up, yelling 'swim away!' at Cardiff supporters.

The clubs have not faced one another since a 3-0 Swansea victory at home in February 2014, just before Cardiff was relegated from the Premier League.

One day. We will get to experience the vitriol these two cities have towards each other in a derby match one day.

Severnside Derby vs. Bristol City

Although Cardiff has a bigger rivalry with Swansea and Bristol does as well with the Bristol Rovers, this rivalry – more than a century old – has become a matter of national pride: Wales vs. England.

The Robins, as Bristol City are known, first played Cardiff in 1915 and defeated the Bluebirds in an FA Cup match five years later in 1920. Each side has dominated the series for long stretches at times. Cardiff went unbeaten in the rivalry from 1958-1968, and Bristol City had an even longer unbeaten run, from 1971-1992. Cardiff City holds a slight edge in the series, 37-34, but Bristol City has won seven of the last 10 matches.

The most noteworthy aspect of this rivalry is it has never been played in the top flight. Neither club has appeared in the First Division/Premier League very often. In fact, Bristol City has not been in the top flight since 1979-80 when it was relegated for the first of three straight seasons down to the Fourth Division.

Both clubs played each other as recently as 2017-18 in the Championship, however. The clubs split their matches that year, and Bristol City finished in 11th place, 23 points behind 2nd-place Cardiff. The Robins did have the satisfaction, however, of a run to the League Cup semifinals, where it lost to eventual champions Manchester City.

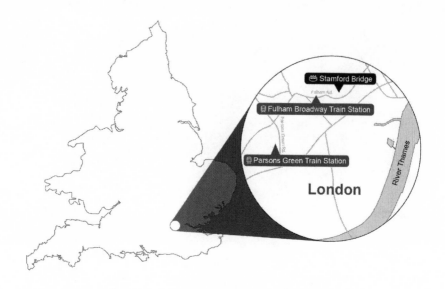

Chelsea Football Club

Year Founded: 1905

Colors: Royal Blue and White

Nickname: The Blues

Stadium: Stamford Bridge

Address: Fulham Road, Fulham, London, SW6 1HS, UK

Capacity: 40,853, 8th largest stadium in Premier League

2017-18 Average League Attendance: 41,281, 8th in Premier League

Trophies:

Premier League/First Division (6): 1954-55; 2004-05; 2005-06; 2009-10; 2014-2015; 2016-17

FA Cup (8): 1969-1970; 1996-1997; 1999-2000; 2006-07; 2008-09; 2009-2010; 2011-2012; 2017-18

Football League Cup (5): 1964-65; 1997-98; 2004-05; 2006-07; 2014-15

UEFA Champions League (1): 2011-2012

UEFA Europa League (1): 2012-2013

UEFA Cup Winners' Cup (2): 1971; 1998

Current Ownership: Roman Abramovich

Current Manager: Maurizio Sarri (1st season)

2017-18 Finish: 5th in Premier League (21W, 10L, 7D)

FA Cup: Won the Final, 1-0, over Manchester United

League Cup: Lost to Arsenal in semifinals, 2-1 aggregate

Champions League: Lost to Barcelona in round of 16, 4-1 aggregate

The Sports Tourists' Tips for Chelsea

Visit the Chelsea Museum on Matchday

It's pricier, but if you are a long-time supporter, or simply want a comprehensive presentation of Chelsea's past and present, you may wish to consider a Matchdays at The Museum experience. This package combines pre-match casual dining and a complimentary bar of beer, wine and soft drinks with a behind-the-scenes mini-tour and the chance to explore and learn about the history of the football club in the Chelsea FC Museum. The tour takes you onto the Stamford Bridge ground, where you can sit in the players' seats and traipse down the same path as Antonio Conte. The museum offers a thorough presentation of Chelsea's soccer history, and the experience includes a visit with a former Blues legend. Our first visit included a cameo by Ron "Chopper" Harris, the club's all-time leader in appearances, and a devastatingly physical defender from the 1961-1980 (hence the nickname -- look up his take down of Georgie Best if you are bored one day).

Stay at Stamford Bridge

Chelsea makes it convenient for supporters to stay at Stamford Bridge, as the Millennium & Copthorne Hotels at Chelsea Football Club are located on the grounds, placing you mere seconds away from the stadium itself. Because of the amount of stops heading west, even if you don't stay at Stamford Bridge, it's worth it to find an Air BnB on the west end if you're going to see Chelsea specifically.

Butcher's Hook Pub

Chelsea offers numerous (over 40) pub offerings within half a mile of Stamford Bridge. Although you have a plethora of options on Fulham Road, King's Road, North End Road and Chelsea and South Kensington, for historical purposes, don't forget to stop in to the Butcher's Hook (477 Fulham Road, SW6 1HL). Located opposite Stamford Gate, on the corner with Holmead Road, and previously named the Rising Sun, this is where the club was founded in 1905.

Try This Shortcut to Get on the Tube Quicker

With Chelsea normally in the mix for multiple domestic titles and European competition, heavy crowds are expected at all matches. Depending on how crowded it is after they have concluded, you may want to go south for one stop once you get on the Tube at Fulham Broadway. This puts you on the far less crowded south platform, and your wait time to get on the Tube is considerably lessened. Get off at Parsons Green, one stop down, and then return north. It will still be packed when you get to Fulham Broadway again, but this time, you will already have a spot on the Tube, and you will have saved some time in the process.

Our Chelsea Experience

Fans of other Premier League clubs should beware. This season ends in an odd year and Chelsea has a brand-new coach. The last two times that happened, the Blues won the Premier League with relative ease.

A third title this season would recall the San Francisco Giants feat of winning World Series in three straight alternating years, 2010, 2012 and 2014.

While there were likely some issues of motivation, as well as free agency complications that would explain the Giants feat, those titles were all earned under the same manager, Bruce Bochy. In Chelsea's case, the psychological background of the alternating titles seems to be directly related to a change in manager.

The first title comes with a bit of an asterisk because Jose Mourinho wasn't brand new. He is Chelsea's most successful and famous manager in history. The club brought him back for the 2013-14 season, but he didn't actually win his third league title until his second season, 2014-15, after he got through some roster churn.

The next year, the Mourinho effect rapidly wore off. Young starlet Eden Hazard looked labored instead of brilliant and the Blues sunk to 10th in the league – their worst finish since Russian bazillionaire Roman Abramovich took over the club. Mourinho was dismissed for Italian Antonio Conte.

Cue the sun peeking out from the clouds, bluebirds singing and a regenerated Chelsea in Conte's first season. In fact, the last time we visited Stamford Bridge in April 2017, the West London club was in euphoria, just a win away from clinching the Premier League title. Outside the Fulham Broadway station fans waiting for a District Line train back to the center of London happily sang, "Antonioooo" over and over. It seemed the love affair would never end.

Hazard moved from promising young player to Player of the Year candidate and leader of a World Cup contender in Belgium. Under Conte, the claim was he'd been freed up from Mourinho's shackles.

One year later, everything had changed. The embattled Conte had gone from a warm, excited coach to a grumpy man with bags around his eyes and what appeared to be a two-pack a day smoking habit. Chelsea had fallen out of the top four and finished fifth, out of a Champions League spot. To make matters worse, they were eliminated from the Champions League in the first round of the knockout stage, 4-1 on aggregate to Barcelona. Meanwhile Liverpool would advance to the final after knocking Man City out in the quarters.

Predictably, Conte was let go and replaced midway through the summer by another chain-smoking Italian, Maurizio Sarri. Sarri came from Napoli where he'd coached the club to a second-place finish in last year's Serie A campaign.

Even more unique about Sarri, he had never played the game at a high level and he hadn't spent his whole life in big time soccer, like most modern-day coaches. He was a successful banker who moonlighted as a coach for low-level Italian sides. At 45 years old, he got his first Serie B (Italian Second Division) job at Pescara. He worked his way up to Napoli in 2015 – his 18th club. Now he's arrived in England with – stop me if you've heard this before – a refreshing attitude and a new system to get the most out of Chelsea's players.

And already the signs of an alternating three-peat were on display. Most people had forgotten about Chelsea's winning pedigree – eleven members of the most recent championship team are still here. And seven members of the title-winning squad under Mourinho in 2015 are still around.

The new coach had already sparked some life back into the Blues with an unbeaten start to the season. In the fortnight before our visit to Stamford Bridge, Chelsea won a Europa League road game in Greece, drew 0-0 in a laborious performance at West Ham then handed Liverpool its first loss in any competition, 2-1 in the League Cup.

One could say they were unlucky to drop two points to Liverpool in the league the following Saturday after Daniel Sturridge's late, goal of the year candidate. And you could even say a Napoli win at home over Liverpool in the Champions League, with the squad Sarri put together, was a bit of a victory for the Italian as well.

So Chelsea sat in third place, just two points off fellow unbeatens, Liverpool and Manchester City. They were firmly ensconced in a title race, at least for now. And true to the alternating year form, Hazard was back to his sparkling self, perhaps because of Sarri, or perhaps because of increased confidence from a deep World Cup run for Belgium.

He was tied for the Premier League lead in scoring with seven goals and was an early consensus Player of the Year.

What was the difference? Sarri was aware enough not to take too much credit. In fact, he addressed the alternating year phenomenon head on.

"The history of this club is a little bit strange," Sarri told *The Guardian*. "In 2014-15, 87 points, then 50 points in 2015-16 with the same coach and the same group. Then 93 points and 70 last season, again with the same group and same coach."

"A gap of five points might be down to whether you are lucky or unlucky, but the difference in one season was 43. The numbers tell us something. I don't know if it is attitude, because they usually train very well, so the attitude is good. There is probably something from the mental point of view, but I still have to understand why."

Hazard preferred not to look too deep into his turnaround.

"I like to have the ball in the last 30 meters," Hazard told *The Guardian*. "It is completely different from Antonio Conte or Jose Mourinho before."

Unfortunately, Hazard didn't get a start when we showed up – though we'd seen him a bit heavy legged and unable to penetrate at the London Stadium two weeks before.

You see, our visit wasn't for a Premier League match, but for the Europa League, a competition most clubs frown about. But Chelsea has a unique history with the competition and Europe in general. And the fans enthusiasm wasn't dampened at all on a Thursday night at the Bridge vs. MOL Vidi, formerly known as Videoton.

Vidi were the last Hungarian team to reach a European final. In 1985, they beat Manchester United in the quarterfinals to reach the UEFA Cup – the predecessor to the Europa League.

Eventually, Vidi reached the final against Real Madrid. In a two-legged, home and away final, Vidi beat Madrid, 1-0 at the famed Santiago Bernebeu. But they lost at home, falling 3-1 on aggregate.

Before 2009-10, Vidi had only twice finished in the top two of the Hungarian OTP Bank Liga. They've done it now in eight of the last nine seasons, winning three times.

Brief History of Stamford Bridge

The Stamford Bridge Grounds officially opened on April 28, 1877, and was used primarily for athletics (track and field) meets into the 20th century. When the Mears brothers obtained the deed to the ground in 1904, they immediately began looking for a football club to fill it. Fulham FC was offered the chance to play there and declined, leading to the eventual creation of Chelsea FC in 1905.

The Shed End, home to Chelsea's largest and loudest supporters, was built as a terraced area in 1930. It remained the home for the Blues' faithful through the early 1990s, when the Taylor Report, which demanded all stadiums become all-seaters, resulted in the Shed End's demolition. Over the years, Stamford Bridge has evolved from an oval (think race track) shape to the more typical football stadiums of today, and the more recent refurbishments have resulted in fans being closer to the pitch.

It has since been surpassed in size by the new Wembley (Tottenham Hotspur's temporary home for the last two seasons), the Emirates (Arsenal) and London Stadium (West Ham United), and Tottenham's new White Hart Lane will also be larger upon its completion in 2019. However, Chelsea has completed formal applications to build a new stadium at Stamford Bridge with a capacity of 60,000. This could require the Blues to play elsewhere for up to four years, and not move into their new digs until 2023.

Stamford Bridge also offers one of the more unique experiences in English football, as the website, Stamford-Bridge.com explained: "The whole 12.5-acre site has seen the building of Chelsea Village. A leisure and entertainment complex housing 2 four-star hotels, 5 restaurants, conference and banqueting facilities, nightclub, underground car park, health club, club museum and business center. It has come a long way since the original athletics venue was first built in 1876."

"There has never been a better time to be a Vidi fan than right now," Hungarian sportswriter Tomasz Mortimer told the Chelsea program.

Then it shouldn't have been a surprise to see Vidi fans filling up the away section with Hungarian flags. Or to see Chelsea struggle to break down the Magyars for large portions of the game.

There was something in the air it seemed, especially for a Thursday night match against a supposedly lower level team.

Perhaps it was the surprising stubbornness of Vidi. But also, you felt the history of Stamford Bridge and Chelsea Football Club. After all, a game like this might not be a reality without Chelsea. The club has had a big influence on Hungarian football *and* European football, especially in the competition that's become the Europa League.

In 1906, under the tutelage of player-coach John Tait Robertson, Chelsea played three friendlies in Hungary, winning them all easily.

But Robertson's Hungarian adventure was just beginning. After leaving Chelsea for an apparent failure to show up for work regularly, Robertson ended up in Hungary in 1912, as coach of MTK Budapest.

He immediately changed their style of play, emphasizing passing, two-footed play and better control of balls in the air. In the process, he built a club that would finish the 1914 season undefeated for the first of 10 straight titles.

And, with that success, Robertson's style set the precedent for the coming golden years of Hungarian football, including their World Cup final appearance in 1954. That was after they beat England, 6-3, in the so-called "Match of the Century" at Wembley Stadium.

Unfortunately for Robertson, he didn't get to see any of it because he left the club just after the start of the unbeaten season, again for neglecting his duties.

The Chelsea match day program for the Vidi game said, "He was a man of great footballing insight, a heralded visionary and a pioneering force in the early professional era."

The program also quoted an obituary of Robertson, saying, "It was often said by leaders of the game in Austria and Hungary that it was Jacky Robertson who laid the foundations of the cultured football played there."

Of course, Chelsea was always a club with one eye on the continent. In 1954, while Hungary was dominating world football, Chelsea club secretary John Battersby accepted an invitation from L'Equipe magazine to travel to Paris to help form a European competition – what would eventually become the European Cup and then Champions League.

Chelsea was the only English club represented and Battersby was elected to the board, along with his new pal, Real Madrid legend Santiago Bernebeu. And as luck would have it, Chelsea won the league title that season and received an invitation to the first European Champions Cup.

However, English clubs were forbidden from playing in the competition by the Football League the first couple of years, so Chelsea didn't go.

It would take 44 more years for Chelsea to get another invite to what had become the Champions League. And in 2012, they defeated Bayern Munich in its home, the Allianz Arena, on penalty kicks. It was the first and only Champions League title for the club or any club in London.

However, Chelsea had proven to be a success in the secondary European competitions. They won the Cup Winners Cup in 1971 and 1998, while reaching the semifinals in 1995 and 1999. In 2013, the year after their first Champions League title, the Blues won the Europa League, making them the first English team to hold both titles simultaneously.

The driving force behind Chelsea's 1998 win was Gianfranco Zola, the club's pint-sized Italian sparkplug. Zola, a former captain of the club, is now back on the bench as a member of Sarri's staff working with Chelsea's immensely talented first team. This came after a disastrous run as head coach of Birmingham.

"This is a blessing. A dream situation," Zola told *The Guardian.* "And the best reason why I'm throwing everything I have into making the best of this experience for Maurizio Sarri and the club. Everyone knows how much I care about this club, so it's a great opportunity."

"I'm glad for it, I'm very grateful. But now there's lots of work I need to do to deserve it. I'm here totally at the disposal of Maurizio and hope I can give the best of myself for him to be successful. His success will be my pride and happiness."

We traveled to four Europa League and Champions League games over the course of this trip and of the four, the best atmosphere was at Stamford Bridge on Thursday night.

The Matthew Harding stand was packed, as was the rest of this iconic West London stadium. Everyone stood in the Harding stand and you didn't go too long without a song. They pulled out all the old favorites serenading the club's legends: Frank Lampard, Didier Drogba and John Terry.

One other song started creeping in too. "Maurizioooo… Maurizioooo…"

Like someone who'd covered the tattoo of their old girlfriend with the new girlfriend's name, Blues' fans had moved on and were basking in the glory of the unexpectedly hot start to the season.

Unfortunately on this night, it wasn't showing up on the field. Much like the West Ham stinker two weeks before, there was lots of passing but no real penetration. In that West Ham game, new midfielder Jorginho set the Premier League record for most completed passes in a game with 180.

But all that passing led to only a few chances and a nil-nil result. On this night, Sarri had opted to rest Hazard despite putting out a strong lineup otherwise. But as the game went on, the decision was looking like a mistake.

Of course, someone could've handed the ball to Spanish striker Alvara Morata and he still might not have scored. Morata's one-year plus stay at Chelsea had been rough and short on goals. But when he missed a point blank chance in the first half, it seemed like his lowest point.

Maybe the amount of fixtures had caught up with the team. Keeper Kepa Arrizabalaga had arrived as the most expensive goalkeeper in history. And he seemed eager to get involved in the game. As the play stayed in Vidi's defensive end for most of the first half, he went through a full sequence of sprints, up and down the box. When Chelsea was denied a penalty 100 yards away from him, he turned and yelled at the goal line judge on his end.

But twice, when Vidi did attack, Kepa hesitated to come claim the ball. In both cases, Vidi nearly scored as a result of Kepa's slow reactions. Only luck kept the ball out of the net.

Finally in the 60th minute, Sarri put on Hazard. Just his appearance to warm up on the touchline brought roars from the Chelsea crowd. But his introduction to the game was met with electric applause and a buzz of excitement. Hazard didn't disappoint, flitting around with enthusiasm as soon as he came on.

His energy sparked the team and eventually led to the only goal of the contest, a catharsis for Morata.

Hazard drew two defenders down the right side then laid the ball off for Cesc Fabregas, who curled a cross in to the near post. Willian got position on the ball but could only flick behind him with his head. Luckily, Morata was bursting forward with vigor. Just moments before he took an elbow off the face that made the normally mild-mannered Spaniard irate. His revenge came when he got to Willian's ball first and smacked it into the top corner for a 1-nil lead in the 69th minute.

Morata ran towards the goal line, just feet in front of us, and buried his head in his arm and then Willian's shoulder. When he came up, his eyes looked red as if he had been crying. Or else it was the mark from the elbow. Either way, it was an emotional moment for Morata and a breakthrough for Chelsea.

The second goal wouldn't come despite more chances, but Blues' fans left the game secure with their first place position in the Europa League group. Chelsea was right back in the title race and all was good again at Stamford Bridge.

On the way back to the tube station, there were even a few people singing "Mauriziiiiooo…" Things had changed, but in this odd year, much remained the same.

~BM

London Derbies vs. Queens Park Rangers, West Ham, Arsenal and Tottenham

Although Chelsea is not defined by one specific rival, the club's generation of success, combined with a history of hooliganism and academy poaching, has provided contentious relationships with several clubs in and out of London.

The Blues have had several nasty encounters over the years with Queens Park Rangers, located just four-and-a-half miles away. When Blues defender John Terry used racist language to taunt Anton Ferdinand in 2011, it revived a long dormant rivalry.

Chelsea contests the District Line Derby with West Ham, a club whose academy has provided the Blues with many stars in recent years, including Terry, Lampard, Johnson and Joe Cole. The term refers to the line on London's Tube that used to take fans directly between Stamford Bridge and West Ham's old stadium, Upton Park.

Despite long-standing clashes with Manchester United, Liverpool and Leeds United, it is the Blues' battles with North London clubs Arsenal and Tottenham that stand out the most.

Chelsea-Arsenal is a long-running contest that intensified incredibly with Abramovich's arrival, and his subsequent hiring of Mourinho. The Portuguese manager pegged Arsenal and its manager, Arsene Wenger, as principal threats to his desire to build a champion at Stamford Bridge, and he attacked them verbally every chance he could. In addition, the Ashley Cole transfer saga that took place over 2005 and 2006, which led to the Gunners' left back moving to Chelsea after acrimonious circumstances, produced more bad blood between the two sides.

As for Tottenham, the Blues and Spurs have butted heads numerous times since the 80s. It is an increasingly heated rivalry, fueled by hooliganism in the 1980s, jealousy in the 1990s and 2000s, and -- more recently -- a common pursuit of silverware and Champions League football. Meetings between the two clubs invariably deliver controversy and contention by the bucket-load, and an atmosphere of barely contained hostility in the stands, with Chelsea one of several serial offenders when it comes to anti-Semitic chanting, a result of Spurs' historical Jewish connections.

Brief History of Chelsea Football Club

On the evening of March 10, 1905, in an upstairs room at the Rising Sun pub, Chelsea FC was formed. Among the founding owners were millionaire Henry Augustus "Gus" Mears, his brother Joseph, their brother-in-law Henry Boyer, publican Alfred Janes and his nephew Edwin, who ran the Rising Sun.

Chelsea FC was formed to fill Stamford Bridge, a stadium that previously hosted non-soccer events before the Mears brothers, huge fans of the fledgling sport, took control of the stadium's lease in 1904.

There are two Chelsea timelines: BA (Before Abramovich), which featured a few highs and a few trophies, but mostly struggle and, at times, relegation. Peter Osgood, "King of Stamford Bridge," had 150 career goals and scored in every round of the club's 1970 FA Cup win. Jimmy Greaves scored a ridiculous 132 goals in 169 games over four years, including 43 in one season, and Bobby Tambling had 202 goals, leading the club historically for more than 40 years before Frank Lampard surpassed him in 2013.

The Blues won one First Division title during this stretch, in 1954-55, three FA cups and two League Cups. Chelsea made an impact on the European scene, winning the UEFA Cup Winners' Cup, which later folded into the Europa League, in 1971 and 1998.

Then, there is AA (After Abramovich). Roman Abramovich became Chelsea's principal owner in the summer of 2003. The club was in dire financial straits when it was sold to Abramovich, and he quickly paid off most of the club's 80 million pounds of debt and then went on a spending spree before the start of the 2003-04 season, buying big name players like Claude Makelele, Geremi, Glen Johnson, Joe Cole and Damien Duff.

Chelsea reached the Champions League semifinals and finished second in the Premier League in the 2003-04 season, but Abramovich elected to replace manager Claudio Ranieri with Jose Mourinho, who was coming off back-to-back Portuguese Primeira Liga titles and a Champions League crown with FC Porto. Mourinho, in turn, led the club to back-to-back Premier League championships in 2004-05, with a Premier League record 95 points, and 2005-06.

Mourinho departed early in the 2007-08 season. In the time since, eight separate managers (not counting caretakers) have led Chelsea, including a return by Mourinho that resulted in another league title in 2013-14.

The Blues have won five Premier League titles since Abramovich took control of the club, and have added five FA Cups and three League Cups to the trophy case, as well as one Champions League and one Europa League title each. Chelsea has won 15 trophies in 15 seasons during Abramovich's reign.

John Terry captained the club to five Premier League titles, five FA Cups, three League Cups a UEFA Europa League and a Champions League crown, although he technically missed the Champions League final because of a red card suspension. Lampard, a West Ham academy product and Terry's teammate for much of that run, scored a club-record 211 goals.

Chelsea is the last English club and the only one from London, to win the Champions League, defeating Bayern Munich on penalties in 2012. The Blues qualified for the Champions League for 10 consecutive seasons, from 2003-04 to 2012-13. In the first eight seasons, the club reached the semifinals four times and the finals once, in 2008, when it lost a heartbreaker to Manchester United on penalty kicks in the first All-England final, after Terry's infamous slip when taking a penalty. That loss, at Luzhniki Stadium in Moscow, may be the club's most devastating ever.

The Blues would redeem themselves with a classic at Allianz Arena in Munich in 2012, against Bayern Munich. The hosts scored a dagger in the 83rd minute when Thomas Muller tallied the go-ahead goal, but Didier Drogba evened things up five minutes later with a powerful header from Juan Mata's cross.

The match went to penalties and Drogba secured his place in Blues history by converting the winning penalty to give Chelsea its first Champions League crown. Petr Cech was the stalwart in goal during much of the 21st century run, establishing a club record for clean sheets while winning numerous titles. His stoppage time save on Arjen Robben's penalty kept Chelsea alive in that Champions League final, and he stopped Ivica Olic and Bastian Schweinsteiger in the shootout round to secure the win.

The victory over Bayern Munich is the last time an English team has appeared in the finals, through 2016-17. When the Blues won the Europa League the following season, 2012-13, it became the only club to hold the Champions League crown and the Europa League title simultaneously.

Chelsea is involved in a series of firsts. On Boxing Day, 1999, the Blues became the first club to field a starting 11 composed entirely of non-British players. They were the first team to score 100 goals in one Premier League season, 2009-10. Upon winning the UEFA Europa League in 2013, Chelsea became the first English Club (along with Juventus, Ajax Amsterdam and Bayern Munich) to win all four European trophies. Finally, in Chelsea's triumphant return to the top of the Premier League table in the 2016-17 season, the Blues became the first club to win 30 games in one Premier League season.

In 2017-18 Chelsea added an eighth FA Cup, tying the Blues with Tottenham for third in overall titles.

2017-18 Season Review

The club's first season in 22 years without legendary captain John Terry was a bit of a mixed bag.

The defending champions got off to a rocky start. Off the field, star striker Diego Costa refused to play while awaiting a move to Atletico Madrid, which eventually came in January. On the field, the Blues lost their opening game, at home, to expected relegation candidates Burnley. Back to back losses at home to Manchester City and at Crystal Palace pretty much knocked Chelsea out of the title race for good. Especially with Manchester City's record-breaking 22-game unbeaten streak to start the season.

Even an unbeaten run of seven games failed to move Chelsea into the top two. But, Chelsea was having great success in all three of its cup competitions.

Chelsea won a pair of clutch 2-1 games in the League Cup over Everton and Bournemouth on stoppage time goals by Willian and Alvaro Morata, respectively. However, the Blues were knocked out in the semifinals over two legs by crosstown rivals Arsenal. Chelsea could only draw nil-nil at home, but fell 2-1 at the Emirates.

The FA Cup was a different story and brought Chelsea a trophy for a second straight season. But Chelsea's run to England's oldest trophy nearly stalled out early. In the third round, Chelsea drew Norwich away, 0-0, forcing a replay at Stamford Bridge. A Michi Batshuayi goal looked like it would hold up for a 1-nil Blues win, but Norwich's Jamal Lewis equalized in stoppage time. After an extra 30 minutes the game went to penalties, which Chelsea won, 5-3.

The Blues stormed past Newcastle and Hull City before going to Leicester City for the quarterfinals. Pedro's 105th minute goal overcame a late Jamie Vardy equalizer and Chelsea moved on, defeating Southampton in the semifinal.

In the final at a sold out Wembley Stadium, Chelsea beat Manchester United, 1-0, on a 22nd minute penalty by Eden Hazard. The win was Chelsea's eighth FA Cup title, putting the Blues in a tie for third in all-time wins with Tottenham.

Chelsea advanced to the Round of 16 in Europe. The Blues only lost one game in the group phase. Unfortunately it was at Roma, who would win the group. The second-place finish forced Chelsea into a matchup with Barcelona. The Blues drew 1-1 at home, but a Lionel Messi brace led Barca to victory, 3-0, at the Camp Nou.

But, in the midst of all of these ancillary competitions, Chelsea struggled in the league, losing five out of seven games during one late winter stretch, including a 3-nil thrashing at home by Bournemouth and a 4-1 loss at Watford.

A final day 3-nil loss at Newcastle meant Chelsea would miss out on the Champions League in 2018-19. As a result, manager Antonio Conte was let go and fellow Italian Maurizio Sarri was brought in to replace him in the summer.

World class defensive midfielder N'Golo Kante was the club's Player of the Year and would go on to lead France to a World Cup victory in the summer.

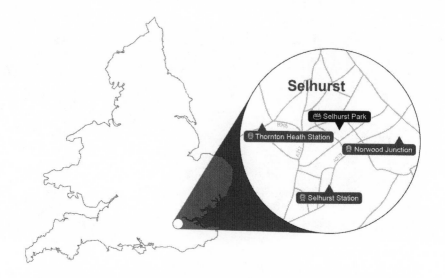

Crystal Palace Football Club

Year Founded: 1905

Colors: Red and blue vertical stripes

Nickname: The Eagles

Stadium: Selhurst Park

Address: Whitehorse Lane, Selhurst, London SE25 6PU, UK

Capacity: 26,074, 15th largest in Premier League.

2017-18 Average Attendance: 25,062, 14th in Premier League

Trophies:
None

Current Ownership: Joshua Harris and David S. Blitzer

Current Manager: Roy Hodgson (2nd season, 12W, 13L, 11D)

2017-18 Finish: 11th in Premier League, 41 points (11W, 16L, 11D)

FA Cup: Lost at Brighton in 3rd round, 2-1

League Cup: Lost at Bristol City in 4th round, 4-1

The Sports Tourists' Tips for Crystal Palace

Best Way to Get Tickets

Most Palace games are sellouts and third-party tickets are hard to get for this club given the relatively small size of Selhurst Park and rabid fan base. You must purchase a Palace membership to be eligible to buy tickets – a silver membership is 25 pounds. We advise you to pick out a game, plan ahead and be prepared to buy tickets the moment they go on sale to all members. Midweek games seem like an easier ticket.

"Glad All Over" is a Must Pre-Game Experience

It is imperative that you arrive prior to kick-off to hear "Glad All Over." The Dave Clark Five track gets the match started on the right foot, and stirs the home supporters into a rightful frenzy. Make sure you know the words to the song before you arrive, so you can get wild with the Palace faithful.

You Have Plenty of Tube Options

Speaking of Norwood Junction, that is just one of the Tube stops that land you close to Selhurst Park, along with Selhurst or Thornton Heath. The Norwood Junction stop, with direct service from London Bridge, places you an easy 10-15-minute walk from Selhurst, good to have a pint or three with your mates. Selhurst and Thornton Heath put you a bit closer to the stadium when you get off, but can take a little bit longer coming from central London. We chose Norwood Junction because its exit was just across the street from one of the more popular pubs, The Cherry Tree.

Stop off at the Cherry Tree Before the Match

We chose the Cherry Tree (32 Station Rd., Woodside, London SE25 5AG, UK) because of its proximity to the Norwood Junction railway station, the closest Tube stop to Palace's Selhurst Park. It takes no more than a minute to go from railway exit to pub entry. The pub has a Polish presence, with flags all over, and is one of the ones that states on the outside that only home supporters are welcome. We found that to be false as a couple of Tottenham lads had their Spurs jerseys on. A decent-sized garden on the side handles either rollover crowds or simply the desire to be outside and get a smoke in. Televisions inside had multiple matches on, which created pockets in those areas.

Erbil Shwarma

Of course, London is a city full of outstanding restaurants with food from all over the world. But if you're looking for a cheap treat, take yourself to the Canada Water underground station, just south of the Thames and only a few stops north of Norwood Junction. When you walk up the stairs out of the station, look for a set of temporary trailers in the square across from the library. One of those trailers is Erbil Shwarma, which is without a doubt the best shwarma you will ever have, served with love and extremely affordable. This is the perfect spot to grab a bite to eat on your way to a midweek game. Tell our friend the three Americans said hello… and make sure you get a touch of sriracha on the top.

Our Crystal Palace Experience

When it comes to Crystal Palace FC, all eyes are on one man. Whether it's at Selhurst Park or on the road, it's the club's controversial star, Wilfried Zaha, who gets all the attention.

Perhaps never has a player better fit the moniker of talisman for his team than Zaha. A talisman is defined as "an object thought to have magic powers and to bring good luck." So essentially, a good luck charm.

But in English football, the talisman is so much more than that. Obviously, without his presence, teams tend to struggle. But, often the talisman is more like a mood ring. As he goes, the team goes. His mood becomes the team's mood.

For Crystal Palace, when Zaha is smiling and enjoying his football, everyone else on the team does as well. When he's driving at defenders, taking people on and scaring the bejeezus out of back lines – his team takes on that mentality too.

But the reverse can be damaging to the team's morale. When Zaha is sulking, moody, alternating between a "who me?" look and an incredulous sarcastic smile, the team's mood is the same way. When he's bickering at officials and his teammates, it poisons the spirit of his Palace side.

Witness the on-field results last season. With Zaha on the field, Palace won 11, drew 11 and lost six, scoring 1.4 goals per game. Without him, they lost every single time and scored just four goals in 10 matches.

Coach Frank DeBoer was fired in the midst of a seven-game losing streak to start the season. But, the Eagles recovered. Mostly because Zaha came back from injury and new manager Roy Hodgson built the entire attack around him.

Zaha was happy and at home. He grew up in Croydon, the south London neighborhood where Palace's home, Selhurst Park is located. He came up through the youth ranks with the club, but in 2013, he left for Manchester United in a blockbuster deal.

At United however, Zahas are a dime a dozen. Perhaps that's an exaggeration because he is a singular talent; fast, quick and with cunning feet, somehow able to elude defenders. He can cross and finish with both feet and he even has the strength to get around defenders.

So of course, he's a rare player and obviously United was willing to pay big money for him at a young age, 10 million pounds. But then, clubs like Manchester United stockpile those kind of players. And Zaha wasn't the golden child he'd always been at Palace. He only made two appearances for United and alternated on loan with Palace and Cardiff City.

Worse yet, he was unhappy. He struggled mentally. He was even the subject of vicious rumors circulating about a potential relationship with then United manager David Moyes' daughter. Rumors he vehemently denied, yet no one at Manchester United stood up for him. To them, he was just another Manchester United player. At Palace, he was the chosen son.

"I'm living in this hell, by myself, away from my family, and I thought, 'If this doesn't make me stronger, what will?'" Zaha told *Shortlist*, a fashion magazine.

"When I was at United I had [money], but I was still so down and depressed. People think your life's different because you've got money and you've got fame, so they don't treat you the same."

So the prodigal son returned to Palace and became the consensus best player in the league not on one of the top six teams.

But there's a price to pay when you're so clearly the most talented player on your team and the talisman. Every single opponent gears their defensive game plan to stop you. And when you're an emotional player like Zaha, they find ways to push your buttons.

When we last visited Selhurst Park in April 2017, we watched Tottenham cut Zaha down to the ground by design. In the first half it was midfielder Victor Wanyama who repeatedly stopped Zaha in his tracks with brutal, borderline illegal tackles.

He finally got a yellow late in the first half and coach Mauricio Pocchetino replaced him with Mousa Sissoko at halftime. The equally powerful defensive midfielder picked right up where Wanyama left off, knocking Zaha down every time he turned on the skill. With Zaha suppressed, Palace lost 1-nil.

Over a season later, the game plan hadn't changed for Premier League opponents. In the week before our matchup, Zaha was on the end of a vicious tackle from Huddersfield's Mathias Jorgensen. He responded with strong words and even stronger play. Eventually, he embarrassed the same player, leaving him in his wake with slick moves before a brilliant, curling finish that would be the only goal in a Palace win. It was Zaha's eighth goal in his last 10 Premier League games, as many as he'd scored in the previous 44.

But Zaha wasn't done making his point. In the post-game press conference, he talked about the blunt force tactics and his perceived lack of protection from the officials.

"I don't even know what to say anymore. I feel like before anyone gets a red card, I'd have to get my leg broken. That's why I lose my head," Zaha said. "But I'm trying to just let my feet do the talking."

His coach, eager to stick up for his best player, echoed those sentiments.
"People are entitled to say what they feel sometimes. I don't think we should be in a rush to criticize someone for coming out and saying something that's heartfelt. And an honest comment," Hodgson said later in the week.

Of course, that kind of public statement can backfire. For one, you never want to let your opponent see your emotions if you can avoid it. It only encourages them to keep doing it to wind you up.

And secondly, you can't always be sure that challenging the officials will get you better treatment. Sometimes, it can harden them to your cause and then what was a neutral arbiter turns into an enemy. Leading into our match, on a rainy, gloomy Saturday afternoon, Newcastle coach Rafael Benitez made exactly that point about the officials.

"I am surprised because usually the FA deal with these things and comments like that," Benitez said. "I have confidence in (referee) Andre Marriner though. He is an experienced referee, even if his record with our players is not great, but I think he will handle it well."

The quote was a subtle jab at the flip side of Zaha's argument, the complaint around the league that he's a diver, something that's dogged him throughout his career. While there's no doubt he is fouled hard and fouled often, sometimes he gives the impression he's making the most of it. Since 2014-15, only Jamie Vardy has earned more penalties than Zaha's 11.

Maybe it's a worthwhile strategy given the dirty tactics used against him. Or maybe it makes defenders feel justified when they foul him. Either way, we were determined to see for ourselves at Selhurst Park. All eyes were on Zaha.

As Americans, we were in for an extra treat. The primary defender responsible for marking Zaha would be American Deandre Yedlin. Yedlin had played well to start the season for

Newcastle and was starting to shed his reputation as a sprinter without much else to his game. But against Zaha's equal speed, jukes and jives, Yedlin was stepping up to a higher level.

Three minutes into the match, Zaha took on multiple defenders, then went down with light contact, drawing a foul. The Newcastle players remonstrated but the ground rules had been set. The match official, Marriner, was going to err on the side of protecting Zaha.

Fifteen minutes into the game, Zaha reached into his bag of tricks and attempted to volley a pass with his heel to breaking left back Patrick Van Aanholt. He was hammered down just outside the box, setting up another free kick for Luca Milivojevic. His shot was on target as he starts to get a feel for the same angle, to the keeper's right, the place where the defense decides to hack Zaha every single time.

For a free kick specialist like Milivojevic, having Zaha as a teammate is a dream come true. In most contests, you might get one or two chances to strike a free kick at the goal from the same area. In this half, Milivojevic got to have target practice. His first few shots were like sighters from a gun, helping him hone in on his target.

In the 36th minute, Yedlin showed he's equal to Zaha in speed, but not guile. A slick little feint drew a trip. The ensuing yellow card was cheered by the Palace crowd, who stood up every time Zaha touched the ball.

"He's just too good for you! He's just too good for you!" rang down from the Holmesdale End. At other points in the game, they broke into, "Nah, nah, nah, nah. Na, nah, nah, nah. Hey, hey, hey. WIlfried Zaha."

A note about the Holmesdale End, where Palace attacked in the first half: It's typically the loudest in the Premier League. And one of the only places where songs are sung completely and don't die out of shyness. The rhythmic chanting nature of Palace's songs make even the most hardhearted fan sing along in their heads.

But despite still putting out great sound, the Holmesdale End had been compromised. You see, most clubs in England have an area behind one end or the other where everyone stands, sings and roots passionately. But at Selhurst Park, there has always been an even more hard-core support base inside the Holmesdale End: the so-called Holmesdale Fanatics.

The Fanatics sat in the lower corner to the keeper's right. And it's because of them that the songs are so loud and the atmosphere so unique at Palace. Much more like an Italian, Eastern European or even an MLS crowd, the Fanatics consider themselves "ultras." They stand and sing and wave flags throughout the entire game, often accompanied by a drum.

Even if you're not a fan of Palace, it's a sight to behold. But the group has grown to over 200 and was looking to move behind the goal. Longstanding season ticket holders in those seats weren't keen on the idea. Talks with the club came to nothing and the Fanatics disbanded before this season.

The difference was noticeable. The singing didn't last as long. And it wasn't as frequent. It seemed the rest of the crowd needed someone else to help them overcome their shyness. After Southampton won at Selhurst Park 2-nil before the international break, goalkeeper Alex McCarthy told *The Independent* the stadium was "less intimidating" and "a lot quieter without [the Fanatics] there."

However, all is well that ends well because shortly after the Newcastle game, the Crystal Palace board said they wanted to bring the noise back. Now, the Fanatics will move to a section in Block E, just behind the goal, after all. Current ticket holders will be placated some way or the other. In fact, many of them may wish to join the Fanatics.

Because as Milivojevic stood over another free kick to the left side of the box with Palace knocking on the door, you wouldn't have noticed the Fanatics were missing.

This time Milivojevic got even closer, clanging the inside of the post and nearly giving Palace a deserved lead for all their possession. It's only the end product that was missing. And the problem seemed to be a lack of understanding between Zaha and Van Aanholt.

On numerous occasions in the first half, Van Aanholt played a ball to Zaha, then failed to make a run for the give and go, leaving Zaha to take on two defenders by himself. Zaha vehemently instructed him with hand signals to play the ball to midfielder James McArthur so Zaha could run off him. The message only seemed to partially get through.

In the second half, Yedlin started to gain in confidence and Zaha became the aggressive defender. Ten minutes into the half, he caught Yedlin with a tough tackle to win the ball cleanly. Yedlin stayed down for a second before gingerly getting to his feet. Zaha recognized the same pain he feels week in and week out and circled back to pat Yedlin on the back in a show of sportsmanship.

But then the frustration started to grow for the talisman. First, he was taken down hard on a clean tackle and laid on the ground annoyed with himself more than the tackle. Another time, he failed to reach a cross from Andros Townsend. And then in the 75th minute, he tried to use his bag of tricks to beat Yedlin, but the American was hip to it. He took the ball from Zaha and forced the Palace star to drag him down for a foul, a call that usually goes the other way.

While Zaha started to lose his sizzle, another Croydon boy was catching the eye, Aaron Wan-Bissaka, Palace's 20-year old right back. Over the recent international break, Wan-Bissaka earned his first cap for the England under-21 team. (Zaha, incidentally, played 13 games for the England squad in his under-21 days, before switching allegiance to the Ivory Coast.)

All game long, Wan-Bissaka had used his speed and understanding of the game to find open positions deep in Newcastle territory on the right side, something Van Aanholt was not doing on the other side. Perhaps sensing this too late – or just put off by Yedlin's growing aggressiveness, Zaha made a belated move to the right side, hoping to link up with Wan-Bissaka.

The game's most heated moment came with Zaha back defending in front of the box. He took a clever touch to back out, already looking up for Wan-Bissaka's run. But before he could get off a pass, he was fouled. Zaha tried to take the free kick quickly, but Newcastle's Kenedy laid on the ball to delay him. Zaha shoved him over and the two players, backed by a number of teammates, squared up with each other.

Two minutes later, Zaha finally got the chance he wanted, the opportunity to stick a dagger through Newcastle hearts. Townsend's cross found Zaha all alone on the right side of the box. He dawdled for a moment, long enough to give the defense a chance to close him out, then fired a low shot wide of the far post.

McArthur tried to rush in and finish it, but it was too far ahead of him. Another late cross from Van Aanholt set up a McArthur-Zaha combo, but it was deflected away. And with that, the game ended nil-nil. The fans left soaking wet and with nothing to show for it.

Zaha trudged off disappointed. Yedlin got some post-game instructions from Benitez, punctuated by a long pat on the cheek from the Spanish manager.

A week later, the talisman showed his ugly side in a Monday night trip to Bournemouth. He openly feuded with Van Aanholt, constantly upbraiding him during every stoppage in play. It got so bad Van Aanholt wouldn't look at him and Zaha had to look to McArthur to deliver his message.

At one point, Zaha turned to someone in the Bournemouth crowd where we sat and told them to "Shut the fuck up." Then he picked a fight with Bournemouth players that nearly spilled over. The dispute continued at the final whistle until Zaha turned on his heels and stormed off into the locker room.

For Palace, the Newcastle loss was part of a six-game run without a League win. (And the streak was still going at the time of publication). And the first of four games without a Zaha goal. As talismans go, he's proving to be the negative kind for the moment. But with a player of his talent, the switch can go on at any time. Crystal Palace fans and Roy Hodgson hope it happens sooner than later.

~BM

M23 Derby vs. Brighton and Hove Albion

Palace is part of what is considered one of the more interesting and, shall we say, weird rivalries, the M23 Derby with Brighton and Hove Albion. The two clubs are separated by 45 miles between East Sussex and South London, with numerous other clubs closer to both.

However, it was these two clubs' ambitions to elevate above the Third Division in the 1970s, the relationship between their two managers at the time, and a hotly contested first-round FA Cup match that cemented this rivalry. Former teammates at Tottenham, Terry Venables was named Palace manager in early summer, 1976, with Alan Mullery appointed to Brighton's managerial post a month later.

The two respectively led their clubs to promotion that year, and the teams played each other five times that season, including two replays of a first-round FA Cup match that ended with much controversy. Palace won that third engagement, 1-0, after a converted Brighton penalty was called back for encroachment by…Palace?

Brighton's ensuing penalty attempt was saved. Mullery chased referee Ron Challis off the pitch to discuss the call. In that same sequence, a Palace supporter dumped a pot of hot coffee on Mullery.

Thus, a rivalry was born. Brighton enhanced it by changing its nickname to the Seagulls to take its rivalry to the air. Both clubs were promoted again, this time to the First Division, at the end of the 1978-79 season.

Although the clubs have only played each other 12 times since 1991, there have been some memorable match-ups. Wilfried Zaha broke Seagulls supporters' hearts with two second-half goals of the second match to lift the Eagles in a Championship playoff semifinal in 2013, eventually defeating Watford to advance to the Premier League for the fourth time.

The two rivals split the regular season series last year, with both in the Premier League together for the first time. Palace drew 0-0 at Brighton before winning a crucial game, 3-2, in April that helped ensure Premier League safety. But Brighton took a third matchup, in the third round of the FA Cup, 2-1 on the South coast.

Brief History of Selhurst Park

Selhurst Park opened in 1924 and was the fourth ground used by Crystal Palace. After the club was forced to leave its first ground, the actual Crystal Palace, due to its use by the military in World War I, the then-Glaziers spent the next decade between Herne Hill and the Nest before a former brickfield was turned into the current home of the now-Eagles.

Selhurst Park has played home to boxing, cricket and polo matches and hosted two 1948 Olympic soccer matches. Palace has shared the stadium with two other clubs -- Charlton Athletic and Wimbledon, which spent a combined 18 years at Selhurst. Charlton had gone into administration and Wimbledon had to leave its home, Plough Lane, since it could not meet new stadium standards.

The record attendance at Selhurst Park was recorded in the club's Second Division-clinching win over Burnley in 1979. A total of 51,801 witnessed the Eagles' 2-0 triumph.

Despite being around for over 90 years, and with Tottenham's old White Hart Lane now demolished, Selhurst Park is still only the 10th oldest stadium in the Premier League.

Portions of it harken to Fenway Park from Major League Baseball. And, not necessarily in a good way. The Arthur Wait Stand has three prominent pillars that make it difficult to take in the full pitch during play. However, the trade-off of the poor sightlines that stems from the low-hanging second tier is the amplification of sound produced throughout the stadium. This especially includes the chants from the rowdy Palace supporters in the Holmesdale Road Stand.

There are two sights at Selhurst Park you won't see anywhere else in English football. Americans will love the pre-match sight of the club's mascot, Kayla, a bald eagle flying around, even though Kayla had to stay away for a while in 2017 because of a bird flu scare. Crystal Palace instituted another pre-match item in 2010 that Americans will appreciate -- the only cheerleaders in all of English football, the Crystals.

Brief History of Crystal Palace

Crystal Palace began life as a castoff, denied membership by the Football League and then refused entry into the Southern League First Division in 1905, forcing it into the Southern League's Second Division, composed mainly of reserve teams of more established clubs.

The club was originally known as the Glaziers. Like so many English football clubs, Palace's nickname represented the primary profession of its players at its inception. A glazier fits glass into windows and doors, which is apt as the club were trying to find a way to fit into the English Football League.

Palace spent more than a half century wallowing in the lower levels. Just eight years removed from their place in the Fourth Division, the Glaziers, in front of 36,126 supporters at Selhurst Park, played its biggest match in club history on Saturday, April 18, 1969. Those supporters were eagerly watching their club take on Fulham in hopes of seeing them clinch promotion to the First Division for the first time.

Brian Dear and Frank Large scored early to give the visitors a 2-0 advantage, and Palace faithful were resigning themselves to rooting for a Charlton Athletic loss later that evening to clinch their club's promotion for them. There would be no need to rely on separate results, however, as Palace stopped playing with its fans' emotions. Goals by Steve Kember, Mark Lazarus, and a winner by Cliff Jackson clinched promotion with a match to spare. The club that had spent virtually all its 60 plus year history in the bowels of English football would now spend its Saturdays against the likes of Liverpool, Leeds and Manchester United.

The Eagles supplanted Glaziers as the club's nickname in the mid-1970s, when former player Malcolm Allison made the change. As the club's manager, he was attempting to enhance Palace's standing within English football, and he chose the name Eagles because that was the same nickname of Portuguese side Benfica, whom Allison recognized as one of the most recognizable clubs in Europe at the time.

This same thought process led to a change in the club's primary colors, which had been claret and blue since its inception, in honor of Aston Villa, which supplied Palace with its first shirts, and whose board founded Palace back in 1905. The colors were changed to red and blue to mirror those of Barcelona, another long-standing European power.

Those moves did not have an immediate impact, as the Eagles dropped as low as the Third Division, but Palace, after experiencing its first four years in English football's top tier between 1969-1973, reached the top level again in 1979.

Jim Cannon, dubbed "Mr. Crystal Palace," made 663 appearances, primarily as a center back, for the club between 1973-1988. He was paired in the back with Kenny Sansom for five successful seasons. They were joined on the 1978-79 team that was promoted to the First Division by Vince Hilaire. He scored 36 goals and assisted on Ian Walsh's winner in a 2-0 victory over Burnley that allowed them to pip new rival Brighton for the Second Division title on the season's final day.

That championship and ensuing promotion brought record-priced transfers and a hot early start in the First Division the following season, leading that Eagles team to be named 'The Team of the 80s' despite the fact it ultimately finished in 13th place.

During that time, two of Palace's forays into the First Division yielded some of the top players in club history. Ian Wright, Geoff Thomas and Mark Bright combined to produce CPFC's best showing ever, a third-place finish in the First Division in 1990-91. Bright and Wright each scored more than 100 goals for the Eagles while playing six seasons for the club.

Wright had a brace in a 3-3 1990 FA Cup tie with Manchester United that had to be replayed five days later, and he has scored the most post-war goals for the club. Thomas captained the club through a promotion to the First Division, that 1990 FA Cup final appearance -- one of only two for the club -- and the third-place finish in 1990-91. He scored 35 goals for the Eagles.

Since 1977, the Eagles have bounced between the Premier League/First Division and the Championship/Second Division, spending a total of 18 years in the top flight.

This current six-year stint in the Premier League is the longest the Eagles have stayed up in the top flight. However, Palace does own the dubious distinction of being one of four clubs to be relegated from the Premier League a record four times, joining Middlesbrough, Norwich City and Sunderland.

2017-18 Season Review

The season started off in the worst possible way for Palace – with seven straight defeats in the league and no goals scored. Former Dutch star Frank De Boer was named head coach in the summer.

De Boer was handed an easy game to open the season at home. By all accounts, Huddersfield was heading right back down to the Championship at the end of the season. Instead, the newly promoted Terriers smashed Palace, 3-0, at Selhurst Park.

Star player Wilfried Zaha played against Huddersfield, but then missed the Eagles' next six games with injury – all losses. It was the worst start to a season in Palace history. After the fourth loss at Burnley, De Boer was fired and much-traveled English coach Roy Hodgson was brought in to stop the bleeding.

Hodgson's second match was a win – over Huddersfield in the League Cup. But Palace still lost its next three league matches, including 5-nil and 4-nil thrashings at Manchester City and Manchester United, respectively.

Chelsea came to town after the international break and things looked grim with Palace four points below anyone else at the bottom of the table. However, the Eagles finally got their talisman Zaha back healthy. And his late first half goal held up for a 2-1 win. The losing streak was over.

Palace would still remain at the bottom of the table until a run of eight straight against non-"Big 6" teams. The Eagles got points in all eight. After the club's first winning streak of the year, back-to-back victories over Watford and Leicester in December, Palace finally climbed out of last. The Watford win was especially memorable with two goals after the 89th minute to overcome a 1-nil deficit.

With only one loss in a stretch of 12 games, Palace climbed as high as 12th place by mid-January. But they weren't safe yet. Another lackluster stretch in February and March dropped the Eagles back into the relegation zone.

Palace was rejuvenated by a Zaha brace in a wild 3-2 win over rivals Brighton and then won four of its last five matches to escape relegation. The Eagles forced Stoke and West Brom into relegation by beating them in the season's last two weeks.

Palace finished an incredible 11th place after starting with no goals or points in its first seven games – a credit to Hodgson and to Zaha's health. He finished as the club's Player of the Year with nine goals. Penalty specialist Luka Milivojevic finished as the leading scorer with 10 goals.

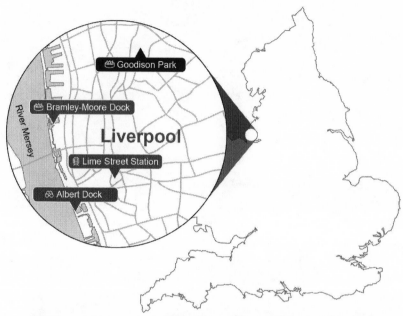

Everton Football Club

Year Founded: 1878

Colors: Royal Blue and White

Nickname: The Blues; The Toffees

Stadium: Goodison Park

Address: Goodison Rd., Liverpool L4 4EL, UK

Capacity: 39,221, 9th largest stadium in the Premier League

2017-18 Average Attendance: 39,043, 9th in the Premier League

Trophies

Premier League/First Division (9): 1890-91; 1914-15; 1927-28; 1931-32; 1938-39; 1962-63; 1969-70; 1984-85; 1986-87

FA Cup (5): 1905-06; 1932-33; 1965-66; 1983-84; 1994-95

UEFA Cup Winners' Cup (1): 1985

Current Ownership: Farhad Moshiri, since February 2016

Current Manager: Marco Silva, 1st season

2017-18 Finish: 8th in Premier League, 49 points (13W, 15L, 10D)

Europa League: Eliminated at group stage; Finished third with four points.

FA Cup: Lost at Liverpool in third round, 2-1

League Cup: Lost at Chelsea in fourth round, 2-1

The Sports Tourists' Tips for Everton

Stay Far Away and Prepare to Take a Cab

There are two main pockets of hotels. The posh ones are down by Albert Dock, along the road that faces the water. Then, more central to downtown Liverpool, by Lime St., the hotels are slightly cheaper. Either way, most hotels are more than a mile walk or a long cab from Goodison Park. Once Everton builds its new stadium at Bramley-Moore Dock, Albert Dock will be the best area to stay.

A Match Day Walk Offers a Serene Setting

Goodison Park is in the middle of a neighborhood on three sides, with Stanley Park and the Anfield Cemetery fronting the fourth side. Stanley Park is gorgeous, and we recommend walking through the paths to see just how close Goodison Park and Anfield are to each other. The park offers beautiful sceneries with abundant flowers, as well as a swing park with a large triangular climbing area that also gives you good views to take pictures of the surrounding area. As the match gets closer, work your way around Goodison and enjoy the sounds and throngs of people among the adjacent streets, which close closer and closer to match time. It feels a little like walking Yawkey Way before a Red Sox game.

Get a Picture with Dixie

Get to Goodison early enough where you can walk around the entire stadium. The club has done a great job encapsulating its history in a timeline that goes around three quarters of the stadium. With pictures and short description labels, you can get a strong sense of the club's history, from 1878 until today. If you are coming from the neighborhood side, large images of former players and managers emerge above the neighborhood skyline and get you ready for the match. Finally, go take a picture with the statue of 'Footballer, Gentleman and Evertonian' William Ralph 'Dixie Dean,' Chelsea's legendary scorer from the 1920s and 30s, that fronts Goodison Road, and serves as a big blue welcome to Goodison Park.

Enjoy a Pint at the Royal Oak

Just a short, seven-minute walk from Goodison, the Royal Oak (272 Walton Rd., Liverpool L4 4BE, UK) is a great pre-and-post match destination to have a pint or three. The pub has space around all four sides of the bar itself, and the front of the pub is open for smokers, and when it gets too crowded inside. Since it is not directly adjacent to Goodison, there is actually space to move around inside, even when it does get packed.

Our Everton Experience

Nil Satis Nisi Optimum is the motto of the Everton Football Club. It's Latin for "nothing but the best is good enough."

But the motto isn't so much a call to excellence, but an excuse to complain for Toffees fans, who perhaps take the saying a bit too literally.

Because for Everton fans, it seems not a single thing the club does is good enough – and every single aspect of the match day experience is open to criticism.

Coming into our Sunday late afternoon match with winless West Ham, Everton had taken a point from every contest. But they won just one and drew three others, including a 1-1 home result against lowly Huddersfield the last time out. At the Royal Oak pub and in the Gwladys Street End before the game, there was trepidation about an injury-hit squad, but not much to moan about results wise.

Instead, the price of chips at the pop-up stands outside Goodison Park – most selling food for charity – got Toffees fans' attention.

"Three pounds for chips and curry??!!" exclaimed at least three different walkups in their incredulous Scouse accent. "Bloody hell!"

But certainly the chips had never been free outside Goodison Park? And inflation had crept in over the last 30-odd years, not over the previous two weeks' international break. You started to wonder? Do Everton fans just like to have a moan?

We'd experienced it in almost every cab ride around Liverpool with Evertonian drivers. Before you could hardly speak, they were complaining about Liverpool FC, unprovoked. But until this performance, it seemed we'd only scratched the surface of the negativity.

Once inside, safely folded into an early-century seat in the upper stand of the Gwladys Street end, the moaning continued.

The overhang of the top stand, which prohibits a view of the clock or scoreboard, is like watching a match through a claustrophobic tunnel. The all-seater environment is made even worse as fans pop up and down in their chairs depending on the excitement of the play. Some fans see potential where others don't and the dance becomes a bit awkward as a few linger on their feet longer.

The first time it happened a few rows behind us, the sarcastic Scouse humor came out.

"Just my luck, I've been sat behind the tallest human alive," one lad half-jokingly complained about the relatively tall bloke standing in front of him. Everyone laughed.

As the match went on and the volume of his complaint increased, everyone got uncomfortable – none more so than the tall lad just minding his business. And that was tame compared to the rest of the contest.

The Toffees' whole back line was out injured, starting with veteran center backs Phil Jagielka and Michael Keane. Stalwart fullbacks Leighton Baines and Seamus Coleman were missing as well.

So it would be a day for youth. But Everton had made lots of noise about their young guns, starting up front with Dominic Calvert-Lewin (21), who was paired with 27 million pound winter signing Cenk Tosun.

In the back, Chelsea loanee Kurt Zouma (23) and promising young defender Mason Holgate (22) deputized in the middle. Everton academy product Jonjoe Kenny (21) was on the right. And the signing of the summer, former Barcelona youngster Lucas Digne (25) started on the left.

In goal, Everton had England's starting keeper Jordan Pickford, who is relatively young himself at 24. So the future was on full display on this day at Goodison Park, mixed in with veterans like Gylfi Sigurdsson, Theo Walcott, Morgan Schneiderlin and Tosun.

Maybe it was the right time to start the youngsters. After all, West Ham had played four and lost four. Coach Manuel Pellegrini, a champion at Man City, was already being wheeled to the old folks home by Irons' fans. None of the London club's new signings had showed much promise. Frustration – and an unexpected relegation battle – was brewing.

So Everton, at home, had thrown out the club motto. Coach Marco Silva was hoping something less than their best would still be good enough. But of course, this is the Premier League. And on this day, it was men versus boys.

Digne and Kenny showed a lot of pluck and hustle, but the bigger players coming at them on the West Ham wing had the better of them physically, particularly the Hammers' new Ukrainian signing, Andriy Yarmolenko.

Despite Digne's best efforts, he was pushed around and bossed by the 6-foot-2 Yarmolenko. Digne is listed as 5-foot-10, but it seemed unlikely when you saw him stand next to the other players.

Unfortunately for the Toffees, it was Tosun, arguably the club's strongest player, who was outmuscled for the first goal. In fact, Tosun seemed completely unable to perform duty one for any center forward: settle the ball and keep it while under pressure. For a lesson in how to do this to near perfection, one only had to look across Stanley Park at Roberto Firmino's performances, week in and week out. The comparison sums up the gap in talent between the two city rivals.

Early in this contest Tosun's first touch under pressure let him down over and over again. And in the 11th minute, rugged West Ham defender Fabian Balbuena knocked him off the ball. Pedro Obiang gathered the loose ball and chipped it over the top, cutting the entire Everton back line out in one pass.

West Ham's star man Marko Arnautovic won the race to the ball, drew Pickford out of the net and with no Everton defender in a hurry to catch up, unselfishly slid the ball across to Yarmolenko for the easy finish.

Everton fans' complaints had already started before the ball even hit the back of the net.

"27 million for that?!" was the general muttering towards Tosun. When angry, English fans have a way of standing up, shaking their head and jolting their arm forward, palm outstretched in disgust, as if gesturing at a replay of the previous error playing in their minds. But it looks like they're just gesturing towards the field in general, as if everything down there is disgusting them.

The gesture was apropos at this moment, as nothing on the field was going right for the Toffees.

Perhaps the worst players were the most experienced. Walcott, a frail sprinter who failed to materialize for Arsenal and England, had never met a challenge he couldn't pull out of. His soft attempts to chase down 50-50 balls helped West Ham grow in defensive confidence. And it set a poor example for the younger players.

Sigurdsson, Walcott, Schneiderlin and Calvert-Lewin were constantly running back and forth across the field to create space, which is good. Except they were occupying the same space at the same time and actually bumped into each other on a couple occasions, prompting frustration in the stands.

Idrissa Gana Gueye, the other midfielder who's gone by all three names at one point in his relatively short English career, was not much better. At least three times, he received a ball with his back to the goal and quickly played a one-touch pass, spinning away to make a run. Except twice he did it with no defender within 10 yards. It would've been easy enough to keep the ball, turn and take the space with the ball himself. But like a robot with limited programming, he just kept performing the same trick.

The second West Ham goal came on a mistake from another big money signing, Pickford, the starting keeper for England's World Cup semifinal run. He dithered for nearly a minute before playing a soft goal kick along the ground to seemingly no one.

Mark Noble stepped in front and drew a foul from the late reacting Digne, but not before sending the ball forward to Yarmolenko. Advantage was played; Yarmolenko cut in on the flailing Everton defenders and curled a shot with his left foot into the top corner.

Holgate, ignoring his own deficiencies, turned and screamed at the England number one, who paced around embarrassed and tried to ignore the anger of his younger teammate.

Digne showed flashes of his talent here and there. He worked down the left side and put a pinpoint cross on Tosun's head. Tosun headed it right into the keeper's chest, prompting more arm waving from the Gwladys Street End.

At one point, two particularly irritated middle-aged men in front of us complained loudly:

"All they want to do is find the easy man on the wing and then cross it. Every time, out to the wing, out to the wing."

Turning towards the field, they screamed, "Play it down the middle!!"

The teenager next to us rolled his eyes and shook his head. Keeping his voice down to avoid unnecessary attention from the obviously inebriated older men, he told us he disagreed.

"This is how we play at Everton. I've been coming for 10-odd years and under every manager, we play the ball to the wings and cross it to the middle for a goal. If they don't think that's how we play, then I don't know what games they've been coming to."

The young lad was onto something. Everton's best players for the last few seasons were arguably their fullbacks, Leighton Baines and Seamus Coleman, both out injured on this day, and former striker Romelu Lukaku, a man easily capable of tucking away a cross with his head.

The teenager was proven right when Everton pulled back some pride – and a little bit of hope – just before halftime. The Toffees had been much more lively after Silva made a 37th minute substitution, taking off Schneiderlin and putting on Bernard. It was an admission from Silva that he picked the wrong central midfield pack.

Bernard, another new signing, was bright and opened up space for the wings to get forward. Kenny laid a beautiful cross onto Sigurdsson's head and he buried it into the top corner. The teenager smiled at us knowingly and rolled his eyes in the direction of the mouths in front of us, who quickly left their seats to beat the halftime rush to the beer line.

For the only time all game, the halftime crowd buzzed with mild positivity. The Toffees weren't at their best, but maybe the substitution had sparked something. Just over ten minutes into the second half, all hopes were dashed.

Obiang and Arnautovic were able to do whatever they wanted, playing a 1-2 and slashing right through the growing space between Zouma and Holgate. Arnautovic's finish squeezed under Pickford's late dive and perhaps that's why there was no return yelling from Pickford at Holgate – both were culpable.

Around that time, the fans in the Gwladys Street End made up for the truce on the pitch. Murmurs of dissension and small arguments were breaking out everywhere. The tantrums peaked – or should we say piqued – when one younger fan with his hood pulled tightly to his head, stood up and shouted at a much older fan at the top of his lungs:
"SHUT THE FUCK UP!!"

The old man stayed in his seat and could only stammer a weak, "No, you shut up," back at him. Even the arguments amounted to nothing at Goodison.

Everton mounted some fight late and substitute Oumar Niasse found himself wide open in the 83rd minute, just below us. Of course, his shot hit the bar.

At that point, Toffees fans streamed out of Goodison Park and who could blame them. Even the man selling programs had a lackluster afternoon, unable to change a ten and so the only memento we took home was the Toffees anger ringing in our ears.

The lack of any coherent game plan, the confusing lineup choices and the poor concentration of the Everton defense all looked like managerial mistakes.

Perhaps its time to give Silva's record a thorough look. After taking Estoril up to the top Portuguese division, an unlikely fifth place finish and Europa League berth, he landed at Sporting in Lisbon. He signed a four-year contract, they finished third and he was fired at the end of his first season for not wearing the club's official suit in one match. From there he went to Olympiacos in Greece. His one year in charge was impressive, winning the Greek title and winning 17 matches in a row in Greece, a 21st century record in any major league until Manchester City broke the record last season. Olympiacos also claimed a win at the Emirates over Arsenal in the Champions League. After all that, Silva quit in the summer for personal reasons.

He turned up in January of the next year at Hull City, where he couldn't keep the Tigers from relegation. Which is fair, you might say, considering a team of Hull's talent level.

Except that Hull team included England starter Harry Maguire, who later signed for Leicester, and left back Andy Robertson, now captaining Scotland and starting for Liverpool in the Champions League final. Both looked like much better players after they left Silva.

He got off to a great start at Watford before being wooed by Everton. His Watford career went off the rails quickly, losing eight out of 11 before being fired on January 21, 2018 for his wayward eye. Watford brought charges to the FA against Everton for tapping up. Tapping up means recruiting him while he had another job.

But why was Silva so in demand in the first place? At Everton he'd gotten results in his first four games, but you could argue they've should've had more with draws at newly promoted Wolves and perhaps soon-to-be relegated Huddersfield. And they blew a 2-nil lead at Bournemouth. The only win came at home against a poor Southampton squad.

Was Silva the "best" man for the job? Was he "good enough"? Time will tell, but on this day's performance, there could be more long days when the likes of Man City, Chelsea and crosstown rivals Liverpool come to Goodison.

We contemplated those matchups as we walked home along the old Merseyside docks of Liverpool. One of these docks, called Bramley-Moore, is set to host Everton's new riverfront Stadium, allegedly as soon as 2021.

There was a lot of excitement about the stadium when we came to Liverpool in April 2017. But for whatever reason, zero progress has been made. The dock was still mostly deserted except for the stack of wood pellets, storage for the lumberyard across the street.

We wondered if there was anything truly positive going on at Everton Football Club. And of course, we wondered if the expectations were lowered, from Champions league to Premier League survival, would that temper the complaining?

Perhaps it was time to change that motto…

~BM

Merseyside Derby v. Liverpool

Everton's Goodison Park and Liverpool's Anfield Stadium are within sight of each other – less than a mile apart --if you stand in the right spot in Stanley Park. With only the park between them, the stadiums' proximity speaks to the extreme closeness of the rivalry, played twice each year as the Merseyside Derby.

It is the longest consecutive running rivalry, as both clubs have been in England's top flight since the 1962-63 season. For years, the rivalry had a separate nickname, the "Friendly Derby," with rival supporters sharing colors at matches. This is no longer the case, as the play on the pitch has gotten bitter in recent years.

Only five players were ejected in the first 88 years of the Derby, but 22 more have gone off in the last 33 years. Walk the neighborhoods adjacent Goodison Park and you will see, almost exclusively, a blue tint on the rowhouses, with an occasional brave red hue mixed in.

Liverpool has dominated the rivalry in recent years. The Reds have a current unbeaten run of 16, tied for longest in the Derby's history. More importantly, Everton has not won at Anfield in the 21st century. Since a Kevin Campbell goal gave Everton a 1-0 victory on September 27, 1999, the Blues have gone 0-10-10 in away matches. The two teams have played to a draw 82 times.

Liverpool holds a 118-82 advantage in the series, boosted by a win in the 2017-18 FA Cup third round. Otherwise, the two teams played to relatively uneventful draws in league play, drawing 0-0 at Everton and salvaging a point at Anfield with a 1-1 draw on a late Wayne Rooney penalty

Although Everton has tallied nine First Division trophies and five FA Cups, those titles have the feel of a little brother when compared to Liverpool's litany of domestic and European trophies, which currently number in the 40s. Neither side has raised a league trophy since Liverpool in 1989-90, but the Reds have won two FA Cups, three League Cups and two European crowns (1 Champions League and 1 Europa League) since Everton won its last trophy, the 1994-95 FA Cup. Liverpool supporters kindly remind their Everton counterparts of this fact at every derby, and probably every other day of the year as well.

"

Brief History of Goodison Park

The "Grand Old Lady," as Evertonians refer to it, Goodison Park is one of the oldest stadiums in all English football, and the fifth oldest in the Premier League. Only Stamford Bridge (Chelsea, 1877), St. James' Park (Newcastle, 1880), Turf Moor (Burnley, 1883) and Anfield (1884) have been around longer than Goodison, which opened in 1892.

According to Everton FC's website, Goodison Park was the "first major football stadium built in England."

The club's website credits Goodison as the "first major football stadium built in England." This included building modern stands and gates and turnstiles at a time when most stadiums had little to none. It was truly an enclosed stadium fit for the burgeoning sport.

Its creation resulted from a feud between the Everton club and former Everton Chairman, John Houlding. In a great example of "He Said, He Said," most historical reports place the blame on Everton's eventual move to Goodison on Houlding, who owned the land at Anfield, raising rent prices every year. As a result, Houlding would soon after found Liverpool, lighting the fires for the rivalry.

The largest recorded attendance at Goodison was, of course, a Merseyside Derby. A total of 78,299 saw Everton take on Liverpool on December 18, 1948, and the two played to a 1-1 draw.

Because of Everton's consistency, Goodison has "staged more top-flight games than any other ground in England…and was the only league ground in the country to have hosted a World Cup semi-final (in 1966)."

Since 1994, and the updating of the Park End, the stadium has remained largely unchanged. It's two tiers three quarters of the way around -- Bullens Road Stand, Gwladys Street Stand and Main Stand – and feels like an old-time football experience inside. That's both a good and bad thing as the seats at Goodison Park are as small and old-timey as anywhere else in the Premier League save Selhurst Park.

With Everton acquiring land at Bramley-Moore Dock to move the Toffees, the time to see a match at Goodison is growing short. The tentative plan is for the club's new stadium to open in time for the 2020-2021 season. Fans and stadium enthusiasts will want to schedule an opportunity to sit in the Howard Kendall Gwladys Street End before the move takes place.

Brief History of Everton

Including the 2017-18 campaign, the Toffees have played in the top flight for a record 115 seasons, 11 more than Aston Villa, and 12 more than neighborhood rival Liverpool. In fact, Everton has only played outside English football's top division for four seasons, 1930-31, and a three-year stretch between 1951-52 and 1953-54 (the league was suspended a combined 11 seasons for World War I and World War II).

Everton has spent 65 straight years in the top flight, second only to Arsenal's 92, and eight years ahead of Liverpool's run of 57 straight. In the club's history, Everton has won nine First Division titles, trailing only Manchester United, Liverpool and Arsenal, while finishing as runners-up seven times. The Toffees have also won five FA Cup crowns, tied for ninth all-time, while finishing second eight times. They also won the 1985 UEFA Cup Winners' Cup.

Everton was founded as St. Domingo's Football Club in 1878, named after the local church that put the club together. Two years later, it was named Everton after the neighborhood the club played in and was one of the 12 founding members of the English Football League in 1888. The Toffees were successful early, winning the First Division in 1890-91, an FA Cup in 1905, and the league again in 1914-15.

The club's fortunes improved further with the acquisition of Dean from fellow local side Tranmere Rovers in 1925. Despite losing a testicle earlier in his career (you read that right), and fracturing his skull in a motorcycle accident in 1926, Dean would define Everton's fortunes for a decade. He led the club to two league titles and an FA Cup crown, scoring a club-record 349 goals in 399 appearances.
The Toffees' legend scored an English-record 60 goals during the 1927-28 season that stands to this day. Everton also won a Second Division title during his time with the club. He has a statue outside Goodison Park that simply says "Footballer. Gentleman. Evertonian." The "gentleman" portion of his plaque is reflected in the fact that he was never booked in any competition, even after having a testicle damaged.

Everton's progress was stunted a couple times in its history. The first came when World War II halted play after the Toffees won their fifth league title in 1939. They would not win again until 1962-1963, under Harry Catterick. The successful manager led the club to an FA Cup in 1966, overcoming a two-goal deficit to Sheffield Wednesday in the process, as well as another league title in 1969-70.

Everton's success ended after the 1970 league crown, as rival Liverpool won eight of the next 14 First Division titles. Catterick's success in the 1960s and 70s was replicated in the 1980s by manager Howard Kendall, who spent six years leading the Toffees. During his tenure, Everton won two league titles in 1984-85 and 1986-87, finishing second to Liverpool in the year between. The club also won the 1984 FA Cup, finishing as runners-up the next two seasons, and the 1985 UEFA Cup Winners' Cup. The team also finished second in the 1983-84 League Cup.

The Heysel tragedy in 1985 prevented Everton from taking part in European play during the height of the club's run in the 1980s. Since Kendall's departure in 1987, only a 1995 FA Cup, under manager Joe Royle, has graced the trophy room.

David Moyes, Roberto Martinez, Ronald Koeman and Sam Allardyce have led the club to no worse than 11th since the 2004-05 season. The Toffees are currently one of only six clubs – Arsenal, Chelsea, Liverpool, Manchester United and Tottenham Hotspur as well – to have played in the Premier League every year since its inception in 1992-93.

2017-18 Season Review

Expectations around Goodison Park were high headed into the 2017-18 season. Dutchman Ronald Koeman was starting his second season at the helm, after a strong seventh place finish the year before, with 61 points and a +18 goal differential.

Sure, leading scorer Romelu Lukaku was gone to Manchester United for 75 million pounds. But Everton strengthened its back line with England keeper Jordan Pickford and defender Michael Keane. The Toffees signed Icelandic hero Gylfi Sigurdsson and speedy former Arsenal star Theo Walcott. And on top of all that, Everton brought back its favorite son: Wayne Rooney. He left for Manchester United as a teenager, but returned as a legend with more to give. Everton now had a platform for further success and a potential move into the top six.

But, the lineup just didn't come off in the early days of the season and Everton was dumped from the Europa League at the group stage after an embarrassing performance. The Toffees lost four of their first five group stage matches, the only point coming in a draw at home to lowly Apollon Limasol of Cyprus.

At the same time, Everton was thrashed in three straight top six matches in August and September, shut out by Chelsea, Tottenham and Manchester United. United poured in four goals, including one from Lukaku. The Toffees won just three times in the first 13 games and Koeman paid the price, despite has previous success.

Disgraced former England coach Sam Allardyce came in to right the ship. No one has been in the top division as many years in a row as Everton's current 64-year run so no one takes relegation that seriously at Goodison Park. Still, the Blues sat in 16th place when Allardyce took over on November 30.

True to his style, Everton grinded out results. Allardyce went unbeaten in his first six games, after a win for caretaker manager David Unsworth. It was the best streak of the season and righted the ship.

Still, the Toffees never really challenged for Europe and failed to win a game against the top six, losing eight and drawing four, including two Merseyside Derby draws.

Everton was knocked out of the League Cup in the third round by its crosstown rivals, 2-1, on a late goal from newly signed Virgil van Dijk.

Rooney led the team in scoring with 11 goals, but was sold to DC United in the summer. Goalkeeper Jordan Pickford was the club's Player of the Year. He started every Premier League match and had 12 clean sheets in all competitions. He went on to star for England at the summer's World Cup

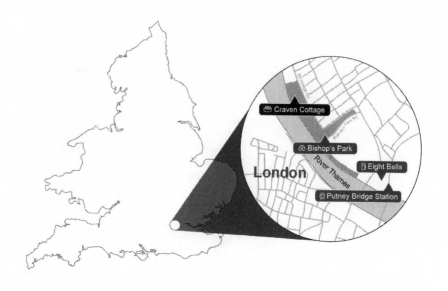

Fulham Football Club

Year Founded: 1879

Colors: Red, Black and White

Nickname: The Cottagers; The Whites

Stadium: Craven Cottage

Address: Stevenage Rd., Fulham, London SW6 6HH, UK

Capacity: 25,700, 16th in the Premier League

2017-18 Attendance: 19,896, 14th in the Championship

Trophies

None

Current Ownership: Shahid Khan

Current Manager: Claudio Ranieri (1st season)

2017-18 Finish: 3rd place in English Football League Championship, 25W, 8L, 13D; Won promotion via playoff, defeated Aston Villa, 1-0, in playoff final.

FA Cup: Lost in third round vs. Southampton, 1-0

League Cup: Lost in second round vs. Bristol Rovers, 1-0

The Sports Tourists' Tips for Huddersfield

Don't Stress Too Much About Tickets

If you're a Fulham fan and already a member, tickets should be plentiful when they go on sale to members. And you'll have a few days to decide. This is not a club you need to wait around the computer at 9 a.m. in order to secure your tickets.

Even if you're not a member, we still don't expect you to have any trouble. Most Fulham home games are not currently sellouts and tickets are available to the public a few weeks and even days before the match.

This makes Fulham a great place to go to on a lark. Its bucolic west London setting, Premier League status and friendliness to Americans makes it a perfect place to visit, no matter who you root for.

Stop off at the Eight Bells

You want history? You want that tight, intimate feeling of a London pub before a match? Well, you got it. Visit Eight Bells (89 Fulham High St., Fulham, London, SW6 3JS), the epitome of a tavern. This makes sense as it has been around since 1629, when it was known as the Blue Anchor.

The pub is located just minutes from the Putney Bridge tube station, the closest stop to Craven Cottage. You can stop in briefly for a pint (we recommend grabbing a London Pride) or stay a while, especially with a few tables outside, and watch the Cottagers' supporters scramble toward the match.

Walk Along the Thames to Craven Cottage

After having a pint or three at the Eight Bells, head over to Craven Cottage by taking one of the best paths available in the Premier League, the embankment pathway along the Thames River.

It is a mile walk between Putney Bridge station/Eight Bells pub and Craven Cottage. Virtually all that distance can be covered by walking on this pathway, which winds its way through Bishops Park for the last half of the walk.

We have done it twice and, rain or shine, it is magnificent. We attended two Saturday matches, which means that, while you are walking along the Thames, you will see rowers galore on the water. There were even boat races our first time there. There was a kind of Oxford vs. Cambridge feel even though it was just secondary schools competing. This walk definitely meanders through a unique setting.

Take the Craven Cottage Tour

We took this tour our first trip to England, when we were not sure if Fulham was going to get promoted after the 2016-17 season (they didn't) and we did not think we could get tickets to the first leg semifinal match the next day against Reading (we did).

Just go their link to find out available dates and times. Tours are 15 pounds each for adults, and totally worth it. You meet at the Café at Craven Cottage and a guide will take you on a comprehensive 90-minute tour. If you get lost, meet at the Johnny Haynes statue, the long-time Fulham great who scored 150+ goals in more than 650 appearances for the club.

This journey includes a stroll through the actual cottage itself, where you see Fulham's manager's office, as well as the seats that are reserved for the families of current players.

For Americans, one of the best parts of the tour is seeing photos of Brian McBride and Clint Dempsey during the club's more recent successes.

Don't Hurry Back to the Tube

As with any other Premier League match in London, heading to the tube immediately after its conclusion is a no-no. It is a shit-show environment with nasty, drunk fans supporting both teams cutting and cursing non-stop.

You can head back to the Eight Bells for another pint, but it was packed out the door both times we tried. On our last visit, after the draw with Watford, we walked over to Bellillo (255 Munster Rd., London, SW6 6BW), which is one of a host of restaurants within a half mile to mile of Craven Cottage, so you can grab a bite anywhere. You may need a reservation at Bellillo, but we got lucky with a 10-minute wait.

The menu choices won't blow you away, but the food is good and the customer service is better. We had the arancini (stuffed rice balls) for an appetizer and then got talked into the montanarona, which is a fried pizza with fresh buffalo mozzarella and more.

It was a simple meal that hit the spot and cleared the tube by the time we got back.

Our Fulham Experience

Traveling throughout England as an American in love with soccer/football earns you a number of responses from the locals.

In some places, you get quizzical 'What are you doing here?' looks. In others, fascination with your interest and where you're from, although when anyone mimicked our American accents, it made it sound like we were all from Texas.

In others, you have to prove yourself worthy of the locals' respect with your level of soccer knowledge. This may be technical – understanding the acute differences between a 4-4-2 and a 4-3-3 and when each formation is best employed. Or, it can be historical – knowing how long a club has been around, who its greatest players are, what its recent history has been, etc.

Most club's fans have welcomed us with open arms throughout our two trips. None more so than Fulham, one of the few places where American players have established enough of their own history on the pitch to gain a serious following by the supporters.

In fact, the club that plays in the Cottage along the Thames is known slightly different in the United States.

Fulhamerica.

This is due to the positive performances of several US players in a Fulham kit over the past two decades.

Since 1999, Americans have tallied more than 750 appearances for the club and played crucial roles in both Premier League and Europa League success, as well as the club's most recent promotion from the EFL Championship.

The beginning of this talent transfer across the pond occurred fairly quietly. Marcus Hahnemann, one of a bevy of talented US goalkeepers coming up the ranks in the 1990s, joined Fulham in June of 1999. He made little impact over a handful of games, but he did end up making more than 250 appearances for Reading.

Other Americans, like Emerson Hyndman, Eddie Lewis, Eddie Johnson and Kasey Keller made appearances and contributions for the Cottagers over the years, but three Yanks would stand above the rest for their accomplishments in a Fulham uniform.

Carlos Bocanegra and Brian McBride both came over from MLS in the January transfer window of the 2003-04 season. The two US Men's National Team mainstays were at different points in their careers. Bocanegra, 24 at the time, was already an established defensive presence heading into his peak years.

McBride, However, appeared headed towards his soccer twilight at the age of 32.

The two Americans featured in several important Fulham moments over the next four years. Bocanegra starred as both a defender and a holding midfielder and became a versatile and invaluable contributor during his time at Craven Cottage.

McBride became a fan favorite for the same reason he is one of our all-time favorite US Men's players. He is fierce and brave and regularly ended matches with blood present somewhere on his face or the back of his head.

His relentless pursuit up top earned him numerous goals with the US team and the Columbus Crew. Then, Fulham became the beneficiary of his unabating style.

In the middle of the 2006-07 season, Fulham added another American from the New England Revolution on a 2-million-pound transfer thought to be too steep at the time: Clint Dempsey.

That season was the first of two consecutive campaigns where the Cottagers faced relegation from the Premier League. McBride led the team with nine goals.

Dempsey scored just one, but it came in the final game of the season, against Liverpool. Needing at least a tie to stay up, Dempsey scored the lone goal in a triumph over the Reds.

The following season featured much of the same. Keller came aboard for a year, and his clean sheet against Portsmouth on the final day of the season again ensured Fulham's Premier League survival. Dempsey had six goals on the year while McBride and Bocanegra each completed their four-year stays in Fulham.

On March 16th of that season, against Everton, Fulham made American history. Keller, McBride and Johnson started that day, and Dempsey and Bocanegra later came off the bench for coach Roy Hodgson. Five Americans playing on a Premier League side in one game.

As sportswriter Steven Keehner wrote, "It remains a high watermark in the history of US stars abroad."

To understand McBride's popularity, consider this: One of Fulham's most popular current VIP packages features seats that allow you into McBride's Bar.

According to Fulham's website, "Named after Fulham's American hero, Brian McBride, this spacious sports bar is a great place to enjoy lively banter and discuss all the match action."

How much for a McBride's VIP ticket to one match? For the 2018-19 season – 219 pounds. How much for a season VIP pass

West London Derby

The west London Derby is one of the more lightly regarded derbies in English football, and includes any of four clubs playing against each other: Brentford, Chelsea, Fulham and Queens Park Rangers.

Of those, Fulham has faced Chelsea the most, 83 times, with little success. The Cottagers have won just 11 times, with Chelsea victorious 46 times. The Blues have a current 17-game unbeaten streak against Fulham, with the Cottagers' last victory coming in a March 2006 Premier League contest.

Fulham and Brentford have played to a nearly even record. Fulham holds a slight edge in the series, 21 wins, 20 losses and 17 draws. However, the Bees own the recent matches in the series, winning four, drawing three and losing to the Cottagers just once in four seasons in the Championship between 2014-18.

Fulham own a slight, 16-14 series edge over Queens Park Rangers, including three wins and a draw in six matches in the Championship the last three years.

Over time, the clubs involved just have not played each other that much, and there is little in the way of vitriol spewed by players or fans at the other. In fact, in 2011, *Sportskeeda* ranked the west London derby as the fifth best out of five London derbies overall.

that includes McBride's Bar? For the 2018-19 season – 2,799 pounds.

Not bad.

Bocanegra and McBride left in 2008, as did Keller, who spent just the one season at Craven Cottage. Johnson would stay with the club through 2011, but only made 19 appearances, spending the majority of his time with Fulham on loan to clubs like Cardiff City and Preston North End.

That left Dempsey as the sole American making significant contributions, and the young Texan made the most of the spotlight. He finished the 2008-09 season with eight goals and three assists as Fulham, which finished seventh with 58 points, recorded its highest top-flight finish in club history.

The 2009-10 season may have been even better, despite a 12th-place Premier League finish. The Cottagers competed in the Europa League and made it all the way to the final before losing late to Atlético Madrid, 2-1. Along the way, Dempsey had his defining moment in a Fulham jersey.

In the Europa League round of 16, Juventus posted a 3-1 win against Fulham in the first leg at home in Turin. Then, Juve scored the first goal at Craven Cottage two minutes into the second leg. Cottagers fans can be forgiven if they started focusing on the rest of the Premier League season at that point.

But Fulham responded. First, Bobby Zamora in the ninth minute. Then, Zoltán Gera in the 39th. Then, after the half, Gera again in the 49th, this time on a penalty kick. That left the door open for a moment of greatness.

Dempsey took it. In the 82nd minute, just outside the top right side of the box, Dempsey turned and chipped a shot over Juventus goalkeeper Antonio Chimenti for the winning goal. It was a beautiful finish and a spectacular moment for Americans and Fulham fans alike.

For Dempsey, who finished second in scoring for Fulham in 2009-10, the high level of production continued. He had 13 goals and eight assists in 2010-11 as the Cottagers finished eighth.

Then, in 2011-12, as Fulham finished ninth, Dempsey led the club with 17 Premier League goals, putting him fourth in the league that season behind Robin van Persie, Wayne Rooney and Sergio Aguero.

Dempsey had 23 goals and six assists in all competitions that year. That output led to a 7-million-pound transfer to Tottenham after the season, but Dempsey will always be remembered in England as a Cottager.

His 50 Premier League goals are the most in club history. McBride, who scored 32 Premier League goals for the club, is tied for second with Belgian Steed Malbranque.

His performance in a Fulham uniform earned him the highest praise from perhaps Fulham's best player ever, all-time leading scorer Gordon Davies:

"He was a player I really enjoyed watching at Fulham. I wasn't sure how he would fare when he first arrived given that the standard in the Premier League is a lot higher than in America," Davies said. "But from Day One, he showed that he had the ability, the work rate and the nous in and around the box. I'll never forget his goal against Juventus, which had me jumping around like a nine-year-old boy in my living room."

Take the Craven Cottage tour one day and you will see countless pictures of Dempsey and McBride celebrating big goals and big wins. As an American, it is a great opportunity to puff out your chest with pride.

2017-18 Season Review

A season that finished with the club's first appearance at Wembley Stadium in 43 years started with a whimper. Fulham went winless in the season's first month and won just four of its first 17 matches. A 1-nil defeat at relegation-bound Sunderland in mid-December had the Whites mid-table near the middle of the season.

Sheyi Ojo and Floyd Ayité scored in a 2-1 home win over Barnsley two days before Christmas that set off the longest unbeaten run in club history. Aleksandar Mitrović came over on loan from Newcastle in late January and scored 12 goals in the club's final 14 regular season matches.

The Cottagers did not lose for four and a half months. During that time, Fulham won 18 and drew five in a 23-game unbeaten streak. However, a 3-1 loss at Birmingham City on the final day of the regular season left the club in third place. For the second straight season, Fulham would have to go the playoff route.

Slaviša Jokanović's club lost at Derby County, 1-0, in the first leg of the semifinals. Ryan Sessegnon, who led the team with 16 goals and added six assists, scored in the second leg at Craven Cottage, as did teammate Denis Odoi, who tallied the winner in the 66th minute to send Fulham to Wembley Stadium for the first time since the 1975 FA Cup final.

Scotsman Tom Cairney scored six goals all season, none bigger than his goal in the 23rd minute of the playoff final against Aston Villa off a Sessegnon assist. Goalkeeper Marcus Bettinelli and Fulham's defense made the goal stand up despite playing down a man the last 20 minutes. It was the team's 16th clean sheet of the season, the 12th since midseason. The Cottagers were going back to the Premier League.

Why bring all this up?

Because we received an extra bonus ahead of our match at Craven Cottage on September 22nd. We knew we would get to see Watford, which won four straight to start the season and currently sat fifth in the table after a 2-1 loss the week before to Manchester United.

Now, after an announcement just days ahead of the match, we were going to see Dempsey as well. He was being honored at halftime for his Cottager career.

It would be a bittersweet moment. We saw Dempsey at the end of June in Seattle in a Cascadia Cup match against the Portland Timbers.

It was a cracker of a game. The Timbers took the lead three separate times in a 3-2 victory. The Sounders responded twice, and also introduced Peruvian Raúl Ruidíaz at halftime, an addition that would aid the then-slumping Sounders in a run to the MLS Western Conference semifinals.

What we also saw was the last run of Dempsey, which we didn't know at the time. He looked old and was even booed at times at home after his giveaway resulted in one of Portland's goals.

Two months later, Dempsey retired, after 15 professional seasons. He is tied with Landon Donovan for the most national team goals with 57 and is the only American to score in three consecutive World Cups.

He had 79 goals and 45 assists in MLS play, winning an MLS Cup with Seattle in 2016 after starting his career in New England. His 50 Premier League goals are also the most for an American, so the reasons for his halftime honor were obvious to us.

Seeing him was an extra treat, but seeing the Cottagers was why we were there in the first place. We hopped off the tube at Putney Bridge, had a pint at the Eight Bells and then worked our way through a steady drizzle to Craven Cottage, watching rowers thrash the waters of the Thames along the way.

After a 13-year stretch in the Premier League ended with relegation following the 2013-14 season, Fulham had competed for four seasons in the Championship. The club performed poorly its first two years down, finishing 17th and 20th and almost dropped another level, to League One.

Serbian Slaviša Jokanović took over the club midway through the 2015-16 season and was determined to get the Cottagers back to the Premier League. He had already accomplished the feat with Watford, guiding the club to a second-place finish in 2014-15, although his reward for achieving promotion with the Hornets was a pink slip.

He led Fulham to a sixth-place finish in 2016-17 and a trip to the playoffs. We were at Craven Cottage when the team hosted Reading in a playoff semifinal. It was an uneven performance that resulted in a 1-1 tie thanks to a second-half goal by Tom Cairney.

The Cottagers lost, 1-0, in the second leg, and had to wait a year for another opportunity. After an uneven showing in the season's first half that left Fulham mid-table, a club-record 23-match unbeaten streak propelled the team into third-place and another playoff appearance.

This time, the Cottagers would advance, defeating Derby County in the semifinals and Aston Villa in the final. Another

Tom Cairney goal, this time in front of nearly 90,000 at Wembley, gave Fulham the 1-nil result it needed. It was the club's first appearance at Wembley in more than 40 years, since the 1975 FA Cup final.

Jokanović had Fulham back in the Premier League, and American owner Shahid Khan made sure that he would not make the move empty-handed.

The Cottagers spent more than 100 million pounds in bringing in a dozen players over the summer. The biggest moves involved the additions of Ivorian Jean Michaël Seri, German André Schürrle, Spanish goalkeeper Sergio Rico, Argentinian Luciano Vietto and former Burnley and Swansea City center-back Alfie Mawson.

However, the most important signing was the permanent move of Aleksandar Mitrović from Newcastle. The Serbian came over on loan at the start of February and promptly scored 12 goals in 17 league appearances as part of Fulham's unbeaten run. He signed a five-year contract with Fulham worth more than 20 million pounds.

The deal was announced at the end of July and the first positive response we received on the signing came in, of all places, San Francisco. We were grabbing breakfast at historic Boudin Café on Fisherman's Wharf when the cashier noticed the Fulham jacket I was wearing. His English was strong, but all he said was, 'Fulham?'

When I said 'yes,' his response, with a smile from ear to ear, was, 'Mitro!'

Apparently the young man had attended primary school with young Mitro. Although still 24 years of age, Mitro is no longer young. He is a 6-foot-1, 180-pound tank up top, his head and legs firing missiles at will.

We were excited to see Mitro, Seri and the rest of the upgraded Fulham squad take on a Watford side that was impressive early in the Premier League season.

The last time Watford played Fulham at Craven Cottage was nearly four years ago in the Championship, and the Hornets came away with a 5-0 victory, thanks largely to a hat trick by captain Troy Deeney.

Early in the match, we saw just how in-form the current club was.

Off a long throw-in that resulted in multiple missed Fulham clearances, Watford's Andre Gray took a pass from Will Hughes and slotted it past goalkeeper Marcus Bettinelli 90 seconds into the game for a 1-0 Watford advantage.

Allowing an early goal has been something of a bad habit for Fulham, which surrendered a goal 97 seconds into the contest the week before to Man City's Leroy Sané. It was a scene all too familiar to FFC Radio man, "Gentleman" Jim McGullion.

"The most frustrating thing is that, not for the first time, we made things harder for ourselves by giving away a sloppy goal," McGullion said. "At least one goal in every game so far has come from a Fulham man making an error of judgement or giving possession away cheaply. Whilst its very early days and we've used a lot of new players, we really need to tighten things up and eradicate those kinds of mistakes because at this level you'll almost always get punished...if we continue letting in goals at the current rate, we'll end up in big trouble."

Fulham had a great opportunity to equalize in the 12th minute when a pass from Schürrle sprung Vietto up on the left side, but Watford keeper Ben Foster ably came off his line for the initial stop, with Vietto going wide right on the rebound.

Watford owned the majority of the first half, with missed attempts and multiple saves by Bettinelli the only thing keeping the Hornets from at least a three-goal advantage. Fulham's first 45 minutes were more notable for the team's defensive miscues, including poor marking by Seri, a horrific back pass by Mawson and bookings to both Fosu-Mensah and Mawson.

At halftime, Jokanović made two substitutions, bringing Denis Odoi and Floyd Ayité on for Mawson and Kevin McDonald.

"I made two changes. I would have made four if I could," Jokanović told *The Guardian*'s John Brewin after the game.

Many in the stands did their usual sprint for booze around the 40th minute, but we stayed in our seats to view the rare halftime scene – an American honored by a Premier League club.

Dempsey stood near the manager boxes as a video tribute showed his greatest goals in a Fulham uniform – including the Juventus tally and the relegation-saving winner against Liverpool. He had his usual faint grin and both clapped for and saluted the Fulham supporters, who chanted his name and clapped in return.

It was a sight to behold, and hopefully a harbinger of more American success here in the future.

Fulham surely built off that celebration, for the Cottagers were a completely different club in the second half. Mitrović nearly evened the game in the 49th minute, rising above Watford defender Craig Cathcart, but his header went over the bar.

The game remained this way until the 78th minute when a Schürrle shot was blocked into the path of Vietto, who beat Watford right back Daryl Janmaat to the ball before sending a low cross in to Mitrović, who simply let the ball glance off his leg past Foster.

The Guardian jokingly observed that Mitrović, now with five league goals on the young league season, currently had one more than his former club, Newcastle.

As the match hurried to a close, Mitro nearly added to his tally sending another blazing offering off his head that Foster just barely tipped off the bar in the 90th minute.

The game ended in a draw, and represented one of the few high points for the Cottagers in the first third of the season. Fulham lost its next six matches, including defeats to relegation favorites Cardiff City and Huddersfield, allowing 18 goals total over that span.

In fact, the club allowed 28 goals through its first 10 league games, tying an infamous Premier League record.

The poor defensive showings and the negative results cost Jokanović his job after 12 games. Italian Claudio Ranieri, who coached Leicester City to the Premier League title in 2015-16 and most recently led French side Nantes, took over just before Thanksgiving. The Cottagers responded immediately with just their second win, 3-2 over Southampton.

The team can only hope more American help is on the way. Tim Ream has made more than 100 appearances for Fulham since coming over from Bolton in 2015. The defender was the club's player of the year in 2017-18 after making 48 appearances and returned from injury soon after our appearance at Craven Cottage.

San Diego native Luca de la Torre had a goal and two assists in Fulham's 3-1 third-round League Cup win over Millwall. And youngster Marlon Fossey, originally from Los Angeles, was making a name for himself on Fulham's U-18 and U-23 squads the past few years before a torn ACL at the start of the 2018-19 season sidelined him.

Fulhamerica is alive and well at Craven Cottage. Fulham itself just needs to do the same.

~BB

Brief History of Craven Cottage

The Cottage has been home to Fulham since 1896, although the club spent the 2002-03 and 2003-04 seasons at Loftus Road, home to Queens Park Rangers, as the Cottage was renovated into an all-seater stadium.

The land was purchased in 1894 and the stadium became Fulham's third official home ground, following Half Moon (1891-95) and Captain James Field (1895-96), although the team did play at several locations between 1879-1891.

Stands were built and demolished until 1905, when the West London and Fulham Times reported that Fulham officially obtained a 99-year lease on Craven Cottage, allowing more serious development to take place.

Architect Archibald Leitch, the man responsible with designing seemingly every major English football ground during this time period, was hired and oversaw the completion of a 5,000-seat stand (now the Johnny Haynes Stand) and the cottage itself, which housed, and still houses, the clubs' changing rooms.

Large crowds, thanks to standing terraces, attended matches regularly prior to World War II. To this day, the largest Craven Cottage crowd, 49,335, was for a 1938 match against Millwall. The stadium was used as a military training ground during the second World War, as were so many of the stadiums in and around London.

The backside of the Johnny Haynes Stand houses the club café, guarded by the Johnny Haynes statue, with ticket offices and the team's store further down. The outside of that stand looks similar to the warehouse at Baltimore's Oriole Park at Camden Yards.

For nearly 70 years, the stand backing on to the River Thames was simply terracing, allowing for an open view of the river, and lovely winds to come into play. That changed in 1972, when the Riverside Stand (then known as the Eric Miller Stand) was completed.

The last big change took place when the club finally reached the Premier League. Due to policy changes created by the Hillsborough tragedy in 1989, all stadiums in the Premier League have to be all-seaters.

That required two years of renovation, forcing the Whites to share Loftus Road with Queens Park Rangers. Now, back home for 15 years, and back in the Premier League, Craven Cottage is one of the more uniquely beautiful stadiums we experienced.

Brief History of Fulham

Research has confirmed that Fulham was formed in 1879 as Fulham St. Andrew's Church Sunday School FC by worshipers at the Church of England on Star Road, West Kensington.

The club is the oldest London side in the English Football League, although it turned professional after Arsenal.

By 1888, the club had shortened its name to Fulham, and began calling Craven Cottage home in 1896. Admitted to the Southern League's Second Division in 1898, Fulham quickly earned promotion to the First Division by 1903. After winning two consecutive Southern League Division One titles, Fulham moved to the Football League in 1907, and was assigned to the Second Division.

Between 1906-07 and 1948-49, the club spent 27 seasons in the Second Division and four a step down in the Division Three South. The two world wars canceled a total of 11 seasons in between.

The club finally broke through during the 1948-49 season, winning the Second Division. The Cottagers pipped West Brom by a point on the final day of the season, and earned promotion to the First Division for the first time. Although the club was only up for three seasons, the 1950s were an exciting time for Fulham.

Bobby Robson, who later managed the 1990 England World Cup team to the semifinals, was signed by then-manager Bill Dodgin as a 17-year-old in 1950. He paired with Johnny Haynes and Bedford Jezzard up front and scored 141 goals in 636 games for Fulham.

Jezzard was no scoring slouch himself, tallying a post-war record 39 goals in the 1953-54 season, including a record nine-match scoring streak. He finished with 142 goals in under 300 games with the club. Haynes, known as The Maestro, came to Fulham around the same time as Robson, as a 15-year-old in 1950. He would go on to set the club record with 158 goals in 658 games for the Cottagers, despite a tragic car crash that limited the tail end of his career. A statue of Haynes stands outside the stand bearing his name at Craven Cottage.

The Cottagers earned promotion to the First Division again following the 1958-59 season, when they finished second behind Sheffield Wednesday. Fulham would spend nine years in the First Division, the club's longest stretch in the top tier for more than 30 years.

Jezzard, who became manager of the club in 1958, and later Vic Buckingham, oversaw this golden period. Fulham's heart at this time was George Cohen, a right back deemed by England coach Alf Ramsey as "England's greatest right-back," who led the club for more than a decade. Graham Leggat was an offensive force during this time as well, scoring more than 130 goals for the club.

Dark days followed, as Fulham, starting in 1967-68, was relegated twice in two years, all the way down to the Third Division. Over the next 33 years, the Cottagers would split their time between the second and third divisions while also spending three years in the Fourth Division in the late 1990s, then known as Football League Division Three.

Fulham reached its only FA Cup final at this time when, as a second-division club, it lost to West Ham, 2-nil, in 1975.

Late in the 1970s, the club signed Gordon Davies, who would play for Fulham for two separate spells, as did Robson. He scored 178 goals for the Cottagers, still a club record, although he was unable to lift the club back to the top flight.

Fulham almost went out of business entirely in 1987 thanks to a misguided attempt by club ownership to purchase Queens Park Rangers and merge them with the Cottagers. Former player Jimmy Hill stepped up and led a group that rescued the club.

Fulham's low-point occurred during the 1995-96 season, when it finished 17th in Division Three, only a few spots away from losing Football League status for the first time.

Egyptian Mohamed Al-Fayed purchased the club in 1997 and, through wise spending and player transfers, Fulham went on a scintillating run, earning promotion three times in five years, ultimately to the Premier League in 2001.

The Cottagers didn't just survive in the league; they lasted 13 years before relegation. During that time, the club experienced perhaps its best seasons ever.

Fulham finished top-half of the Premier League table four times, with its best finish a seventh-place showing in 2008-09 under Roy Hodgson. That finish put the club into Europa League play the next year, where they knocked off Shakhtar Donetsk, Juventus, Wolfsburg and Hamburg to reach the final, losing, 2-1, to Atlético Madrid.

One of the greatest moments in the history of the club occurred in the round of 16. After losing, 3-1, at Juventus in the first leg, Fulham stormed back at Craven Cottage. Bobby Zamora scored in the ninth minute to offset an early David Trezeguet goal for Juve.

Hungarian Zoltán Gera scored twice in 10 minutes spanning both halves and then, in a splendid individual moment, American Clint Dempsey scored on a chip from just outside the penalty box in the 82nd minute. While Juventus players stood stunned, Dempsey went behind the goal and celebrated with his teammates and Fulham's supporters.

In the final, a Diego Forlan goal in the 116th minute, his second of the game, broke Fulham's hearts and prevented the club from hoisting its first major trophy as Atlético Madrid won at HSH Nordbank Arena in Hamburg.

The Cottagers stayed up another four years before relegation following the 2013-14 season. Pakistani-American businessman Shahid Khan, owner of the NFL's Jacksonville Jaguars, took control of the team ahead of that season. He did not acquit himself favorably that first year, firing two managers before the club finished 19th and dropped down.

Fulham struggled its first two seasons back down in the Championship, finishing 17th and 20th. Serbian Slaviša Jokanović took over midway through the 2015-16 season and guided the club to the playoffs the following season, falling to Reading in the semifinals.

The Cottagers earned a trip back to the Premier League with a tremendous close to the 2017-18 season. Fulham went on a club-record 23-game unbeaten run and the team knocked off Derby County in the semifinals and Aston Villa in the final at Wembley.

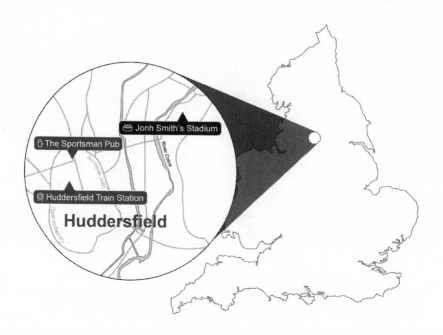

Huddersfield Town AFC

Year Founded: 1908

Colors: Blue and White Vertical Stripes

Nickname: The Terriers

Stadium: John Smith's Stadium

Address: Stadium Way, Huddersfield HD1 6PG, UK

Capacity: 24,500, 17th in the Premier League

2017-18 Attendance: 24,012, 16th in the Premier League

Trophies

First Division/Premier League (3): 1923-24;
1924-25; 1925-26

FA Cup (1): 1921-22

Current Ownership: Dean Hoyle

Current Manager: David Wagner, 4th Season
(53W, 49L, 26D)

2017-18 Finish: 16th place in the Premier League
(9W, 19L, 10D)

FA Cup: Lost in fifth round vs. Manchester United,
2-0

League Cup: Lost in third round at Crystal Palace,
1-0

The Sports Tourists' Tips for Huddersfield

John Smith's Ticket Demand Rising

In previous seasons, Huddersfield tickets were plentiful and easy to get, even without a membership. But this season, we were forced to buy a membership and once it was our turn to purchase tickets for Tottenham's visit... very few were available.

Tickets are still cheap, thanks to owner Dean Hoyle's promise to keep tickets low-priced even after promotion. But the John Smith's Stadium is a busy place these days. As a second year in the Premier League began, more and more locals wanted to come out and see the show. Being the only Premier League team in Yorkshire doesn't hurt the demand either.

Start at The Sportsman

If you're arriving in Huddersfield by train, or staying in the city center, you should start your match day at The Sportsman pub. It's a three-minute walk from the train station and less than a mile from the John Smith's Stadium on the other side of the River Colne.

The Sportsman is a perfect combination of game day atmosphere with good beer and food options and came highly recommended by locals. If you want to drink closer to the stadium, there's the Rope Walk in the shopping center out front of the John Smith's.

Branch Out and See a Rugby League Game Too

Huddersfield is known as the birthplace of Rugby League. What most Americans know as rugby is called Rugby Union and is played in American colleges and at the international level. Rugby League is played under different rules to make the game much faster. Think the constant play of soccer meets the hard hitting, passing and running game of American football. The Huddersfield Giants play in the Super League. The season runs from February until October, so be sure to check the schedule if you're going during those months.

Our Huddersfield Experience

Even in late September, with the Premier League season less than 20% complete, two names were already on everyone's tongue with it came to relegation.

Neil Warnock's Cardiff City team, who seemed surprised, even a bit annoyed, to find themselves outside the championship...

And Huddersfield Town, Yorkshire's lone representative at the top level. Most people were shocked when coach David Wagner was able to keep the lowest-scoring team in the Premier League in the top division last season.

Yet here the Terriers were a year later, still swinging at the highest level.

But was this club's best moment in time coming to a close? The unique story of a close-knit club rising from obscurity to the highest level, fueled by a local owner, a young genius manager and a bargain-priced roster was just too good to be true for too long.

It seems strange – foolish even – to predict who's going down just seven games into the season. Especially when you consider on our last trip to England, the last two relegation teams were still a mystery to most pundits in early April.

But as we left the hotel on a bright sunny Saturday to see the Terriers host title contenders Tottenham, the results did not look hopeful for Huddersfield.

In its first six games, Huddersfield Town picked up just two points, thanks to draws with Everton and fellow stragglers Cardiff City. Worse yet, goals did not appear on the horizon. Already the Terriers had been shut out in three games, all at home, never scoring more than one goal in any game. In fact, Huddersfield hadn't scored at home since April 14.

Another loss and Huddersfield would drop more than three points behind the 18th place team and even farther away from 17th place and safety. For the proud people of Yorkshire, that could mean potential disaster.

Athletically, Yorkshire has an attitude much like Texas in the US. Yorkshiremen believe themselves tougher, with more heart than the average Englishman. Yorkshire and grit roll off the tongue like Yorkshire and pudding. Yorkshire pudding, for those who don't know, is a delicious type of roll on the side of a roast, usually great for sopping up gravy.

As *The Daily Mail* said, "Had 'God's Own County' been a republic, it would have finished 12th in the London 2012 Olympics medal table, ahead of South Africa, New Zealand, Spain and Brazil. And there was a time when residents believe the County Cricket title was theirs to keep on a rolling basis. Coming first is in the genes."

For years Yorkshire was well represented in the Premier League. Often, at least three or four of Yorkshire's 10 professional clubs played at the top level. But in 2004, mighty Leeds United, the standard bearer for the area, went down. And only three years earlier, they'd played in the Champions League semifinals. Many thought they would bounce back quickly. But 14 years later, they're still waiting.

As of publication of this book, Leeds was in pole position to be promoted back up next year, but it's a long season. Yorkshire hasn't had two teams in the Premier League at once since 2001. In five of the last 14 seasons, Yorkshire has been completely shut out of the Premier League.

It didn't happen once in the 21 years prior...

Were Huddersfield and Newcastle to go down this season – with no one else from Yorkshire or the Northeast (Sunderland, Middlesbrough and Newcastle) getting promoted... it would be the first time in the history of English football these two proud regions would have no team at the top level.

The damned thing about it is Yorkshire football had a resurgence on the international stage this past summer during the World Cup. No area of England had more players on the roster than Yorkshire's six. If you add two more players from the Northeast, this potentially Premier League barren area carried the standard for the English national team.

Breakout central defender Harry Maguire, speedster Jamie Vardy, fullbacks Kyle Walker and Danny Rose, plus defenders John Stones and Gary Cahill, all hail from Yorkshire. (Cahill actually grew up on the border in Derby.)

Maguire pointed out the rugged nature of all these players during an England press conference:

"There are quite a lot of Yorkshire lads in the squad and they all tend to be defenders or defensive midfielders. It must be something from the culture of the area. I'm sure there are other parts of the country who are more than capable of getting in a physical battle, but I'm sure we're all up for it, definitely."

Brief History of the John Smith's Stadium

After 86 years at Leeds Road, Huddersfield Town moved into the John Smith's stadium in 1994, except then it was called the Alfred MacAlpine Stadium, the name of the contractor who built it. In 2004, Galpharm Healthcare was the sponsor. And since 2012, local brewer John Smith's name has adorned the ground.

The stadium was a joint effort between the Terriers and the local rugby league powerhouse, Huddersfield Giants. With a capacity of 24,169, the stadium ranks 16th in the Premier League.

When the stadium opened, Huddersfield was in League Two and only drew 13,334 fans. During the first season in the Premier League, the Terriers averaged 24,012 fans a game.

Despite Huddersfield's low level in football at that time, the city's status as the birthplace of rugby league meant the stadium was built to host World Cup matches for both rugby league and rugby union. As a result, it was one of the first modern stadiums in England and won the RIBA Building of the Year award in 1995.

The structure is open in all four corners and has arched white roofs over each section, giving it a unique look. In order to become Premier League ready, the team put in new grass, new floodlights and larger press boxes.

There's some cool perks to joining the Premier League as well. In 2018, the John Smith's Stadium made its debut in the popular EA video game, FIFA 2018.

Tottenham's arrival had stirred memories of England's remarkable run to the World Cup semifinals. And one of those Yorkshireman, Doncaster-born Rose, was in the starting 11.

And of course, Tottenham's star and England's top man, Harry Kane was sure to draw a lot of interest.

With the early results so poor, we expected there to be a lot of nail biting and tension around Huddersfield. But both before the match at The Sportsman's Pub and on our arrival at John Smith's Stadium, no one was focusing on the negative. And the thought of

Huddersfield in the Championship seemed far from everyone's minds.

Over and over the mood from Terriers' supporters was one of optimism and excitement at still playing in the top level against teams like Tottenham.

You never know what to expect when a load of Cockneys turn up in the gritty north, but to our pleasant surprise, the atmosphere seemed cordial everywhere. Dare we say, the way it ought to be. Dozens of Yorkshire's finest – giant scary looking police officers, many of them on horseback – lined the streets to keep the peace. Inside the Sportsman, there was no need for security. Many of the Huddersfield fans sat in a reserved room while the Spurs' fans milled about in the pub area.

In the back garden, tables alternated between the navy blue of Spurs and the brighter blue version of Huddersfield's uniforms. Spurs fans slapped their "Spurs on Tour 2018" stickers on the air conditioning unit, but no one seemed to mind. It was really the perfect Saturday afternoon at the pub.

The beer selection was outstanding and definitely punched above its weight compared to more famous pregame pubs in bigger cities. The bar was properly staffed with someone always ready to fill a glass. And between the relentlessly talkative Yorkshiremen and the Cockneys, conversation was never a problem.

We enjoyed it so much, we left with the last wave of stragglers making the mile walk northeast of the city center to the John Smith's Stadium.

Huddersfield has a gem to visit. John Smith's is one of the most visually unique stadiums in the Premier League. It's built down in a valley and the arching beams pop up above the parking lot, where you can also get a glimpse of the seats.

The Terriers share the stadium with Huddersfield's first love, the Huddersfield Giants rugby league team. The unique game of rugby league was created in Huddersfield and continues to be popular there, even in a country mostly obsessed with the more well known rules of rugby union.

On the way into the stadium we passed a light post with a sticker on it. It was the coach, Wagner, making a series of bizarre faces, like sticking his tongue out. The caption on the sticker read, ironically, "We shouldn't be losing to teams like Huddersfield."

With all that's happened in the last couple of years, there's one thing all Huddersfield fans are united by: their undying belief in Wagner and his almost magic abilities.

The former Jürgen Klopp assistant – and German-American who played eight times for the USA from 1996-96 – was having a hard time stirring up offense this season. And yet the fans, who had been waiting five months for a home goal, were patient. They never turned on him. They know just what a miracle they're living and they had a refreshing sense of perspective.

In the Britannia Rescue family stand at the John Smith's, plenty of fans didn't care about the standings. They were here to see their Premier League heroes. The large contingent of children was wide-eyed when Kane came towards our end in the first half.

There was a sign with a polite request to watch your language in this section, and it all had a very Norman Rockwell feel to it.

The Guardian's match report opened, "A sylvan setting makes the John Smith's Stadium one of the most pleasant places to spend an autumnal Saturday afternoon, and the appetite for Premier League football among proud and impassioned supporters remains undimmed. Yet with Huddersfield still bottom of the table and now going into October without a win, the script is badly in need of a change."

Unfortunately, as soon as the 25th minute, it became clear the script wasn't going to change on this day. Terriers' defender Terence Kongolo, featured on the match day program cover, went down with an injury attempting to tackle Lucas Moura on the edge of the box. Moura was left wide open to pick out Kane with a delicate chip to the back post. The England striker powered it home with his head.

Despite lots of Huddersfield possession and some serious work rate from Australian Aaron Mooy, the Terriers were down again. The crowd shrugged as if expecting it.

Just nine minutes later, the same forgiving crowd was on its feet and testing that foul language rule. And it was a Yorkshireman at the center of the controversy, Rose, Tottenham's fullback.

After Kongolo's injury, Florent Hadergjonaj came on as a sub. And he was completely bamboozled on the second goal. Rose's run and Heung-min Son's clever ball put Rose goal side of Hadergonaj, driving along the end line. Hadergjonaj reached out to slow him down, getting a light hand on Rose's shoulder. The local boy immediately flopped to the ground like a fish out of water to earn the penalty. So much for Yorkshire grit.

Kane crushed the penalty into the top corner, like he always does, and the rest of the game played out quietly. A worn out Spurs team went into a shell and the Terriers failed to break them down.

With no natural game breaker, we could see it was going to be a long year for Huddersfield. On this beautiful afternoon, with the sun shining and the crowd chipper, it made you sad to think about a year from now. Huddersfield could be back in the championship. Wagner could be gone to a bigger club, several of whom would likely line up for his services. Stars like Mooy and defender Christopher Schindler could be sold on to greener pastures. All the joy and togetherness built by Wagner – gone in the flash of an eye. And along with it, Yorkshire's long-prominent role in English football.

Thankfully, most in the crowd weren't having such sad thoughts. Or at least they didn't show it.

Huddersfield's magical journey continues for at least six more months – and no one is worried about the end for now.

~ BM

Brief History of Huddersfield Town

Huddersfield Town was one of the iconic teams of English football after World War I, back when teams from the north, especially Yorkshire, dominated the game. The club was founded in 1908, perhaps an afterthought in the shadow of Rugby League, the version of that sport invented and passionately supported in Huddersfield.

The football club played at Leeds Road from around the time it was founded until 1994 when Huddersfield Town opened the MacAlpine Stadium, now called the John Smith's Stadium through sponsorship.

One of England's greatest coaches of the interwar era was Herbert Chapman. He took over at Huddersfield Town in 1921, as the Terriers entered First Division competition for the first time. In his first full season, 1921-22, Chapman's Town team won the FA Cup, 1-0, over Preston North End on a penalty by Billy Smith. And thus begun an era of dominance rarely matched at any other time in English history.

The Terriers finished third in the league the next season before going on a run of three straight Football League titles from 1923-24 through 1925-26. Chapman – who introduced concepts like floodlights, on-field communication between players, as well as fitness and diet requirements. He called for a European Cup competition 20 years before it happened.

However, Chapman would leave for Arsenal before Huddersfield's third title. The team he put together, paced by Huddersfield's all-time leading scorer George "Bomber" Brown, won a third title in 1925-26. Brown showed up at training straight from the coal mine as an 18-year old, looking for a tryout. He went on to score 159 goals in 229 games, knocking in 35 goals in 41 games during the three-peat season of 1925-26.

The Terriers were loaded with talent, like Scotsman Alex Johnson, who scored a hat trick for Scotland's "Wembley Wizards" team that crushed England, 5-1, in a famous matchup. Captain Tommy Wilson and club legend Roy Goodall – both top five in all-time Huddersfield Town appearances – were giants in the back.

After three straight First Division titles, Huddersfield finished second the next two seasons. The Terriers also reached the semifinals or beyond of the FA Cup for three straight seasons, losing in the finals to Blackburn in 1928 – the last of the Rovers six FA Cups; the semifinals to Bolton Wanderers in 1929; and the 1930 final to Chapman's Arsenal – the first of Arsenal's record 13 FA Cups.

After that, the run was pretty much over. The Terriers remained in the First Division, finishing second in 1933-34 and third in 1935-36. Huddersfield reached its fifth FA Cup final in its history in 1938, but couldn't get a second trophy, losing to Preston North End, 1-0, in extra time. After World War II, the club's fortunes suffered.

But they had a chance for renewal when Bill Shankly – a former Huddersfield Town player who started for Preston North End in the 1938 FA Cup final – took over early in the 1955-56 season. Later that same season, Huddersfield was relegated from the First Division for the second time in five years.

In 1956, Shankly signed a wispy teenager named Denis Law, who immediately made his mark as a 16-year old, scoring in an FA Cup fifth round game against Peterborough United. By 1959, Shankly had Huddersfield climbing up the Second Division table. But the Huddersfield board would not spend money for more players and Shankly was lured to Liverpool.

Shankly would go on to get Liverpool promoted before winning three First Division titles, two FA Cups and a UEFA Cup on Merseyside. Law would leave for Manchester City shortly after as well, and eventually win two First Division titles, an FA Cup and a European Cup while scoring 159 goals for Manchester United. Oh what could have been for Huddersfield Town.

The Terriers came back up to the First Division for two years, 1970-71 and 72-73 before dropping two divisions in the next four years. They would languish in unfamiliar obscurity until winning the League One playoff in 2011-12.

Huddersfield barely hung on in the Championship for four seasons, finishing no higher than 16th. But with the hire of German-American coach David Wagner in 2015, Huddersfield made a surprising run to finish fifth in 2016-17, winning a pair of epic penalty shootouts to earn promotion to the top division for the first time since 1972.

Last season, despite being tied for the fewest goals scored and the worst goal differential in the league, Huddersfield claimed a couple famous scalps on the way to finishing 16th. The Terriers had done the impossible all over again.

West Yorkshire Derby –
vs. Leeds United and Bradford City

Any time the Terriers play Leeds United or Bradford City, it's known as the West Yorkshire Derby. Huddersfield is just 12 miles from Bradford and only 14 miles separate the John Smith's Stadium and Leeds' home at Elland Road.

West Yorkshire is full of passionate fans, but unfortunately, these matchups have rarely been played for high stakes beyond local dominance. Because of the up and down nature of the clubs, they haven't been in the same division often.

Huddersfield's rivalry with Leeds heated up in 2016-17, however, with the Terriers sweeping both matches in the Championship, solidifying their overall edge in the series with 32 wins to 27 for Leeds. Huddersfield went on to promotion and Leeds fell out of the playoff race.

In February's match at the John Smith's both managers were sent to the stands after David Wagner ran down the field to celebrate a goal, then was bumped and confronted by Leeds' coach Garry Monk on his way back to the Huddersfield bench. A melee ensued, but Christopher Hefele's late goal secured all three points for Huddersfield.

Even uglier was an incident in the home crowd that saw a Huddersfield fan unfurl a Turkish flag to mock two Leeds supporters who were stabbed to death at the 2000 UEFA Cup semifinal in Istanbul against Galatasaray. The fan was ejected and charged by police.

Huddersfield also hold the edge against Bradford City, 20 wins to 13. However the clubs have only played 11 times in the last 20 years, and didn't play at all for 53 years between 1922 and 1975. The last meeting was a 2-1 Huddersfield Town League Cup victory in 2013.

The series with Bradford is not without controversy either. In February 1997, Huddersfield defender Kevin Gray's violent tackle broke the leg of Bradford City striker Gordon Watson, the highest-priced signing in club history at the time. Watson was never the same again, but did win a case against Gray for damages and was paid a 900,000 pound settlement. It's one of only two times that's ever happened in English football. The BBC called Gray's tackle, "the most expensive tackle in history."

All three cities are also huge rivals in rugby league.

2017-18 Season Review

After scuffling its way to promotion in the Championship playoffs via two penalty shootouts, not many expected Huddersfield to stay in the Premier League beyond one season.

The Terriers did it – finishing 16th – despite tying relegated Swansea for the fewest goals in the league with 28. Only similarly relegated Stoke City had a worse goal differential than Huddersfield's negative-30.

The Terriers opened the season with a shocking 3-nil win at Crystal Palace. They followed with a 1-0 win over Newcastle in the first home Premier League game in John Smith's Stadium history. In fact, Huddersfield earned points in five of its first six games. After six weeks Huddersfield was in eighth place, heady territory for the Yorkshire supporters.

The club's biggest win came on October 21 at home against second-place Manchester United. Huddersfield took the fight to United with goals by Aaron Mooy and Laurent Depoitre in the first half. Marcus Rashford's 78th minute goal made everyone nervous, but Huddersfield hung on for the win with wild celebrations by coach, players and fans.

Eventually, the Premier League season ground down the limited depth of Huddersfield. The Terriers only won three games after December 16, losing five in a row to start the year. The losing streak dumped them into the relegation zone for the first time.

They responded with two wins in a row, 4-1 over Bournemouth and a crucial 2-1 win over relegation rivals West Bromwich Albion. The Terriers never fell back into the fray again, staying just above the line for an unlikely 16th place finish.

United got a measure of revenge when they knocked Huddersfield out of the fifth round of the FA Cup, 2-0. The Terriers advanced that far after a dramatic fourth round win over Birmingham City. Huddersfield put in three goals in extra time to win 4-1.

Central defender Christopher Schindler, the man who scored the winning shootout goal in the playoff final, was the team's player of the year. Steve Mounie was the club's top scorer with nine.

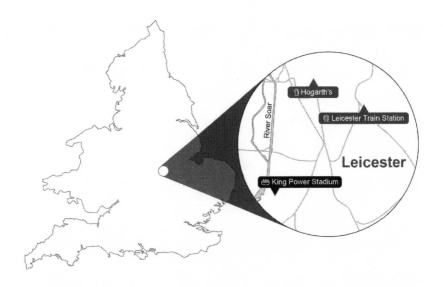

Leicester City Football Club

Year Founded: 1884

Colors: Royal Blue and White

Nickname: The Foxes

Stadium: King Power Stadium

Address: Filbert Way, Leicester, LE2 7FL, UK

Capacity: 32,273, 12th in Premier League

2017-18 Average Attendance: 31,631, 10th in Premier League

Trophies:

Premier League/First Division (1): 2015-16

League Cup (3): 1963-64; 1996-97; 1999-2000

Current Ownership: Vichai Srivaddhanaprabha

Current Manager: Claude Puel (2nd season, 13W, 13L, 9D)

2017-18 Finish: 9th in Premier League, 12W, 15L, 9D

FA Cup: Lost in quarterfinals vs. Chelsea, 2-1 (AET)

League Cup: Lost in fifth round vs. Manchester City, 1-1 (4-3 in penalties)

The Sports Tourists' Tips for Leicester City

Get Value in Your Stay in the City

If you are looking for a reasonable rate for your wallet, and a manageable distance from King Power Stadium, stay at the Ramada Encore Leicester City Centre (84-90 Charles Street, Leicester LE1 1GE, UK). It is located just .3 miles from the Leicester Railway Station, and just over a mile away from King Power. You are close enough to get to the match in 20-25 minutes by foot, but far enough away from the madness post-match. There are several restaurants and pubs on Belvoir Street, adjacent to Charles Street, to whet your whistle before or after the Foxes play.

Hogarths Puts You in the Middle of Everything

Hogarths (5-9 Hotel St., Leicester LE1 5AW, UK) is a big pub with a lively atmosphere and a layout that withstands heavy crowds well. We went on a Tuesday night for the second leg of the Champions League quarterfinal against Atletico Madrid, a match we could not get tickets for. It was a healthy crowd by kickoff, with one long bar on the right. In the front left corner is a larger viewing area, with a couple more side areas with booths on the left side, as you head to the back. It took a couple minutes to get pints at the bar once the match started, but everyone was in a convivial mood, chanting and singing.

Get Close to the Action at King Power

King Power is one stadium we would recommend getting a seat close to the action. We got lucky and landed seats in Tier 1 of the East Stand, in Row A. Normally, we like sitting at least a few rows back and above to get more of an elevated view of play as the ball goes from side-to-side, but King Power does an excellent job of giving you unobstructed views down at the bottom. More importantly, the location of our seats put us perfectly in-between Leicester City and the visiting supporters, and the bevy of opposing chants fired at each other landed perfectly on our section.

Stop by the King Richard III Visitor Center

We happened upon it by accident in our quest to find Hogarths on the night of the Atletico Madrid match. The King Richard III Visitor Center (4A St. Martins, Leicester, LE1 5DB) tells the story of the King's life, as well as his death at the Battle of Bosworth Field in August 1485. The center also recounts the incredible recent discovery of his body beneath a municipal parking lot next to the Leicester Cathedral in September 2012. For over 500 years, his remains lay undiscovered. It should not take you more than 90 minutes to walk through, but for us, it was an incredibly interesting random piece of history.

Our Leicester City Experience

Just two years ago, Leicester City experienced the greatest of fairy tales, winning the Premier League against all odds.

Now, at the tail end of October 2018, they experienced the greatest of tragedies.

Vichai Srivaddhanaprabha, Leicester's owner since 2010, died in a helicopter crash following his club's draw with West Ham on Saturday, October 27th.

The billionaire entrepreneur routinely left King Power Stadium, home of the Foxes, by helicopter to return to his residence in London. On this evening, according to reports, his helicopter immediately crashed after it had risen above and cleared the stadium, killing all five aboard.

With the crash taking place not long after the game's conclusion, a number of fans were still in the area, including Tim Acott, a long-time Leicester supporter. He told The Guardian:

"It just came out of the stadium already spinning, then down to the ground. Just in a spiral. It hit the ground with a big bang then burst into flames. It's over on the other side of the car park, I don't think there were people there. I'm shaking like anything."

The owner's loss was mourned by countless people, from Leicester players – most notably goalkeeper Kasper Schmeichel – to Thai and British royalty, to local Leicester fans and Thai citizens who took great pride in his success, both in the retail industry as well as with his club.

Even Claudio Ranieri, the coach he fired the year after he led Leicester to the championship, arrived to pay his respects. Riyad Mahrez, a player Vichai sold to Manchester City in the last year, pointed up to the sky after scoring a goal for City against Spurs at Wembley in honor of his 'friend.'

Though not American, the Thailand native lived the most American of dreams. An entrepreneur by trade, he opened his first duty-free store in 1989 and built it up into a retail empire, eventually naming his business King Power. His shrewd acquisitions of retail space in Thai airports led to a dramatic rise in his fortune. At the time of his death, he was worth $3.3 billion, according to Forbes.

"He is a self-made man, worked hard and loved friends dearly," said Anutin Charnvirakul, leader of the Bhumjai Thai political party. "We just lost someone who made big contributions to the public. I am sure his legacy will live on."

Srivaddhanaprabha took on another great challenge when he purchased Leicester City for 39 million pounds in 2010. His connection to the club began in 2007 when his company became the shirt sponsors for the Foxes.

At that time, the club had never won a championship in the top tier. Outside of three League Cups, the last coming in 1999-2000, Leicester had won nothing of note at the highest English football levels.

More importantly, the club was mired in the EFL Championship at the time, having only recently been promoted from the third tier. Srivaddhanaprabha spent more than $150 million of his own money to stabilize the club during its ascent to the Premier League.

It was unheard of to think that Leicester would compete with Chelsea and Manchester United and the rest of English soccer royalty. And yet, it did. At 5,001-1 odds ahead of the 2015-16 season, Leicester's title, won with two games in hand, is considered one of the greatest stories in not just soccer, but all of sports history.

It was authored by the likes of star players Mahrez, Jamie Vardy and Wes Morgan, and orchestrated by coach Claudio Ranieri. But it was Srivaddhanaprabha who provided the foundation. Under his guidance, the club is now worth 371 million pounds.

Thailand is a soccer-mad nation, sporting the jerseys of the world's biggest clubs throughout the country. However, after Srivaddhanaprabha's purchase of Leicester, those royal blue Foxes jerseys became more prevalent than Man U and the rest.

Although nearly 6,000 miles separate King Power Stadium from Thailand, the triumphant Foxes were treated as national heroes when Srivaddhanaprabha brought the team home after winning the Premier League in 2016. A victory parade was held in Bangkok and the trophy made in appearance in front of thousands.

The bridge between the two was expertly built by Srivaddhanaprabha, seen at numerous games supporting his team over the years. He was considered a hands-on owner who extended that involvement directly into the Leicester community.

He supported numerous local charities as well as Leicester supporters themselves, taking care of travel costs to away games at times and providing free beer and food on others.

He mirrored those relationships with his players, buying them cars and exuding general love that was returned poignantly upon his passing. In fact, many of the Leicester players flew to Thailand after playing Cardiff to attend part of his funeral proceedings.

East Midlands Derby
vs. Derby County and Nottingham Forest

Whenever Leicester competes against either Derby County or Nottingham Forest, the match is considered the East Midlands Derby, reflecting the region in which the three clubs are located. Both Derby County and Nottingham Forest are roughly an hour's drive away, with Forest being the club that has historically earned more wrath from the other two.

Derby County has won 46 matches against 34 losses versus Leicester, with 28 draws. However, the Foxes are unbeaten in five matches, having last lost in March of 2013. Andy King, Wilfred Ndidi and Demarai Gray scored as Leicester City won a 3-1, fourth-round FA Cup replay win over Derby County in February 2017.

The Foxes have a closer career record against Nottingham Forest, winning 40, losing 39 and drawing 27. The clubs have not met since a 2-2 draw in the Championship in February 2014. Leicester City was promoted to the Premier League after that season. Forest is the author of Leicester's biggest loss, however, a 12-0 shellacking in 1909.

The Foxes also take part in the M69 Derby with Coventry City, named after the motorway that spans 24 miles between the two cities. Leicester City owns a 37-25 advantage in this rivalry, with 24 draws. The clubs have not met since March 2012, as Coventry City was relegated to League One that spring and League Two following the 2016-17 season.

It is a relationship between owner and fans, and owner and players, rarely seen in professional sports. The Guardian's Stuart James noted that, when the club won, Srivaddhanaprabha noted that "Our spirit exists because of the love we share for each other."

Former Arsenal and Palace great Ian Wright noted how rare this is for an owner on his radio show.

"Normally with football clubs, it's just take, take, take from the fans," Wright said on BBC Radio 5 live Sport. "But what he (Srivaddhanaprabha) has done at Leicester City Football Club is the benchmark for how it should be done.

"How many owners have we seen so visibly give something to the fans like that? Give something to them? None. I don't know any. Who, I'm talking about generously give everybody when you get in there you get a beer, you get food, you get this…give them something. To the players, give them cars, just give. The community, just constantly giving.

"Talking about somebody who's just like… You know he put Leicester properly on the map in the respects of the way people see Leicester now and the way people will continue to see Leicester. That will continue, I believe, and he's a major part of that. For me, as an owner, if you're coming in and you are going to put your money in and you're going to really give a community something then what he has done for Leicester is, for me, the benchmark of how it should be done."

Srivaddhanaprabha's tragic death occurred three weeks to the day after we made our visit to King Power. At the time, we were only focused on how Leicester had reverted back into a fairly obscure mid-table club, banking on continued poor performance by the bottom half to stay where it is, having only garnered 44 and 47 points the last two seasons, respectively.

The Foxes are also on their third manager since their title season. Claude Puel, who replaced Craig Shakespeare, came on board late in October 2017. At that time, he was actually the club's third manager in less than a year, thanks to Ranieri's dismissal less than a year after his team's miracle win.

Leicester played Everton in our early October match. We had seen the Foxes knock Wolves out of the League Cup 11 days early at Molineaux Stadium in a staid affair. We also saw Everton again no-show at Goodison Park in a 3-1 setback to West Ham in mid-September.

With a steady drizzle complementing the first wave of colder English weather this fall, this match, as it drew closer, was not on we had circled on the calendar.

In fact, our only previous appearance at King Power Stadium resulted in Leicester's 6-1 undressing by Harry Kane and Spurs that put an exclamation point on the post championship season's transition back to reality.

2017-18 Season Review

Three extra points translated to three places higher in the table for Leicester City, which has followed its miracle 2015-16 championship season with two middle of the table performances.

The Foxes again replaced a manager during the season, as Craig Shakespeare was sacked in mid-October, just months after signing a three-year contract. Leicester had won just one of its first eight matches and were sitting at 18th in the table at the time of his release.

A week later, former Southampton skipper Claude Puel was placed in charge. The Foxes pulled five wins and 17 points from his first eight matches in charge, moving up to eighth.

Leicester City stayed in roughly the same place the rest of the year. The club won just once, albeit a 3-1 victory over Arsenal in the home finale, and pulled just four points total in the final seven games of the season. Despite this, and confirming the abundance of mid-table mediocrity this year, Leicester still finished ninth with 47 points.

Puel has often been criticized for a plodding style of play that has made watching his clubs something of a chore. That style helped lead to his dismissal from Southampton after one season despite an eighth-place finish and spot in the League Cup final. However, moving Leicester up several places (they were 14th when he took charge) was enough to bring him back for 2018-19.

Jamie Vardy again led the Foxes in scoring with 20 goals, and Harry Maguire proved a smart signing coming off a 17-million-pound transfer from relegated Hull. Riyad Mahrez was again creative, but rumors of his transfer to Man City began early in the season and both hovered over him and weighed on the club the rest of the season.

The Foxes reached the quarterfinals of both the FA Cup and League Cup, and could have gone further in both. Leicester knocked off Sheffield United, Liverpool and Leeds before losing to Man City on penalty kicks in the League Cup. The club defeated Fleetwood Town in a replay, Peterborough United and Sheffield United again, before losing to Chelsea, 2-1, in extra time in the FA Cup.

The Foxes' performance early in the season fit with what most prognosticators had predicted. They won four of their first seven matches, knocking off Huddersfield, Newcastle and Wolves – all promoted within the last two seasons – and Southampton, which often looks like a club that wants to go down a tier.

Leicester's losses were to Liverpool, Man U and Bournemouth, one of the clubs vying to replace Leicester as Premier League darlings. In fact, it is fair to say the Cherries already have that distinction.

The crowd noise was definitely muted a bit by the weather, but with Everton an evenly matched opponent, Leicester supporters had a positive air about them. Positive air, that is, until the seventh minute, when Richarlison scored for Everton. The Brazilian is a favorite of manager Marco Silva, having followed him from Watford to Everton. His countryman, Bernard, danced on the left side into the box and found him up and beyond the far post for the finish. The goal, Richarlison's fourth of the season, quieted the crowd for an extended period.

Sticking with the one-name theme, Ricardo got the Foxes on the board a few minutes ahead of halftime. Coming down the left flank, he feigned a shot with his right foot to shake off a defender, deftly moving to his left foot for the equalizer to the near post.

Morgan, continuing to show signs of decline in the back, earned two yellows by the 63rd minute to leave Leicester a man down. As the game proceeded toward its final 15 minutes, the Foxes, and their supporters, were anxiously hoping for a draw.

That dream disappeared quickly thanks to a cracker by Everton's Gylfi Sigurðsson in the 77th minute. He took possession of the ball with his back 40 yards to the goal, turned, shed his defender, dribbled a couple times and fired a blazing shot into the upper left-hand of the corner past Schmeichel.

As we left King Power, we noticed very little about Leicester fans. In fact, it was the boisterous nature of Everton's followers – loud and singing all the way to the Leicester train station and then all the way on the train to Liverpool – that stood out.

One of our lasting images of that game was Schmeichel's head hanging down in disbelief after Sigurðsson's winner.

What we could not have realized at the time was that we would see the image of Schmeichel in a similar pose following Srivaddhanaprabha's death. The two were close and Schmeichel went to Twitter to share his feelings:

"I cannot believe this is happening. I am so totally devastated and heartbroken. I just cannot believe what I saw last night. It just doesn't seem real."

Schmeichel continued: "It is difficult to put into words how much you have meant to this football club and to the city of

Leicester… You cared so deeply for not just the club but for the entire community… You went above and beyond in every aspect."

And then, Schmeichel turned personal:

"Never have I come across a man like you. So hard working, so dedicated, so passionate, so kind and so generous in the extreme. You had time for everyone. You touched everyone. It didn't matter who it was, you had time for them. I always admired you as a leader, as a father and as a man… Without you and your family, all this, everything we did together everything we achieved would never have happened."

We were wondering what our Leicester storyline was going to be for this edition. Never did we imagine it would be this.

Leicester's League Cup match with Southampton the following week was postponed, but the Foxes did travel to Cardiff the following week to face the Bluebirds in a 1-0 win. The players wore t-shirts with Vichai's face on it, under the words 'The Boss.' In addition, Leicester fans traveling to Cardiff were given a free breakfast at King Power Stadium, along with a special tribute shirt, before they departed on their journey.

Around the league, players wore black armbands as a mark of respect, and a minute of silence was observed ahead of all matches. The Premier League is amazingly adept at these moments, with the entire stadium going silent until a whistle allows supporters to get back to their songs and chants.

Leicester won on a Demarai Gray goal in the 55th minute and played to a scoreless draw with Burnley in front of thousands of mourning fans at King Power the following week. The club's place in the middle of the table seems secure, but with the untimely passing of their beloved owner and spiritual leader, a period of stressful transition is sure to ensue.

~BB

Brief History of King Power Stadium

King Power, located at Freeman's Wharf, adjacent to the River Soar, was the long-planned replacement for Filbert Street, which was home to the Foxes from 1891-2002.

When it first opened in 2002, the new ground was named Walkers Stadium after the English snack company that paid for the naming rights. Naming rights were sold to King Power ahead of the 2011-12 season.

Despite only existing for 15 years, King Power has witnessed several landmark moments in Leicester's history, including three league championships in three separate divisions. The Foxes won League One in 2008-2009, then posted a team-record 102 points while winning the Championship in 2013-14, before winning the Premier League in 2015-16.

During those three seasons, the Foxes won 42 matches and lost just four at King Power. After losing to Arsenal at home early during the club's title-winning 2015-16 campaign, Leicester closed the season on a 15-game unbeaten streak at King Power, which included 10 wins.

With a current capacity of 32, 273, King Power is the 12th largest stadium in the Premier League in the 2018-11 season. The four stands at the stadium are all connected, meaning when it is loud there, it is extra loud there, as there are literally no openings anywhere for sound to escape.

Perhaps the most poignant moment in the stadium's brief history came after Leicester had clinched the Premier League title in the spring of 2016. The Foxes secured the title five days earlier when Chelsea and Spurs played to a 2-2 draw, but this was the first time the team had played since then, and the last time that season it would play at home, where Leicester went 12-1-6 in league play that year.

Prior to the team's 3-1 win over Everton, Italian tenor Andrea Bocelli, accompanied by countryman and Leicester manager Claudio Ranieri, sang an exquisite version of "Nessun Dorma", followed by "Con Te Partiro" to a delighted crowd.

Brief History of Leicester City

Contrary to popular worldwide belief, the Leicester City FC timeline did not begin with the long-shot Premier League-winning side from 2015-16.

The club was formed, as Leicester Fosse, in 1884, and previously had its best performance in the top flight in 1928-29, when it finished as runners-up with Arthur Chandler, Hugh Adcock and Len Barry.

Chandler played in the 1920s and 1930s and is Leicester's all-time goal-scoring leader with 273 (259 league, 14 FA Cup). He also led the club to a third-place finish in 1927-28.

Arthur Rowley is second in career scoring for Leicester with 265 goals (251 league, 14 FA Cup), but he has the most league goals in English Football club history with 434. He led the club to two Second Division titles in 1953-54 and 1956-57.

The Foxes lay claim to England's two greatest netminders. Gordon Banks manned the goal for Leicester City between 1959-67, making 356 appearances, during which time the club won a League Cup and made two FA Cup finals, as well as another League Cup final. He was named FWA Footballer of the Year in 1972, won the World Cup with England in 1966, and made one of the best saves of all time, stopping Brazil's Pele at the 1970 World Cup finals. He was replaced in goal by Peter Shilton, who still owns England's international caps record at 125.

The Foxes spent 24 seasons in the First Division between 1957-58 and 1987-88. Gary Lineker, a homegrown product who won the World Cup's Golden Boot in 1986 for England, scored 103 goals in 216 appearances for the Foxes between 1978-85. He is now the host of BBC's Match of the Day, a long-running flagship football show. Steve Walsh followed Lineker and made 450 total appearances and scored 62 goals as a punishing defender for the club between 1986-2000.

The tail end of Walsh's career coincided with the Foxes' most impressive run in the past 25 years. Leicester has made four forays into the Premier League since its inception in 1992-93. Current Ireland national team manager Martin O'Neill led the club to four straight top 10 finishes between its call-up in 1996-97 through 1999-2000. They also won the League Cup twice, and finished as runners-up on another occasion during that time. Muzzy Izzet, Emile Heskey and Matt Elliott formed the nucleus of those squads.

Leicester struggled with finances in the early 21st century, briefly going into administration in 2002. The Foxes made it back to the Premier

Leicester struggled with finances in the early 21st century, briefly going into administration in 2002. The Foxes made it back to the Premier League in 2003, but dropped back down to the Championship after one season, and found itself in League One for the first time ever in 2008-09. Promoted back to the Championship after one season, the Foxes won the Championship in 2013-14, survived relegation from the Premier League in 2014-15 with a Great Escape, and followed with possibly the most unlikely season in English Football history.

The Premier League championship season featured amazing performances from several players, most notably Jamie Vardy and Riyad Mahrez, who were acquired for a combined 1.45 million pounds. The club broke the Premier League record for highest points jump in one season by any team, going from 41 to 81. That record was immediately broken by Chelsea in 2016-17 (50-93, +43). The exploits and accomplishments of that side will forever live in Leicester City lore.

The Foxes have spent all but one season in club history in the top two tiers of English football. Although the championship in 2016 represented their first top flight crown, Leicester has won seven Championship/Second Division titles, with the most recent coming in 2013-14. The club finished first the lone season it dropped down to League One, in 2008-09. Prior to winning it all, the closest the Foxes had come to top-flight glory was the second-place finish in 1928-29, and a fourth-place finish in 1962-63.

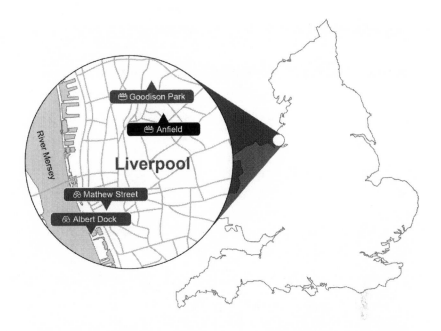

Liverpool Football Club

Year Founded: 1892

Colors: Red and White

Nickname: The Reds

Stadium: Anfield

Address: Anfield Road, Liverpool, L4 OTH, UK

Capacity: 53,394, 5th in Premier League

2017-18 Average Attendance: 52,958 6th in Premier League

Trophies:

Premier League/First Division (18): 1900-01; 1905-06; 1921-22; 1922-23; 1946-47; 1963-64; 1965-66; 1972-73; 1975-76; 1976-77; 1978-79; 1979-80; 1981-82; 1982-83; 1983-84; 1985-86; 1987-88; 1989-90

FA Cup (7): 1964-65; 1973-74; 1985-86; 1988-89; 1991-92; 2000-01; 2005-06

League Cup (8): 1980-81; 1981-82; 1982-83; 1983-84; 1994-95; 2000-01; 2002-03; 2011-12

Champions League/European Cup (5): 1976-77; 1977-78; 1980-81; 1983-84; 2004-05

UEFA Cup/Europa League (3): 1972-73; 1975-76; 2000-01

Current Ownership: John Henry, Fenway Sports Group

Current Manager: Jurgen Klopp (4th season, 81W, 30L, 44D)

2017-18 Finish: 4th in Premier League, 21W, 5L, 12D

Champions League: Lost in final to Real Madrid, 3-1

FA Cup: Lost in 4th round vs. West Brom, 3-2

League Cup: Lost in 3rd round at Leicester, 2-0

The Sports Tourists' Tips for Liverpool

Expect to Spend More Money on a Ticket

Get a membership card as soon as possible and plan ahead because most games will sell out quickly. Your best bet is to prepare to spend more money to get a hospitality ticket, which usually comes with some form of pre-match meal and drinks, and a visit from a former Liverpool player. The price ranges from 200 pounds to 600+ pounds, depending on the type of ticket. This is not the only way to get tickets, but in our experience, is the most likely path for any of the big Premier League games or Champions League. You still will need a membership in order to purchase those tickets, in most cases.

Stay Downtown and Walk to Anfield on Game Day

Anfield is on the northern end of town, and most of the hotels are in the center of town or near the Albert Dock. Our suggestion is to stay near Lime Street and take the 2-mile walk to Anfield, or take a cab. The train system is not like London, and the buses tend to get clogged on match day. Bring some rain gear and walk up the hill towards Anfield. It's well worth your time.

Visit the Pubs Near Anfield – But Prepare for Unmanageable Crowds Inside

There are a number of pubs around Anfield that will be packed with people on match day, so get there as early as you can if you want to be able to get to the bar and order a drink. We tried a couple but found The Albert to be the most fun. ALL of them were not just crowded, but overcrowded, so be aware.

This is another reason a hospitality ticket can make your game experience that much more enjoyable. It gives you a place to drink beers and make conversation –without feeling like you're about to get trampled.

Go to Anfield Before Match Day

Anfield on match day is a crazy, chaotic experience. Take some time while you're in town and visit Anfield the day before or after the match. You'll be able to visit the team store without huge lines. Get your picture taken with Bill Shankly's statue and take some time for quiet reflection in front of the memorial for the 96.

Cavern Club

If you're in Liverpool for a weekend, you should definitely take in Matthew St, and the Cavern Club, the original home of the Beatles. Make sure you grab dinner at Casa Italia, a long-time fixture of the area and some of the best "homemade" Italian food in England. Look out the window to your left and you'll see a poignant statue of "Eleanor Rigby," the fictitiously lonely lady in The Beatles' song. Don't worry about the lines, they clear up quick and the service is fast.

Try Lark Lane – the Alternative to Matthew St.

Tourists party on Matthew St. – and it's worth doing at least once. But if you're looking for a good time in a more low-key, quintessentially Liverpool setting, go east to Lark Lane, a street full of pubs and eateries where far more locals hang out and the prices aren't through the roof. For a delicious coffee or handcrafted cocktail, we recommend the Writer's Block, a comfy shop with great service.

Merseyside Maritime Museum

A great way to understand the history of Liverpool and the Merseyside in general is to visit this excellent museum on the Albert Dock. Yes, everyone wants to go to The Beatles Story, but that's more a tourist trap. The Maritime Museum shares the good and the bad of this shipping town, including its key role in the international slave trade. The World War II Naval section and ship replicas are worth an hour or two of your time alone. Even better, the museum is free.

Our Liverpool Experience

It's hard to make out the words when you hear it on TV, but in the stands at Anfield, the club's newest song resonates with both power and beauty:

We've conquered all of Europe
We're never gonna stop,
From Paris down to Turkey
We've won the fucking lot.
Bob Paisley and Bill Shankly
The Fields of Anfield Road,
We are loyal supporters
And we come from Liverpool
Allez Allez Allez
Allez Allez Allez
Allez Allez Allez
Allez Allez Allez!

When Liverpool supporters look back on how fun these first few seasons have been under Jürgen Klopp, and how much hope was re-instilled in the legendary club, this song may sum it up.

Like most chants/songs sung in the terraces, this is not an original. Napoli supporters sang it first, or at least their version (Un giorno all'improvviso) of it.

It comes from a 1980s song, L'Estate Sta Finendo (The Summer is Ending), by the Italian disco band Righeira.

This specific version was conceived in pubs around Anfield. That is an accomplishment in and of itself, because simply breathing and being able to move while in those packed establishments is already a noteworthy feat.

The song was first heard during Liverpool's 5-0 victory at Porto during the first leg of the Champions League round of 16 and followed the Reds through subsequent triumphs over Manchester City, then Roma.

It became Liverpool's official anthem on the march to Kiev and the Champions League final against Real Madrid. The song is joyful and perfectly characterizes the club's play under Klopp, as well as connects the current club with iconic Liverpool sides from years past.

The fervor with which supporters sing the song, aggressively and loudly, matches the exciting attacking style of play Klopp employs.

Despite failing to produce a trophy in his first two and a half seasons at Anfield, Klopp's Reds are must-see entertainment on a weekly basis.

Their attacking style is easy on the eyes. It's produced great victories like the club's 4-3 triumph over Man City that ended its 22-match unbeaten streak – including a Premier League-record 18-match winning streak – in January 2018.

However, it's also contributed to the club regularly dropping points to the Premier League's bottom feeders. Those results and poor showings have provided fuel for Klopp's detractors. They theorize that, when playing a more talented opponent who is willing to open up, the Reds seize on that opportunity and score, but when a club closes up shop and parks the bus, Klopp's side cannot penetrate and is left exposed during costly counter attacks and set pieces.

That theory has its merit, but only to a degree. Under Klopp, Liverpool has produced two consecutive top four finishes, thus qualifying for Champions League group play both times.

Liverpool's fans have been supportive, showing up in force for every game. However, they do have high expectations of winning trophies on a regular basis, which has been lacking.

Liverpool has now gone without a trophy of any kind since winning the League Cup in 2012. Before that, the last trophy to grace their case was the FA Cup in 2006. These two six-year droughts represent the longest consecutive trophy-less years at Anfield since Liverpool went 17 years between First Division titles (1946-47 to 1963-64).

These Reds are good, very good, but will they ever be great? Will they ever hoist a trophy of any kind, or will players have to leave the club to do so as Philippe Coutinho did when he left Merseyside for Barcelona in January 2018?

They feel sooooooo close. And they came so close in Kiev, despite losing star forward Mo Salah to a shoulder injury early in the match. Sadio Mané knotted the contest at one in the 55th minute, and Reds' supporters allowed themselves a brief moment of hope that a sixth Champions League/European Cup trophy could be coming home.

Gareth Bale's heroics for Madrid, combined with Liverpool goalkeeper Loris Karius' miscues, rid them of that dream in a 3-1 defeat, but the Allez Allez Allez chant symbolized the sweet run nonetheless.

Klopp and Liverpool took those vibes into the offseason, where the biggest goal was to establish more depth.

Brief History of Anfield

One of the most iconic stadiums in Great Britain, Europe and world soccer for that matter.

Anfield hosted a game on the very first weekend of the English League, on Sept. 8, 1888. But it was Everton who hosted Accrington, not Liverpool.

By 1892, Liverpool FC was formed and played their games at Anfield. And in 1906, the club built a large standing-room only area for the fans. They called it the "Spion Kop" because the steep stand was reminiscent of a cliff of the same name in South Africa, the setting for a fierce battle during the Boer War.

A number of stadiums throughout England named their stand after this battle... but Liverpool's is the most famous.

Eventually, the Kop, as it's known, became the most rambunctious stand in English football. As Liverpool rose to new heights in the 60s, 70s, and 80s, the sound of Liverpool's "Kopites" singing "You'll Never Walk Alone" became sweet music to the ears of fans all around the world. And is still one of the guaranteed goose bump moments in any fans' life.

In 2016, the club completed an expansion of the Main Stand that added 8,500 seats. And they're planning to add another 4,825 seats to the Anfield Road stand as well.

The club has struggled mightily any time several matches are scheduled close together under Klopp, specifically the heavy slate of games scheduled between Boxing Day and the first week or two in the new year.

Klopp satisfied these goals with his offseason spending spree, made easier with the money brought in from Coutinho's transfer.

The Reds had already inked Naby Keita from RB Leipzig in a deal that was finalized early in the 2017-18 season...

They added defensive midfielder Fabinho from AC Monaco...

And they brought the powerful Swiss right winger Xherdan Shaqiri from relegated Stoke City.

But the biggest display of Klopp's intention of taking the Premier League crown was his signing of Brazilian goalkeeper Alisson from AS Roma for 67 million pounds, a record at the time for a netminder.

Alisson, who surrendered seven goals to the Reds in the Champions League semifinals, was ecstatic to join Klopp's side:

"I'm really happy, it's a dream come true to wear such a prestigious shirt for a club of this size that is used to always winning," Alisson told Liverpool's club website.

"In terms of my life and my career, it's a huge step for me being part of this club and family."

Alisson's transfer was meant to have the same kind of impact in the back as fellow Brazilian goalkeeper Ederson's signing with Premier League champion Man City did prior to the 2017-18 season.

With Simon Mignolet and then Karius providing shaky service between the pipes, Klopp had no choice but to make a move.

Klopp also made a monstrous move to shore up the defensive ranks. He went all out to firm up the back line that would now be playing in front of Alisson. Twenty-six-year-old Dutch defender Virgil van Dijk moved from Liverpool farm club Southampton to Merseyside for 75 million pounds – a record transfer for a defender – in the January 2018 window.

This was the worst-kept secret in the Premier League as Liverpool was pursuing van Dijk for more than a year, even dodging sanctions from previous associations with him while he was still under contract with the Saints.

Van Dijk's contract dwarfed the previous record signed by Kyle Walker with Man City, but Liverpool saw the Dutch giant as a stabilizer and difference-maker and, more importantly, a leader.

"With the history at the club and everything around it... it is just a perfect, perfect match for me, and for my family as well," van Dijk told *The Guardian*. "I think this is the right time for me to be here and to develop all sorts of aspects to my game. I am looking forward to doing that, that's the main thing."

The defender could not have had a better debut as he scored an 84th-minute winner over rival Everton in a third-round FA Cup match. The Reds allowed just 10 goals in the 14 Premier League games van Dijk played in after his transfer.

His presence allowed Klopp to put his best back four – center backs van Dijk and Joe Gomez and outside backs Andy Robertson and youngster Trent Alexander-Arnold – out on the pitch. Dejan Lovren and Joel Matip would have to settle for reserve roles better suited for them with this club.

The moves had a positive impact on the club, as Liverpool started the 2018-19 season on a tear, winning six straight and outscoring opponents, 16-3.

The most impressive result was a 2-1 decision over Spurs at Wembley in September, the site of a 4-1 shellacking the previous season. Klopp's defense was getting the job done. His offense, which featured seven different scorers in the first six games, was in a groove as well.

In addition, Liverpool opened its latest Champions League run with a mesmerizing 3-2 victory at Anfield over Paris Saint-Germain that featured an injury time winner from Roberto Firmino.

The joyful start came to a halt with a disappointing third-round League-Cup loss to Chelsea, followed by a draw against those same Blues three days later, featuring a classic 89th-minute equalizer from Daniel Sturridge. Then came a 1-0 Champions League defeat in Naples to Napoli, and suddenly the Reds were a bit off the beat.

That is where the club stood when we ended our second journey through the Premier League with a cracker tilt at Anfield in early October. Liverpool against Man City. The defending champions against the club believed to represent the greatest threat to its goal of repeating.

Liverpool had defeated Pep Guardiola's side three straight times, including both legs of their Champions League quarterfinal triumph, and were certainly not intimidated by the record-setting champions, especially when they would most likely be without the services of Belgian Kevin De Bruyne.

City has not won at Anfield since 2003, and Klopp was determined to keep that streak going.

It helps that Klopp is the only manager with a successful record against Guardiola, so much so that his biographer, Raphael Honigstein, says that Klopp is Guardiola's "kryptonite."

The two faced off several times in Germany – Klopp leading Dortmund against Guardiola's Bayern Munich side – splitting eight matches before Klopp departed for Liverpool.

"It never got personal between the two of them," Honigstein said. "If anything, they were very complimentary of each other and their tactics."

By the time City came calling in October, Klopp owned a record of eight wins, one draw and five losses against Guardiola.

City already claimed a victory by just making it to the stadium in one piece. In their previous trip to Anfield, the Citizens' bus was attacked with beer cans and bottles by Liverpool supporters as the route was known ahead of time. It was kept secret this go-around.

Anticipating that German Leroy Sané would start on the wing for City, Klopp installed Gomez on the wing and Lovren in the center. Alexander-Arnold has struggled against wingers with blazing speed and Sané is one of the fastest players in the game.

Guardiola opted instead to leave Sané on the bench, and the chess match ensued. The Reds controlled a blistering pace in the game's first 15 minutes. Salah, who broke the Premier League-record with 32 goals in his Liverpool debut, sent a shot wide in the fourth minute.

The crowd responded with yet another repurposed 1980s ditty.
Mo Salah, Mo Salah, Mo Salah,
Running Down the Wings
Salah, ah ah
Egyptian King

The song came from James' hit single "Sit Down" in 1988 and was applied to Salah during his record run. The band's vocalist, Tim Booth, a big Leeds supporter, understands and appreciates why his song has caught on with Salah.

"Liverpool supporters have always been some of the best in the world; as a neutral, they've always been the fans I've respected the most because they get behind their team no matter what," Booth told Liverpool's club site.

"I've always had a good soft spot for Liverpool and their ability to find a witty song – so great, they can have it… But one of the greatest footballers in the world can have it, when he's playing such beautiful football it's a pleasure."

Other than a nearly grievous mistake by Gomez in sending the ball back into the middle in the 20th minute, Liverpool looked tremendous.

Unfortunately, the Reds then suffered the loss of their unsung hero, James Milner. The versatile footballer was one of the youngest to ever play in the Premier League, debuting with Leeds as a 16-year-old in 2002. He spent time at Newcastle and Aston Villa and played nearly 150 matches for Manchester City before joining Liverpool in 2015.

In three plus years with the Reds, Milner has done a bit of everything, from spending a year as a solid left-back, to playing up on the wing, to simply getting the job done from his preferred midfield position. He has the kind of soccer quads that look like they want to push through the skin every time he goes full sprint.

He may not have the talent ceiling of many of his teammates, but he represents Klopp's heart, and his hamstring injury in the 28th minute, with Keita brought in to replace him, sucked the air out of Liverpool's lineup.

City began to take more and more of the momentum, although the Citizens put no shots on goal until the final third of the match. Riyad Mahrez, the Leicester City transfer so instrumental in the Foxes' miracle Premier League victory in 2016, began to create space in Liverpool's defensive third.

He got a couple of shots on goal before Gabriel Jesus replaced Sergio Aguero in the 65th minute. Aguero is a monumental hero from City's three titles, but he has yet to score in 10 appearances at Anfield.

Alisson exhibited his value, pushing away first a cross from Bernardo Silva and then a follow-up by Mahrez to the near post. The game appeared to be heading for a scoreless draw when Sané came on for former Red Raheem Sterling – to a smattering of boos – and immediately pushed the pace.

His efforts were rewarded several minutes later. He took a pass from David Silva into the box and was taken down almost immediately by van Dijk.

Most people, watching on television, only see the final attempt on a penalty kick. They often miss some of the drama surrounding it, as was the case here.

Aguero is City's feature penalty taker, but he was out. Gabriel Jesus had come on earlier and expected to take the kick, but was told not to by Benjamin Mendy – at Guardiola's request – to the Brazilian's dismay.

He slowly walked away as Mahrez stepped to the spot… and sent his attempt several rows into the stands. It was his fifth miss in eight Premier League attempts.

That took the air out of the tires for everyone and the match finished scoreless. The draw put City back to the top of the table, with Liverpool falling to third behind Chelsea on goal differential. Draws can always leave both sides feeling unfulfilled, but we knew we had seen two giants compete.

The result was an appetizer for what should be a season-wide battle at the top between at least those three sides. Those clubs continued undefeated through the first 11 matches, the first time three clubs had done so since 1978-79.

"The level of the Premier League now is ridiculous, it's relentless really," Joe Gomez told the *Evening Standard*. "You can't slip at any point or teams will capitalize… We have to remember that, regardless of who we are facing. Every point is so important."

Dropping points anywhere could mean an end to a title run Liverpool so desperately wants.

~BB

Merseyside Derby vs. Everton

The so-called "Merseyside Derby" is a crosstown rivalry at its best.

Besides the fact that both teams play on opposite sides of Stanley Park, this is also the longest-running rivalry in England's top league, where both teams have resided since 1962-63.

The players on the pitch, many of them local, don't hold back in the Merseyside Derby. And it shows as no other fixture in English soccer has resulted in more red cards given. Though, it was originally called the "Friendly Derby" because the town is littered with families who are split between red and blue, and often go to the games together.

Liverpool has the edge in overall wins (92-66), including a 2-1 win in the third round of last year's FA Cup. The clus drew both of their league matches, extending Liverpool's record undefeated streak to 17 matches, going back to October 2010.

Northwest Derby vs. Man United

The North-West Derby pits the two greatest clubs in English history against each other. Liverpool and Manchester United have won a combined 38 league titles, 19 FA cups and eight European cups.

Manchester United's legendary coach, Sir Alex Ferguson, famously pledged to *"knock Liverpool off their f***ing perch"* when he took over in the 1980s, and in some ways, he was successful.

United lead the all-time series 80 wins to 65, with 55 draws. But, the large chunk of that deficit was created during the Premier League era, with United dominating the league at times and Liverpool unable to win a title.

It makes sense that two successful clubs from the same corner of the world would develop an often-bitter rivalry. In fact, the rivalry is so contentious that these clubs don't even do business. Phil Chisnall was the last player to transfer between the two – and he left United for Liverpool in 1964!

The clubs played to a scoreless draw at Anfield early in the 2017-18 season. Manchester United won, 2-1, at Old Trafford in March.

Brief History of Liverpool Football Club

The club was formed after a dispute between brewer John Houlding and the Everton Football Club. Houlding would later become mayor of Liverpool. But at this point, he was a board member at Everton. More importantly, he was the club's landlord.

In the late 1880s, it was Everton that played at Anfield, on the west side of Stanley Park. As the team gained more fans, Houlding raised the rent. On top of that, he insisted that only his beer was sold at the stadium.

By the end of the 1891 season, the rest of the Everton board had enough. They refused to pay the rent increase or buy the land from Houlding. They broke away and purchased another property on the east side of Stanley Park. This was to become Goodison Park, where Everton plays now.

Left with a stadium and no team, Houlding formed Liverpool FC on March 15, 1892. At that point, the club played in the Lancashire League. But within eight seasons Liverpool won its first title in the top division.

One of England's iconic clubs, Liverpool has spent 102 of its 114 seasons in the top division. They won four titles before World War II, but it took the club's lowest moment to create a truly dominant force.

In 1954 Liverpool were relegated to the second division, where they toiled for eight years. But that mediocrity led them to hire Bill Shankly, a quick-witted Scot who rebuilt the club from the ground up in his own image. The team won the second division going away in 1961-62, earning promotion back to the Premier League. What they did next is legendary, as Shankly's Reds won the League in their first year back. Even better, they took the trophy from their more powerful crosstown rivals, Everton.

Thus began an era of intercity dominance that still remains, leading Shankly to proclaim: *"There are only two sides in Liverpool. Liverpool and Liverpool reserves."* Under Shankly's reign, Liverpool won three league titles and most importantly, its first European trophy. Shankly assembled one of the more talented coaching staffs in history, who developed the Liverpool Way in a cramped storage room, stuffed with the player's cleats...

The "Boot Room" insured that Liverpool's greatness would carry on beyond Shankly's retirement. His assistant Bob Paisley took over in 1974 and carried the Reds to even greater heights. Between 1976 and 1990, Liverpool were simply the best club in the world, winning four European Cups and 10 of 15 First Division titles, the last coming in 1989-90.

Since the creation of the Premier League, however, Liverpool have failed to win a title, a sore point for the home fans and a sticking point for rivals. Liverpool was able to win one major trophy in memorable fashion, however.

The 2005 Champions League final in Istanbul saw Liverpool fall behind 3-0 at halftime to Italian power AC Milan. The rest is history, as the Reds found three second-half goals to tie the game before winning in a dramatic penalty shootout and completing one of the most unlikely comebacks in European history.

2017-18 Season Review

The Reds achieved another Top-4 finish in league play and nearly added to its European trophy haul, losing to Real Madrid in the Champions League final.

Jurgen Klopp's club never sat outside the top half of the table and were the only Premier League club to go undefeated at home (12W, 7D). Roma transfer Mohamed Salah had a fantastic first season with Liverpool, scoring a Premier League-record 32 goals and winning the Professional Footballers Association (PFA) player of the year award. The Egyptian totaled 43 goals and 14 assists in all competitions in a dream debut.

The team was a scoring machine, tallying 84 goals, second in the league behind Manchester City's league-record 106 goals. The front three of Salah, Sadio Mane and Roberto Firmino is as dynamic and exciting to watch as any, more than making up for the loss of Philippe Coutinho to Barcelona.

The Reds only allowed 38 goals, tied for fourth-best in the league. The long-awaited transfer of Virgil van Dijk from Southampton in the January window transformed a consistently shaky defensive side. The center back played in 14 league games for Liverpool after his transfer, with Liverpool allowing just 10 goals in those contests.

Academy product Trent Alexander-Arnold and Hull Transfer Andy Robertson helped solidify the back line, and Robertson's crosses into the box were a joy to watch for Liverpool supporters.

With City having its record campaign, winning a first Premier League title was never realistic, but the Reds faltered again against lower table competition, preventing a higher finish. Liverpool lost at Swansea and played to draws at Newcastle and at home against Stoke, as well as both matches against West Brom. In fact, the Reds only garnered nine of a possible 18 points against the three soon-to-be relegated sides.

Liverpool did play some great soccer against the top sides, handing City one of their only two league losses in a 4-3 thriller at Anfield in January and pounding Arsenal, 4-0, at home early in the season. A 4-0 win over Brighton to close the campaign clinched fourth place and a second consecutive season of Champions League play.

Although Liverpool went out early in both the League Cup (third round to Leicester, 2-0) and FA Cup (fourth round to West Brom, 3-2), the Reds had a Champions League season to remember. The club scored 47 goals – including qualifiers – and reached the final against Real Madrid in Kiev.

Unfortunately, Salah went out early with a shoulder injury, Loris Karius made two amazing blunders in the back and Gareth Bale scored a goal for the ages in a 3-1 triumph that gave Madrid its third consecutive Champions League crown.

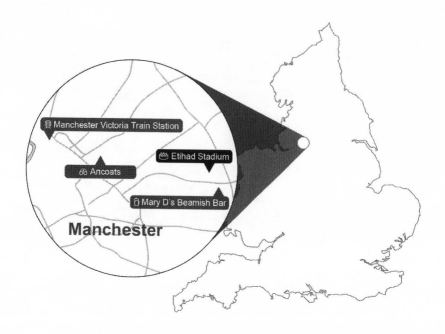

Manchester City Football Club

Year Founded: 1880 (as St. Mark's)

Colors: Sky blue and white

Nickname: The Citizens

Stadium: Etihad Stadium

Address: Ashton New Road, Manchester M11 3FF, UK

Capacity: 55,017, 5th in Premier League

2017-18 Attendance: 54,054, 5th in Premier League

Trophies:

First Division/Premier League (5): 1936-37; 1967-68; 2011-12; 2013-14; 2017-18

FA Cup (5): 1903-04; 1933-34; 1955-56; 1968-69; 2011-12

League Cup (5): 1969-70; 1975-76; 2013-14; 2015-16; 2017-18

European Cup Winners Cup (1): 1969-70

Current Ownership: Shiekh Mansour

Current Manager: Pep Guardiola, 3rd season (79W, 17L, 17D)

2017-18 Finish: Won Premier League, 32W, 2L, 4D

Champions League: Lost in quarterfinals to Liverpool, 5-1 aggregate

FA Cup: Lost in fifth round at Wigan, 1-0

League Cup: Defeated Arsenal, 3-0, to win League Cup

The Sports Tourists' Tips for Manchester City:

City Tickets Are Surprisingly Easy

Given the level of entertainment we saw at the Etihad Stadium, tickets are surprisingly easy to acquire, even for some of the bigger games. With Pep Guardiola in charge and a host of exciting players, you would expect the stands to be filled to the brim.

But for a midweek Champions League match against Lyon, the first of the group stage, whole sections were empty. We got great seats in the lower level, right behind the net for 40 pounds a piece. The price would be significantly higher for teams like Man United, Liverpool or Arsenal in the same situation. Hard to believe, but you can see the best in the world against the best in the world easier than expected.

The Best Pre-Match Bar in England

When we walked in the front of Mary D's Bar on Grey Mare Road, it appeared we were going to get the same thing we got at most other game day bars in England… no room to stand, a long wait for drinks, and a generally sardine can atmosphere of annoyance and aggression.

Instead, as we kept walking to the back section of the bar, we were pleasantly surprised by the positivity and fun everyone was having. The back is a huge area, with a massive floor in the middle, plenty of room to stand and multiple bars ready to serve you. It had the feel of your favorite college dance club as opposed to 300 people crammed into your Grandma's living room. There was a DJ playing all of the City fans' favorites to get them warmed up for the last home game of the season. And there is Blue Moon on tap, something rare in England.

A Taste of Maine Road at the Etihad

Just across the street from the South Stand of the Etihad Stadium is the Maine Road Chippy Shop, named for City's previous home. On game night, it was packed with people lined up down the street waiting to order or sitting on the curb, absorbed by their chips with curry sauce.

Rudy's is Worth Getting There Early

The Etihad Stadium is located on the Northeast periphery of Manchester and we found the best neighborhood to stay is Ancoats. It's an up and coming area of old brick mills and storage houses turned into apartments and cool clusters of restaurants and pubs located along a pathway of canals. The popular Northern Quarter is only a short walk away as well.

The pick of the bunch in Ancoats is Rudy's Neapolitan Pizza. The melt in your mouth crust convinced us to devour three pies in a matter of minutes.. One thing to note: You'll want to get there early in the dinner hour. They do not take reservations and by 6:30 p.m., the wait can be as long as two hours.

Our Manchester City Experience

World champion is a fickle distinction.

When was the last time the World Series champs played a team from Japan or the Dominican Republic?

When was the last time the NBA champion had to go through Panathinaikos, Maccabi Tel Aviv or BC Barcelona to hoist the Larry O'Brien Championship trophy?

When it comes to team sports, world champions are rarely ever truly resolved. The World Cup comes along every four years for soccer and rugby, and a world champion is declared. But those are for countries, not clubs.

In soccer, the truest evaluation of greatness in today's game is not necessarily measured in league championships... At least not for European clubs.

Winning the Premier League, Bundesliga and La Liga are all fine and good, but for a European club to be revered as a world champion, it needs to win that "other league."

The Champions League.

Now, an argument can be made that since top clubs like Palmeiras, Gremio and Flamengo in Brazil, River Plate and Boca Juniors in Argentina and other South American clubs do not compete because they are not Europe-based, the Champions League does not truly crown a world champion. Clubs from North America and Africa do not compete either.

Fair enough. But the competition's winner is regularly regarded as the best on the planet. Real Madrid (13 titles) has won three straight, although a fourth will be difficult with Cristiano Ronaldo now donning a Juventus kit.

AC Milan, Bayern Munich, Barcelona, Ajax; all are Europe's soccer royalty. All are near the top in number of European Cups/Champions League titles won.

England has several clubs in this discussion as well. Liverpool leads the UK with five championships, followed by Manchester United with three and Nottingham Forest, which won back-to-back titles under legendary coach Brian Clough in 1979-80, with two. Aston Villa (1982) and Chelsea (2012) have one each.

You know who has not won?

Manchester City.

This stands out specifically because of the club's domestic success the last decade. The Citizens have won three of the last seven Premier League titles and achieved a double each time, winning the FA Cup in 2011-12 and the League Cup in 2013-14 and 2017-18.

In fact, Manchester's 2017-18 season, domestically, was one for the ages. City set numerous league records and put themselves in the discussion for greatest Premier League side ever.

Pep Guardiola's club won 18 straight, a Premier League record, scored 106 goals, allowed just 27 and totaled 100 points, the first time a Premier League club has reached the century mark in points. In fact, only two clubs were able to best City on the season, Manchester United and Liverpool.

However, the Reds bested them somewhere else as well… the Champions League.

After winning its group and easily handling Basel in the round of 16, City drew Liverpool in a quarterfinal match-up, and the clubs met in Anfield for the first leg in early April.

Jürgen Klopp's club blanked City, 3-0 on goals by Mo Salah, Alex Oxlade-Chamberlain and Sadio Mané. It was just the fifth time all season, including league games and domestic cup competitions, that City had been shut out.

Things did not get better in the second leg, as Liverpool won at the Etihad, 2-1. Gabriel Jesus scored two minutes in to give City the spark it would need to mount a thrilling comeback, but Liverpool held. Second-half goals by Mane and Roberto Firmino sealed City's fate. It was one of only three losses the Citizens would suffer at home all season in all competitions.

So, another double, but another early exit from the Champions League for City. That has become the norm for the club.

With Arsenal's string of 19 straight Champions League appearances snapped following a fifth-place Premier League finish in 2016-17, City is now the longest tenured EPL club. They are making their eighth straight appearance in the competition and ninth overall, with the first coming way back in 1968-69 when it was known as the European Cup.

The club's success on English soil has not translated to European play, with City failing to make it out of the group stage twice. The club has also been knocked out of the round of 16 three times. Besides the quarterfinal loss to Liverpool, the club has a semifinal appearance in 2015-16 where it lost on an own goal to Real Madrid at Santiago Bernabéu.

Has all of this European failure sparked discontent off Maine Road? Not hardly.

City's supporters love, love, love winning the Premier League, and they love it when their club hoists either of the domestic cups. But, when it comes to European play, the fans simply don't care. In fact, if it were up to them, City would not take part in those competitions.

This perspective comes with a great deal of history, all of which occurred in the past several years.

It started in 2011-12. That year, City finished third in Group A, behind Bayern Munich and Napoli. The third-place team drops down to the Europa League at its knockout stage.

City's round of 32 opponent was FC Porto, a Portuguese club with a long history of success. During the first leg, at Estádio do Dragão in Porto, the home supporters hurled racial epithets at City's Mario Balotelli and Yaya Toure, who are both black. The Italian Balotelli was the primary victim as Porto's supporters made monkey chants throughout the match with video evidence posted on YouTube.

As a result, Porto was fined 20,000 Euros by UEFA. *The Manchester Evening News* noted at the time that this was "half of the fine recently imposed on Arsenal manager Arsène Wenger for confronting a referee and criticizing him after a match."

City advanced, winning that game, 2-1, then pounded Porto at the Etihad, 4-nil. Their Europa League round of 16 opponent was Sporting Lisbon, another Portuguese side. In the first leg, at Sporting's Jose Alvalade Stadium, City failed to make it back onto the pitch in time for the start of the second half. The club was 30 seconds late.

UEFA's fine for that 30-second tardiness: 30,000 Euros.

That was the first in a series of instances that made City fans believe that UEFA was against them.

In 2014, UEFA rolled out a series of fines against clubs they believed were violating the Financial Fair Play regulations. The base aspect of those regulations is simple; clubs are not allowed to spend more than they earn, so as to prevent potential catastrophic implications down the road.

City was one of seven clubs affected and, along with Paris Saint-Germain, was the hardest hit. According to *The Guardian*, UEFA had concerns over both combined financial losses over previous seasons as well as the 350 million-pound sponsorship deal the club had with Etihad.

Brief History of the Etihad Stadium

The Etihad Stadium is an impressive sight from blocks away. It rises up from a fairly flat, undeveloped piece of land in the northeast of Manchester along the Ashton New Road.

Tall, angled masts connected to cables make a very distinctive roof. Adding to the effect are a series of eight spiral staircases, spaced around the stadium. The Etihad Stadium looks like a fantastic spaceship, especially at night when it's lit up in Manchester City's sky blue colors.

The Etihad, as it is known through sponsorship, was originally called the City of Manchester Stadium and opened for the 2002 Commonwealth Games as the main track and field arena. As part of the agreement not to waste the stadium, Manchester City was given a lease with the City of Manchester Council. The club had to pay 20 million pounds to refit the stadium for football, by removing the track and adding another tier of stands. The vast majority of the cost, however, was paid for by local taxpayers and profits from the sale of lottery tickets.

After the refit, the stadium was handed over to Manchester City for the start of the 2003-04 season. After 80 years at rundown Maine Road, City had a beautiful park to call home. The Sky Blues opened the stadium with a 5-0 thrashing of Wales' New Saints in a UEFA Cup qualifier. However, Man City struggled that season and finished just two spots above relegation.

In 2008, Shiekh Mansour bought the team and started buying up much of the land around the stadium for future development purposes.

The Etihad Stadium's biggest moment came in 2012 when Sergio Aguero scored his famous 93:20 goal to win the league in the dying moments over Manchester United.

One very interesting thing about the Etihad Stadium are the louvres in the corners that can be opened up on non-match days to allow wind to flow through the stadium, which is good for growing grass. City has gotten accolades for the quality of the Etihad's grass, especially because it helps the club's passing and attacking style.

The club reluctantly accepted the sanctions, which included a 49-million pound fine and transfer restrictions, as well as roster limitations that affected City's Champions League prospects at the time.

According to the *Manchester Evening News*, this was "an initiative that set out with the good intention of stopping clubs from spending beyond their means (that) evolved into a means to stop clubs like City and Paris St. Germain, with rich owners, from benefiting from investment."

The sanctions were harsh, but accepted, until, in 2016, when UEFA announced that it was "relaxing" the financial fair play rules, but only for clubs with new outside investors. This meant that AC Milan, a long-time Italian power, would be in the right with its new Chinese investors, but City and PSG would still be punished.

This fueled "the feeling that FFP is simply a ploy to try and stop the new rich from outgunning the traditionally rich."

As if all this was not bad enough, the straw that broke the camel's back is simply known as the Moscow incident. In October 2014, in another group stage game, City travelled to Russia to take on CSKA Moscow at the Khimki Arena. The Arena was to be empty as part of a three-game punishment to Moscow for its supporters' issues with racism and hooliganism.

The announcement was made late enough that several dozen City supporters had already made travel and hotel arrangements. They were left on the outside looking in.

But you know who wasn't? CSKA Moscow fans, who utilized creative methods (including purchasing press credentials) to get in and watch the match themselves. It was a joke, and UEFA refused to compensate City supporters who made it to Moscow. They even lessened the CSKA Moscow ban from three matches to two.

This was more than enough to turn City fans off from the Champions League completely. "It's mainly about the way our fans were treated in Moscow," said Albert Mombelli from the 1894 Group, a large Manchester City supporters group. In Mombelli's interview with the *Manchester Evening News*, he continued:

"It was even more disappointing when it was obvious that there were CSKA fans at the game, while our supporters were even stopped from watching it from an office block next to the ground. With UEFA, it's all about sponsors and money, and they don't really care about the fans."

Some City fans made it into Khimki dressed in Moscow police uniforms, before getting tossed out. But it did break a tremendously dedicated streak in the process.

Sean Riley is a City fan who had not missed a game in 25 years – 1,258 games to be exact. That streak came to an end in Moscow. "City fans and Bayern fans (CSKA Moscow's next opponent) were punished for doing nothing wrong," Riley told the *Manchester Evening News*. "It's about supporters who go the extra mile to watch their team, being denied the opportunity through no fault of their own."

To add insult to injury, UEFA recently changed its coefficient points system when it comes to determining seedings for the Champions and Europa Leagues. Instead of rewarding clubs based on current European successes, it would now factor in a club's historical success.

This meant that City could still be hurt by clubs like Manchester United, who have achieved less recently than it had.

Why bring all this up?

Since City fans believe that UEFA is against them, they always boo the Champions League anthem when it is played before the start of those matches. UEFA considered fining City for this act, before thinking better of it.

Our trip to Manchester to see the champions would not be for a Manchester Derby, or to see City take on Liverpool (although we did see those two match up at Anfield).

No, we went to Etihad in mid-September to see the Premier League champions take on Lyon from France's Ligue 1 in their 2018-19 Champions League group stage opener. Although we knew the stories, heard about the booing and understood the anger City supporters had toward UEFA, we were excited to see one of the world's best clubs in its first step in a quest to get a trophy that has eluded it.

City was off and running again, unbeaten in its first five, winning four. Leroy Sané, David Silva and Raheem Sterling had each scored in an easy 3-0 decision over Fulham the previous weekend. Many in the area felt this was going to be the year City changed its European fortunes.

We thought we were coming upon a fired-up Wednesday night crowd that had hit Happy Hour early to lather up for a beating of the French club that was just seventh in league play after a middling 2-2-1 start.

We even – GASP – purchased a pair of those sky-blue City scarves on our walk to the Etihad. However, on the way in, we were exposed to the kind of night it was going to be… the most disappointing night of our whole trip.

Two straight incidents set the tone, and they both involved getting into the stadium. The first issue we had was being stuck in the middle between incompetent City fan and impatient City fan.

2017-18 Season Review

The 2017-18 Manchester City team will go down as one of the greatest Premier League sides of all time, joining Wenger's 2004-05 Invincibles and Alex Ferguson's treble-winning 1999-2000 Man U side.

City won its third Premier League title in seven years and set several league records in the process. The Citizens won 32 games, including 16 on the road. They topped the table by 19 points over second-place Man U. They scored 106 goals and had a goal differential of +79. They won 18 straight. All league records.

In Pep Guardiola's second season with the club, City ended any doubt who would win the title early on, jumping out to a 22-game (20W, 2D) unbeaten streak to start the season. The Citizens didn't just win, they destroyed teams – Liverpool (5-0); Watford (6-0); Palace (5-0); Stoke City (7-2); Everton (7-1). City averaged nearly three goals a game and scored at least three goals 21 times.

The club was in first place by mid-September and never relinquished that spot in the table. City clinched the championship with five games to play, equaling a league record.

Sergio Aguero led City with 21 goals, winning his third title with the team in the process. Kevin De Bruyne led four City players at the top of the assists table with 16. Leroy Sané had 15 while David Silva had 11. Raheem Sterling had a complete season with 18 goals and 11 assists.

Ederson answered the club's biggest question heading into the season at the goalkeeper position. His 16 clean sheets were good for second behind Man U's David De Gea.

Manchester City's bid for an unbeaten season ended in January at Anfield with a 4-3 loss to Liverpool. The Reds also ended City's run in the Champions League, scoring wins in both games of their quarterfinal match-up.

City's weirdest and most disappointing result came in the League Cup, where the club lost in the fifth round to eventual League One champs, Wigan, 1-0. However, City did achieve the double by defeating Arsenal in the FA Cup final in Arsène Wenger's last match in charge of the Gunners, 3-0.

Incompetent City fan is actually a fan we came across at numerous stadiums throughout the UK. This is due to a new ticket-taking method. Instead of just showing your ticket and getting passed through, like fans did before, you now have to slide the barcode of your ticket underneath a reader before you can enter.

Other than the folding process being occasionally cumbersome, it is quite an easy endeavor. In fact, we have been doing it in the US for several years already. But, in the UK, there are still fans at each location that treat the process like rocket science.

One such fan was in line in front of us at the Etihad. He couldn't figure out what to do, and got agitated when anyone tried to assist him. Meanwhile, the folks behind us kept elbowing us in our backs to push forward. Where were we supposed to go?

On top of all that, one slick City fan was going to skip the line and try to slide in front of us and go in. When we stopped her and said, "get back in line," she called us "fucking tourists!"

If getting inside the stadium was an ordeal, supporting City during the match was a chore.

The Guardian's Paul Wilson would later say the match was City's "most inept performance of the season, the English champions being made to look amateurish at times by the side that finished third in Ligue 1 last season."

Guardiola himself would not witness this debacle from his usual sideline perch. He was serving out yet another UEFA penalty, this time a one-game suspension for criticizing officials in the second leg of that quarterfinal defeat to Liverpool.

Mikel Arteta is a former Everton and Arsenal defensive midfielder who was passed over in his bid to replace Wenger with the Gunners. He was calling the shots for Man City from the bench on this night, as the suspended Guardiola watched from the stands.

Because of that, we were also penalized. We expected to see a City side that was now speaking fluent Pep, but, after the predicted booing during the Champions League anthem, the first half was a collection of giveaways you wouldn't see in League One. Lyon would make the Citizens pay in the 26th minute.

Another giveaway, this time by Fernandinho, led to a series of mistakes in the back. The last, a whiffed attempt by Fabian Delph to clear the ball, allowed Lyon's Maxwell Cornet to send a shot low and to the right of Ederson, Man City's goalkeeper. It was 1-nil to Lyon and the small contingent of traveling supporters chanted and cheered with glee below and to the right of us in the South Stand.

"You have zero margin in the Champions League," Arteta told Wilson. "If you lose concentration, if you don't win the duels, you pay the price."

Seventeen minutes later, Nabil Fekir took the ball away from Fernandinho, again in a giving mood, around midfield. Fekir was electric for our visit. He made a direct run to the goal and scored ahead of defender John Stones, giving Les Gones (The Kids) a 2-nil lead at the break.

Fekir gained headlines in England for his initial signing with Liverpool over the summer, only to be denied thanks to previous knee injury concerns. The knee apparently held up well as he scored 23 goals for Lyon over 40 games in 2017-18, and it held up even better as the attacking midfielder played for France's World Cup champions.

Apparently, we weren't the only ones disgusted. As we walked into the men's room at halftime in the supposedly smoke-free stadium, a cavalcade of smokers puffed vigorously on their cigarettes or vapes. It was an ugly setting that paired perfectly with the display on the field.

A few women even lingered by the urinals in the men's room, puffing away; an off-putting faux pas in such a class stadium.

Sané was subbed on in the 55th minute for City. We continued to be baffled at his exclusion from Guardiola's starting lineup after being excluded from Germany's World Cup roster entirely last summer. And we all saw how that turned out for Germany, the most disappointing side at Russia 2018, didn't we?

He changes the game. His passing, his vision, his speed. Everything. He is criticized for his body language at times, but we are certainly proponents of letting his positives outweigh his negatives on the pitch. That was the case in this contest, as the speedy midfielder penetrated Lyon's back line time and again.

Yet, even with his presence, it was a former Manchester United man, Memphis Depay, who almost put Lyon up three goals. The forward, sporting red hair as a reminder of his United connections, was a thorn in City's side all night. He took a pass from Tanguy Ndombele and sent an offering at Ederson that the Brazilian barely tipped off the post in the 60th minute.

Yet, City fans could hardly be bothered to boo him – something typical when a former player of a rival shows up in town.

Aguero, City's long-time, beloved killer up top, came on with a sore ankle in the 63rd minute to provide another boost. His club got within one four minutes later thanks to Sané. He scampered down to the left baseline, beating two Lyon defenders, before sending a pass in to Bernardo Silva, who scored to cut the deficit in half.

Sané continued to threaten, and his City teammates did the same… all to a collective yawn by City's supporters, As *The Guardian*'s Jacob Steinberg noted in his game breakdown.

"There's been a very strange, flat atmosphere at the Etihad this evening. There's no energy from City's fans. They sound bored."

We noticed the bland atmosphere as well, and began taking video of City supporters leaving a tight game in the 80th minute, much to the dismay of the City supporter behind us, who began questioning our criticism of his fellow fans.

"They're plastic," we said.

To which he replied, "it's only Champions League, mate."

Aguero and Kyle Walker took multiple shots on goal late that either went high or wide, or were easily stopped by Anthony Lopes, Lyon's netminder. His last stop on Aguero, in the 90th minute, was possibly his best of the night, and the Citizens fell short, 2-1.

City may win the Premier League again. It currently sits top of the table after going unbeaten again in its first 12 matches. The club may win a domestic cup or two. A double or triple may be in the offing.

In fact, this may still be the year the Citizens break through in the Champions League. Despite losing the opener to Lyon, Guardiola's side held on to defeat Hoffenheim and throttled Shakhtar Donetsk by a combined 9-nil score in two straight matches to take the lead in their group.

But, if City ends the 2018-19 campaign without a victory, or even an appearance in the final at Metropolitano Stadium, home to Atlético Madrid, it's all good.

To City fans, it's just Champions League, mate.

~ BB

Manchester Derby vs. Manchester United

While this crosstown rivalry has reached new levels in recent years, it's been going on since 1881 when Newton Heath beat St. Mark's, 3-0.

136 years later, those two teams are now known as Manchester United and Manchester City, and have played 177 games against each other overall. United have the advantage, as expected, with 73 victories to 52 for City. United's legendary coach Matt Busby played over 200 games for City.

Before World War II, many of the city's football fans supported both clubs, a tradition perhaps started by an 1894 benefit game between then-Newton Heath and Ardwick, to make money for victims of the Hyde Road mining disaster, which happened near Ardwick's stadium. The two clubs met in the FA Cup for the first time in 1891, with Newton Heath winning 5-1 in the first round.

City's had its moments, however, most famously at the end of the 1973-74 season when former United player Denis Law back-heeled a goal for City that confirmed relegation for United and set off a riot at Old Trafford.

More recently, the rivalry has played out with the backdrop of the title race as City famously held off United for the Premier League title in 2012 in the final moments of the season. The win rubbed it in the face of United coach Alex Ferguson, who dismissively called City "noisy neighbors." In 2011, City won the FA Cup semifinal over United, 1-0, on its way to winning the title.

Now, two of the world's most famous coaches, Pep Guardiola and Jose Mourinho are in Manchester and have renewed their personal rivalry that began in Spain when Guardiola led Barcelona and Mourinho, Real Madrid. In the first three meetings between them last season, City won 2-1 at Old Trafford and drew 0-0 at home in a game that saw United's Marouane Fellaini sent off for head butting Sergio Aguero. However, United took the honors in the fifth round of the League Cup, beating City 1-0.

In summer 2017, the two played in Houston, Texas as part of a US tour, marking the first Manchester Derby played outside of England.

The two Manchester Clubs split their 2017-18 matches. David Silva and Nicolas Otamendi scored as City defeated Man U at Old Trafford, 2-1, in December.

However, Jose Mourinho had the last laugh of the season as Paul Pogbal scored a brace and the Red Devils handed City one of only two league losses on the year, 3-2, at the Etihad in April. Manchester United's win prevented City from clinching the Premier League title against their rivals.

Brief History of Manchester City

These days Manchester City spends million of pounds a year fielding one of the most talented teams in the world, and all mostly to escape the club's status as the little brother in the city of Manchester. But it wasn't always that way.

What became Manchester City Football Club started a team representing St. Mark's Church in the east Manchester neighborhood of West Gorton in 1880. Unemployment was high and so was gang membership and alcoholism. The church started a team to try to keep men off the streets and out of gangs. Eventually, the team became Ardwick FC in 1887 and moved into a stadium at Hyde Road. In 1894, the club changed its name to Manchester City to represent the whole town – eight years before crosstown club Newton Heath changed its name to Manchester United.

In 1898-99, City won the Second Division and were promoted to the top level for the first time, led by leading scorer and captain, Billy Meredith. Despite playing as a winger, Meredith led the team in scoring four times in nine years, a rare feat at that time. City went back down to the Second Division after the 1901-02 season, but popped right back up after winning the Second Division title the next year.

This was to become a trend for City. Ten times the club has been relegated from the top division of English football. And in all ten instances, the club never spent more than four seasons at the lower level before earning promotion back to the top. Four times, City jumped right back up the next year.

The Citizens won the first trophy ever for the city of Manchester in 1904 as Meredith scored the lone goal in a 1-0 FA Cup final victory over Bolton. The next season, Meredith was accused of trying to bribe an opponent from Aston Villa into throwing the game to help City finish higher in the standings. Meredith was banned for 18 months. During his ban, he was sent to Manchester United where he made 365 appearances. In 1921 – nearly 50 years old – he returned to City where he finished with 390 appearances.

In November 1920, the Main Stand at Hyde Road was destroyed by fire. And in 1923, the club moved to Maine Road where it played until moving to the City of Manchester Stadium in 2003.

To underscore City's up and down existence, we present the year 1926. City recorded another first over Manchester United – the first Manchester team to play at Wembley in the FA Cup final, which they lost 1-0 to Bolton. The Citizens also put the worst derby defeat on Manchester United in history, 6-1. And for all that – they were relegated to the Second Division.

City went to back-to-back FA Cup finals in 1933 and 34, losing the first to Everton and England captain Dixie Dean. The next year, City fielded a team with future United manager Matt Busby in it. Fred Tilson scored two late goals to make up for goalie Frank Swift's early mistake, giving City a 2-1 win over Portsmouth. Swift – then a teenager – would go on to captain England. He was working as a journalist when he died in the Manchester United Munich Air Disaster, a crash that Busby survived.

Peter Doherty's 32 goals fired City to the First Division crown in 1936-37, the first for the club. The Citizens went to consecutive FA Cup finals again in 1955 and 56. And again they lost the first, this time to Newcastle United, a famous game because it's the last trophy Newcastle won, a rut that's just hit 62 years. The next season City won its third FA Cup title, 3-1, over Birmingham City.

Before the current run, Manchester City's most glorious moments – and some would say it still takes the cake – was its European Cup Winners Cup run in 1970. Of course, it being City, just three seasons prior the Sky Blues won the Second Division to gain promotion. Two seasons later, they beat Newcastle on the last day of the season to claim the 1967-68 First Division title, the second in their history and the last league title before Sergio Aguero's famous 93:20 victory. The next season, Man City beat Leicester City 1-0 on a Neil Young goal to win the 1969 FA Cup – and earn an automatic berth in the European Cup Winners Cup.

Led by Young, Colin Ball and Sam Lee, City charged through the tournament, dominating at home in the two-leg, home and away format. City drew mighty Athletic Bilbao in Spain, 3-3, before winning 3-0 at home. The Citizens crushed Belgium's Lierse SK, 8-0, and scored an extra time goal in the second leg at home against Academica de Coimbra, to win 1-0 on aggregate and advance to the semifinals.

After losing the first leg of the semifinal 1-0 at Germany's Schalke 04, City romped to a 5-1 win at home to earn a finals berth. Manager Joe Mercer had predicted the team would attack in the final against Poland's Gornik Zabrze and so they did, even in a driving rain and sloppy conditions at the Prater Stadium in Vienna, Austria.

Young scored the opener 12 minutes in and Lee converted a penalty just before halftime to give City a commanding 2-0 lead. Gornik pulled one back in the second half but City hung on for its only European crown to date. City did the double by winning its first League Cup in 1970 as well, but also finished just 10th in the First Division, signaling a quick end to that era.

In 1997-98, City were relegated to the third division of English Football, the lowest the club had ever fallen. The Sky Blues climbed out quickly and two seasons later were back in the Premier League. That lasted one season, as an 18th place finish saw them relegated. But one year later, in 2001-02, City won the Championship and promotion back to the Premier League. The Citizens haven't gone back down since.

In 2003, the club moved into the City of Manchester Stadium, now called the Etihad Stadium. In 2008, Shiekh Mansour, an oil man from Abu Dhabi, bought the club and invested millions of his own money to buy players and upgrade personnel.

Manager Roberto Mancini led City to the fifth FA Cup title in its history in 2011, 1-0 over Stoke City. Yaya Toure scored the game's only goal with a powerful shot in the 74th minute. The next season, Aguero's goal at 93:20 on a wild final day of the season won City its first Premier League title, pipping Manchester United on basically the last kick of the season.

Since then, the Citizens won a double – Premier League and League Cup – in 2013-14, and another League Cup in 2016, the same year they made the semifinals of the Champions League before losing to eventual champion Real Madrid.

They added another double this season, winning the Premier League in record fashion and handling Arsenal for their third League Cup title in five years.

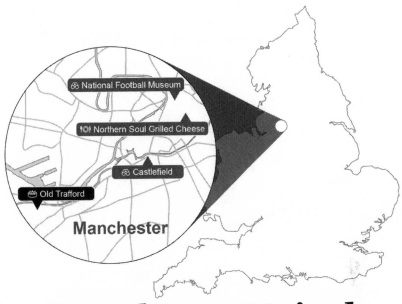

Manchester United Football Club

Year Founded: 1878

Colors: Red and White

Nickname: The Red Devils

Stadium: Old Trafford

Address: Sir Matt Busby Way, Stretford, Manchester M16 0RA, UK

Capacity: 74,879, 2nd largest stadium in Premier League

2017-18 Average Attendance: 75,102, 1st in Premier League

Trophies

Premier League/First Division (20): 1907-08; 1910-11; 1951-52; 1955-56; 1956-57; 1964-65; 1966-67; 1992-93; 1993-94; 1995-96; 1996-97; 1998-99; 1999-2000; 2000-01; 2002-03; 2006-07; 2008-09; 2010-11; 2012-13

FA Cup (12): 1908-09; 1947-48; 1962-63; 1976-77; 1982-83; 1984-85; 1989-90; 1993-94; 1995-96; 1998-99; 2003-04; 2015-16

League Cup (5): 1991-92; 2005-06; 2008-2009; 2009-2010; 2016-2017

UEFA Champions League/European Cup (3): 1967-68; 1998-99; 2007-08

UEFA Europa League/UEFA Cup (1): 2016-17

UEFA Cup Winners' Cup (1): 1991

Current Ownership: Manchester United PLC, led by Malcolm Glazer, since May 2005

Current Manager: Jose Mourinho (3rd Season, 75W, 19L, 24D)

2017-18 Finish: 2nd in Premier League; 81 points (25W, 7L, 6D)

FA Cup: Lost to Chelsea in final, 1-0

League Cup: Lost at Bristol City, 2-1, in fifth round

Champions League: Lost to Sevilla in Round of 16, 2-1 aggregate

The Sports Tourists' Tips for Manchester United

How to Get Tickets for Manchester United

After a few tries, we've cracked the code when it comes to Manchester United tickets. The first thing is, budget high. If you are willing to spend 200 pounds or more per ticket, your options open up. The Red Café hosts three course meals for VIP United guests, then you get a seat in the Sir Alex Ferguson Stand. But even with the expensive tickets, you have to be aware of when tickets go on sale. And you will absolutely want to purchase a Manchester United membership as soon as possible before your trip. Tickets will sell out for almost all games.

Get There Early and See the Munich Memorial

With a capacity surpassing 75,000, Old Trafford is the closest thing resembling an NFL stadium, and it got crowded early. Arrive an hour before and walk around the large stadium to get to the Munich Memorial, which honors the 23 people – including eight players – who died in a plane crash coming home from European play on February 6' 1958. If you go to the memorial on the anniversary of the crash, you will likely find supporters solemnly singing "The Flowers of Manchester" around the exact time, 3:04 p.m., the plane crashed.

Stay in Castlefield and Take in Manchester's History

We stayed in an AirBnB for a week during our time in Manchester. It was located roughly two miles from Old Trafford, in the Castlefield neighborhood, less than a quarter mile from restaurants, pubs and the Roman Fort on Duke Street. The location allowed us an easy stroll into the heart of downtown, along historic canals lined with old brick buildings, and we were also able to stop by the ruins of the Castlefield Roman Fort, located near the Bridgewater Canal. The remains of the 2,000-year-old fortress also include colorful information panels nearby.

It is not a lengthy visit, but the fort is one of those stops on our trip that reminded us how young our country really is.

Get a Grilled Cheese and a Shake

We came upon a series of little pop up food joints on Church Street, and the one we kept going back to was Northern Soul Grilled Cheese (10 Church St., Manchester M4 1PN, UK). The menu is written in chalk above the cash register and offers eclectic versions of the cheesy favorite. Order 'The Soul' which includes a secret three-cheese blend, and down it with an Oreo milk shake. Their shakes are thick, creamy concoctions that take time to enjoy, so do so while looking out on the foot traffic passing by. And now they have a location right next to the Manchester Piccadilly station.

Stop by the National Football Museum

If you have an extra day in Manchester, go to the National Football Museum (Urbis Building, Cathedral Gardens, Todd St., Manchester, M4 3BG, UK). Entry is free, although a 6-pound donation gets you a program and a ticket to lift the replica League and FA Cup Trophies they have on site. The museum offers a comprehensive history of football, through the eyes of English players, supporters and leagues. Interactive games, documentary footage and hordes of jerseys provide a detailed, colorful setting to enjoy the beautiful game.

Our Manchester United Experience

By the end of 90-plus minutes of Champions League football on an almost perfect fall night at Old Trafford, it became painfully clear the greatest club in Premier League history was in a full-blown crisis.

As the whistle blew on a listless, nil-nil draw against Valencia, the 14th place team in Spain, boos rang out from the packed house – many of whom were positively excited just two hours before.

How did it get to this point? How had Manchester United become a shell of its former self?

Obviously, it didn't just happen in one 90-minute period. Mutiny was already afoot in the fortnight before Valencia came to town for the second game of the group stage of the Champions League.

In the prior week, United's best player – or at least it's most expensive – Paul Pogba, had publicly questioned the cautious approach of legendary (notorious?) manager Jose Mourinho. He was promptly stripped of his captaincy.

Before the game, former player and youth team coach Paul McGuinness, working for the club as an ambassador in the fancy Red Café, indirectly questioned the manager's approach as politely as possible.

"We're Manchester United; we like to go on the attack."

During the Valencia game, former star Paul Scholes – an 11-time Premier League champion with the Red Devils – questioned the manager on TV and not very politely.

"His mouth is out of control and he's embarrassing Manchester United."

But as much as all of those people are a part of the fabric of Manchester United, it's the fans who are at the heart and soul of the club. Sure, everyone makes that claim, but at this club its true. United had a massive following long before the TV money and the slew of championships and the foreigners who flood in for every game.

And when the fans staged a mutiny, it felt like the situation had reached a point of no return.

Jose Mourinho had to go. Who knew when or who would replace him, but the club wouldn't have its identity again until the problem, the cancer, the scourge Mourinho had become, was removed.

What was the mutinous refrain, shared by current players, former players, the fans… what was the magic word that sparked a rejection of everything Mourinho represented? The one that got Pogba censored because it was so grating to Mourinho's ears.

Attack.

Attack. Attack, attack, attack.

To understand this request – and United as a club – it helps to understand the context.

Sir Matt Busby was United's manager from 1945-1969 (plus a half season in 1971) and probably the most responsible for the philosophy of modern-day Manchester United. And in the 1968 European Final against Benfica at Wembley Stadium, United went up 1-nil early in the second half thanks to a Bobby Charlton header.

Most teams in a big game like that would've shut it down and played defense to protect the lead, like say, Mourinho's famous Chelsea, Inter Milan and Real Madrid teams. But Manchester United is not most clubs.

United fans, and Busby, weren't happy to rest on their laurels. Instead, the fans reminded Busby's Babes of their own philosophy, by chanting the very phrase that so offended Mourinho.

"Attack, attack. Attack! Attack! Attack!"

The attacking philosophy may have led to a Benfica goal, but in extra time, United, led by George Best, scored three goals and won its first European crown (and the first for England), 4-1.

Of course, all teams want to attack and score goals. But United sought to do it in a more emphatic manner than anyone else. And attacking football has become synonymous with the club. Like Barcelona, United couldn't just win, they had to win with style.

How did this philosophy become the core of the club's ethic? Perhaps it was a result of the terrible tragedy that happened a decade before Busby's babes triumphed in Europe.

The infamous Munich Air Disaster happened after a plane carrying United's team back from European competition against Red Star Belgrade crashed upon takeoff, killing eight first team players as well as 15 staff and press.

Busby survived. As did the man who led the club on the pitch for the 1968 victory, England World Cup winner Sir Bobby Charlton.

But perhaps this tragedy gave the team their attacking philosophy. No one understood better than Busby, Charlton and Manchester United: life is short, tomorrow is never guaranteed. So why sit back and defend when you can keep pushing forward?

Maybe the philosophy just sprung from the incredible amount of attacking talent Busby gathered at the club. Charlton, George Best, Denis Law. These were the so-called "Flowers of Manchester," the team that lifted the club back from the ashes of Munich to the celebrations of Wembley. With that kind of talent on the pitch, its no wonder fans chanted "attack, attack, attack."

Fast forward to the Sir Alex Ferguson era – and by the way, if you're great at United, you get knighthood. Knighthood isn't bequeathed because of scrappy 1-nil wins. It's given because of true greatness and fearlessness going forward.

Ferguson's philosophy was always that the best defense is a great offense that moves forward at any opportunity. And he kept up Busby's tradition by signing players with unmatched attacking quality. Eric Cantona. David Beckham. Ryan Giggs. Cristiano Ronaldo.

United became so well known for their relentless 90-minute approach and late winning goals, the last few minutes of the game was referred to as "Fergie time."

But in 2013, after 13 Premier League titles, five FA Cups and three European championships, Ferguson retired. He would eventually get a statue and a stand named for him. The obvious question was how would United continue to stay on the front foot.

Who would come in and push them forward next? But this was no longer a United run by the fans, their concerns for the style of play were pushed aside.

The goal became to protect what you already had. Both on the field and in the front office.

Manchester United is another cautionary tale of foreign ownership, in this case, American. The financial details of the club are quite boring, but here's the simple version:

The Glazer family, led by patriarch Malcolm, bought the team and then used it as leverage to borrow more money at favorable rates. United is the main collateral for their empire of debt. They also own the Tampa Bay Buccaneers, by the way.

Now, United is very much a business with a brand to uphold and an expected amount of revenue. That means decisions have to be made for all kinds of reasons and not always the quality on the field. Like bringing in Paul Pogba and Alexis Sanchez. Like hiring Mourinho in the first place. He was the best man available and Man United as a business had to be seen getting the best person available. Especially after the experiment with David Moyes and Louis van Gaal went wrong.

For years, one of Britain's most astute football men, Ferguson, decided everything at the club. Now, this committee approach had weakened the authority of the coach.

But still the club spent money on big name players. The need to sell jerseys, expensive VIP tickets like the ones we had, and TV airtime around the globe, was prominent.

Moyes and Van Gaal appeared to have handpicked their rosters. But in the end, it wasn't good enough. Now Mourinho, three years into the project, was having a different problem. Did he even want these players? Were they signings given to him by club director Ed Woodward? Over 419 million pounds had been spent on transfers already in the Mourinho era. But was it enough?

In the case of Pogba, the biggest signing of them all at 94.5 million pounds, Mourinho's disdain seems clear. After Pogba questioned his philosophies in so many words, Mourinho sat him for the League Cup game. From the stands he posted an Instagam photo of him laughing while United were losing. Mourinho seemed incensed and in an exchange caught on camera, the coach called his star out at practice. In the video, he seems to insult Pogba, who stands there looking surprised.

Mourinho complained about needing more central defenders, a direct swipe at the skills of Eric Bailly and Victor Lindelof, two high-paid young players Mourinho raved about before signing. So that's on him. Just about the only player he has any praise for this season is Luke Shaw, the fullback who previously served as Mourinho's whipping boy for two years. It was like bizarro Mourinho.

Earlier in the year, after more questioning he didn't appreciate, Mourinho got up and walked out of a press conference after holding up three fingers and explaining that's how many Premier League titles he'd won. More than anyone else in the league combined. "Respect, man. Respect. Respect. Respect," Mourinho sneered at them vacantly as he walked out.

Days later he didn't look slick when he arrived at Wembley Stadium to see England vs. Spain. Attempting to step over the rope to the VIP area, his feet got caught and he tripped, stumbling forward a couple of feet before falling over himself.

It seemed a bit symbolic of United, in the same way as Arsene Wenger's inability to zip his coat symbolized Arsenal's issues.

Wins at Watford and Young Boys of Switzerland had seemed to clear up their troubles. But then they lost to Mourinho's former player, Frank Lampard and Derby County in the League Cup.

United arrived at the London Stadium on the weekend and were thrashed by West Ham, 3-1. West Ham's coach is of course, one of the other men to win a Premier League title, Manuel Pellegrini. He clapped and encouraged throughout the game. Mourinho glowered. West Ham gave a supreme effort winning a vast majority of 50-50 balls. Man United looked like an ineffective defensive shell of themselves.

Now, Spain's Valencia had come to town. Though a big name in European football, probably the fourth or fifth most recognizable team from La Liga, Valencia was 14th in the league tables. And they were barely scoring. In the Ferguson days, this would've been a lock for United.

But before the game at the Red Café in Old Trafford, not everyone was so sure. Opinions were split on whether it was Mourinho's fault or Pogba and the players. You could sense plenty of support for the coach in the crowd before the game as well.

Despite that support, lots of people, backed by odds makers, wondered if a loss to Valencia meant the end of Mourinho at United. He had signed a long-term extension in January, but how long could United deal with results like this before it affected the brand?

Right from the start, it didn't appear to be United's night. The game was delayed over five minutes because United had arrived at the stadium late. There was lots of construction around the southwest of Manchester (and to be frank, everywhere in Manchester. The City Center is a kaleidoscope of cranes.)

Apparently not happy with just criticizing his own team, Mourinho brought the Manchester Police into question after the match.

"We left the hotel at 6 p.m., hoping that 30 minutes would be enough and it normally is," Mourinho said. "But this time, the police refused to do an escort so we came by ourselves. It took, from the Lowry Hotel, 75 minutes."

"UEFA were nice and the referee was nice to allow us to start the game five minutes later because we needed time to be prepared. We anticipated it could have been dangerous, in the sense of arriving late, but we were informed that the police refused a police escort."

The Manchester police, however, issued this statement through *The Guardian:*

"Escorts were provided only 'on occasions when there is intelligence or information suggesting a risk of threat or harm to the players. Greater Manchester Police had previously used police vehicles to accompany the team's coach but after a review of our core policing responsibilities it was decided that we would no longer provide this service at every fixture."

Contrast that reaction with the national concern over Manchester City's bus when the Premier League champions went to Liverpool and you can see how far United have sunk in the pecking order, even in its own city.

Once the players did make it on the field they were their same tentative selves from the weekend. Valencia was quicker to loose balls. They made short direct passes and moved up the field. United appeared to be playing in slow motion.

Mourinho was doing lots of cajoling and gesturing from the touchline. But without being able to hear him, and with only the United players' reactions as your guide, you'd have thought he was yelling, "Stop! Stop! Hold the ball! Don't move!"

United would win the ball deep in its own half. Players like Marcus Rashford or Alexis Sanchez would burst forward down the wing as Valencia sleepwalked back in defense. But the sprints were worthless, the ball never came.

Usually it was Nemanja Matic or Pogba with the ball, looking up, almost waiting for Valencia to get back before they moved forward, like it was the gentlemanly thing to do. It wasn't just disappointing, it was depressing to watch. And a crowd hoping to see a performance like at Watford instead saw a damp rag. All of that talent, speed and skill, and it was like no one had any idea how to use it. Valencia was ecstatic to pick up a point and never seriously threatened.

A beautiful night and an electric atmosphere had gone stale. United fans typically hold their tongues. To their credit, they're not known for overreacting. All of those Ferguson years had taught them the value of stability. But towards the end, after another glacial counter attack, they snapped.

"Attack! Attack attack attack!!" they screamed. It didn't last long, but it was the first direct rejection of Mourinho's style from the people that mattered. And it was followed by loud boos at the end of the match.

Forget Scholes, Pogba and the rest of the pundits. The fans were demanding more now. Something had to change.

~BM

Brief History of Manchester United

Like many football clubs in the United Kingdom, Manchester United was formed as a place where workers could play. Originally known as Newton Heath LYR (Lancashire and York Railway), the club included railway yard workers who wanted to face workers from other companies.

The club became known as Manchester United in 1902, after John Henry Davies, a local brewery owner, invested in the club and changed its name. Man U took advantage of a bustling industrial worker population, numbering nearly two million, with newfound leisure hours in Manchester after the turn of the century. Backed by money and large crowds, the club won two First Division titles in three years, as well as an FA Cup in 1909. However, Manchester United spent most of its time through the end of World War II in the bottom half of the First Division, as well as nine seasons in the Second Division.

Sir Matt Busby was hired following the end of World War II, and he dramatically changed the club's fortunes. Under his 24-year stewardship, the club won five First Division crowns and two FA Cups, and he chose the nickname Red Devils as an intimidating option based off the successful local rugby club.

Busby's greatest accomplishment, however, was leading his club through its darkest hour. He led his youthful "Busby Babes" squads to two league crowns in the 50s, resulting in its first ever appearances in Europe. After defeating Red Star Belgrade, 5-4, in European play, Manchester United was involved in a tragic air crash, known as the Munich Air Disaster, on February 6, 1958.

Twenty-three people perished, either in the crash or from resulting injuries, including eight players. This included Tommy Taylor (131 goals) and Duncan Edwards (debuted at age 16), along with left-back Roger Byrne (280 appearances). Busby himself was badly injured, but he recovered over time and led Manchester United for more than another decade.

Busby developed a wealth of talent over his time at Old Trafford, including Bobby Charlton, a Munich crash survivor who would go on to lead the 1966 English World Cup champion side, while scoring 249 goals in 758 appearances for Man U. Those totals are now both now second in club history. He is one of only three Englishmen, along with former teammate Nobby Stiles, and Ian Callaghan, to have won both the World Cup and the European Cup.

Northern Irishman George Best, "El Beatle," had 179 goals while dazzling individually. Watch his highlights on YouTube. He was a truly incredible talent.

Busby's retirement at the end of the 60s led to a mostly dormant period, in terms of trophies. Wilf McGuinness, Frank O'Farrell, Tommy Docherty, Dave Sexton and Ron Atkinson combined could only muster three FA Cups through the 1985-86 campaign. In the fall of that year, Sir Alex Ferguson, a Scot like Busby, was hired over from Aberdeen and began a reign of unprecedented English football success.

Ferguson did not retire until after the 2012-13 season. Under his leadership, Manchester United won 13 Premier League crowns, surpassing Liverpool for the most top-flight league trophies in the process (the club now has 20 overall). The club also won five FA Cups, four League Cups and two Champions League titles during the Ferguson era.

Under Ferguson, a multitude of stars emerged following the game-changing transfer of Eric Cantona from Leeds in the fall of 1992. Cantona was followed by "Fergie Fledglings" David Beckham, Phil and Gary Neville, Nicky Butt and Paul Scholes, part of the so-called Class of 1992, and they combined to score 155 goals for the Red Devils. Wayne Rooney is now the club's all-time leading scorer, surpassing Charlton with 253. His 198 Premier League goals going into the 2017-18 season currently trail only Alan Shearer.

Cristiano Ronaldo was electric, Bryan Robson was a true leader, and Denis Law was prolific, scoring 237 goals. Ryan Giggs is now considered the standard bearer for the club, scoring 168 goals in a club-record 963 appearances. Manchester United won 13 League cups and two Champions League crowns during his time. He leads the Premier League era with 632 appearances and 162 assists.

David Moyes lasted less than a year following Ferguson. Dutch manager Louis van Gaal came on and lasted two, winning an FA Cup. Under Jose Mourinho, United won the Europa League title and the League Cup in 2016-17, but have failed to marshal a title challenge and have been surpassed by Manchester City.

Brief History of Old Trafford

The first pitch Newton Heath played on, at North Road, was "cloaked in smog from a nearby chemical plant." The club's second ground, on Bank Street, was more of a "village hall." After Davies purchased the club and removed all debts, he moved to build a new stadium near the Manchester Ship Canal, and directed famed football stadium architect Archibald Leitch to "create the finest stadium in the North."

Old Trafford, with space available for more than 80,000 people, opened with United losing to Liverpool, 4-3 on February 19, 1910. The ground set an attendance record in 1939, as 76,962 watched Wolves take on Grimsby Town in an FA Cup semifinal that March, but dark days loomed.

Due to its proximity to the canal, as well as the Trafford Park industrial estate, Old Trafford was a popular target of Hitler's Luftwaffe during World War II. In March 1941, bombs "wrecked most of the main stand, the dressing rooms and offices, and scorched the pitch." The resulting damage forced United to move to Man City's then-home, Maine Road, for nearly a decade. With support and pressure coming from fans, Old Trafford was rebuilt and reopened on August 24, 1948, with Man U defeating Bolton.

The club's extended success under Sir Matt Busby, combined with hosting multiple matches during the 1966 World Cup, led to further expansion and innovation at Old Trafford, with floodlights, private boxes and a souvenir shop among the newer implementations at that time.

That innovation continued throughout the 1970s and 80s, with the introduction of English football's first club museum, and into the 90s, when Ferguson began United's march to world dominance. The stadium hosted matches at Euro '96, and staged the 2002-03 Champions League final between AC Milan and Juventus, and now seats more than 75,000. Charlton called Old Trafford the "theatre of dreams" in John Riley's book, *Soccer*, and it has played witness to many dreams coming true in its 107-year history.

Manchester United's stadium is representative of the power the club wield throughout England and the world. Old Trafford is as much of a survivor as those who have played, managed and spectated within its walls.

Manchester Derby vs. Manchester City

Only four plus miles separate Old Trafford from the Etihad, home of Manchester City. The Red Devils own a 73-52 advantage over their Mancunian rivals, with 52 draws mixed in.

The first match between the two took place in November 1881, when City were known as St. Marks West Gordon going up against the railway team of Newton Heath, which won that first tilt. For many years, both sides cheered on the other after matches as it was a Manchester win regardless.

Things began to change when Busby, whose playing career ironically consisted of time at two clubs, Man City and Liverpool, was hired by Man U. Busby's teams rose to prominence in the early 1950s, then emerged from the 1958 Munich airplane crash that claimed the lives of 23 people, including eight players as well as Frank Swift, a noted football journalist who, as a player, expertly manned the goal for Man City for 16 years.

The club continued winning, taking their first European Cup (now Champions League) with a win over Benfica in 1968. That same season, City pipped their cross-city rivals by two points for the First Division crown, their first in 31 years and last for 44 years. Led by the 'Holy Trinity' of Charlton, Best and Law, United had won two of the previous three First Division titles.

United dropped after Busby's retirement, and Law was unceremoniously allowed to leave for City prior to the 1973-74 season. The Red Devils struggled all year, and were facing relegation when meeting City at the end of the season. Law, who had 12 goals that season for City, scored late on a backheel to give City the lead. Immediately following the goal, fans at Old Trafford rushed the field, and the game was called off, with the current result standing, securing United's relegation. The following season was the only one United would spend below the top flight in 80 years, between 1937-38 and 2017-18.

This rivalry has taken on more meaning this century, starting with Man U's Roy Keane taking out Alf-Inge Haaland in a nasty payback challenge in a 1-1 draw in 2001. Following Man City's purchase in 2008, the derby took on added significance with world-class talent evident on both sides. Rooney scored perhaps his trademark goal in a 2-1 victory over Man City in February 2011, an overhead kick that is played over and over leading up to the derby nowadays.

This was mostly a one-sided affair in United's favor until recent years, as Man City has won nine, lost six and drawn two since the 2011-12 season. That was a memorable season for City for many reasons. The club turned the tide with a spectacular 6-1 thrashing of Ferguson's side in October, ending a horrific stretch of one win in 27 meetings at Old Trafford for City. Skysports noted that this was the "worst home defeat since February 1955" for United. A header by Belgian international Vincent Kompany late in the first half secured a 1-0 triumph for City in the return match at Etihad at the end of April, setting the stage for the most dramatic of endings to the season.

After securing a season-ending victory at Sunderland, United watched on the Stadium of Light's video screen as Eden Dzeko and Sergio Aguero scored two goals in two minutes – the second coming at the now-famous time of 93:20 – to defeat Queens Park Rangers and win the league title for City on goal differential over United. Both clubs had 89 points.

After the Red Devils rebounded to win the league title in Ferguson's final season in 2012-2013, City propelled itself to another title in 2013-2014. They won 27 games that year and swept United, winning by three goals at home early in the season, and again at Old Trafford at the end of March, led by Dzeko's brace.

Last season United was one of only two teams to defeat Manchester City in the Premier League. Yet United finished a Premier League record 19 points behind first-placed City.

Northwest Derby vs. Liverpool

Manchester United's rivalry with Liverpool is based on the history of the clubs, as well as the cities themselves. Not happy with rising rents at Liverpool, Manchester opened its own canal in 1894, taking trade, and jobs, away from Merseyside. The two representative clubs have not been fans of each other since.

Under Sir Alex Ferguson's leadership, Manchester United surpassed Liverpool domestically with 20 Premier League/First Division crowns to Liverpool's 18. However, the Merseyside faithful kindly remind Red Devils supporters that they own European superiority, with five Champions League/European Cup titles to Manchester United's three.

Man U currently owns an 88-75 edge in victories over the Reds, with 65 draws. Ferguson gave his club the decided advantage in the rivalry, going 30-19, with 14 draws against Liverpool.

This can be a nasty affair, with Liverpool supporters often sarcastically bringing up the Munich Air Disaster in chants and songs, and Man U faithful responding in kind with the same tone on the Hillsborough Disaster.

2017-18 Season Review

Manchester United only spent two weeks of the entire 2017-18 season outside of the top two in the league. Unfortunately, the club only spent four weeks in first place.

The Red Devils opened the season with three straight wins before losing at Stoke City. That loss and a nil-nil draw at Liverpool four weeks later dropped United to second place for good. Thanks to Manchester City's 22-game unbeaten streak to start the season, United remained stuck behind its crosstown rival – the eventual champions – all year long.

In the teams' head to head matchups, United lost at home, 2-1, in December. The Red Devils claimed a small victory in April, beating City 3-2 at the Etihad. It was one of only two league losses for city. Besides United, only Liverpool in the Champions League beat City at home.

Surprising losses at Huddersfield, Newcastle and Brighton, plus a home loss to eventually relegated West Bromwich Albion were the big reason why City finished 19 points ahead of second-place United, a Premier League record.

The Red Devils won their relatively easy Champions League group over FC Basel, CSKA Moscow and Benfica. However, the weakness of their group showed when Sevilla bounced United from the Round of 16. After drawing nil-nil on the road, United lost 2-1 at home in the second leg and failed to advance in the knockout round.

Manchester United was bounced out of the League Cup in the fifth round, but made a dominant run to the FA Cup final at Wembley Stadium. In wins over Derby County, Yeovil Town, Huddersfield Town and Brighton & Hove, United did not give up a goal through the quarterfinals.

The Red Devils beat Tottenham in its own home, Wembley Stadium, 2-1, in the semifinals on goals by Alexis Sanchez and Ander Herrera. But United was handcuffed in the final, losing 1-nil to Chelsea, ending the club's hopes of tying Arsenal with the most FA Cups, 13.

Spanish goalkeeper David De Gea was named the club's Player of the Year. His 18 clean sheets earned him the Premier League's Golden Glove and he was named to the league's team of the season for the fifth time.

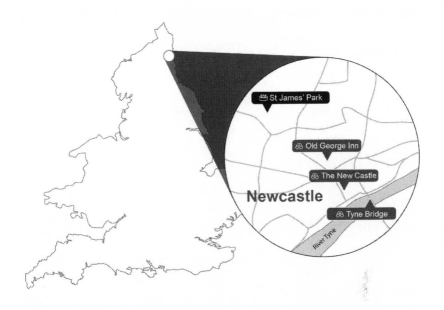

Newcastle United Football Club

Year Founded: 1892

Colors: Black and White Vertical Stripes

Nickname: The Magpies

Stadium: St. James' Park

Address: Barrack Road, Newcastle upon Tyne NE1 4ST, UK

Capacity: 52,354, 7th in Premier League

2017-18 Average Attendance: 52,297, 7th in Premier League

Trophies:

First Division/Premier League (4): 1904-05; 1906-07; 1908-09; 1926-27

FA Cup (6): 1909-10; 1923-24; 1931-32; 1950-51; 1951-52; 1954-55

Current Ownership: Mike Ashley

Current Manager: Rafael Benitez, 4th season (49W, 37L, 19D)

2017-18 Finish: 10th in the Premier League (12W, 18L, 8D)

FA Cup: Lost in fourth round at Chelsea, 3-0

League Cup: Lost in second round vs. Nottingham Forest, 3-2 (AET)

The Sports Tourists' Tips for Newcastle

Expect Tickets to Be Scarce

When purchasing tickets, each ticketholder must have a Newcastle United membership, which will cost around 20 pounds per person. Then ticket sale dates are staggered, starting with the most seasoned St. James' Park veterans down to members with no ticket history, and then general sale.

Because of promotion to the Premier League, we expect Newcastle tickets to sell much quicker than they did last season when the team was in the Championship (and still nearly sold out), meaning you have two options: Use LiveFootballTickets.com and prepare to pay up to get a seat *or* try to get tickets to a League Cup or mid-week Premier League game against a lesser opponent that might not sell out.

Gaze up at St. James' Park From The Strawberry

For pre and post-game entertainment, not many pubs are better positioned than The Strawberry. St. James' Park looms over the Newcastle supporters' pub, which is just down the stairs and across the street from the Stadium. It gets crazy packed, but if you're there early enough – or you can make it out of the game quick enough – you'll witness people watching on the highest level as thousands of fans march up and down the steps.

Ain't No Party Like a Newcastle Party

Newcastle is a prime party destination for English people, not to mention Scottish and Irish. Every weekend, throngs of Londoners descend on Newcastle to soak up the cheap drinks and party atmosphere. We were there the weekend Newcastle University students returned for the fall, so there was even more excitement in the air. There's pubs everywhere, particularly east of Newcastle Central train station and just on the Newcastle side of the River Tyne. But trust us, if you're not sure where to go it won't take you long to figure it out. On Friday and Saturday nights the streets are constantly full of partygoers, moving from bar to bar.

For a Lower Key Party, Head to Historic Old George Inn

History is ever present in Newcastle, even in the pubs. At the back of the historic cloth market sits the Old George Inn, which has been in business since 1582. King Charles I, while awaiting execution at an open prison nearby, used to frequent the Old George. The three-story pub has a bar on the second floor, but a fireplace and TVs down the stairs – making it a bit of a pain when you want to order, but well worth the comfort. Take in the place on a non game day when you want to have a quality beer and bite to eat in a comfortable historic setting.

Walk Through the Castle

The best way to understand the amount of history in this Northeast locale is to consider the name of the town. There's not much new about the "New" Castle. In 1080, it was built on the site of an old Roman settlement called Pons Aelius, which had a fort and small settlement surrounded by walls. The most recent update was the Black Gate – built in 1250 by Henry III.

The majority of the Castle grounds and walls are open to the public at all times. It's hard to miss as the Castle sits right at the entrance to town, next to the main bridge across the River Tyne into Gateshead.

Take a Day Trip to Edinburgh, Scotland

Newcastle's extreme north location in England makes it the best place for you to plan a day trip to Scotland. Edinburgh and Glasgow are both easy 2-3 hours drives north, but in Edinburgh there's lots of impressive architecture and pubs to explore downtown, including the iconic Edinburgh Castle on the top of the hill. On the edge of town is Arthur's Seat, a challenging mountain climb that provides views of the North Sea and the town of Edinburgh from the steep, narrow top.

Our Newcastle Experience

Geordies can be difficult to understand. Their native Newcastle accents can strangle a word or two – at least to our American ears.

But mention the name of Newcastle United owner Mike Ashley, and their responses are quite clear.

"He's shite!"

"It's criminal what he's done to the club!"

"Keegan should batter him senseless!"

And that came from calm, sober supporters at The Strawberry two hours before a fall match at St. James' Park between Newcastle and Arsenal.

Wherever you go, the London native's name is met immediately with whistles and catcalls from members of the Toon Army, Newcastle's mighty followers.

When battling against relegation in the Premier League isn't enough for supporters…

When you ostracize one of your club's living legends, and it is public knowledge…

And when so many threats are made against you that you don't attend a match for your own club for more than a year…

Isn't it time to consider selling?

Ashley has explored that possibility, but for now continues to stand defiantly against all those who would see him removed as NUFC's owner.

The historic club is currently the only Premier League representative from England's northeast. Situated just over 100 miles south of Edinburgh and roughly 125 miles northeast of Huddersfield, the next most northern EPL entrant, Newcastle is the sole Premier League representative of this proud region.

Newcastle supporters consistently come out in drovers. They do this despite Ashley's stagnant leadership, especially when it comes to supporting current manager Rafa Benitez. The veteran gaffer, who most notably led Liverpool for six seasons, took on the challenge of Newcastle late in the 2015-16 campaign.

Unfortunately, the Magpies were relegated. Benitez could have looked for coaching opportunities at a higher level elsewhere, but he chose to stay and lead the club forward.

He wanted them to move back up immediately, and that is what they did.

Newcastle won 29 games, totaled 94 points and secured the EFL Championship for the second time in eight years – the only two seasons it had dropped down to England's second tier.

Benitez had his side primed and ready to compete in the premiership…

But Ashley failed to provide him with the resources to improve his club. A Championship-winning side needs to add Premier League-caliber players to contend at the next level. Ashley and his lackies in charge of the club did not, and still do not, allow Benitez to make those Premier League moves.

In fact, Benitez and Ashley hardly speak. At the start of the 2017-18 Premier League campaign, *The Guardian* reported that Benitez and Ashley "do not talk on the telephone. Instead, Lee Charnley, Newcastle's managing director, serves as a conduit, passing messages between the two."

Benitez has lamented his lack of transfer fund resources since he set foot in Tyneside. According to him, when he's been given money to spend, it has been on players that are not his first choice. Players like Joselu, who do not have Benitez' confidence.

"We have to improve the team but I am signing the players I can, not the players that I want – although that does not mean I don't like the players I have," Benitez told *The Guardian*. "The reality is that, if you cannot pay 25 million pounds, you have to go for a different kind of player. To buy quality you have to pay; we haven't done that."

Those kinds of statements and a poor early start to the 2017-18 season took all the air out of the championship-winning tires. The club then embarked on a nine-match winless streak that left Newcastle in the drop zone.

Benitez was able to pick up January transfer window reinforcements like Kenedy and goalkeeper Martin Dubravka. A late-push, despite the club's third four-match losing streak of the season, put the Magpies in 10th place, albeit with a less-than-stellar 44 points.

The position actually spoke more to the mediocrity of the Premier League's mid-table than anything Newcastle accomplished. Twelve wins and 18 losses left the club better than 10 other Premier League sides. Not really something to pump your chest about.

Brief History of St. James' Park

St. James' Park has hosted football in some shape or form since 1880. The name comes from St. James' Chapel and Hospital nearby the park area on Leazes Terrace. A large part of the park – now called the Gallowgate End – was built on a former hanging ground.

Newcastle Rangers practiced on the plot of land in 1880 and Newcastle West End played games there for a time. But in 1892, Newcastle East End took over the lease of the small park with seats before changing the club's name to Newcastle United. By 1905, the park held 60,000 people and had a swimming pool in one end.

What the stadium looks like now – a giant set of steel girders rising high up into the Newcastle sky, looming above the town – is nothing like the compact, small-stand stadium it started as. Rather than parkland, there are office buildings and a huge mall in front of the stadium now.

Somehow Newcastle and its various owners found a way to continuously modernize the stadium, turning it into one of the Meccas of world football. With a current capacity of 52,354, it was by far the largest stadium in the Championship last year and currently sits seventh in the Premier League.

But it's the passionate support of the fans that – save for one down period in the 1970s – have filled the stadium to the brim throughout its 125-year history. Despite the loss to Arsenal, the Toon Army mostly stayed through Ciaran Clark's late goal – there were only minor patches of empty seats when the final whistle blew.

For most clubs, surviving that first year in the Premier League is the main goal. After that, teams can build and look for more success up the ladder. But Newcastle isn't most teams. The club has been in the Premier League for 24 of 27 seasons, including the 2018-19 campaign. The three years the Magpies weren't in the premiership all featured championship seasons in the second tier.

Despite not winning a First Division title since 1926-27, Newcastle is routinely in the top tier, and recognized as one of the most famous clubs in all of England.

Nickeling and diming just won't cut it. Going into the 2018-19 season, Benitez is in the final year of his contract. Ashley actually offered both a long-term, 5-year extension and a shorter 1-year extension in the summer of 2018, but the Spaniard balked as soon as any talks of larger transfer budgets and improved support systems like training grounds and the club's academy went nowhere.

Rumors abounded in the past as to why Benitez has even stayed this long. Many tapped into his romanticism for the game of football, his love of the Premier League, the close proximity (three-and-a-half-hour drive) to his Merseyside-based family and his belief that he can make Newcastle contenders again.

The Magpies have not seriously contended for a Premier League crown since 2002-03, when the club finished third, 14 points behind champion Manchester United.

For that to occur though, the biggest summer signing splash cannot be West Brom's Salomon Rondon, who only came on after Newcastle's sale of Aleksandar Mitrović to Fulham was finalized. The big Serbian was an offensive revelation for the Cottagers, scoring 12 goals in their run to promotion to the Premier League.

It was the same old story as the 2018-19 season began. Benitez publicly predicted a relegation battle, and he could not have been more right. Newcastle opened the season winless in its first five matches, including a second-round League Cup ouster by Nottingham Forest for the second consecutive season. That loss represented the club's third loss to lower-league competition in the past four years.

Sure, the Magpies lost 2-1 to Top-6 clubs Chelsea, Man City and Spurs each, but they also drew with relegation favorite Cardiff City. With one point from its initial four matches, we came upon St. James' Park on a mid-September afternoon sprinkled with hope, but tethered down more with cynicism over a club that may be heading back down in the spring.

We had a few pints at The Strawberry and watched Liverpool get the better of Spurs at Wembley, and chatted with members of the Toon Army that made it up Barrack Road early for the reverie.

Saying "Can I get you a pint?" sparked positive energy. Bringing up Ashley's name was like slapping their mother right in front of them.

"He needs to sell the club and get out of here," remarked one Tooner in an Alan Shearer jersey.

"He needs to sell and then disappear into thin air, mate," said another, wearing a Kevin Keegan throwback.

Keegan is another stain for Ashley. Although he only played a couple seasons for the Magpies in the early 1980's, Keegan was revered by Newcastle supporters. He scored 48 goals in 78 games and helped Newcastle earn promotion to the top tier after a six-year absence.

On top of that, Keegan managed the club during a hugely successful stint over nearly five years, which started with saving the club from dropping to the third tier for the first time ever to competing for Premier League titles.

He resigned early in 1997 despite the club's presence again near the top of the table. After stints at Fulham, the English National team and Manchester City, Keegan returned to Newcastle in January 2008 after nearly three years away from management. He again had a positive impact on the club, steering them from possible relegation to 12th place.

That is also when Keegan first came into Ashley's stratosphere. Keegan began complaining about – shocker – Ashley not supporting him with transfer funds needed for acquisitions ahead of the 2008-09 season. Keegan left the club and a dispute ensued over what he was owed, taking more than a year to resolve.

Keegan released a book in October 2018, *My Life in Football*. Excerpts were released before we arrived in Newcastle. He has vowed never to return to St. James' Park while Ashley still owns the club and has only made one appearance since leaving in September 2008, and that was in disguise for a private function.

Keegan, who won two million pounds to end that dispute, said that "I will always be persona non grata as long as the Mike Ashley regime remains in place... The sad thing is that I would not want to go back anyway... that policy is set in stone until Ashley is gone."

With these warm and fuzzy feelings in place for a club currently 18th in the table, we headed to our seats in St. James' Park early, and the pre-match atmosphere was loud.

Songs were blaring...

Credence Clearwater Revival's "Born on the Bayou"...

The Animals, long-time NUFC supporters (lead-singer Eric Burdon was a ball boy at St. James' Park) belted out "We've Gotta Get Out of This Place"...

Then some Hendrix...

Then Beatles...

Then Newcastle's anthem – "The Blaydon Races." A new version of this 19th century folk song was taped in 2017 ahead of the Magpies' Good Friday match against Leeds, which we attended.

2017-18 Season Review

The season got off to an ominous start, as the winners of the 2016-17 English League Championship did little to improve themselves, stifling excitement about the club's chances of moving up the table. As Sky Sports' Phil Thompson noted, "a summer of relative inertia in the transfer market meant that some of the optimism had been sapped from supporters early in the campaign and relegation was a real fear at the halfway stage."

The club won three in a row early in the season, including two victories over soon-to-be relegated Swansea City and Stoke City. Newcastle promptly went through a nine-match winless streak, losing eight and earning just one point. A 1-0 defeat to Arsenal just before Christmas left Rafa Benitez' side in the drop zone.

Newcastle continued to scuffle, earning just 10 points in its next eight games, but a 1-0 shutout of Manchester United – the club's first win at St. James' Park in four months – sparked a mini resurgence. After drawing with Southampton and a loss at Liverpool, the Magpies defeated Southampton, Huddersfield, Leicester and Arsenal in a row, its longest winning streak of the campaign.

Another four-match losing streak – Newcastle's third of the year – quieted things down, but a 3-0 win over defending league champion Chelsea to close the season left the club in tenth place, the first newly promoted club to finish in the top half of the Premier League table since West Ham (also 10th) in 2012-13.

Newcastle went 8-7-4 at home and 4-11-4 away, scoring just 39 goals away throughout the season. Captain Jamaal Lascelles took a step forward as the team's leader with a strong defensive campaign and Ayoze Perez led the club with 10 goals overall, eight in league play. The club had short stays in both the League Cup, losing late. to Nottingham Forest, 3-2, and the FA Cup, falling to eventual cup champion Chelsea, 3-0, in the fourth round.

Flags were waving everywhere and a sea of black and white vertical stripes were arrayed throughout St. James' Park, with just a speck of red and white from the Arsenal-clad followers in the upper tier of the Leaves End.

The Magpies responded by taking the fight to Arsenal right away. New manager Unai Emery's side was on its heels early as Newcastle brought the pressure and the chances.

Jacob Murphy tested veteran Arsenal keeper Peter Čech with a header from the left side, but none of the chances found the back of the net. Despite this, Newcastle looked and felt like big winners in the first 45 minutes.

However, something happened at halftime. First, Benitez was forced to remove skipper Jamaal Lascelles due to an ankle injury he sustained in warm ups. Lascelles admirably attempted to play through this injury in the first half, albeit poorly. Benitez substituted Ciaran Clark for him at the break.

"He was trying in the first half and we had to make the substitution, so, in the end, it was one less option for us to change things during the second half," Benitez said.

Whether it was Lascelles' substitution or too many orange slices in the locker room, the Magpies were not ready at the start of the second half.

Arsenal dominated from the opening kick and were rewarded a couple minutes in when Pierre-Emerick Aubameyang was taken down by Federico Fernandez, leading to a beautiful, 30-yard free kick goal by Granit Xhaka (pronounced Shaka) – what fans refer to as one of his XhakaBOOMs!

Newcastle keeper Martin Dubravka got a hand to it, and maybe should have gotten a little more. His defense did not help. The pressure they applied in the first half, squeezing Arsenal's forwards and midfield, was not present in the second half.

Nine minutes after Xhaka's tally, oft-criticized German Mesut Ozil scored on a rebound of Alexandre Lacazette's initial attempt, slipping a soft left-footer past a shielded Dubravka.

Aubamayeng almost made it 3-0 in the 60th when he was found out on the left wing and dribbled in, only to send his offering wide right. In fact, Arsenal had several chances to add to their advantage, to the delight of the away fans in the upper echelons of the Leazes Stand, who awoke from their slumber to chant "Arsenal!...Arsenal!...Arsenal!..."

Newcastle was listless and uninspired, although Perez and Joselu both had shots stopped by Čech, until an extra-time goal by Clark, who headed home a cross from Fernandez in stoppage time.

The club lost 2-1 yet again, their fourth defeat in five EPL games so far this season, to drop to 19th in the table. Only Burnley, with a worse goal differential, separated the Magpies from the bottom.

This five-match start was tied for the worst Premier League opening performance for Newcastle under Ruud Gullit in 1999.

The issues from the match stayed with Newcastle fans long after its completion. The Royal Victoria Infirmary was an unlikely home for us on our first match night in England, but such are the wears from trans-Atlantic travel.

Not unlike in the US, when waits in emergency rooms can be excruciatingly long, we stayed in the reception area for a little more than four hours before being seen.

During that time, a host of Newcastle fans made their entrance into the infirmary area, victims of alcohol consumption and bitterness, which led to everything from broken hands, arms and ribs to bloodied faces.

Some came in from a typical wild Saturday night out in Newcastle, but the rest was the result of a long day cheering for a winless side.

And it would not get any better. The following week, Ashley looked on as his side played to a scoreless draw in London at Palace. Watching his club in person for the first time in more than a year, he was booed relentlessly by his own fans.

Losses at home to Leicester City and Brighton followed, as well as a defeat at Manchester United and a scoreless tie on the coast at Southampton. Dubravka encouraged a players-only meeting after the Leicester loss, and Benitez himself was being somewhat jeered, as fans and even players began questioning some of his substitutions.

This is the worst league start for Newcastle since 1898, and the Magpies are in danger of getting relegated for the third time in Ashley's 10 years of ownership. Bear in mind that *The Chronicle* noted in October that Newcastle had only been relegated four times total in the club's previous 117 years.

Everyone wants Ashley to sell the club. Articles pop up talking about potential buyers, or even takeovers. Others take wistful walks down "What Could Have Been?" lane regarding Man City owner Sheikh Mansour's interest in buying the club from Ashley before making the move for City.

Until change at the top happens, it is fair to say that Newcastle, and its Toon Army, are stuck in limbo.

~BB

Brief History of Newcastle United

The history of Newcastle United is equal parts glory and mediocrity. Unfortunately, the vast majority of the mediocrity – and very little of the glory – has come in the last 62 years.

Newcastle United is one of the top FA Cup teams historically – with six victories and 13 overall finals appearances. However, the last of those Cups came in 1955. And it still holds as the last major trophy won by the Magpies. But in the early days of the Football League, the power was in the North – and arguably no one was more powerful than the coal miners on the River Tyne – Newcastle United.

An early predecessor, Newcastle Rangers, was the first to play near Leazes' Terrace, which the locals started calling St. James' Park, in September 1880. But Newcastle United, as we know it today, was formed out of a merger between two clubs, one on each side of town. In 1882, a number of smaller clubs banded together to form Newcastle East End. In 1886, a fledgling club called West End Football Club took over the lease at St. James' Park.

The two clubs joined the Northern League, instead of the Football League. Soon, there was an arms race in the city of Newcastle. Newcastle East End became a limited company in 1890, hoping to use the investment money to buy players. West End tried to do the same thing, but lost the race. Soon, East End took over West End's St. James' Park lease and what was left of the club, changing its name to Newcastle United in 1892.

Newcastle United tried to gain admission to the First Division of the Football League in 1893, but was only given a place in the Second Division – joining the lower league the same season as Liverpool and Arsenal. A year later, the red jerseys of East End were replaced with the current white and black vertical stripes.

Interestingly, Newcastle's early years were spent in a vain quest to win England's biggest trophy, the FA Cup, similar to the Magpies vain quest of today.

Newcastle earned promotion to the First Division in 1899, through a series of what were called "test matches" – essentially, like a promotion playoff today. This began a nearly 20-year run when Newcastle United was a fixture in the top 10, and even top five of the Football League.

The Magpies loaded up with talented local Northern players, like Jock Rutherford and captain Colin Veitch, who played every position except for goalie, and off the field, helped fund the Newcastle People's Theatre. Newcastle won the Football League for the first time in 1904-05, then did it again in 1906-07 and 1908-09. In the meantime, the Magpies were experiencing frustration in the FA Cup.

Newcastle went to the FA Cup final three times in four seasons, but lost to Aston Villa (1905), Everton (1906) and Wolves (1908). Finally in 1910, the Magpies broke through. But even that first win required a replay against Burnley, after a 1-1 draw in the first game. Newcastle wasn't over its hoodoo, going back to the final in 1911, only to lose a replay to Bradford City.

The Magpies added FA Cup victories in 1924 and 32. And paced by 39 goals from Scotsman Hughie Gallacher, United won the Football League title for a fourth time in 1926-27. To this day, it's the club's last top division title. After relegation and a brief spell of Second Division football before and after World War II, Newcastle established themselves as the so-called "Cup Kings," an ironic moniker now but well-deserved in the early 50s.

Coach Stan Seymour – a Newcastle player in the 20s and 30s – recruited future club legend Jackie Milburn. Milburn would become the club's all-time leading goal scorer in League play. He's second overall in goals in club history. But it was the FA Cup final where Milburn made his mark, taking two splendid goals, including a long-range strike considered one of the best in history, to win the 1951 FA Cup, 2-0, over Blackpool.

The next year, Chilean George Robledo gave Newcastle a 1-0 victory over 10-man Arsenal to win back-to-back FA Cups. Milburn was at it again in the 1955 final, scoring the fastest goal in FA Cup history 45 seconds in to lead the Magpies to a 3-1 victory over Manchester City. The win tied Newcastle with Aston Villa with six FA Cups, the most in all of England.

But for the Magpies, 1955 was the last time they would win a major title. The club has reached the final three times since – and lost all three. In 1995-96, under the ownership of John Hall, Newcastle United were called "The Entertainers," thanks to the exciting attacking play of the club's all-time leading scorer Alan Shearer, Les Ferdinand and David Ginola. Coach Kevin Keegan had the Magpies poised for a first Premier League title.

But, a late-season collapse punctuated by a 4-3 loss to Liverpool saw Newcastle give up a big lead and lose to Manchester United. The Magpies would finish runner-up that season and the next, unable to break through.

In 1999, Sir Bobby Robson took over after the disastrous Ruud Gullit era and steered Newcastle back towards the top of the table. After a fourth place finish in 2001-02, the Magpies qualified for the Champions League, where they became the first team to lose its first three group stage games and still qualify for the knockout round

Newcastle finished third place in the Premier League during that Champions League season of 2002-03. The next year, they were knocked out of the Champions League early, but made a run to the semifinals of the UEFA Cup before losing to Didier Drogba and Marseille.

In 2007, sporting goods' millionaire Mike Ashley took over the club and fortunes have suffered since. The Magpies were relegated in his second season in charge, 2008-09 before popping back up the next season.

But a failure to properly invest has resulted in only two Top 10 Premier League finishes under Ashley – fifth place in 2011-12 and 10th place in 2017-18. Newcastle was relegated again in 2015-16, but came right back up after winning the English League Championship title under coach Rafa Benitez.

Tyne-Wear Derby vs. Sunderland

The Tyne-Wear derby pits Newcastle, situated on the banks of the River Tyne, against Sunderland, located 12 miles away on the River Wear. Both towns were built on the coal trade. And the citizens can't even agree on what type of mining lamp to use.

Newcastle's residents are called Geordies, supposedly because of their preference for a lamp designed by George "Geordie" Stephenson. Sunderland's miners preferred the Davy lamp – a replica of which is outside Sunderland's aptly named, Stadium of Light.

As you can imagine, this fierce Northeast rivalry goes far beyond the football field. According to Richard Stonehouse in *The Guardian,* it started because Newcastle was loyal to the crown and in those days, the city's merchants were given exclusive coal rights – much to the chagrin of Sunderland's coal traders.

When the English Civil War started in 1642, Newcastle supported the King. Sunderland joined Oliver Cromwell's Parliamentarians, eventually leading to the Battle of Boulden Hill in 1644. Sunderland's residents, with the help of Scots, won the battle and the Scots colonized Newcastle for themselves.

356 years later, a group of Sunderland fans armed with bats and bricks took a ferry to Newcastle and met a small army of Magpies' hooligans to fight. Dozens were arrested and one man left brain-damaged.

But despite all the fighting off the field, the derby hasn't meant much on the pitch. Neither team has won a trophy in 43 years and often, the derby is a relegation six-pointer. However, the historical results are an even split right now with 53 wins a piece and 49 draws. Newcastle has failed to win any of the last nine matchups, including a five-game Premier League losing streak.

Incredibly, in recent years, four different Sunderland coaches (Paolo di Canio, Gus Poyet, Dick Advocaat and Sam Allardyce) all faced Newcastle in their second game in charge – and all four won.

It may be a while before the two teams face each other again. Sunderland was relegated two consecutive seasons, falling from the Premier League down to League One ahead of the 2018-19 season. Unless Newcastle is relegated and Sunderland promoted – which is not out of the realm of possibility on both accounts – cup matches will be the only potential opportunity to witness this game.

Newcastle fans took special joy in Sunderland going down again. When Newcastle was relegated from the Premier League after the 2015-16 season, Sunderland fans told the Toon Army to "enjoy Burton."

Newcastle supporters have made sure to let the Mackems know that they will be enjoying those matches with the Brewers in League One.

The most memorable derby in history came in 1990 when the two met in a two-legged playoff semifinal. After a 0-0 draw at Sunderland's Roker Park, Newcastle gave up four away goals in the second leg and missed out on promotion at the hands of its rivals, sparking infamous rioting and pitch invasions in the last 20 minutes of the game.

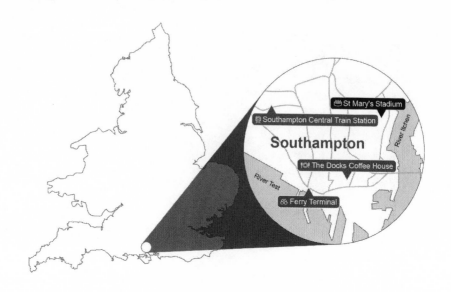

Southampton Football Club

Year Founded: 1885

Stadium: St. Mary's Stadium

Colors: Red and white vertical stripes

Nickname: The Saints

Address: Britannia Road, Southampton S014 5FP, UK

Capacity: 32,384, 11th in Premier League

2017-18 Attendance: 30,781, 11th in Premier League

Trophies:

FA Cup (1): 1975-76

Current Ownership: Gao Jisheng

Current Manager: Mark Hughes, 2nd season with club (3W, 5L, 2D)

2017-18 Finish: 8th in Premier League, 12W, 16L, 10D

FA Cup: Lost in semifinal at Chelsea, 2-0

League Cup: Lost in second round vs. Wolverhampton, 2-0

The Sports Tourists' Tips for St. Mary's Stadium

Wait for General Sale

You can purchase a membership to Southampton for just 30 pounds. And the membership will get you an extra three days priority on tickets rather than general sale. But, for the moment, Southampton isn't selling out. And if you have no ticket purchase history with Southampton, you'll still be at the bottom of the priority pile even if you buy a membership.

Instead, just sign up for a free Supporter Number and wait for general sale, when you'll be able to buy tickets without a membership. Most games – outside of matchups with the big six – will still have limited tickets available when it goes to a general sale.

Get to the Chapel Arms Pub Early on Game Day

While most of the pubs are farther west of St. Mary's Stadium, the Chapel Arms Pub is only a five-minute walk away. It's not very big, so it gets extremely crowded on game days. But if you get there early enough (2 hours-plus), it's a fun place to pregame before you go to St. Mary's. And for as crowded as it gets, bar staff are some of the friendliest we saw.

The Docks Coffee Shop

This gem is in the south end of town, just a couple blocks away from the Southampton docks. The owners, an American expat and his English wife, brew the best coffee in town with personal care. On top of that, there are all kinds of great bites to eat for breakfast or lunch. Rather than give your money to a bland chain store coffee shop, head to the Docks instead, clear your head, read a book or check your email. Then go for a walk along the shore when you're done.

Walk the Old Walls and Get in Touch with English History

As it became important as a port city for England, Southampton also became a target for French raiders from across the English Channel. As a result, extensive stone walls and towers were built throughout the city. Many of them are still standing, dating back to the 14th century. Download the free self-guided walking tour online, or if you want to learn more, visit the Tudor House and Garden for 5 pounds.

Day Trip to Isle of Wight

Southampton has one of England's busiest ferry ports, giving you access to other cities via the water. If you're in Southampton for more than two days, it would be a shame if you didn't take a ferry to Cowes, on the Isle of Wight. The ferry takes a little over an hour, and you can easily walk all around the town of Cowes. Filled with restaurants, pubs and shops on old stone roads, you'll get a good sense of the "Island life", English style.

Our Southampton Experience

Just a few minutes after the conclusion of a thrilling Monday night football game at the St. Mary's Stadium in Southampton, we ventured out into the busiest section of the port city.

Upper Bar Street, as its called, is chockfull of restaurants of all shapes and sizes. Burgers, Cuban, Portuguese, pizza – we had our pick. Enthralled with the match and put off by the halftime lines at the stadium, we were happy we waited to eat. Look at all the choice in front of us.

But, this is England after all, and everything was not what it seemed. The game began at 8 p.m. and after a half-mile or so walk back into the center of town, the clock had just struck 10. Unbeknownst to us, this was the witching hour in Southampton and it turns out – almost all of England.

We tried to walk right into the first restaurant, a highly recommended pizza place with hours posted until 11 p.m.

"Sorry, kitchen's closed," they told us, as we looked at a full dining room. Of course, we could still get drinks if we wanted.

Next door down, more of the same. Over and over again, we were turned away looking for food, but encouraged to come in and have a drink. We found a steakhouse open until 11 p.m. a short walk away. We arrived at 10:25 p.m. The doors were locked as a couple tables finished their meal. The server wouldn't even look at us as we knocked on the door.

And it wasn't just us. Hundreds of Saints' fans swarmed down Upper Bar St. looking for a bite and were turned away. It's almost like the business owners preferred not to make money on food. Drink, as always in England, was readily available any time.

We doubled back to discover even Taco Bell and Burger King were closed. Beyond disgruntled, we trudged back to the hotel, defeated. Then we saw it, our last hope, a well-lit Chinese restaurant with the doors wide open, plenty of people inside and posted hours of midnight.

We walked in triumphant and then saw the look on the hostess's face.

"I'm sorry, our kitchen is closed."

By this time, we were hangry – a combination of hungry and angry for those who don't know – and after a few cross words we left wholly unsatisfied.

Why do I tell this tale of woe?

For a couple of reasons. First, this is both a book about soccer and a book about being a tourist in England. And one thing many Americans will find surprising when you visit England is how early most restaurants stop serving food.

This wasn't just a Southampton problem either, we found it happening all over the country. Even in London. When the bar staff come over and remove the condiments from the table, that's your signal: you missed out on food.

In Brighton, out watching a Champions League game, the kitchen closed before halftime. Outside of the really touristy areas in Liverpool, it was hard to find an open restaurant. In Newcastle, good luck eating after 8 p.m.

Even in London, a town that can appear as bustling as New York City at times, plenty of kitchens in populated areas close down earlier than expected. It can take some getting used to and some planning for Americans, where even a staid fast food franchise like Chick Fil A is open until 10 p.m. and there's a late-night diner in almost every small town.

The other reason we tell this story about Southampton's restaurants is as a parable for the Southampton Football Club.

You see, far too often in the last few years, the Saints have left fans unsatisfied and hungry for more. And under manager Mark Hughes, a former player for the club, the Saints have closed up shop too early, over and over again.

On this Monday night, the same old story played out under the bright lights of St. Mary's Stadium, hard by the River Itchen. The opponent was Brighton and Hove Albion, who came into town from just about 60 miles east along the South Coast.

But whatever you do, don't call this a South Coast derby. Or at least, that's what we read in the lead-up to the game, particularly in an opinionated article by Scott McCarthy in *The Brighton and Hove Independent*.

The argument was that both teams already had Derby matches. Brighton had an organic hate fest with Crystal Palace that started back in the 1970s and heated up in the last few years as both teams fought for promotion to the Premier League.

For Southampton, its rivalry went much further back. There are two major ports on the South Coast and have been for years – Southampton and Portsmouth. And the enmity extends beyond football.

Brief History of St. Mary's Stadium

Southampton is a port city, surrounded by water on three sides. But for 103 years, the Saints played at the Dell, a non-descript stadium in the middle of the city, far from the water.

In 2001, Southampton moved to a more fitting location, St. Mary's Stadium, on the banks of the River Itchen. The modern stadium is closed in on all sides, so there isn't a great view of the water from inside. But most fans walk to the stadium and the sight of cruise ships in port and water nearby gives it a much more authentic feel.

St. Mary's Stadium has the 10th-largest capacity in the Premier League, capable of holding 32,234.

The St. Mary's had an auspicious beginning as Southampton failed to win any of its first five Premier League games there in the fall of 2001. Coach Stuart Gray was fired and Gordon Strachan, now coach of Scotland, was brought in to sort out the mess. On top of that, a pagan witch came to ward off evil spirits. Eventually, a then club-record crowd watched Southampton beat Charlton, 1-0, for its first win in the new home, leading Strachan to say of the witch:

"If she's that good she can take training for the next two weeks and I can get on with my golf while she gets rid of the ghosts. Maybe she can play up front."

St. Mary's Stadium has carried on a history of innovation in the town. The Dell was the first stadium in England to install floodlights. And St. Mary's was the first in all of Europe to install LED floodlights in 2014, which create a brighter atmosphere on TV and use less energy.

Strikes and disputes on the dock between the two towns' workers flared up seemingly every decade since 1912 when Southampton's crews refused to work on the Titanic's sister ship, the Olympic, after a number of men from the town died on the Titanic.

Instead, Portsmouth-based staff were brought in to replace them in a rowboat under the cover of darkness so they wouldn't be attacked. The disagreement between the two towns is real.

But Portsmouth had dropped out of the Premier League like a rock. Though after a few years of floundering, Pompey was leading League One at the time of publication. Still, the only chance Portsmouth and Southampton had of playing any time soon was in a Cup draw.

Should St. Mary's Stadium only get one derby atmosphere every decade or so? What's the point in preventing rivalries?

On Brighton's side, *The Independent's* argument was that the distance between the South Coast cities – 68 miles – prevented the rivalry from developing. But then why was the 50 miles between Palace and Brighton normal?

And of course, in America, the idea that two teams couldn't be rivals because 68 miles is too far apart would seem patently ridiculous. Tell that to Boston and New York, Philly and New York, LA and San Francisco. But in England, over 60 miles there's likely dozens of small fiefdoms, each extremely protective over their perceived differences from the rest. How can you reach a rivalry with Brighton when you're stuck on Portsmouth?

Obviously, the Southampton fans didn't see it our way because the atmosphere in the stadium was mild at best. To be fair, the Saints barely stayed up the year before and hadn't exactly gotten off to a flying start this season.

Going into our Monday night match, Southampton had just four points. The Saints failed to win any of their first three before beating this same Brighton team in the League Cup and then defeating Crystal Palace on the road. And they were the only team in the Premier League who'd failed to score a first half goal all season. So Southampton was getting leads in the second half, then closing up shop too early and losing them.

Southampton has dropped 26 points from winning positions since the beginning of last season. And manager Mark Hughes had been unable to hold a favorable position for 13 of his last 14 matches headed into the Brighton game.

What was the problem? Obviously, Southampton seemed to find its way in front at some point. Why couldn't they keep it going?

The evidence points to a couple of problems, a lack of discipline being the main culprit. Against Leicester City earlier in the season, a 1-1 draw was in the bag, even down a man. Then Leicester scored two minutes into stoppage time.

South Coast Derby vs. Portsmouth

Like many on-filed rivalries in England, the South Coast derby between Southampton and Portsmouth started as an off-the-field dispute.

The maritime history and competition between the two towns naturally leads to disputes. One of the biggest came in 1912, after the Titanic – with a mostly Southampton-based crew – sank. Other Southampton-based sailors refused to crew the Titanic's sister ship, the Olympic, because of the lack of lifeboats. Portsmouth's sailors were happy to do it instead, provoking a reaction on the Southampton docks.

Southampton historian Genevieve Bailey told the BBC:

"The Portsmouth crews arrived in the dead of night by sea because it would have been too dangerous for them to arrive in the city by road."

In the early days, Portsmouth supporters began calling Southampton's team and fans SCUM, or Scummers, a reference to the Southampton Company Union Men who often came to Portsmouth on work. Southampton fans, for their part, call Portsmouth fans "Skates," a derogatory term for sailors, since the Royal Navy is based out of Portsmouth.

The teams first met in 1899 and have played 139 games against each other at all levels with Portsmouth holding the edge with 62 wins, although Southampton has more First Division wins.

With Portsmouth's club in financial decline and Southampton on the rise after its own financial troubles, the two haven't met since 2012 in league play.

One major point of contention centered on the always-controversial Harry Redknapp, who managed Portsmouth before leaving to take over Southampton in 2005. After failing to keep the Saints up in the Premier League, Redknapp went back to Portsmouth and helped them avoid relegation the next season.

Redknapp also coached Bournemouth, whose newfound Premier League status has started a potential second South Coast rivalry with Southampton. However, Saints' fans take a more bemused view of Bournemouth and still consider hated Portsmouth to be their one true rival.

Last May, Manchester City was able to take all three points in a 1-0 win with a Gabriel Jesus goal in the 95th minute. Two weeks before that, Everton earned a 1-1 draw in the 96th minute.

Breakdowns in the moment you should be the most solid point to the coach.

The Saints crowd sat on their hands early in this one. In fact, it was hard to tell what it would take to get the St. Mary's faithful excited and out of their seats. Maybe they just assumed there was going to be no first half goal, like usual.

But in the 35th minute, Pierre-Emil Hojbjerg shocked us all. He opened the club's first half account with one the best goals we saw all trip.

A shot from Mohamed Elyounoussi was blocked and bounced all the way to the deep Hojbjerg, nearly 35 yards from goal. He settled the ball and all alone, took a moment to calibrate. As the defender arrived too late, Hojbjerg unleashed a hard, low shot straight as an arrow towards the far post. At the last moment it turned inside, easily beating the keeper for a 1-nil lead.

It was a big moment for Hojbjerg, who was sent off against Leicester in late August after earning his second yellow card for diving. The sending off played a large role in Leicester's late win.

The rarity of a Saints' first half goal was only matched by the exquisite nature of the finish itself. So of course, the lone first half goal of the season would be nominated as the Premier League's goal of the month for September. (It lost to Daniel Sturridge.)

On the other side of the half, Southampton kept going for it – and got a reward when Gaetan Bong tripped up Danny Ings in the box. Ings coolly buried his penalty and the crowd was enthused.

But, just like when we laid eyes on the restaurants of Upper Bar Street, the door was about to slam shut on Southampton's optimism.

All game long, giant Brighton defenders Shane Duffy and Lewis Dunk were blocking shots and menacing Southampton's less physically gifted forwards. In the second half, after an apparently heated halftime talk with Hughton, Dunk and Duffy made themselves an offensive menace as well.

In the 67th minute, Duffy buried a header off a well-taken free kick by Anthony Knockaert. Duffy got open early, using his strength and height to get away from the Saints' markers.

With the one-goal lead, Hughes panicked and shut up shop early. But the move was nonsensical as many Saints' fans pointed out after the game in the walk to the city center. As defensive substitutes, he put on James Ward-Prowse and Steven Davis, both after the lead was trimmed to 2-1. Both midfielders are amongst Southampton's smallest players.

There was no counter to the threat Brighton posed with its size. And it burned Hughes in stoppage time – again.

Brighton kept knocking on the door on set pieces, drawing a couple tough saves from Saints' goalie Alex McCarthy. But in the 90th minute, disaster struck.

When another brilliant out swinging corner from Knockaert hung dangerously over the box, Ward-Prowse found himself isolated against Duffy. Knowing he was never going to win a battle in the air, Ward-Prowse shoved him with all his might.

And it worked. Duffy went face first on the ground, right in front of the referee, Anthony Taylor. Brighton was awarded a penalty. Glenn Murray tucked it away comfortably in stoppage time. And Southampton, yet again, dropped points from a winning position. That's 11 points lost since Hughes took over in March.

"We obviously went into the game with the intention of winning," Hughes said after the game. "But it wasn't to be."

"We've just got to find a way to manage games to a conclusion – to a winning conclusion. Because we did a lot of things well tonight, but at a key moment in the game, we've just got to see it out.

"In the end it feels like a defeat, and probably a victory for Brighton."

In the end, it meant defeat for Hughes too. Mired in the relegation battle, Saints' management made a change just before the book went to press and fired Hughes. As his replacement, the club hired Austria Ralph Hasenhuttl, who recently took RB Leipzig into the Champions League.

~BM

Brief History of Southampton FC

The roots of Southampton FC started with the St. Mary's Church Young Men's Association, who began playing friendly games along the River Itchen in 1885. By 1894, the club was called Southampton-St. Mary's and joined the Southern League. By 1896, the club shortened the name to Southampton and established itself as a dominant force on the South Coast.

The Saints won six of the next eight Southern League titles and reached two FA Cup finals (and a semifinal) in an era when northern teams dominated the competition. In 1898, Southampton moved away from the river to the middle of town at a stadium called The Dell, which the club called home for 103 years before moving to St. Mary's Stadium, back on the River Itchen, in 2001.

When the Football League and Southern League merged in 1920, Southampton's fortunes began to tank and the Saints spent the next 46 years one to three levels below the top division of English Football. In fact, when Ted Bates took over as manager in 1955, Southampton was playing in the South Third Division. Over his 18-year career in charge of the Saints, Bates took them up three more levels and into the First Division for the first time in 1966.

Led by prolific goal scorer Ron Davies (153 Saints' goals, second best in club history), Southampton qualified for a major European competition for the first time in 1970, playing in the UEFA Cup the next year. Bates resigned midway through the 1973-74 season and handed the reins to Lawrie McMenemy. Bates finished with 346 wins as a manager and a statue of him sits outside St. Mary's Stadium.

Unfortunately, Southampton would get relegated that season, but two years later, the Saints would achieve their crowning moment, with Bates on the sidelines as McMenemy's assistant coach. Despite finishing ninth in the Second Division in 1976, Southampton reached the FA Cup final at Wembley Stadium against Manchester United.

As 7-1 underdogs with the bookies, the Saints played outstanding team defense and frustrated the Red Devils. Still, the goal would not come. But in the 83rd minute, a long ball over the top sprung a questionably offside little midfielder named Bobby Stokes. Stokes coolly settled the ball and steered it into the far corner with his left foot to score the game's only goal. The Cup went to Southampton and Bates was the first to shake McMenemy's hand when it was over.

The celebration parade afterwards was "the biggest event in Southampton ever," according to McMenemy. The players took a detour before the parade to the Ford plant in town. The manager, worried his workers would all call out sick on the day of the parade, asked McMenemy to bring the trophy by the plant beforehand. True to his word, McMenemy brought the bus to the factory in the early morning with the players and trophy in tow, giving the workingmen a thrill.

The next year, Southampton reached the quarterfinals of the European Cup Winners Cup and in 1977-78, won promotion to the First Division. In 1979, the Saints finished runner-up to Nottingham Forest in the League Cup. McMenemy began to establish the club's academy as a developer of young talent. And then he sprinkled in talented veterans like Phil Boyer, Alan Ball, England goalkeeper Peter Shilton and England legend Kevin Keegan.

Southampton qualified for the UEFA Cup in three of four seasons between 1981-82 and 1984-85. In 1983-84, the Saints finished second in the league and reached the semifinals of the FA Cup. The club continued its run after McMenemy stepped down, and was part of the first Premier League season.

The club developed thrilling offensive players like Matthew Le Tissier and a young Alan Shearer. Le Tissier, from the Channel island of Guernsey, became the Saints' all-time leading scorer with 161 goals, many of them extraordinary. Shearer was developed at Southampton as a youngster, but had his better days at Blackburn and Newcastle. In recent years, the club's academy produced talents like Gareth Bale, Adam Lallana and Alex Oxlade-Chamberlain, who all found stardom after being sold to other clubs.

In 2002-03, led by James Beattie's 24 goals, the Saints finished eighth in the league and again reached the FA Cup final, losing 1-0 to Arsenal at Millennium Stadium in Wales. However, by 2008, the club was relegated down two levels and put in financial administration, docked 10 points to start the League One season.

During the 2009-10 season, German financier Markus Liebherr took over the club and got the team on solid financial footing. Coach Alan Pardew overcame the points deduction and led the team to a Football League Trophy (a tournament for the two lower divisions of the Football League.) Rickie Lambert scored 36 goals that season and led the team in scoring the next two seasons as coach Nigel Adkins got the Saints promoted two straight years, back up to the Premier League.

Since then, first under Mauricio Pochettino, then Ronald Koeman and Claude Puel, Southampton in the top 10 for four straight seasons, qualifying for the Europa League in two of those years. Unfortunately, the Saints last season was a fight to stay in the league.

2017-18 Season Review

The 2017-18 season was an unpleasant grind at the St. Mary's Stadium. The Saints failed to launch in the league and sold their best player after fighting to keep him for over a year. But, the fans got an FA Cup semifinal day out at London's Wembley Stadium and for a moment were allowed to dream of a trophy.

In all, Southampton can consider its season a victory, first for staying up in the Premier League. The Saints won just seven games all season long – and only three of those against teams that didn't get relegated. At one point, Southampton went 13 straight league games without a win and only beat two teams between October and March, West Bromwich Albion twice and Everton at home.

Mauricio Pellegrini lost his job in March after one win in 18 in the Premier League and former Saint Mark Hughes – recently fired by Stoke – took over. A tough early schedule for Hughes dropped the Saints to 18th and potential relegation with just five games to go.

But Southampton scrapped for results. A nil-nil draw at Leicester followed by a 2-1 win over Bournemouth on Dusan Tadic's two opportunistic goals. The Saints then drew at Everton to set up a showdown at the Liberty Stadium with fellow relegation rivals Swansea. A win would clinch safety, but as the nervous nil-nil draw dragged on, a goal seemed unlikely. Until late sub Manolo Gabbiadini jumped on a rebound of a Charlie Austin shot and ensured safety with the only goal in a 1-nil win. The win also confirmed relegation for both Swansea and West Brom.

Even as the drama unfolded in the league, Southampton's form was decidedly better in England's oldest tournament, the FA Cup. After wins at Fulham and home to Watford in rounds three and four, the Saints took down West Brom for a third time, 2-1, at the Hawthorns to reach the quarterfinals.

Hughes' first game in charge was a 2-nil win over Wigan Athletic in the quarters, clinched with a late Cedric Soares goal. Southampton was headed to a semifinal at Wembley Stadium against mighty Chelsea. But Chelsea dominated possession and kept Southampton's offense at bay, winning 2-nil in front of 73,416.

Austin and Tadic led the club in scoring with seven goals each. Not surprisingly given the club's anemic offense, goalkeeper Alex McCarthy was awarded Southampton's Player of the Year. Hughes kept his job for the time being. He was eventually fired and replaced by Ralph Hasenhuttl just before the book went to press.

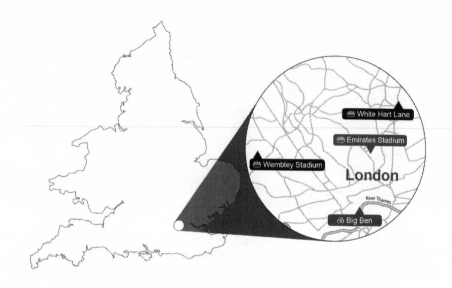

Tottenham Hotspur

Year Founded: 1882

Colors: White and Blue

Nickname: The Spurs. The Lilywhites

Stadium: Wembley Stadium

Address: London HA9 0WS, UK

Capacity: 90,000, Largest stadium in Premier League, and all of England

2017-18 Average Attendance: 70,642, 2nd in Premier League (tickets are capped at 51,000 for certain games)

Trophies:

English Premier League/First Division (2): 1950-51; 1960-61

FA Cup (8): 1900-01; 1920-21; 1960-61; 1961-62; 1966-67; 1980-81; 1981-82; 1990-91

League Cup (4): 1970-71; 1972-73; 1998-99; 2007-08

UEFA Cup/UEFA Europa League (2): 1971-72; 1983-84

UEFA Cup Winners' Cup (1): 1963

Current Ownership: English National Investment Corporation (ENIC), headed by Joe Lewis and Daniel Levy, since June 2001

Current Manager: Mauricio Pochettino (5th Season, 121W, 47L, 50D)

2017-18 Finish: 3rd in the Premier League, 23W, 7L, 8D

Champions League: Lost in Round of 16 to Juventus, 4-3 aggregate

FA Cup: Lost to Manchester United in semifinals, 2-1

League Cup: Lost in fourth round vs. West Ham, 3-2

The Sports Tourists' Tips for Tottenham Hotspur

Catch a match at Wembley in 2018-19 (For now)

Spurs supporters have been anxiously awaiting entering their new cathedral – New White Hart Lane. It was supposed to open for a Premier League match with Liverpool on Saturday, September 15. Oops!

The delays have become somewhat comical, with social media and YouTube offering many theories, many ridiculous, as to why the new stadium is not yet ready for the public.

The delay forced Spurs to host a League Cup match at Stadium MK, home of lower tier MK Dons, but it has also meant more matches in England's ultimate football cathedral. Wembley Stadium has continued to serve admirably as a home ground for Spurs, although it has a slightly smaller capacity for league matches.

Light the Torch When You Get to Wembley

During last year's FA Cup semifinal against Chelsea at Wembley Stadium, The Torch, a pub at 1-5 Bridge Street, was named as one of Spurs' official pubs for the match. Sounds like that tradition has continued into this season, with the Crock of Gold also a hot spot for Tottenham fans on Wembley game days. Originally called The Olympic Torch during the London games, The Torch has food and drink options for everyone. Like all game day pubs, it can get crowded early. To get to The Torch (and the Crock of Gold), simply get off at Wembley Park and walk the opposite way from the stadium. The pubs are about a block away from the Tube station.

Get Ready for the New White Hart Lane in 2018-19 (Maybe)

We still believe that you will be able to see Spurs in their new home sometime before the end of the 2018-19 campaign. A failure to do so would be a systemic failure by all those involved in the massive construction project.

London is easily accessible by flight, so come for Wembley now, then go back for the new White Hart Lane in Spring 2019. The new stadium, located right next to where its predecessor stood for 118 years, will hold roughly 25,000 more seats, making it one of the largest stadiums in England. Spurs fans take pride in the fact that their side have never played further than 100 yards from where the club was formed under a lamppost along Tottenham High Road. Spurs are Tottenham through and through.

Do Not Sing the Song with Them

Like every other club in England, Spurs have a stable of catchy songs and chants that are heard throughout matches. Our favorite involved Dele Alli and his value, as compared to Arsenal's Mesut Ozil. However, there is one song that you will hear, and hear sung loudly and passionately, that you should not take part in. It is called "Being a Yid," and it is tied to the club's historical Jewish connections. Many clubs have derided Spurs for that association, with anti-Semitic references and chants at numerous matches over the years. Spurs fans have embraced this song as a way of embracing their heritage, but it is still inappropriate (read online for debate for and against singing the song) to sing, especially if you are an outsider. As our mate Steve told us, 'for every person I know who sings that song, I know 10-15 who don't. Don't sing it!"

Do Go to No. 8 Hostel

There are many great pub options before or after matches. The Bill Nicholson Pub (102 Northumberland Park, N17 0 London, UK) is named in honor of Spurs' great manager who won two league titles and eight major trophies while serving the club in different capacities for over 60 years. It is a rowdy locale and for Spurs supporters only, so be ready to sing and have a pint.

If you are looking for ample space, good music, televisions showing Bundesliga matches, and a large outdoor area, this is the place for you. There are several bars inside and outside, so your wait for libations is short, the restrooms are convenient, and you can get into 20 different conversations. The staff are friendly and efficient – everything you want from your servers.

This is also for supporters only, so make sure you have either your membership card or your match tickets to gain entry.

Our Tottenham Experience

Construction delays cause headaches for everyone involved. Projects that should have been completed months, even years ago, sit unfinished, waiting for the last brick to fall into place.

Reasons for these delays abound. Money. Unions. Cost overruns. Incompetence. Illegal activity.

One of the greatest examples of this is Boston's Big Dig, the city's Central Artery and Tunnel project that seemingly took decades to complete.

The Boston Globe, in a look back in 2015, described the Big Dig thusly: "It didn't simply take more time than expected; it was eight years behind schedule by the time it was done. And it didn't just have flaws. There seemed to be mistakes at every turn, making the price tag even more laughable, from design blueprints that did not line up properly, to the faulty mixing of concrete, to, most tragically, a ceiling collapse that killed a car passenger in one of the new tunnels."

The cost for the project grew from an early estimate of $2.6 billion to nearly $25 billion, and was the source of both jokes and enmity in and around the state of Massachusetts for what seemed like eons.

But, if you are driving in downtown Boston nowadays, despite the usual rush hour issues, you can now appreciate what was accomplished.

Spurs fans are certainly hoping to have that experience sooner rather than later.

A Tottenham side that may be the best in generations has realistic hopes of winning its first top flight crown in more than half a century this season. But it has been undermined by, of all things, the delay in opening of the club's new stadium, a rebuild of the old one, White Hart Lane.

Supporters are stuck daydreaming about walking up High Road and celebrating their new ground while stuck on the Jubilee Line en route to yet another "home" match at Wembley Stadium.

There are worse things than having to play in England's most revered cathedral, but Tottenham supporters are tired of trekking out to a ground meant more for domestic cup championships, promotion finals, national team matches… and NFL games.

You see, everyone expected Tottenham to be playing in its new home by now, so when the Philadelphia Eagles were scheduled to play the Jacksonville Jaguars at Wembley in late October 2018, it was originally no big deal.

Except, now that Tottenham was still a temporary tenant, Spurs and Premier League champs Man City were set to face each other the next day at Wembley. The sight, on television, was comical.

The NFL shield and American football lines were still present, and the field looked like it was torn to pieces. The day before, Carson Wentz and Blake Bortles were tossing touchdown passes on the same patch of land talents like Harry Kane, Christian Eriksen, Sergio Aguero and David Silva were running on 24 hours later.

For Americans watching, it looked like an Oakland Athletics game at home at cavernous O.co Coliseum the day after the Raiders had battled the Broncos.

"It was…as raggedy as an under-funded high school, and still had the damn yard markers on display and everything," wrote local journalist Gavin Evans. "This amateurish-looking clownery was *not* the fault of poor scheduling… and instead appears to be a result of construction delays."

Evans is right, of course. Spurs and City were supposed to clash under the lights of new White Hart Lane, a towering complex that is due to seat 62,000, a 50%+ increase over its predecessor.

The last match Spurs played at old White Hart Lane was May 2017, after which the stadium closed its doors following the team's first undefeated season there in more than 50 years.

The new stadium was scheduled for completion ahead of the 2018-19 season. After one delay, Spurs were slated to open the new White Hart Lane on September 15, 2018 against Liverpool. That was the first weekend we would be in England on this trip, and we gave serious consideration to making the grand opening our first match.

Good thing we didn't. The opening was delayed yet again, due to supposed safety issues, to October. The club issued an announcement in mid-August:

"Delays are common, certainly for builds of this size and complexity. However, we are hugely frustrated that this has occurred at such a late stage. Whilst we would have been able to mitigate other areas, we simply cannot compromise safety. This decision was unavoidable."

Then, in October, the opening was delayed again until at least mid-January 2019. Don't hold your breath Spurs fans.

Yes, the new stadium is complex. It is large, state-of-the-art and has additional construction requirements like a retractable roof. With a large and lengthy NFL contract in place, the American football field requirements may have added some foreign elements to the construction plans as well.

But was everything affecting the delay unavoidable?

A scathing article in *The Telegraph* in September detailed some peripheral issues with on-site workers. Industry magazine *Construction News* issued accusations against Mace, a global consultancy and construction firm responsible for the building of White Hart Lane.

"There were people off their heads, drinking cans first thing in the morning before going on to site and snorting coke in the toilets."

The article continued, addressing communications issues:

"It is alleged that Mace's role as a construction manager, with subcontractors dealing directly with the club rather than answering to Mace themselves has contributed to a lack of co-ordination on the site of the stadium… leading to a source alleging 'what should take a week normally takes a month, because of the sheer scale of it, but also because the communication is horrendous.'"

These delays were both frustrating and somewhat embarrassing for Spurs. The club was forced to move numerous Premier League and Champions League matches back to Wembley. Even worse, a third-round League Cup match against Watford had to shift to Denbigh and Stadium MK, home of MK Dons, currently competing in League Two.

These construction delays exacerbated a growing, irritating situation with Spurs. The club is in the middle of its best stretch of top-flight finishes since the Bill Nicholson-led clubs that won Tottenham's last first division crown in 1960-61. That team, featuring the likes of Danny Blanchflower, Dave Mackay and John White, also won the FA Cup that season as Spurs became the first club to achieve the Double since Aston Villa in 1896-97.

In a four-year stretch, between 1959-60 and 1962-63, Spurs finished third, first, third and second, respectively. Nicholson won eight trophies in 16 years during Tottenham's golden age.

Under the guidance of Argentinian manager Mauricio Pochettino, Tottenham has finished third, second and third in the

Premier League the past three seasons, placing the team near the top of the table where they feel they belong.

More importantly, Spurs have finished ahead of hated rivals Arsenal the past two years, starting with 2016-17, when the club ended 22 straight years of St. Totteringham's Day, the unofficial holiday when Arsenal secures a higher finish than Tottenham.

Spurs have been the talk of the north London the past few years, yet no trophies have been hoisted, at White Hart Lane or otherwise. In fact, the club was again knocked out of the FA Cup semifinals in 2018. It was the eighth straight time Spurs were knocked out when reaching that far... and it was at Wembley.

Man City was dominant under Pep Guardiola last season and Jürgen Klopp has brought excitement back to Anfield. Chelsea has another first-year manager pushing the Blues to championship heights in Maurizio Sarri. Arsenal also has a new man in place, Unai Emery, who does not want the Gunners placing behind Tottenham for a third straight season.

With those clubs representing just a portion of the top-level competition, what did Spurs do in the offseason to keep pace?

Nothing.

For the first time since the present transfer window process was set in place ahead of the 2002-03 season, a Premier League club – Tottenham – did not add any players. Despite finishing 23 points behind City, in third place, Spurs opted not to improve the roster in any way, shape or form.

This inactivity on both the transfer and the construction front created a unique environment around the club heading into a season that still had high expectations for trophies. It could best be described as a malaise.

Pochettino has looked dismayed and disinterested at times. The Real Madrid job opened up in the fall with Los Blancos sacking new gaffer Julen Lopetegui. Despite signing a contract extension in May, Pochettino's name was immediately associated with the opening.

Meanwhile, his current club started the season about where it would expect to. Spurs picked up 15 points in its first seven matches, but did lose at Watford and at Wembley to Liverpool. Tottenham sat in fourth place, again hovering on the periphery of Premier League royalty, but not quite in the room.

Spurs had an inauspicious start to Champions League play. Last year, Tottenham was grouped with Real Madrid and Borussia Dortmund and given no chance of advancing out of the group, so the club promptly won it before getting knocked out by Juventus in the round of 16.

This year, despite being drawn with Barcelona and Inter Milan, Spurs were given a much better chance of advancement. They opened their campaign in Turin against Inter and suffered a disastrous result. Leading 1-nil thanks to a Christian Eriksen goal in the 53rd minute, Spurs appeared headed for a crucial three points on the road.

However, goals by Mauro Icardi in the 86th and Matias Vecino in extra time in the 92nd sent Pochettino and his club packing empty handed.

Two weeks later, on October 3rd, we were in London to see how Tottenham would respond in its next Champions League outing...

Against Barcelona...

And Messi.

We have seen enough soccer to understand and appreciate the different levels of play. We have covered high school soccer for more than a combined 30 years, collegiate soccer for more than 20, and have watched or covered various tiers of American soccer, from the United States Adult Soccer Association to the National Premier Soccer League to the United Soccer League and MLS.

We have seen many Premier League and EFL Championship matches. Over all these years, we have witnessed good soccer, bad soccer ad everything in between.

However, never before in person had we witnessed the likes of Barca.

You can hear about him, read about him and watch him on television, but seeing Lionel Messi – La Pulga – play live was an otherworldly experience.

Barca had already toyed with PSV Eindhoven in a 4-nil win to begin their own Champions League season, and manager Ernesto Valverde's club arrived in London with all the confidence you would normally expect from the perennial title contenders despite a poor recent run in La Liga play.

Getting to Wembley was an effort, with London's tube service strained to capacity for the massive match. Instead of getting there 90 minutes ahead of the match to have a pint with some friends, we got there 15 minutes before kickoff.

Americans have a strong point of reference for what constitutes massive crowds. Spend a fall Saturday in places like Ann Arbor, Michigan; State College, Pennsylvania; Columbus, Ohio and

Baton Rouge, Louisiana, and you know the feeling of more than 100,000 riled up fans ready to go for some college football.

That is how it felt to be outside Wembley, working our way in. Spurs fans were excited. They were ready to go. Barca supporters, known as Barcelonistas were noisy and boisterous. It was a glorious pre-match atmosphere.

Then the game started. Less than 90 seconds in, Spurs netminder Hugo Lloris, who had a dreary early start to the season off the field with a DUI in London in August, came out too aggressively to try an intercept a pass from Messi to Jordi Alba. The Spaniard calmly tucked it over to recent Liverpool expat Philippe Coutinho for the early Barca advantage.

The crowd was stunned. Annoyed. Pissed off.

"What was that shit Hugo?," belted a demoralized supporter a few rows over.

The first Barcelona goal was ugly. The second was simply divine.

Messi again figured into the sequence, sending a cross into the box to biter/crier extraordinaire Luis Suarez. He chested the ball down to Coutinho, whose attempt glanced off a Spurs defender. The ball caromed right back to Coutinho, who sent the ball back out to the top of the box to Ivan Rakitić. Without hesitating, the Croatian sent a laser just off the inside of the left post for a 2-0 lead in the 28th minute.

As the game progressed, Messi consistently showcased his otherworldly talents. His passes are crisp and always reach the intended target. His runs into space without the ball and his ability to create any space on the ball is incredible. There is nothing to say from an observer's perspective about Messi's play that has not been said before. It was simply a treat to watch him in action.

He started the second half with a fervor, hitting the left post twice in a four-minute span that let the Spurs fans around us know they might be lucky to get out of Wembley just surrendering four or five.

But Harry Kane, a man whose confidence as a striker matches his output, shocked Barca moments later by cutting back from his left to his right foot and sending a shot low and to the far post, past a diving Marc-André ter Stegen, cutting the lead in half.

However, just as Spurs supporters sat back down after celebrating their homegrown lad's retort, Messi responded again. Just four minutes after Kane's tally, Alba crossed a ball on the ground into the middle toward Suarez, who let it go through to a collapsing Messi for the 3-1 advantage.

The pace and technical skill were exhilarating. Every time it looked like Barca would make a mockery of the contest, Spurs responded. It was Erik Lamela's turn to answer in the 66th minute, beating ter Stegen with a deftly placed shot that deflected off Barca center back Clément Lenglet to again bring the match to reasonable terms.

Yet every time Spurs offered that flicker of hope, Messi squashed it with authority. In the 89th minute, Alba took possession of the ball and again sent it into the box to Suarez, who again let it go through to Messi. He had the easiest finish of the night to conclude affairs.

There was a mixture of responses from fans exiting Wembley into the warm October evening. Barcelonistas chanted and screamed and whistled and danced around with great merriment. Spurs fans simply looked exhausted.

Maybe they were tired from the club's ultimately futile performance against a world power...

Of course, they may also have been weary anticipating the long commute back home. Wherever that may be.

~BB

Brief History of Old White Hart Lane

While we join Spurs fans in anxiously awaiting the opening of new White Hart Lane, here lies the history of its old home.

Tottenham played at Northumberland Park until the refreshment stand accident on Good Friday 1898, in the match with Arsenal, forced the club to look elsewhere. Spurs found a solid plot of land behind White Hart Pub, located on Tottenham High Road. It had previously been a nursery owned by brewery chain Charringtons.

In 1904, the West Stand was built. A bronze cockerel was placed atop the stand at the end of the 1909-10 season in honor of Harry Hotspur, who was fond of cockfighting.

Profits obtained from the club's 1921 FA Cup win were used to build a split-level covered terrace at the Paxton Road end, and two years later, the Park Lane end was constructed. The East Stand followed in 1934. At that time, seating and terracing provided a capacity of 80,000.

During World War II, the ground was taken over by the government and turned into a factory for making gas masks, gunnery and protection equipment. From 1950 through 2017, except for the 1977-78 season, White Hart Lane hosted nothing but First Division matches.

Spurs went undefeated at White Hart Lane in the 1964-65 season, a feat they would repeat 52 years later. The club won both of its UEFA Cups at home. An Alan Mullery header clinched the inaugural 1972 competition against Wolves on 3-2 aggregate and, 12 years later, Tony Parks made two saves on penalties as Spurs defeated Anderlecht.

The stadium changed drastically over the years, with stands torn down and rebuilt, and the capacity eventually reduced to just over 36,000. With other powerful English clubs building new stadiums, Spurs decided to improve their ground as well, building a new facility right next to old White Hart Lane. It is scheduled to open ahead of the 2018-19 season, and will hold roughly 61,000.

Tottenham provided its fans with a final season to remember at White Hart Lane. Spurs went undefeated at home in league play, winning 17 and drawing two. The club defeated Arsenal at home, 2-0, at the end of April, to clinch a spot ahead of the Gunners for the first time in 22 seasons.

Brief History of Tottenham Hotpsur

Spurs were initially formed by 13-and-14-year-old schoolboys from Tottenham Grammar School and Saint John's Middle Class School in 1882. Legend has it they held discussions under a lamppost on Tottenham High Way, just 100 yards or so away from where White Hart Lane would be located when in it opened in 1899.

The team became popular quickly and played future bitter rivals Arsenal (then known as Woolwich Arsenal) in front of 14,000 at Northumberland Park on Good Friday in 1898. The refreshment stand collapsed under the weight of fans climbing on top it, and that day produced the desire to move to a new ground, eventually landing Spurs at White Hart Lane a year later.

The club turned professional at the end of 1895, and won its first league title, the Southern League, in 1900. Spurs followed that up with their first FA Cup win in 1901. As they were not yet in the Football League at the time, they became the only non-league side to win the cup when they defeated Sheffield United in a replay. Spurs have gone on to win eight FA Cups in its history, third behind Arsenal (13) and Manchester United (12).

Tottenham joined the Football League and won election to the Second Division in 1908-09 before immediately moving up to the First Division the following season. Following World War I, Spurs won the 1921 FA Cup over Wolves, and bounced between the top two divisions through the end of the 1940s. The hiring of Arthur Rowe as manager in 1949 sparked a Spurs revival.

Rowe won the Second Division in his first year, 1949-50, and his Spurs followed that up by winning the First Division crown in 1950-51. Future World Cup-winning manager Alf Ramsey and Bill Nicholson were on those teams. During Rowe's tenure, his clubs were known for their "push-and-run" style which involved players in triangles. One player quickly laid the ball off to a teammate and then ran past the marking tackler to collect the return pass. This effective and stylistic play became known as the Spurs Way.

The club finished second under Rowe in 1951-52. He would soon be forced to leave the club due to health concerns associated with the stress of managing the team. Spurs finished second again in 1956-57 under Jimmy Anderson, but it was the hiring of Nicholson early in the 1958 season that led to Spurs' greatest run. Tottenham won the league again in 1960-61, followed by another FA Cup title in 1962, and the UEFA Cup Winners' Cup in 1963. Nicholson's side also won the FA Cup in 1961, becoming the first team since Aston Villa in 1897 to win the double.

Jimmy Greaves scored the first goal of the 1962 FA Cup final victory. Greaves would go on to score a club-record 266 goals overall, 220 in league play. Greaves is the highest goal scorer in the history English top-flight football, with 357 goals scored for Spurs, Chelsea and West Ham.

Spurs won another FA Cup in 1967 with some younger players, including Steve Perryman, who would play in a club-record 655 matches over 19 seasons. The team won the 1971 League Cup when Martin Chivers recorded a brace in a 2-0 win over Villa, and again in 1973 in a 1-0 victory over Norwich City.

In between, the club won the first of two UEFA Cups (now Europa League) with a 3-2 aggregate victory over fellow English side Wolves.

Nicholson resigned early in the 1974-75 season, replaced by Keith Burkinshaw. The club was relegated to the Second Division after the 1976-77 season. The following year was the only season between 1949-50 and 2017-18 that Spurs were outside the top flight.

The early 1980s were notable because of Argentinian national team additions Osvaldo Ardiles and Ricardo Villa who, along with midfield stalwart Glenn Hoddle, led the club to FA Cup wins in 1981 over Man City and 1982 over QPR. In a sign of things to come, Irving Scholar floated the club on the London Stock Exchange in 1983, the first to do so. Spurs won the UEFA Cup in penalties over Anderlecht in 1984, its last European triumph.

Tottenham recorded its last FA Cup win in 1991. The club helped push the Premier League forward, as it was one of five teams that heavily favored the separation from the Football League. Top players Gary Lineker, Paul Gascoigne, David Ginola, Jurgen Klinsmann and Gareth Bale have starred for the club in the past 30 years, but the only new trophies have been the 1999 and 2008 League Cups.

However, under Argentinian coach Mauricio Pochettino, Spurs are currently undergoing a renaissance. The team has moved from sixth in 2013-14 to second in 2016-17, Tottenham's highest finish in the league since 1962-63, before adding a third-place finish in 2017-18. Harry Kane won the Premier League's Golden Boot two of the past three seasons and leads a cadre of young Spurs stars looking to win the club's first top-flight title since 1961-62.

North London Derby vs. Arsenal

Spurs have notable rivalries with other London clubs West Ham United and Chelsea, but it is the North London Derby against Arsenal that takes the prize. The two sides first faced each other in 1896 in the United League, and the first notable contest came in April 1898, when a scoreless draw played at Tottenham's Northumberland Park was attended by 14,000 people, and the refreshment stand collapsed when spectators climbed onto the roof. Some injuries occurred, and Spurs were forced to look for a new ground, eventually landing them at White Hart Lane a year later.

The first Football League match took place in December 1909, with Woolwich Arsenal (as the Gunners were known) winning, 1-0. The rivalry picked up when Arsenal moved from Manor Ground to Arsenal Stadium in Highbury, which was only four miles from White Hart Lane. Then, after World War I, the First Division was expanded to 22 teams, and the league voted on what two teams would be added. Chelsea was the first, and Arsenal, despite finishing fifth in the Second Division the previous season, was the second. The Gunners won an 18-8 vote over Spurs and have been in the First Division ever since.

The teams rarely played between 1928 and 1950, as Spurs spent all but two of those seasons in the Second Division. Relations between the two clubs improved immediately after World War II because Tottenham allowed Arsenal to play matches at White Hart Lane, as Highbury was requisitioned by the Air Raid Protection (APR) Station, and subsequently bombed.

Since 1950, however, the clubs have been in the same level every year except 1977-78, when Spurs were back in the Second Division. Since that first league match in 1909, Arsenal hold a 76-57 advantage, with 49 draws. The clubs split their league matches in 2017-18, each winning at home.

This is one of those rivalries where, when a player goes to the other side, he is ridiculed by his former club's supporters. The most famous example of this involves the last player to move from Spurs to Arsenal, defender Sol Campbell. After spending nine seasons with Tottenham, Campbell negotiated with the Gunners before joining the club ahead of the 2001-02 season. Over the next five seasons, whenever the two teams matched up, Campbell was referred to as 'Judas' by Spurs' faithful.

Around the same time, Arsenal owned the longest stretch over Spurs that either side has experienced in the rivalry. Tottenham won at White Hart Lane, 2-1, on November 7, 1999. The would go winless in the next 21 derby matches before winning again in January 2008.

Arsenal faithful have come to celebrate St. Totteringham's Day as the day each season when the Gunners cannot mathematically be caught by Spurs. They celebrated that day for 22 consecutive seasons until late April 2017, when a 2-0 win by Tottenham in the last North London Derby at old White Hart Lane clinched Spurs' place ahead of Arsenal for the season. Spurs have now finished ahead of Arsenal each of the past two seasons.

A lesser-known celebration occurs on April 14th, known as St. Hotspur Day, recognized as such for the club's 3-1 FA Cup semifinal over the Gunners in 1991. It was again celebrated on April 14, 2010, when Spurs defeated Arsenal in league play, 2-1.

2017-18 Season Review

The most common word describing Spurs' 2017-18 campaign was transition. Spending the season playing "home" matches at Wembley felt a bit off after a brilliant, undefeated run at home the final season at old White Hart Lane.

While construction continued on the club's new White Hart Lane, Spurs fell nine points off their 2016-17 finish to finish third in the table, but that was good enough to qualify for the Champions League for the third straight season.

Tottenham lost to Chelsea and drew Burnley for an inauspicious start at Wembley, but the team would only lose at their temporary home again one more time all season, in April to Manchester City.
Mauricio Pochettino's side had an undefeated six-match run early in the season, including an impressive 4-1 victory over visiting Liverpool, and posted an even more impressive run of 14 unbeaten in the middle of the season that established them back in the top four discussion. That run included home wins over Arsenal and Man U a draw on the road at Liverpool and a road win at Stamford Bridge over Chelsea.

A loss late in the season at West Brom threatened the club's top four standing, but wins at Wembley over Newcastle and Leicester to close the season confirmed a third-place showing.

Harry Kane led the club with 30 goals, finishing second in the league. Heung-min Son added 12 goals while midfield maestro Christian Eriksen had 10 goals and 10 assists. Goalkeeper Hugo Lloris tied for third in the league with 15 clean sheets.

Ajax transfer Davinson Sanchez helped offset the loss of Kyle Walker to Man City. He paired with Jan Vertonghen as a strong presence in the back, even with the prolonged absences of Toby Alderweireld and Danny Rose due to injuries. Spurs conceded just 36 goals, good for third in the league.

Despite drawing Real Madrid and Borussia Dortmund in its Champions League group, Spurs went undefeated to finish at the top of their table. They defeated Madrid at Wembley, 3-1, and won both home and away against Dortmund.

Tottenham then got Italian power Juventus in the Round of 16 and drew at Turin, 2-2. Son scored in the first half of the return match at Wembley, but Gonzalo Higuain and Paolo Dybala scored three minutes apart in the second half for Juventus to advance.

The team's stay in the League Cup was short-lived, with an unimpressive 1-0 win over Barnsley in the third round and an even more unimpressive 3-2 defeat to West Ham in the fourth round.

Spurs advanced much further in the FA Cup, albeit with much unnecessary difficulty. Tottenham defeated AFC Wimbledon before needing to go to replays to defeat Newport County and Rochdale in the fourth and fifth rounds, respectively. The team then blanked Swansea in the quarterfinals before falling to Manchester United in the semifinals, 2-1.

This marks the eighth straight time Spurs have lost when they have reached the FA Cup semifinals. The club has not won at this stage since a 3-1 victory over rival Arsenal in 1991, the last time Spurs won the FA Cup.

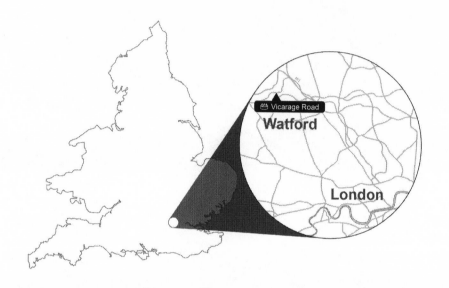

Watford FC

Year Founded: 1881

Colors: Red and Yellow

Nickname: The Hornets; The Golden Boys

Stadium: Vicarage Road

Address: Vicarage Rd., Watford, WD18 0ER, UK

Capacity: 21,000, 19th in Premier League

2017-18 Average Attendance: 20,181, 19th in Premier League

Trophies:

None

Current Ownership: Gino Pozzo, since June of 2012

Current Manager: Javier Gracia, 2nd season (4W, 8L, 3D)

2017-18 Finish: 14th in the Premier League, 11W, 19L, 8D

FA Cup: Lost at Southampton in the fourth round, 1-0.

League Cup: Lost vs. Bristol City in the second round, 3-2.

The Sports Tourists' Tips for Watford

Stay in London

Watford is close enough, 17 miles to central London that you can stay in the city and just take a train to get there. Watford itself is quaint, but with its proximity, and the convenience of transport, you might as well stay in the city, where there is much more to do.

Take the Right Train to Watford Junction

First, get to Euston, the train station hub where you will depart for Watford Junction. However, don't just rush to get on the first train available to Watford. There is a time-saving trick here. There are express trains that will go directly to Watford, a 20-minute ride, as opposed to some other trains that, due to many additional stops along the way, take more than an hour. Take five minutes to read the board at Euston, or ask their Customer Service desk, which is manned by knowledgeable, helpful, and pleasant staff.

Go to a Midweek Game at Vicarage Road

This was advice passed down to us -- go to Vicarage Road during a midweek night match. You will love it. And we did. Again, the convenience of getting to Watford, even during rush hour of the work week, combined with the intimate setting of 21,000 at the stadium, made a win over West Brom that much sweeter. Grab a burger at one of the outside vendors and enjoy the peaceful pace of the Hornets' supporters as they stroll on by.

Dance to "I Just Can't Get Enough"

Yes, this is the club that Sir Elton John built, but after a Hornets home win -- and they had their most top-flight home wins in 2016-17 in 30 years -- dance with the home faithful to Depeche Mode's "I Just Can't Get Enough." It has a great beat, and if you look carefully, you might see Troy Deeney shimmy once or twice. It may not be on the level of Sinatra's "New York, New York," or The Standells' "Dirty Water" in terms of closing out a home win, but Depeche Mode will have you in a joyous mood as you exit Vicarage Road.

Special Family Tip: Go See Harry Potter

Just four miles northeast of Vicarage Road lies Warner Brothers Studios Tour London (Studio Tour Drive, Leavesden, WD25 7LR), where you and your family can go on The Making of Harry Potter tour. The worldwide literary phenomenon sparked eight movies, and this lot tour takes you through sets, set props, original drawings and models, and much more. For anyone who loves the books, the movies, or both, and especially if you share a special connection with your children through these stories, take a bus or train from London and spend some time reliving memories. Grab some butterbeer ice cream at the café.

Our Watford Experience

The spokes of the City of London's giant wheel are many and extend in every direction.

The names of these supposedly sleepy suburbs read like tombstones in a graveyard, vaguely familiar for reasons you do not know. Forgotten pieces of your subconscious.

Reading. Woking. Stevenage. Luton. Wycombe. St. Alban's. Harrow. Guildford. Aldershot. Hempstead. Grays. Gilingham. Maidstone. Even Cambridge, Milton Keynes and Oxford.

All have their own history and uniqueness. The people who live there certainly don't see themselves as an afterthought. But to the cruel eye of the traveler, these hundreds of specks on a map - so close to the real action of London - are easily forgotten.

Their only recognition is often a quick glance at a block of nondescript homes from the window of a speeding train on its way to somewhere more important.

Because of England's football tradition, each of these towns typically has its own football club. But the reality of the Premier League is that it's only reserved for the big players, the big money. And so those names pop up here and there in a mid-round FA Cup game, but are quickly forgotten again.

Except one…

Of the hundreds of London suburbs, only one can claim Premier League football:

Watford FC.

What makes the hamlet of Watford so different from all these other football commuter towns?

The truth is, not much from a city perspective. There's a High Street and a Market Street, like everywhere. There's a sparkling new mall and construction popping up all over as you walk from one side of town to the other in just about 15 minutes. The spill off of London money and jobs is present in the headquarters of JD Wetherspoon and the UK headquarters of Hilton, Total Oil and Costco. There's an old church and an old graveyard, like any English town. And a bustling class of foreign-born citizens too.

But there's no unique vibe, no discerning feature that would make Watford different from any other.

Except its football team. In fact, Watford's presence in the Premier League *is* the unique feature of this town. The miracle of Premier League participation is enough in and of itself. Watford has fought its way back up to the top level three times in the last 20 years.

But on a blindingly sunny September Saturday, after the first international break of the season, Watford weren't just in the Premier League – they were on top of it.

After a home upset of Tottenham a fortnight before, the Hornets had picked up every single point possible to start the year. Four wins from four. Only Liverpool and Chelsea had matched them. And only goal differential kept Watford technically behind those two giants.

Still the Hornets were two points ahead of one of the world's most heralded teams, Manchester City. And on this day, Watford was hosting 10th-place Manchester United and its embattled manager, Jose Mourinho. It was a moment this club and its fans relished. The possibilities seemed infinite. And the atmosphere in the town rose to the occasion.

Already bustling on a market Saturday, the yellow and black vertical striped jerseys were everywhere, sparkling in the sun. Steel drums played, kids laughed and young men paraded in the middle of the street. They drank beers and acted out for reasons they didn't understand. Excitement and hormones are a potent mix.

The NBC Sports crew was in the house too. After Watford's hot start, the game was moved to a primetime 5:30 p.m. British Standard Time start – the last game of a day that began with Tottenham-Liverpool at Wembley Stadium, just a few miles south.

Hopes were high and the current run of success was all down to the man in charge – Javier Gracia. The Spaniard's name looks in need of an autocorrect, but in fact it is Gr – not the standard Garcia. He was the first manager to end one season and start the next at Watford in eight years. And his methods were clearly paying off.

Before the match he was honored as the Premier League's Manager of the Month for August. He'd started the same lineup in all four matches to start the season, including playing two strikers up front, in what seems a novelty now in the Premier League – especially for so-called foreign coaches.

Those two strikers, Watford's stalwart captain and fan favorite Troy Deeney, and Andre Gray, were perhaps in the best form of their lives. Both players have bulked up at times in their careers. The Andre Gray we saw at Burnley two seasons ago was full of graft, but didn't quite have enough speed or guile to get by

Manchester United's last defenders. This season he looked trim and at the races going forward.

Deeney has a reputation for being a brute strength type of striker and has had well-publicized battles with his weight. But under Gracia, he was still running, still battling for a full 90 minutes.

M1 Derby vs. Luton Town

Although the Hatters have been the lower ranked team (they currently reside in League One of English football after winning promotion with a second place finish in League Two in 2017-18. Luton Town leads Watford in the series history, 36-28, with 23 draws.

The clubs are 19 miles apart via the M1 Highway, with places like Slip End, Elmstead and Redbourn between them. Although Watford won the first match between the clubs in 1885, the first official results came when they met in Division Three South twice in four days in March 1921. They met 35 times in that division between 1921-1937, with one FA Cup clash in there, and the Hatters held the slight edge at that time.

It would take more than 26 years before the teams faced each other again, in October 1963, as Luton Town remained in a higher division the entire time. The rivalry picked up the pace when the clubs were ascending toward the First Division at the end of the 1970s, into the 1980s. In First and Second Division games and a handful of FA Cup matches, between 1979-1988, Luton Town held a decided 14-6 edge, with four draws.

This is a quieter rivalry, as only some reports of hooliganism in the late 1960s grace its history. More importantly, with Luton Town's drop in levels, the teams have not met since 2006, when both clubs were in the Championship for one season.

It's not easy for a coach to come in and make an impact on a group of players when so many others have come and gone so quickly. There are now 100 pounds per minute fines for players who arrive late to training. Extracurricular fitness measures like yoga are required. Gracia had established a rules-based order and accountability around the club. And he is going to stick to it, no matter what the situation.

Gracia cut his teeth in La Liga, bouncing around from Almeria to Osasuna to Malaga. He played in Spain as well at six different clubs, with 106 appearances at Real Sociedad and 100 at Athletic

Bilbao. Before he moved to Watford, he was managing Rubin Kazan in the Russian League.

La Liga writer Guillem Balague described Gracia like this on *Goal.com.*

"However, while Gracia may seem mild-mannered and softly spoken, this is a man who hails from Pamplona, where running through narrow streets in front of a host of fairly cheesed-off bulls is considered to be an annual rite of passage for testosterone-fueled males.

Indeed, when asked about whether he was afraid of failure after taking the Rubin job, Gracia replied, 'We run in front of bulls; what is there to fear anywhere else?'"

Defender Craig Cathcart told *The Telegraph*, "If you don't do yoga you get fined – which some of the lads aren't happy about – but these are things to help us."

"He's really humble. Even if you are not in the team no one is complaining because you know the manager is doing his best and he's a nice guy. You can talk to him and there's no problem to knock on his door and ask 'what can I do to get in the team?' Everyone respects him and I think that comes from how he respects every player. That's the way you want a manager to be. The squad seems to be a lot tighter-knit this season."

Gracia gained trust from his players after taking over at a low moment for the club in the 2017-18 season. After a flying start under coach Marco Silva, a surprisingly hot commodity hired from Hull after he couldn't save them from relegation, things went sour quickly.

Silva, by most accounts, was approached by Everton to replace Sam Allardyce in midseason and seemed eager to leave. Watford put a stop to it, but clearly something caused a distraction. Watford lost eight of its next 11 games, winning just one during that stretch. The early season's star man, Richarlison, scored five goals in his first 12 games, and then failed to score again.

Silva was eventually fired for his wayward eye on January 21. The situation has only gotten more acrimonious as Everton quickly hired Silva in the summer, then plucked Richarlison away as well.

Watford has demanded punishment from the Premier League for Everton's "tapping up" of Silva. Tapping up means they approached him while under contract at another club without the club's permission. The Silva distraction nearly got the Hornets relegated. The club's officials have said a fine isn't good enough

– they want points deducted as Everton's overtures took away from their own results as well.

Amidst the drama, it was the little-known Gracia who was brought in to stop the rot in the season's backstretch. His personal relationship with Watford director Gino Pozzo helped him get his foot in the door. In fact, Pozzo had nearly chosen Gracia over Silva in the first place.

The club's performance, while not always pretty, kept Watford up with 15 points and just five losses in the last four months. It was enough to take Watford just over the mythical 40-point line and a 14th place finish. And it was enough to give Gracia a full summer to prepare, the first Watford manager afforded that luxury in eight years.

That faith had clearly been justified as here we were; a full month into the season and Watford was playing meaningful football against world-class opponents.

As I walked into the Red Lion Pub directly across the street from Vicarage Road, I spotted a guy in full Boston Red Sox regalia.

There's something about traveling to a foreign country and seeing a resident of that country who's clearly a fan of an American sports team that warms your heart. Apparently, my Troy Deeney jersey made him feel the same way.

We traded compliments on our way into the pub and the next thing we knew, our new mate Mark bought our first round, introduced us to his friends and we started discussing all things sport and Watford.

Mark was a lifelong Watford fan – even though he hailed from Croydon, just a stone's throw from Selhurst Park, the home of Crystal Palace.

Clearly, the hullabaloo around Palace his whole life had turned Mark off rather than on. He despised Palace, and in recent years he had even more reason to.

Palace's Wilfried Zaha is public enemy No. 1 in Watford after his dive, according to Watford fans, earned Palace a penalty and the only goal in the 2013 Championship playoff final at Wembley, keeping a strong Watford squad down for one more year.

The Hornets came up two seasons later, but Zaha's alleged transgression hasn't been forgotten. Just last April, Zaha was booked for diving at Watford. And he was pilloried on Boxing Day 2016 by Watford's mascot, Harry the Hornet, who walked up behind him then dramatically flopped to the ground like a fish out of water after Zaha had earlier been booked for diving.

It was reminiscent of some of the best American mascots antics, like the San Diego Chicken or the Philly Phanatic. But, in England, outside of Watford, the act was met with anger, especially at Palace. Then Palace coach Sam Allardyce called it "out of order." And current coach Roy Hodgson, when asked about the mascot's antics at the beginning of this season, called him "disgraceful."

Brief History of Vicarage Road

Vicarage Road opened in 1922, with an August match against Millwall. The Hornets had previously played at Cassio Road. With a capacity of just 21,000, it is the second smallest in the Premier League, but it fits its role as a community ground perfectly. The ground quietly emerges while walking up Vicarage Road, is easily accessible, and provides a quality viewing experience from any of its four stands.

Watford made the intimate locale a place to be in the late 1970s through the 1980s, as the club won its way into the First Division for the first time. The stadium has been completely revamped since then, which came after the club's emergence as a top side. The Vicarage Road Stand and Rookery Stand are two former terrace areas that were updated in the 1990s following the Taylor Report, which required all-seater stadiums.

The Graham Taylor Stand, so named in honor of the Hornets' long-time successful manager, is an upgrade of the Shrodells Stand, which was an upgrade of the Union Stand that came over to Vicarage Road from Cassio Road. It is the only two-tiered stand in the stadium. The Rookery stand is where the home fans sit and where we sat for our Saturday afternoon vs. Manchester United. The crowd is loud and passionate and close to the field. There isn't a bad view in this whole stadium.

The most recently upgraded stand is the Sir Elton John Stand, which opened in December 2014. Named for the club's long-time owner and chairman, the stand sits across the way from the Graham Taylor Stand. Lyrics from John's hit "Your Song" can be seen on the wall from the opposite stand.

Harry the Hornet was a big topic of conversation pregame at the Red Lion, or at least, the man inside the suit, lifelong Watford fan Gareth Evans. Just two days before the Manchester United match, Evans stepped down as Harry, a role he'd carried on for 10 years.

Harry would go on, but Evans would go back to his seat in the Rookery End with the rest of the Watford hardcore.

But talk mostly centered around the day's opponent, Manchester United, and their cavalcade of stars. After beating Tottenham, Watford's fans were in no mood to concede ground and you could feel the belief growing as we walked into the ground.

Unfortunately, Manchester United came in like a wounded animal in a corner as well, after a series of negative results and a number of unpleasant press conferences from manager Jose Mourinho. A win was necessary for the Mancs men and they used their talent to take control of the game early.

After a great shot by Deeney forced a save from United's David DeGea, it was one-way United traffic. Ashley Young, a former Watford youth player, was booed with every touch. But he began exerting his influence on the game with his passing ability.

Yet Gracia's men were organized. The central defenders, Cathcart and Christian Kabasele, blocked shots and used their smarts to intervene before world class players like Alexis Sanchez, Paul Pogba and Romelu Lukaku could shift into goal scoring mode.

The real hero though, was veteran goalkeeper Ben Foster, who denied both Sanchez and Pogba at close range in the first 20 minutes.

Unfortunately, unless Watford began to control the ball and press forward, the dam would eventually break. And in the 35th minute, break it did. Young, a recent World Cup starter, sent yet another inviting cross that eluded Watford's defenders, dinked off Lukaku's chest and in. Three minutes later, defender Chris Smalling was allowed to settle the ball off his chest, swivel and finish the volley for a 2-nil lead.

Another wonder save by Foster on Pogba at point blank range saved the game from being out of reach before the half.

For all their grit and endeavor, the Hornets were down two goals. The fans' disappointment was evident. My new mate Mark came and found me near the beer stand, right as I listened to a group of friends laugh at their mate for his halftime commentary.

"If it hadn't been 1-nil, it wouldn't be 2-nil." It sounded simple, but he was right. The first goal gave United the impetus for the second.

By the start of the second half, the steam had blown off and the positive support was back in full force. And the fans were quickly

2017-18 Season in Review

The Hornets season started sweetly, but quickly went sour, forcing yet another change at head coach.

Portuguese coach Marco Silva took over in the summer and Watford looked to have a platform to move forward as a club. Already, it was the club's third straight season at the top level, something they hadn't accomplished since Graham Taylor's reign in the 80s.

Thanks to signings like Tom Cleverley and Brazilian striker Richarlison, the Hornets got off to a flying start, earning a 3-3 draw with Liverpool on opening day and a stoppage time win over Arsenal on a Cleverley goal. With that win in mid-October, Watford sat in fourth place. But things started to go downhill from there.

Somewhere along the way, Everton reached out to Silva, looking to replace its coach, Ronald Koeman. Watford objected and refused to let go of Silva, but the team's performance dropped. Richarlison had five goals by November, but failed to score again.

The club lost 11 of its next 16 games after the Arsenal victory, winning only twice more before Silva was fired for his wayward eye and the distraction it caused. Enter Javi Gracia, a relatively unknown quantity. The Spaniard was hired in late January with the Hornets in 10th place and rapidly fading from the European positions.

A 4-1 win over Chelsea in his second game in charge helped, but the results never really improved and Watford used its hot early start to hang onto a disappointing 14th place finish, enough for Gracia to keep his job heading into the summer – the first for a Watford coach in eight years.

Powerful midfielder Abdoulaye Doucoure started all but two Premier League games and led the team in scoring with seven goals, earning the club's Player of the Year honors.

rewarded. Abdoulaye Doucoure drove at the United defense, pushing them back towards the end line before cutting the ball back for the wide-open Gray. His finish made it 2-1 and the Rookery end went berserk.

The ruckus celebration of jumping and shouting and hugging and highfiving had me seeing stars by the end. The excitement was literally concussive. And it willed the Watford players forward. I've only been in that situation a couple of times and it's amazing. You can feel the home end sucking the players toward the goal in front of them. The energy was unbelievable.

United staggered under the sound of Vicarage Road. And after a meaty challenge from Nemanja Matic on Watford's Will Hughes drew a second yellow and the red card ejection, Watford went all out for the point to keep their unbeaten streak alive.

It almost worked as Kabasele won a header off Hughes' free kick delivery in the dying minutes, only to see De Gea paw it away with an outstretched arm. Heads went in hands in the Rookery End, but only briefly. The applause for the home effort was lusty and the players' appreciation was equal, despite their disappointment at getting nothing in spite of their second half effort.

As Mark and I walked down the road back to the Red Lion, one veteran supporter remarked to no one in particular.

"Head up lads, we've just dropped our first points of the season to United at home – *and we expected to win.*"

Other heads nodded in agreement. Watford was living in a new world.

Back at the pub, my new friend and I threw back a few more beers. Mark told me he'd been to all 92 Football League stadiums, quite a feat. I asked him his favorites – Villa Park in Birmingham was his choice. Though he mentioned there's nothing like a roast pork bap (sandwich) from Barnsley.

Then I asked him the big question, one pertinent for American fans everywhere. Why Watford? I understood his disdain for his neighborhood club, Palace. (They weren't liked at Arsenal and Brighton either.)

But why choose Watford over all the other clubs?

"It's a bit easy to root for a team like United, isn't it?" Mark said. "This club won my heart because it doesn't come easy. You have to earn it at Watford, even with everything against you."

The Hornets had certainly earned it to this point of the season. Mark and his mates were hoping for more, but even if they didn't get it, they'd still hold their heads high at Vicarage Road. For now, Watford FC was still the exception to the rule – the only London suburb with Premier League football.

~BM

Brief History of Watford FC

Formed as Watford Rovers in 1881, the club came about through a group of teenagers who wanted to have organized matches at nearby Cassiobury Park. The club became fully professional and joined the Southern League in 1896-97. They were successful early, winning six league titles by 1914-15.

Watford moved to Vicarage Road, its current home, in 1922. After the Southern League moved to the Football League in 1920, the club spent nearly 40 years in Division Three South, finishing as high as fourth three times, including three straight seasons from 1936-37 through 1938-39. Tommy Barnett was a notable goal scorer on those early Watford sides, tallying 144 league goals and 163 overall in 442 appearances between 1928-39.

Cliff Holton scored 105 goals for Watford, including 42 league and 48 overall in the 1959-60 season, both club records. That performance helped bring the club up from the newly-formed Fourth Division, back to the Third Division. At the end of the 1960s, Watford moved up to the Second Division for the first time.

By 1975-76, the Hornets had dropped back down to the Fourth Division. Three individuals changed the fortunes of the team at this time. Singer Elton John purchased the club and became chairman in 1976. A year later, he appointed Graham Taylor, formerly of Lincoln City, as manager. And, Luther Blissett, who joined the team in 1975, emerged as a bona fide star.

Blissett, a Jamaican-born striker who would notch 14 caps for England's national team, went on to score 186 goals in 503 appearances over three stints with Watford, both club records. His first run with the Hornets, which lasted until 1983, coincided with the team's first foray into the top flight. Ross Jenkins scored 142 goals for the club over an 11-year period that culminated in the team's second-place finish, behind Liverpool, in its first year in the top flight in 1982-83.

As Taylor and Blissett led the team from Fourth-to-First Division in a five-year span, another young star joined the club near its apex. John Barnes, another Jamaican-born prodigy, debuted for the Hornets in 1981 at the age of 17 and scored 85 goals in six years, before joining Liverpool and winning two First Division titles with the Reds.

In addition to the rise to the First Division, Watford also made its first appearance in the FA Cup final in 1984, losing to Everton, 2-0. The Hornets also made their only appearance in Europe, at the UEFA Cup. They defeated Kaiserslautern and Levski Sofia before losing in the third round to Sparta Prague.

Taylor departed for Aston Villa in 1987, the same year Barnes left for Liverpool. The following season, the Hornets were relegated to the Second Division, and dropped another level before Taylor rejoined the club in 1997 for another historic four-year run. Hired again by John after he had purchased the club for a second time, Taylor led the club to two promotions in two years. Watford made its Premier League debut in 1999-2000. The Hornets finished last and Taylor left after the 2000-2001 season with a club-record 353 victories.

Watford spent 14 of the next 15 seasons in the Championship, emerging just once, under manager Aidy Boothroyd, to play in the Premier League in 2006-07. Led by Troy Deeney's 21 league goals, the Hornets finished second in the Championship in 2014-15 to earn automatic promotion to the Premier League for a third time, and the club managed to stay up for the first time.

Deeney, who has been with Watford since 2010, is the fourth Hornets player to reach the century mark. He has scored 113 goals in his career for the club going into the 2018-19 season.

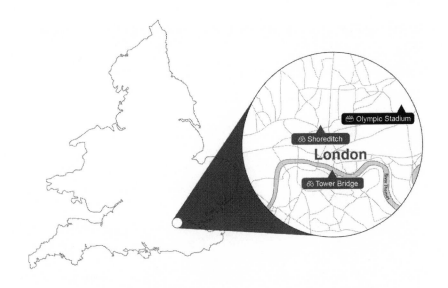

West Ham United

Year Founded: 1900

Colors: Claret and Blue

Nickname: The Irons; The Hammers

Stadium: London Stadium

Address: Queen Elizabeth Park, London, E20 2ST, UK

Capacity: 60,000, 4th in Premier League

2017-18 Average Attendance: 56,896, 4th in Premier League

Trophies:

FA Cup (3): 1964, 1975, 1980

European Cup Winners' Cup (1): 1965

Current Ownership: David Sullivan

Current Manager: Manuel Pellegrini, 1st season

2017-18 Finish: 13th in Premier League, 10W, 16L, 12D

FA Cup: Lost in fourth round at Wigan, 2-0

League Cup: Lost in quarterfinals, 1-0, at Arsenal

The Sports Tourists' Tips for West Ham United

How to Get Tickets

In order to purchase a home ticket, you'll need to be a Claret member first, which cost 40 pounds in 2018-19. Keep in mind that every ticket must go to a member. So even if one person is a member, they can't buy four tickets unless the other three people are also members.

The good news is, with so many seats at the London Stadium, you shouldn't have a problem finding a game with tickets available. Certain London contests and games against the big clubs like Man United and Liverpool, or the FA Cup, will be harder. For Chelsea, a crosstown rival, we still found three seats in the same section, albeit not in the same row.

Skip the Pub… Just go straight to the Stadium

Yes the London Stadium is not Upton Park. But it is a modern stadium built for major events like the Olympics. Everything you need to get a ready for a game is right outside the stadium. Dozens of food options and places to buy beer and drinks. It being the main venue for the Summer Olympics, the walkways are big, wide-open thoroughfares with lots of space to hang out, catch up with friends and enjoy the pre-game atmosphere. It's also very busy at ticketing windows, so make sure you get there early to pick up your tickets, then grab a pint.

If You're Going to the Pub, Go to the Carpenter's Arms

It's a decent hike from the Olympic Park, so make sure you don't get caught short. Have your ticket ahead of time and leave when you see everyone else leaving. Or better yet, go after the game. It's all West Ham fans; so don't go to cause trouble if you're an away fan. But if you're a West Ham supporter, come on in, buy someone a drink and have a great time. On a sunny day, the patio is hopping.

Lots of funky places to eat in Shoreditch

Our favorite was The Cereal Killer, a retro café in the Shoreditch neighborhood that serves cereal of all kinds. In fact, almost any cereal you can think of, they have. You can mix and match with all kinds of additional toppings. Downstairs the "benches" are actually kids' beds with cartoon sheets from the 80s. It's a trip down memory lane for anyone of a certain age – like us – where Saturday was about cartoons and cereal.

Voodoo Ray's Pizza

One thing about traveling anywhere in the world is that you can generally always find a decent slice of pizza somewhere. And if you know ahead of time, which pizza is good and which is bad, it will make your trip a whole lot easier. Trust us, being able to dig into a familiar slice is comforting on the road. Voodoo Ray's is that slice of pizza in East London amongst a lot of wannabes. There's a location in the Shoreditch Box Park, a unique shopping plaza right next to a graffiti decorated set of 5-on-5 soccer fields more than a city block large. There is also a location in Camden Town, where you can grab a slice after seeing a concert.

When in Rome...

When attending a game inside the London Stadium, you need to prepare to act how everyone in your section is acting. If they are singing and standing, then feel free to sing and stand and express yourself. But if you end up in a quieter, seated section, be respectful of the people near you and stay a bit more low-key. Be aware of your surroundings and act accordingly.

Our West Ham Experience

When we last visited the London Stadium, West Ham United was mired in a late season relegation battle. The play on the field was scrappy under battling coach Slaven Bilic and there was no real obvious hope for an infusion of talent.

It all played out seemingly a mile away in the upper level of the former Olympic Stadium. The locals, with nearly a full season of the cavernous stadium under their belts, treated their mostly antiseptic new home with a mixture of boredom and anger. It was safe to say everyone missed Upton Park.

Last season, the second in the former showcase stadium of the 2012 London Olympics, was a nadir for the club and its owners, David Gold and David Sullivan, who bought the team in 2010. And during a 3-0 loss to Burnley in March, the fans boiled over. Ugly scenes from England's recent past flashed on the screen once again. Fans in the stands surrounded the owner's box in a threatening manner, hurling projectiles. Captain Mark Noble wrestled his own supporters on the pitch to prevent further vandalism. The corner flag was ripped out and paraded around in an aggressive fashion.

The supporters' complaints were plentiful. And the opponent, Burnley, didn't help. While West Ham had spent gobs of money trying to reach Europe and failed, Burnley accomplished the feat with a threadbare lineup and barely any spending. The difference was leadership.

But the main argument around the ground was more about the stadium's atmosphere and how that affected the club's soul, not necessarily the team's record. The pitch was far away from the stands. Seating had been shuffled since the club left Upton Park in 2016. Sometimes the problem was, simply, some people wanted to sit and watch the game, some wanted to stand and sing. That's why the supporters' section in most stadiums is in one end, for the most enthusiastic. At the London Stadium, it was in scattered pockets.

All in all, the deal to move into the stadium was a bonus to West Ham United from the owners' standpoint. The club only ponied up 15 million pounds – just 5.5% of the 272 million pound cost to convert the stadium for soccer. That's not even including the multi-billion pound cost to build it originally.

Those savings gave West Ham the flexibility to spend money on players, a luxury Mauricio Pochettino does not have right now as Tottenham builds a brand-new White Hart Lane. Nor did Arsene Wenger have the same fiscal flexibility when Arsenal was building the Emirates. With a virtually no-money down commitment, West Ham can improve its talent and open a new stadium at the same time. Or so the theory went.

Both of the two coaches mentioned competed or are competing for trophies while moving in. West Ham has not.

But sometimes you get what you pay for. And part of the Irons' sweetheart deal meant the club didn't have to pay for maintenance or security of the stadium.

As a result the stadium's employees work for the London Metropolitan Authority, the group charged with running the stadium for owners E20, LLP. Incidentally, E20 LLP is facing financial insolvency, in part because of the ill-advised deal they made with West Ham, likely leading them to pay bottom dollar for workers, like the stewards and gate staff.

Scuffles between fans and stewards were common in the first two years of the London Stadium. Usually because they were being asked to sit down when they wanted to stand. A West Ham United employee would've understood how to defuse the situation.

On our trip to Stamford Bridge, we observed a top-notch steward put out fires quietly all evening without causing a ruckus. He talked to people, politely but firmly, he moved around the crowd and most importantly, he had CFC and a Chelsea logo tattooed on his neck. He was one of them. The cheaply hired London Stadium staff were most definitely not "one of them" to Irons fans.

On our day out at London Stadium, a miserably rainy Sunday contest against that same Chelsea team, we encountered some clueless organization from the London Stadium staff outside. To print our will call tickets, we were directed to one line. Once in the line, we were told we had to go to another window halfway around the stadium.

When we got to that line, we waited 20 minutes before the woman at the window told us the other window was the right place after all and we should've stayed there. She put us in a line off to the side to wait for her to print the tickets. Time ticked on.

The Dockers Derby vs. Millwall

Fans who have seen the movie *Green Street Hooligans* will have a small inkling of the ferocity and violence associated with this game between two teams founded on the East London docks.

Named the No. 1 rivalry in London football by *The Telegraph*, and perhaps the most notorious in all of England, it started as a rivalry between two factions of dockworkers. Millwall's faction centered on the Isle of Pigs and eventually, just south of the River Thames in the Surrey docks. West Ham supporters were based on the northern, Royal Docks.

The violence was on the field mostly in the early days as the teams met 60 times in 16 years from the first game in 1899 in the Southern League, with Millwall largely getting the better of it. Things heated up after a 1926 dockers' strike in which Millwall-affiliated workers crossed the line and went to work, sparking outrage the West Ham fans still sing about to this day.

In the 60s, the two clubs' fans became proxies in a notorious London gang war, with the Kray brothers (played by Tom Hardy in the movie *Legend)* supported by West Ham fans and South London's Richardson gang supported by Millwall.

In the 1970s and 80s, as hooliganism rose in England, these two clubs were at the center of it, with a stabbing death in 1975 and a riot almost every time they played.

The two have played only seven times in the new millennium, and only 11 times since 1990, due to rarely playing in the same division. But in August 2009, some of the worst violence in recent memory happened at a Millwall-West Ham League Cup game, with riot police called in both outside and inside the stadium as planned fights harkened back to the hooligan days, and another fan was stabbed.

Millwall leads the overall series with 38 wins to West Ham's 34 in 99 matchups. Interestingly, only once has one done the double over the other in the same Football League season when West Ham won both First Division meetings in 1918-19.

The match had already begun. Every single person in line around us had suffered the same fate.

None of the workers involved wore West Ham colors or West Ham branded shirts. They were strictly London Stadium employees unaware of the rush of football fans at the start of a game. Despite all their fancy equipment, these folks could've learned a thing or two from the older local ladies at Burnley, who got things sorted quickly with a far less modern will call booth. A little bit of coordination and understanding goes a long way.

Off to that kind of disastrous start, in that kind of weather, we held our breath for the mood inside. What we found was a pleasant surprise.

Our seats were behind the net in the end where West Ham would shoot in the first half. The crowd around us was lively, throwing in a couple more versions of the Irons' anthem "I'm Forever Blowing Bubbles," which made up for the pregame version we missed in the ticket line.

Even better, from our row up, everyone was standing. Below us were plenty of seated people. But no one was bothered either way.

"We've sorta figured it out," the middle-aged woman next to us said. "The people who want to sit, sit together. And the people who want to stand find a place too."

And it's true, we didn't see any of the unrest from last season or our previous visit. The crowd was excited, loud and under control at the same time. And there were more of them. The man next to me was a Cockney who moved to Sweden nearly 30 years ago.

"At Upton Park, it was really hard for me to get tickets. Especially to come all that way," he told me. "This is only my 20-year old's second game. It's not the same atmosphere as I grew up with. But there's more tickets available."

According to West Ham United's own internal figures, the club now has 52,000 season ticket holders. That's over 15,000 more people than could fit in Upton Park.

All of this was part of the plan for West Ham, to make them a big club, in terms of spending, stadium size – and hopefully, trophies as well.

That didn't always come off in the last couple years, but this offseason was perhaps the best of the Gold/Sullivan era. And maybe the pressure from the fans last season was necessary, who knows?

Last year, the club signed flamboyant striker Marko Arnautovic from Stoke City for 24 million pounds. He flattered to deceive under Bilic, but started to thrive later in the year under Scot David Moyes.

This offseason Arnautovic was joined by Brazilian Felipe Anderson, an immensely talented attacking midfielder signed from Lazio for 36 million pounds, the club's transfer record.

Brief History of the London Stadium

After 112 years in the unfriendly confines of Upton Park, also known as the Boleyn Ground, West Ham United is starting its second season in the spacious new London Stadium.

Originally called the Olympic Stadium, the gigantic arena was built for the 2012 London Olympics. The opening and closing ceremonies were staged there. And the Olympic-sized track hosted all of 2012's track and field events, including Usain Bolt's record-breaking performance, and Brit Mo Farah's 5000m and 10,000m double victory.

After the Olympics, West Ham was part of a bidding process to procure the stadium for football use. The Hammers beat out Tottenham for the right to call London Stadium home, leading to Tottenham's decision to rebuild and expand White Hart Lane.

West Ham shares the stadium with Great Britain Track and Field. So while the London Legacy Development Corporation spent over 272 million pounds to make the stadium more attractive for football, West Ham can't take the track away. And that adds a lot of distance between the stands and the field.

The stadium cost over 700 million pounds to build. But West Ham only had to pay 15 million pounds of the conversion cost – and a rent of 2.5 million pounds a year. If the Irons are relegated, the rent payments are cut in half, to 1.25 million pounds a year. If the club were sold any time in the first 10 years of the lease, West Ham would owe an undisclosed one-off repayment to the LLDC, who own the stadium.

The London Stadium boasts a football capacity of 60,000, now the third largest in the Premier League. However, it is built in a deep bowl and has the track attached, making fans in the higher rows feel too far away.

Many fans have complained about the lack of atmosphere and noise, especially when compared to years at Upton Park. But the modern touches are impressive, with food and drink options ringing the spacious area outside the stadium. On top of that, the closest London Underground station, Stratford, gets 58 trains an hour coming in on game days, easing the flow of traffic.

Ukrainian winger Andriy Yarmolenko, long sought after by Premier League teams, joined from Borussia Dortmund for 17.5 million pounds.

Out went seemingly bargain basement coach Moyes and in came Manuel Pellegrini. The Chilean won the league with Man City then gracefully managed his exit after Pep Guardiola's hire made him a lame duck. Since then, Pellegrini had been in China, but he resurfaced in East London for a reported seven million pound yearly salary.

Clearly, West Ham was going all in. But the season started about as disastrously as our attempts to enter the London Stadium. The Irons lost their first four league games and were facing a road trip to Everton that could mean a fifth straight loss – the worst start to a campaign in West Ham history.

The fans were getting anxious. The new signings weren't firing. And after the Everton game loomed home contests with Chelsea and Manchester United. Could West Ham be buried in the relegation zone by the end of October – and after spending nearly 100 million pounds this summer?

It certainly seemed possible. But before the Everton match, Pellegrini wasn't panicking.

"Doubt my methods?" Pellegrini asked in a press conference. "No. I always trust in what I do because I have 35 years in this."

In the locker room however, lifelong Hammer Noble jumped on his team after the previous loss to Wolves. *The Guardian* reported:

"The club captain watched from the bench at the London Stadium and he felt an obligation to shake things up after witnessing another leggy performance. Noble's anger filled the home dressing room and the worst part for the rest of the squad was that they could not argue with the midfielder's criticism."

Whatever happened, it worked. He watched as West Ham stormed Goodison Park, dominated Everton and walked out 3-1 winners. Arnautovic shined at every turn. Yarmolenko scored his first goal for the club – and then his second. Arnautovic sealed it with a third after unselfishly setting up Yarmolenko's first.

According to the coolly confident Pellegrini, the win was always in the bag.

"I was very confident before the match that we would get the result we needed at Goodison Park. I had seen the confidence and belief in the players on the training pitch, along with their desire to give a reaction after the defeat against Wolves here in our previous match," Pellegrini wrote in the match day program for our visit against Chelsea.

"I also said before the game last week that it was important that we all continue to trust in the project that everyone at the club has invested in. Much was said and written during the two-week international break, but we must not concern ourselves with external pressures. I put pressure on myself to keep working in the right way and that does not change based on winning or losing a game."

Noble added, in his captain's notes:
"[Pellegrini] wants to play a certain way and even those four defeats weren't going to change that philosophy. Sometimes it will work and sometimes not, but consistency is the key and on Sunday, it looked as though everyone knew their jobs."

So the sun had finally come out on West Ham's season, just as we arrived for the visit of Chelsea, the league's in-form team, right in the thick of the title race with Man City and Liverpool.

Were Pellegrini's tactics too old school? Would he be found out as past his prime on this Sunday afternoon, his 65th birthday?

Strangely enough, the sun came out against Chelsea as well. No, West Ham didn't score goals galore. But the actual sun, hidden for three days leading up to the match, showed its face early in the first half. And the rest of the London afternoon turned out glorious.

That doesn't mean we saw attacking football or goals galore. We saw a nil-nil game.

Now, there are all types of nil-nil games. The ones in gross weather where the whole game is played in the midfield. There's scoreless draws where a really good team plays lethargically and can't create chances against a packed defense. And then there's nil-nil games where you leave and can't believe there wasn't a goal.

This game was one of the latter. And West Ham's most valuable players were three new signings who'd flown under the radar, and a young player who might be looking for an exit.

In the summer, the Irons brought in 6'4" defender Issa Diop from Toulouse for 22 million pounds. The 21-year old has turned out to be a steal, especially once he really gets the hang of the English game. He's partnered with Paraguayan Fabian Balbuena, a rugged aggressive defender with bravery and smarts. He came from Brazilian giant Corinthians, yet he's settled into the Premier League admirably.

In front of those two defenders was 20-year old Declan Rice. The club's back-to-back Young Player of the Year winner had been moved from central defender to the back of the West Ham midfield. After a shaky first couple games, he'd taken to the position like a duck to water. In the Chelsea game, he was masterful, even while facing players like Hazard, Willian, Jorginho, Alvaro Morata and N'Golo Kante.

Rice is currently on a contract more fit for a young squad player and wants a significant increase in pay. His contract is up next year. The club, so far, aren't keen to acquiesce. Former Premier League player and commentator Danny Murphy, who is also represented by the same agent as Rice, told *Talksport* he was "amazed West Ham haven't got a new contract sorted."

The club complained about the comments. But their own right back, veteran Pablo Zabaleta, said much the same.

"He is in the last year of his contract, so West Ham need to think about his situation because, even though he is young, he looks so mature and is proving he can perform for the team. He is one of those young players you like to look after and help with all the information you can give him."

All those players worked overtime to shut down the Chelsea attack – and the Premier League's most dangerous player, Eden Hazard. They threw their bodies in front of shots and aggressively pushed up their line to keep Chelsea's forwards moving. They used their strength to unsettle a less than rugged group of Blues' attackers.

And it worked. Chelsea midfielder Jorginho set a Premier League record by completing 186 passes. But Chelsea, unbeaten in all competitions to that point, only had a couple of scoring chances. But boy were they first-class chances.

Luckily West Ham had another key signing behind them. And it was new keeper Lucas Fabianski who they could thank for preserving the shutout. Fabianski, a long-time back up at Arsenal, has made more saves than any goalkeeper in Europe's top five leagues over the last five years, mostly the result of battling relegation with Swansea for three seasons. Already this year, only Burnley's Joe Hart has faced more shots in the Premier League.

In this contest, Fabianski had to make two dramatic saves late to preserve the point and the shutout. When Alvaro Morata broke through the line, he found himself at point blank range. Fabianski sold out, made himself big and stopped the flick with his face.

Moments later, Willian curled one to the far post, but Fabianski sprung all the way across the box to his left to tip it away. The crowd roared its approval.

Unfortunately, horrible misses by Michail Antonio and Yarmolenko – he headed a ball five feet wide of an open net – cost the Irons' three points. Yarmolenko added injury to insult a week later when he ruptured his Achilles. He'll miss six months.

But, a draw with Chelsea was nothing to shake a stick at. A week later, the Irons beat Manchester United. The London Stadium was becoming something of a makeshift fortress. But how long would the truce with ownership hold?

~BM

Brief History of West Ham United

The Irons were formed on the docks of London, first as a company club, Thames Ironworks FC in 1895.

President Arnold Hills, a believer in the Victorian principles of fitness and temperance, started the club to give his workers an alternative to the hard drinking going on in much of the East End. But the dawn of professionalism and a downturn in fortunes at the company led to the disbanding of the company club and the formation of West Ham United in 1900.

Hills, ever the philanthropist, gave his own money to help found the club and gave them use of the Memorial Stadium, built by the Thames Ironworks company. On top of that, a number of players – many of whom still worked at the Ironworks – were on the first roster.

West Ham competed in the Southern League's First Division until after World War I when the Football League expanded and the Irons accepted a place in the Second Division. After three seasons in the top seven of the Second Division, West Ham finished second in 1922-23, powered by Vic Watson's 22 league goals, and earned promotion to the First Division.

Perhaps more importantly that season, West Ham made it's first appearance in the FA Cup final on a momentous day in English history: the first game at Wembley Stadium. Over 240,000 people are thought to have attended that game and only the help of a policeman and his gray mare, "Billy" kept people off the field long enough to finish the game. The Irons lost the so-called "White Horse Final", 2-0, to Bolton. It would take another 41 years for West Ham to finally get its hands on a major trophy.

By 1931-32, West Ham's form slipped to the point it was relegated out of the First Division. Seven straight defeats to start the season sealed the Irons' fate. After another poor start to the next season, this time in the Second Division, long-time manager Syd King left the club. King had been in charge since 1902 – and even played for and served as club secretary for Thames Ironworks FC.

King's drinking had gotten heavier after the relegation season and when he showed up drunk to a board meeting after the poor start in 1932, he was fired. One month later he committed suicide, drinking alcohol mixed with a corrosive liquid.

Charlie Paynter was appointed manager and served until 1950 when his long-time assistant, Ted Fenton took over. Fenton had played for West Ham as a schoolboy and was a believer in the benefit of a club developing its own in-house talent. It was Fenton who turned West Ham into the so-called "Academy of Football," by recruiting young talent – much of it local – and encouraging the players to live and breathe football the "West Ham Way" by adopting the latest tactics and even diet.

In the 1950s Fenton signed young players like Bobby Moore, Geoff Hurst and Martin Peters – all of whom would score in England's 1966 World Cup final triumph over West Germany in Wembley Stadium.

It would pay off with a Division Two championship and promotion in 1957-58. Finally, in 1963-64, as the Academy of Football's first recruits came of age, West Ham won its first trophy – the 1964 FA Cup final. Under Ron Greenwood – who took over from Fenton as coach – the Hammers won the final, 3-2, over Second Division Preston North End on Ronnie Boyce's late header.

The victory earned West Ham a berth in the 1964-65 European Cup Winners' Cup and the Irons marched all the way to the final against Bayern Munich at Wembley Stadium. In what turned out to be a mini-preview of the next summer's World Cup final, West Ham won, 2-0, on a pair of second-half goals by Alan Sealey.

The next season, West Ham went back to the semifinals of the European Cup Winners Cup and the final of the League Cup before losing both. The real victory came that summer when all four England goals in the World Cup final came from West Ham players. And Moore, the team and country's captain, was named Jules Rimet award winner as the best overall player at the World Cup.

While many in East London crowed about West Ham winning the World Cup, the Irons seemed to have far more trouble in the Football League. The "glory" years of the 1960s produced only three top ten finishes, the highest being eighth, in 1961-62 and 1968-69.

West Ham won a second FA Cup trophy in 1975. Moore had left the year before and gone to Fulham, and wouldn't you know it, West Ham lined up against the Cottagers in the final at Wembley, with a 21-year old, 40,000-pound signing from Fourth Division Rochdale, Alan Taylor, netting both goals for the West Ham win.

West Ham again reached the final of the European Cup Winners Cup in 1975-76, falling to Anderlecht in Brussels. After relegation in 1977-78, West Ham won the FA Cup out of the Second Division in 1980, beating heavily favored Arsenal in the final on Trevor Booking's header. One stand of the ground is now named the Sir Trevor Booking Stand.

Since then, the Hammers have been promoted and subsequently relegated from the top division five times, finishing third in the old First Division in 1985-86 and fifth in the Premier League in 1998-99. Another FA Cup victory was thwarted in 2006 by Liverpool's Steven Gerrard, whose out of this world strike in stoppage time sent the game to extra time and eventually penalties, where Liverpool won.

2017-18 Season Review

Manager Slaven Bilic barely survived the previous season, but kept his job by keeping West Ham United in the Premier League.

After only two wins in the first three months of the 2017-18 season, the Irons were in the relegation zone and the powers that be decided to make a change. Bilic was fired and former Everton and Manchester United manager David Moyes was brought in to stop the rot.

Four more games without a win left West Ham mired in 19th place. Then the Irons rode an early Marko Arnautovic goal in a battling 1-0 win over city rivals Chelsea. Moyes followed that with a nil-nil draw at Arsenal and a thorough beating of relegation rivals Stoke, 3-0. That run of games pulled West Ham out of the relegation zone – and the club would not drop that far again.

West Ham did well against its London rivals, including high-priced Tottenham, Chelsea and Arsenal teams. The Irons lost only two games against London rivals, getting a least a point in the other six games.

Perhaps the Irons two most remarkable games of the year came a month apart against Tottenham. The Irons nearly came back from down 3-0 in league play at London Stadium before losing,, 3-2. A month later in the League Cup, West Ham again rallied against Spurs, this time after falling down 2-0 at Wembley Stadium. Angelo Ogbonna's 80th minute header off a corner was the Irons' third of the half and completed the comeback. At the time, many thought the win saved Bilic's job. But he was fired three weeks later. West Ham eventually lost to Arsenal in the League Cup quarterfinals.

The London Stadium was home to some ugly scenes during a March 10 match against Burnley. The Irons were beaten 3-0, their third loss in a row, and the West Ham crowd went into full protest mode over a number of grievances. Many fans went on the pitch. Others gathered around the directors' box and threatened owners David Gold and David Sullivan. Cooler heads eventually prevailed and a truce held the rest of the season.

A final day win over Everton earned West Ham a 13th-place finish. Arnautovic, who caught fire after Moyes was hired, finished as the club's Player of the Year and leading scorer with 11 goals.

Somehow the Irons firmed up, getting one or three points from six of their last seven games, including gutsy nil-nil draws vs. Everton and at Stoke, and a pair of 1-0 wins vs. Swansea and Tottenham, the latter killing off Spurs' title hopes once and for all.

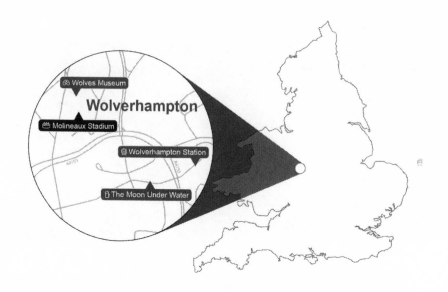

Wolverhampton Wanderers FC

Year Founded: 1877

Colors: Black and Gold

Nickname: Wolves

Stadium: Molineux Stadium

Address: Waterloo Road, Wolverhampton, WV1 4QR UK

Capacity: 32,050, 13th in Premier League

2017-18 Average Attendance: 28,298, 3rd in Championship

Trophies:

First Division (3): 1953-54; 1957-58; 1958-59

FA Cup (4): 1893; 1908; 1949; 1960

League Cup (2): 1974, 1980

Current Ownership: Fosun International, Guo Guangchang

Current Manager: Nuno Espirito Santo, 2nd season (33W, 9L, 10D)

2017-18 Finish: Won the Championship, 30W, 7L, 9D

FA Cup: Lost in third round replay at Swansea, 2-1

League Cup: Lost in fourth round penalty shootout at Manchester City, 0-0

The Sports Tourists' Tips for Wolverhampton

Make Sure You Have a Ticket First

Wolverhampton is a bit out of the way when it comes to other Premier League teams. And it's a community that supports its team. So tickets are hard to get. In our experience, most games do have limited seats still available at general sale.

Your best bet is to get your membership early and keep an eye on the various on-sale dates for each level of Wolves' supporter. If seats do come available to the general public, they likely won't last long, so you'll want to be on top of it early.

If you're flexible, look out for League Cup and FA Cup home games. But don't expect to show up on match day and find tickets. Wolves' fans are excited about being in the Premier League and turning up in droves.

Wolves Museum is the Best of Its Kind

Located around the back of the Molineux Stadium by the ticket offices, the Wolves Museum is a real gem. It's more than just the history of this proud club. Because the history of Wolverhampton is entwined with the history of the English game itself.

Wolves are one of the founding members of the Football League, one of the first to play under lights and the second English club to play in Europe. They even won a trophy in America. You can learn about all of this and more in the Wolves museum.

There are also plenty of interactive games for the kids (ok, and for the adults too) including your opportunity to serve on both sides of a penalty shootout with Wolverhampton's all-time greatest strikers and goalies. Good luck stopping Steve Bull. There's even a massive theater showing giant movies of Wolves' past glories.

Admission is cheap, just 7 pounds for adults and 4.50 pounds for kids. Or, you can get a family ticket for two adults and two children for just 18 pounds. You'll need about one or two hours to go through. The museum is open on Friday (12 p.m.-5 p.m.), Saturday (11 a.m. – 4:30 p.m.) and Sunday (11 a.m. – 3:30 p.m.) when there is no match.

On match days, the museum's hours vary based on the day of the week, but the museum closes 90 minutes before kickoff. It opens at 9 a.m. on Saturdays and 10 a.m. on Sunday match days. For Monday/Tuesday games, it opens at 3 p.m. and for Wednesday-Friday matches, the museum opens at noon.

Avoid the Old Stine and Go Straight to the Stadium

We asked around about good local pubs and got a lot of recommendations to swing by the Old Stine. This neighborhood pub was hard to find – literally one sign on the main street pointed us in the *opposite* direction – and it's about a mile in the opposite direction of the stadium from the rest of the hotels.

The service was rude and clearly not welcoming to new guests. The locals were nice enough, but two Americans and a Canadian at the Old Stine might as well have been aliens. And it immediately sparked loud conversations about how foreigners were ruining the game.

The truth is, there aren't many great pubs in Wolverhampton and the atmosphere around the stadium is hopping pregame. It's worth it to go up there, grab a pork bap or go inside. The hallways are spacious, there are plenty of pie options and cold pints. The atmosphere was far more welcoming and inclusive than at the Old Stine.

Do yourself a favor… learn the words to "Nuno Had a Dream" before you go. You'll be hearing it all night, in and out of the stadium.

Our Wolverhampton Experience

A good mate of ours once told us a story about a particularly controversial moment from her teenage years. Eager to chaperone her friend on a date with a boy she met online, she negotiated England's complicated train system, going from East London to the Midlands town of Wolverhampton and back. The trip went off without a hitch – or any suspicion on her parents part.

But alas, she failed to destroy the evidence and her mother, searching for something in her room, stumbled on the offending train tickets.

The punch line came when her mother stormed in on her, exclaiming, "Wolver-bloody-Hampton?! You've been to Wolver-bloody-Hampton?!" And so the town has been known in their house since.

Early in the 2018-19 Premier League season, you could imagine similarly incredulous exclamations coming from the back rooms of Manchester.

The Wolves were back in the Premier League and not afraid to make their presence felt. Portuguese manager Nuno Espirito Santo's squad were the only ones to take points off Manchester City in the season's first seven matches – earning a 1-1 draw at a noisy Molineux Stadium.

They went to Old Trafford to take on Manchester United, in form after wins at Watford and Young Boys. There was even a thaw in relations between manager Jose Mourinho and star Paul Pogba.

Wolves threw a monkey wrench in all that with a thoroughly dominant performance that deserved a victory, but ended up in a draw. Nuno's squad was so good, they tore apart United's thin cohesion. Pogba complained about tactics in the post-game press conference and Mourinho stripped him of the vice captaincy in the game's wake.

While those results may have raised some eyebrows around England, they are not a surprise for Wolverhampton's management. This is precisely what they came to Wolves to do – build a team that could compete with the best.

After all, by Wolves' reasoning, if Burnley could make it to Europe last year, why can't they?

The Wolverhampton Wanderers revitalization project began in earnest over three years ago when Chinese conglomerate Fosun International bought the club. Once a proud club, three-time First Division champion and four-time FA Cup winner, Wolves had fallen on hard times. Up and down from the Premier League, they never seemed to make it stick for long. The lack of resources was a big reason. With Fosun International in charge, that problem quickly changed.

Many foreign owners stay far away in the distance. But after one season, Fosun International's man, Jeff Shi, moved from China to Wolverhampton. And he reached out to Portuguese connections to find his best player, Ruben Neves, and manager, Nuno Espirito Santo.

You see, throughout last season's dominant Championship campaign, a new song became popular at the Molineux Stadium.

"Nuno had a dream,

to build a football team,

with Chinese owners and a wonder kid from Porto.

With 5 at the back,

and pace in attack...

We're Wolverhampton!

We're on our way back!"

Aside from the quibble over whether to sing three or five at the back – Espirito Santo plays three defenders and two high fullbacks – the song perfectly tells the story of the key factors in Wolves rise.

Neves is the wonder kid from Porto and the team spent 15.5 million pounds to pry him away from there before the start of last season. Shi also added Premier League veteran goalie John Ruddy and Jota, the team's other Portuguese talent on loan from Atletico Madrid.

But this team was built on the vision of Nuno, perhaps the most interesting coach in the Premier League right now. He is Portuguese, raised on tiny Principe Island, just off the West Coast of Africa and thousands of miles away from the Portuguese mainland.

"I grew up with no shoes because my house was there and the beach was there," Nuno told *The Guardian.* "There were no cars and we played. It was paradise."

He grew up to become Jose Mourinho's backup goalkeeper on Porto's 2004 Champions League winning team. He later managed at the same club before coming to Wolverhampton, of all places.

In fact, as we mentioned, Wolves have built up a considerable Portuguese contingent. Jota and Neves both came from the Porto setup. Joao Moutinho has played at Sporting and Porto. Helder Costa played at Benfica and goalie Rui Patricio played his entire career at Sporting before heading to the Black Country. Moutinho and Patricio are European champions with Portugal and were signed in the summer to bolster the roster.

The Patricio signing was particularly bizarre as he was signed for free after claiming hardship to break his contract and leave Sporting of Lisbon. The hardship? The owner, Bruno de Carvalho called his whole team "stupid" and suspended 19 of them after a Europa League loss. And he may or may not have ordered 50 masked assailants to break into the training complex and assault members of the team and coaches.

Now there are seven Portuguese players in the first team at Wolverhampton, plus the manager. It seems strange that these talents from the same area all want to go to an industrial city in the West Midlands. But Nuno had a dream, after all, and the club was clearly upwardly mobile.

And the moves worked. Wolves took the lead in the Championship by Week 14 last season and never looked back. They never lost more than one game in a month and finished with 99 points, a club record for that level.

"We had to take the risk to come here," Jota told *The Guardian.* "Sometimes when you want to achieve something, you have to take a risk. And at that time it was the best thing to do. We came here, we saw the project of the club, we saw the players they bought, so we put our minds in the Championship, focused on [getting to] the Premier League and did our work. In the beginning a lot of people criticized us, including in Portugal. They said: 'You are a great player, and you go there now?' But now I think everyone understands we were right."

Winning helps you get over moving to a new town. But familiarity among your mates helps too.

Brief History of Molineux Stadium

This historic ground has seen its ups and downs, but it will always hold a special place in the history of English football.

The ground at Molineux hosted the very first Football League match every played, on Sept. 7, 1889, a 2-0 win for Wolverhampton over Notts County. It was the only facility in the country designed for the specific purpose of League football. Over 4,000 people attended that first game.

Local citizens had been used to heading to the Molineux Grounds for a day out. The area was originally owned by local merchant Benjamin Molineux, who built a hotel there. In 1860, the estate was purchased by O.E. McGregor and turned into a mini-amusement park. There was a lake for rowboats, an ice skating rink, and of course, a place to play football.

After the Northampton Brewery bought the spot in 1889, they immediately rented it to Wolverhampton, who fixed up the ground in preparation for league play.

Wolves made more football history in 1953 when they installed floodlights and began to host a series of midweek night games with teams from all over the world. The first was played against South Africa. Over the next decade, Wolves would host a number of these games, many of them aired live on the BBC. In fact, Wolverhampton took down Real Madrid at home in 1957 in a famous game for the club.

Many say these night games paved the way for European competition and the eventual Champions League.

Unfortunately, less than 30 years later, the Molineux almost finished the club off. An expensive rebuild of then-outdated stands in the late 70s required massive debt and almost bankrupt the club, who were kept out of receivership by three minutes thanks to a group put together by former player Derek Dougan.

Still, the infamous Taylor Report, which outlawed standing terraces, found the Molineux to be out of date. And another new owner, this time local businessman Sir Jack Hayward, set about building a more modern stadium, raising the seating capacity and renaming the stands.

"Sometimes we fell like we are in Portugal when we have dinner together," Neves said in the same interview. "I had my daughter's first birthday [last month], I brought my family and my fiancée's family from Portugal, and with all the Portuguese players as well there were 30 people."

There is another side to this Portuguese migration as well. All of the players and the coach have the same agent, Jorge Mendes. Mendes is also the agent for Jose Mourinho and Cristiano Ronaldo. And he's served as an advisor to the Wolves owners for the last two years.

Obviously, this relationship has its benefits in the quality of players the club has brought in. But, in the Championship, the other teams sent a letter of complaint about a potential conflict of interest. Nothing has been done about it and it's hard to tell what's illegal.

Needless to say, Mendes' influence has helped shape the club. With the new veteran signings this summer, *The Guardian's* preview called Wolves, "the strongest and most fully formed team ever to come up from the Championship."

But, in a nod to the club's proactivity, seven of the team's starters also played on last year's Championship team. Plus, Nuno began the season by playing the same lineup eight straight times, a Premier League record. When he was named September manager of the month, Nuno gave credit to the team's medical staff.

The philosophy of this team is not to sit back and wait. They're going to play how they want to play, opponent be damned. Against Man United and Man City, they definitely weren't playing for a draw and were actually unlucky not to win.

"We never play like that," Nuno told *The Guardian*. "We will never play like that. It doesn't make sense. How can you build a game plan based on just drawing? You have a corner, you get one goal, you are losing, you lose your game plan. The players look and say 'now what?'

"What you have to become is really strong in what you do. That's the point of building a team. You don't know any other way – it would be absurd to do it any other way."

Managing director Laurie Dalrymple echoed his coach.

"I think the strategy we had… has been about building a squad and a structure we think is going to be viable to take further, beyond promotion," Dalrymple told *The Guardian*. "We want to be excited about the fact we're going to Chelsea, Man City, Liverpool etc. but not overawed by that."

We arrived at the Molineux Stadium on a Thursday night to see Wolves vs. fellow Premier League side Leicester City in the third

2017-18 Season Review

The 2017-18 season was one of the most special in the history of Wolverhampton Football Club.

Coach Nuno Espirito Santo took over, combined with a couple of fellow Portuguese maestros and took Wolves to the most points in club history at the Championship level, 99. The black and gold won the Championship by nine points and earned promotion with four weeks to spare.

It was a season of highlights and very few low points. Playmaker Ruben Neves sprinkled magic all around in his first year with the club. Neves only scored six goals, but it seemed as if each of them was spectacular. All six came from outside the box, starting with a sixth-minute strike in a 3-2 win over early promotion favorites Hull City in August.

But the goal of the year came in April at a wet Molineux Stadium. Up 1-0 on Derby County in the 51st minute, a corner kick was cleared as far as Neves. He juggled it once, turned his body and hit a shot that seemed to defy gravity, tucking under the cross bar for a goal. It was voted the Championship's goal of the season. Neves was named Player of the Year by his club and by the league as a whole.

Three days after the win over Derby County, Fulham failed to win against Brentford and Wolves celebrated promotion. The next week, after beating Birmingham, Wolves clinched the Championship title.

Wolves' dominance was such, the never lost more than one game in any month. And they led the division from week 15 on, never relinquishing first place. Wolverhampton didn't lose between October 28, 2017 and January 13, 2018, winning 10 and drawing three. Just before the streak started, they were eliminated from the League Cup by Manchester City on penalty kicks. Wolves did not give up a goal in open play in the League Cup competition. Just after the streak ended, they were eliminated from the FA Cup by Swansea City on a replay.

Diogo Jota, another Portuguese player, led the team in scoring with 18 goals. Goalie John Ruddy, defender Conor Coady and Neves all made the Championship team of the season.

round of the League Cup, or what's currently called the Carabao Cup through sponsorship.

The League Cup is the lesser of the two English domestic cups, behind the FA Cup in importance. It's comprised of all 92 teams in the Football League only, from the Premier League to League Two. The bigger Premier League clubs enter the competition after the first couple of rounds typically, and Wolves advanced to this point with a second round win over Sheffield Wednesday, 2-0.

But the League Cup isn't just a throwaway competition. It's actually a great place for teams to rotate players, try out young players and reinstate injured players. Different clubs treat the competition with different levels of seriousness, sometimes leading to more lopsided and surprising results.

For Premier League teams brimming with talented, confident players beyond the starting 11, it's a great tool to offer those same players some much-craved playing time.

It's also a great time to bring in new fans as well. Most teams offer far cheaper tickets for the midweek, nighttime League Cup games.

With the stadium now sold out for the Premier League, this gives more people a chance to come see their heroes in a more affordable and less intimidating setting. At the club shop earlier in the day, we bumped into a fellow who was buying up gear for his son.

"I've just rushed over here from work cause he'd kill me if I didn't get him a shirt."

"I've lived in Wolverhampton for 30 years, but I've never been to a game. I'm a bit of an Arsenal fan, if I'm honest," he whispered. "But I figured this was a good chance to see Wolves. And my son absolutely loves them. We're pretty excited we could get tickets."

In the match day program, Dalrymple reached out to people just like our friend at the shop:

"Tonight, we're sure to welcome a few new faces to the crowd – maybe even a few who are visiting for the first time – which was the thinking behind the subsidized ticket prices for this game. The capacity crowds at Molineux in the Premier League have made it increasingly challenging for supporters outside of season ticket holders and loyalty points owners to attend matches, so hopefully tonight is a good opportunity for even more of our fantastic fan base to see the team play live against fellow top-flight opponents Leicester City."

On this night, the 21,562-person crowd (capacity is 31,700) wouldn't see the same Premier League lineup. Nuno started a changed side with only one player from the previous week's draw with United, defender Conor Coady.

So no Nunes or Jota. But, exciting new signing Adama Traore was in the lineup for his first start of the season. Traore was signed from Middlesbrough in the summer for 18 million pounds and is built more like an American football player with electric speed to boot. In fact, sometimes too much speed, according to British Olympian Darren Campbell.

Boro coach Tony Pulis hired Campbell to teach Traore how to run smarter. It worked as Traore was voted Boro's Player of the Year by the fans and players last season. He also won the club's young player of the year award too. He scored five goals and assisted on 10 others as Boro just missed out on the playoffs.

"One of the things I said to him was 'everything you do is 100 mph so you need to know what it's like at 50 per cent, 70 per cent, 80 per cent,'" Campbell told *The Express and Star*.

"It was a case of him getting to know how to use his power and use his speed. Fortunately, he took on the advice and he got his move to Wolves. We knew he was an exceptional talent. He just needed smoothing out a little bit. If you're going to improve, you need to have that level of relaxation. He hadn't scored a goal and once he understood what he had to do, he started scoring goals."

But with such a deep team at Wolves, he hadn't been able to crack the starting lineup. In this game, Traore made his impact, getting open in dangerous positions and driving at the Leicester defense. But with veterans like Jonny Evans and Wes Morgan in the back, Leicester made it hard to break through.

Neither club had much in the way of attack on a chilly night in the two-thirds full stadium. Even after Leicester threw on Jamie Vardy and Wolves subbed in Jota, not much happened. The game ended in a stalemate.

In a new change for the League Cup this season, instead of going to extra time, the game went straight to penalties. In goal for Wolves was last season's hero, Ruddy, now supplanted by Patricio. On the other side for Leicester, the club's backup keeper and a penalty folk hero, Danny Ward.

As a Liverpool loanee to Huddersfield two seasons ago, Ward carried the Terriers to the Premier League, making two penalty saves in a promotion playoff final at Wembley Stadium to beat Reading in a shootout. That was after saving two penalties in the semifinal.

And right in front of our end at the Molineux, he reprised that role. Jota, Traore and Roman Saiss were all stopped. In fact, it was young prospect Benny Ashley-Seal who scored the only goal for Wolves. Ruddy is no slouch and he stopped two penalties of his own. But Leicester prevailed and Ward was carried off by his teammates.

For Wolverhampton, it was the second year in a row the club was eliminated from the League Cup after penalties. Last year, it was to Manchester City, also after a nil-nil draw.

In fact, Wolves hasn't given up a goal in the League Cup in 600 minutes. And not in the six games they've played in the competition under Nuno. The coach was disappointed in the loss, but upbeat on the overall project.

"The most important thing is the boys wait for their chance, the way they work on a daily basis knowing that maybe sometimes they are not an option, but knowing when the chances come, good answers must be given. And they gave a good answer," he told *The Express and Star* after the match.

"The boys did it the same way. Changes don't mean anything for us. We keep the same style, we keep the same ideas and philosophy, game by game, it doesn't matter what competition, we wanted to win. I'm sad that we didn't win, but proud of the way we worked."

After all, it was just the League Cup. And as September turned to October, Wolverhampton still sat 10th in the Premier League, close enough for the Portuguese coach's dream to become a reality.

~BM

Brief History of Wolverhampton Wanderers

Despite having little impact on the Premier League era, Wolverhampton is one of the most important clubs in English history. Wolves were one of 12 founding members of the English Football League, the first competition of its kind in the world. They were also the star of the 1950s, just as interest in football was exploding in the post-war decade.

The club started in 1877 after the headmaster of St. Luke's School in nearby Blankenhall gave his two best pupils each a soccer ball as a reward. These two, Brodie and Baynton, started a team at the school, first called Blakenhall St. Luke's, then the Goldthorn Football Club. In 1879, they joined forces with the Blankenhall Wanderers cricket club to become Wolverhampton Wanderers.

Wolves quickly developed a reputation as a talented team in the uber-talented north. The Wanderers were on of the first clubs to compete in the newly created FA Cup. And in 1888, they joined five other Midlands teams and six teams from the North to create the single-division Football League. Only three of those teams currently play in the Premier League – Wolves, Everton and Burnley.

When it came to picking the founding teams, Wolves had to be on the list after a dominant performance in 1886-87, in which Wolverhampton won 31 of its 40 matches, including all three games as part of Queen Victoria's 50-year jubilee. In their first year in the Football League, Wolves reached the FA Cup final for the first time, losing 3-0 to Preston North End.

Wolves also found their home prior to the start of the Football League, taking over a plot of land in the Molineux Pleasure Gardens. Fitted with a small stand, the stadium hosted the first Football league match, a 2-0 win over Notts County on Sept. 7, 1889. After many renovations and expansions, Molineux Stadium sits on this same plot of land, just off the Central Ring Road.

Wolverhampton broke through for its first major trophy in 1893 with a 1-0 win over Everton in the FA Cup final at Fallowfield in Manchester with 45,000 people in attendance. The players were carried through the streets, many of which were renamed in their honor.

Still, league dominance eluded the club and Wolves eventually dropped to the newly created Division Two in 1906. The lower status didn't stop the club from claiming another FA Cup in 1908, beating heavily favored Newcastle, 3-1, at Crystal Palace.

However, the club would fade from the national consciousness while floundering at the lower level until the early 30s. Major Frank Buckley was brought in to heal what he called the "sick man" of English football. His recruitment of talent worked as he brought in enough new players to push Wolves to the First Division once again.

Unfortunately, Wolves under Buckley became known as nearly men. In 1938, they lost the title on the last day in a 1-0 loss at Sunderland. In 1939 they were trounced in the FA Cup final by Portsmouth, 4-1. They finished runners-up in the league in the last two years before World War II and then lost to Liverpool on the last day to cough up the 1946-47 league title.

But in 1948, Buckley's former captain Stan Cullis took over as manager. One of his first acts was to make 23-year old Billy Wright his captain.

In the spring of 1949, Wolverhampton went to Wembley with their "fast direct attack" against Second Division stragglers Leicester City. Jesse Pye scored two first half goals in front of 96,000, and Wolves won, 3-1. Wright was presented the trophy by a then young Princess Elizabeth. And so, Wolves showed a glimpse of their future glory days.

During the 1953-54 season, Wolves battled their Black Country rivals, West Bromwich Albion, for the title. Fueled by an 18-match unbeaten run, Cullis' men finally won the First Division title by four points. Wolves won two more league titles in 1957-58 and 1958-59, part of a four-year run where they scored 100 goals or more every season.

Wright retired in 1958 at the top of his game. Once rejected by Buckley for being too small, the 5-feet, 8-inches Englishman became the first person in the world to start 100 matches for his country. He captained England 50 times and was given a knighthood for his contributions to football. Both Wright and Cullis have stands named after them in the modern Molineux Stadium.

Cullis was an innovator as well. Between 1953-62, Wolverhampton hosted a series of games with European giants like Real Madrid, Racing Club of Argentina, Spartak Moscow and Hungary's Honved in a game televised on the BBC. The games were played under the lights at the Molineux, making it one of the first stadiums with permanent lights. The success of these games set the stage for European competition and what we know as the Champions League today.

In 1958, Wolves became the second English team to play in the European Cup, after Manchester United. And despite Wright's retirement the previous year, Wolves came extremely close to winning a league title and an FA Cup in 1959-60. Only one team, Aston Villa in 1897, had ever done it.

But Wolverhampton finished second in the league before defeating a hard-luck Blackburn Rovers side in the FA Cup final. Norman Deeley had a brace as Rovers lost Dave Whelan to a broken leg early and played with 10 men the rest of the way. Some say this match helped lead to updated substitution rules as just six years later, the English Football League finally allowed a substitution for an injured player for the first time.

The club's fourth FA Cup signaled the end of an era. Two years later, Wolves were nearly relegated. Cullis was fired after 30 years with the club.

Wolves were eventually relegated for two seasons, bouncing back up in 1967-68. They finished fourth in 1970-71, earning a spot in the UEFA Cup. The "Doog," aka Derek Dougan, had a hat trick against Academica of Portland and Wolverhampton advanced to the final, beating Juventus along the way. Unfortunately, Wolves couldn't overcome their own countrymen, Tottenham, in the final.

Thanks to the goals of John Richards and Kenny Hibbitt, Wolverhampton won two more trophies in the 70s, League Cup victories in 1974 and 1980. Then things turned south quickly for the club. They were relegated in 1982, bounced back for one season and then went as low as Division Four. Serious financial problems plagued the club and Dougan tried to save them, pulling together an investment group from Saudi Arabia, the so-called Bhatti brothers. But the mystery owners eventually disappeared and the big investments never came, putting the club in even more trouble.

In its darkest days, the club signed a promising young player away from rivals West Brom named Steve Bull. The Bull, a stocky, competitive forward, would go on to become the club's all-time leading scorer with 306 goals. And he helped carry Wolves out of the bottom of English football with back-to-back promotions, winning the Fourth Division in 1987-88 and the Third Division in 1988-89.

In 1990, local businessman Sir Jack Hayward poured a large portion of his own wealth into the club, helping build a firm enough footing for a return to the top level, by then called the Premier League. After 11 seasons at the second-highest level, Hayward finally got his wish as Wolverhampton won playoff promotion on its fourth try in 2003.

Wolves scored three first-half goals in a 3-0 cakewalk over Sheffield United, ending the club's 19-year absence from the top. Hayward's thumbs up, caught on camera, gave many Wolves' fans happy tears. It's immortalized on a statue outside the Sir Jack Hayward stand at the Molineux that was unveiled this past summer.

Premier League football didn't stick though and Wolves went down the next year. They later had another three-year stint in the Premier league end in 2011-12. Hayward later sold the club and since 2015, Wolverhampton has been owned by Chinese holding company Fosun International. With more money spent on foreign talent and coach Nuno Espirito Santo, Wolves rolled to 99 points and the Championship title in 2017-18, earning promotion back to the Premier League. And with over 100 million pounds invested in top players, Wolves are hoping to make this promotion stick.

Black Country Derby vs. West Bromwich Albion

Wolves are located in an area of England called the "Black Country", which itself is in the so-called West Midlands. It's called the Black Country for a number of reasons, including the smoke and soot from the ironworks industries that popped up in the area in the late 19th century. It was also a prominent coal area as well.

The two most prominent teams in the Black Country are Wolves and West Bromwich Albion though Walsall is also considered part of the Black Country rivalry. As the sport heated up in the late 19th century, industrial England was at the forefront. And the Black Country was the center of it all. When the nation's football communities got together to create the Football League, Wolverhampton and West Brom were amongst the 12 original teams. As a result, this derby is one of the oldest in the world, with 160 meetings.

The Albion lead the overall series, 64 wins to 53 with 43 draws. The two rivals haven't played since February 2012 because they haven't been in the same division. The height of the rivalry came in 1954 when the two met in the Charity Shield with Wolves the league champions and West Brom the FA Cup champions. More recently, West Brom beat Wolves over both legs of a playoff promotion semifinal in 2007.

The two clubs share much of the same heritage, but root against each other like brothers. Lots of people work together and share the same pubs. Still, the rivalry has turned ugly at times. After an FA Cup replay in the same 2007 season, Wolves fans attempted to attack the West Brom supporters, only to be stopped by police. Instead, they turned their attentions on the police, leading to some of the worst riots in Wolverhampton in decades.

If you ask hardcore Wolves fans, they hate Birmingham a lot more. It's the "city" and not a part of the Black Country.

As one fan told *The Daisy Cutter:*

"West Brom are similar to us. Working class, hard working blokes, like a pint, watch the football, have a bit of banter, shake hands afterwards.

Blues fans are arseholes in the main. Don't get me wrong, Albion is THE derby. I wouldn't give Blues the respect of putting them on that pedestal – but I get more pleasure out of doing them over than West Brom."

The Sports Tourists' Glossary of English Football Terms

10-Man: when a team loses a player to a red card, announcers refer to them as a 10-man side from that point on in the match.

40 Points: the supposed gold standard in points for staying in the Premier League. Since 1995-96, when the Premier League dropped to 20 teams, only three clubs have achieved 40 or more points and been relegated.

Added Time: a half is 45 minutes, but time is added on by the referee to account for time spent on injuries, substitutions and goal celebrations at the end of the half.

Against the Run of Play: when one team scores despite the other team dominating play and controlling the ball consistently in their end.

Aggregate: In club competitions, during the knockout phase, teams often play each other twice, home and away. The winner is decided by adding together the scores of the two matches. If the aggregate score is tied, the winner is normally the club that scored more goals on the road (away goals). If that still produces a tie, two 15-minute overtimes ensue, and then penalties if needed.

All Over the Place: referring to a team that is playing horribly, especially on defense.

Appearance: statistical term for a game played.

Are: in England, a team is plural; that is, you'll hear "Arsenal are really good." In the states, we'd say Arsenal is."

At the Back: a team's defense.

Attack: also called a forward; a player whose duty is to score goals.

Away Goal Rule: tie-breaker used in competitions such as the Champions League. Rewards teams for scoring goals in away matches and is usually the first tie-breaker used in a two-leg aggregate goal competition.

Backheel: a kick where the ball is hit with the heel of the foot.

Back Room: the support staff of a football club.

Ballon d'or: the award given annually to the best player in the world. Conceived by French journalist Gabriel Hanot, the award was originally given to only European players, expanding to players at Europeans clubs and, finally in 2007, to all players around the world. Lionel Messi (5) and Cristiano Ronaldo (4) have combined to win the last nine awards from 2008-16, with Ronaldo a heavy favorite to add his fifth award in 2017.

Booking: a yellow card shown to a player by the referee for a serious foul. Two bookings or yellow cards result in a red card or sending-off.

Boots: cleats.

Box: the 18-yard penalty area.

Boxing Day: the day after Christmas in England, when every team in the Premier League plays. There is typically a full slate of 10 matches on this day.

Brace: two goals in a game scored by the same player.

Bundesliga: Germany's premier league.

Cap: an appearance made by a player for their national team. These players used to get actual caps every time they did made an appearance.

Capitulation: an English term for surrender used in soccer to describe clubs that seemingly gave up against opponents.

Challenge: an attempt to stop or tackle a player.

Champions League: a tournament with all the top clubs from Europe playing against each other. In England, the teams finishing in the Top-4 play in the Champions League the following season. Recognized as the best club competition in the world.

Chance: a near goal.

Cheat: an opposing player who's done something wrong, like faking an injury.

Chips: fries, in England, where chips are called crisps.

Class: skill.

Clean Sheet: a shutout, normally credited to the goalkeeper.

Clear Their Lines: when a defense gets the ball out of its end.

Clearance: a defensive kick that is intended to put the ball out of danger.

Clinical Finish: referring to a well-placed, controlled shot from a scoring position that ends in a goal.

Concede: to allow a goal in.

Consolation: late goal in a loss, as in scoring a goal in the 89th minute when down 5-1.

Corner Kick: a kick from the corner flag awarded to the attacking team when the ball has crossed the goal-line after last being touched by a player of the defending team.

Cover Himself in Glory: do really well, but it is only used by announcers, scribes and pundits in a sarcastic/negative manner, ie. When a goalie lets in a soft goal, he didn't "cover himself in glory."

Cross: a pass from the side of the pitch into the penalty area to find an attacker and score a goal.

Deadline Day: the last day of a transfer window, when many last-minute signings occur. Similar to Major League Baseball's trade deadline.

Defender: a player who tries to prevent the other team from scoring goals.

Delivery: getting the ball to somebody in a scoring position – also called service.

Derby: a local rivalry game – Liverpool vs. Everton, Man City vs. Man United, Newcastle vs. Sunderland.

Dive: a fake attempt at drawing a foul, especially in the penalty box. Also one of the biggest reasons, along with low scores, why Americans have historically disliked soccer.

Dodgy: weak, usually referring to a goalkeeper.

Double: winning two titles in the same season such as the league and the FA Cup. Can also include a Champions League or Europa League title. Man United won a double in the 2016-17 season by winning the League Cup and the Europa League.

Draw: a match that ends in a tie.

End/Stand: sections of stadiums in England.

English Football League: a league competition featuring professional football clubs from England and Wales. Founded in 1888 as the Football League, it is the oldest such competition in the world. Before the Premier League broke away in 1992, it was comprised of the top four levels of English football. Now, it is made up of levels 2-through-4, a total of 72 teams in three leagues.

Equalizer: a goal that cancels out the opposing team's lead and leaves the match tied or drawn.

Europa League: an annual football club competition organized by UEFA since 1971 for eligible European football clubs. Clubs qualify for the competition based on their performance in their national leagues and cup competitions. Formerly called the UEFA Cup.

Extra Time: If a match has no winner at the end of regulation, two additional 15-minute sessions of extra time may be played in some competitions, normally in the FA or League Cup, or European competition. This is not utilized in league play.

FA: Football Association – English football governing body.

FA Cup: a tournament that involves almost every possible professional team in England. The bigger clubs join in the later rounds, and many dramatic matches have been played between Premier League clubs and League Two sides, and even lower. The final takes place in Wembley every May. Arsenal defeated Chelsea, 2-1, in 2017.

FC: Football Club – appears in the team name for most clubs.

Finish: scoring a goal.

Fixture: a scheduled game/match. In England, the home team is listed on the top, when a schedule or result is listed.

Flatter to Deceive: a bust. Used to describe either a young academy star or a transfer who performed well previously, but does not get the job done with his or new club.

Form: a player or club's recent play. Winning five in a row would be good form.

Formation: how the players line up on a field. Only 10 are ever listed, as the goalkeeper is separate. Some popular formations include a 4-4-2 (defenders are listed first, followed by midfielders, then forwards), 4-3-3, 3-5-2, and 4-5-1.

Fortress: when a team is unbeatable at home.

Forward: player whose primary responsibility is to score goals.

Foul: any violation of the rules.

Found Wanting: lacking all that is needed or expected. In football terms, not finishing a goal opportunity.

Free Kick: the kick awarded to a team by the referee after a foul has been committed.

From Nothing: when a team has done nothing all game and then comes out of nowhere to score a big goal.

Full-Time: the point of the game where the referee blows the final whistle and the match is over. This normally occurs after 90 minutes and any added injury or stoppage time.

Gaffer: also known as a manager, the person in charge of a team and responsible for peripheral aspects such as training and adding new players and transfers.

Geordie: slang term for somebody from Newcastle.

Goal Difference: if Team A has scored four goals and Team B has scored one, the goal difference is three. Used to determine who advances in tournament competitions where teams play more than one match against each other.

Goal Kick: a kick taken from the 6-yard line by the defending team after the ball has been put over the end line by the attacking team.

Goalkeeper: the player in goal who has to stop the ball from crossing the goal-line. The only player who can handle the ball during open play.

Going Forward: on the attack.

Great Escape: avoiding relegation when a team looked doomed. Normally does not earn this distinction unless the club was bottom of the table at Christmas or later before reaching safety by season's end.

Ground: really refers to the field, but is used to encompass the stadium and its field (pitch) together.

Hat Trick: scoring three goals in a game.

Have the Wood: Australian and New Zealand slang meaning to have an advantage over.

Having the Numbers: when a team gets the ball and heads upfield with five or six players instead of just one or two.

Head for the Corner: a time-wasting tactic used late in matches by the team winning at the time. It involves taking the ball into the corner and attempting to hold possession as long as possible while forcing a defender to either kick the ball out of bounds or commit a foul.

Header: the shot that occurs when a player touches or guides the ball with their head.

Hit the Beach: not focused. Playing like you are already on vacation (holiday) in the offseason.

Hit the Woodwork: the crossbar or the post of the goal. This expression means a team kicked a ball against the crossbar or post and was very unlucky not to score.

Hold Your Hand Up: this has two separate meanings. The first is when a player admits they have committed a foul. The second is when defenders do it as a ball gets past them to an opposing player they feel was offside at the time.

Hour Mark: 60th minute of a match, when substitutions normally start taking place.

Howler: a basic mistake, normally referring to a goalie's miscue.

Impose Themselves: get into the game after playing terribly earlier.

International: someone who plays for their respective country's national team.

Keep Possession: to be able to keep the ball and prevent the opposing team from touching it.

Kit: uniform, in England.

Kop: a big section of seats behind a goal that seats the most hard-core fans for the home side. The most famous is at Anfield, Liverpool's home.

La Liga: Spain's premier league.

League Cup: Cup competition contested by only the top four levels of the English Football League system, the Premier League through League Two, comprising the top 92 teams currently in England.

Leg: when clubs play each other twice in some competitions, each game is called a leg.

Linesmen: referee's assistant, located on either sideline, whose main duty is to indicate with a flag when the ball has gone out of play or when a player is offside.

Loan: a player being sent to temporarily play for a club other than the one he is currently contracted to. Loans may last from a few weeks to all-season long and can also last for multiple seasons with multiple clubs.

Mancunians (Mancs): slang for somebody from Manchester.

Man-On: shout during a football match to warn a teammate that a player from the other team is right behind.

Mark: guard a player.

Match: two teams playing against each other in a 90-minute game of football.

Match of the Day: a BBC program on Saturday and Sunday evenings that shows highlights, with pundits discussing the teams.

Mental: when fans completely lose it celebrating a goal or win, or in the case of Watford's Troy Deeney, promotion to the Premier League.

Merseyside: a term for Liverpool, which is on the side of the River Mersey. The Merseyside Derby refers to the rivalry matches played between Liverpool and Everton.

Midfielder: a player who plays mainly in the middle part of the pitch.

Minnows: refers to a small team that dreams of taking down a much larger side in a club competition.

Narrow: describes a way of playing where you simply barrel down the middle of the pitch and try to beat opponents with short, quick passes, and rapid movement.

Nil: used to denote zero for a score. Example: 1-nil.

Nutmeg: a trick or technique in which a player passes the ball through an opponent's legs and then collects it from the other side.

Off the Line: when a goalkeeper misses a ball, but a defender is there to clear the ball off the goal-line.

Offside: when an attacking player is closer to the opposing team's goal-line at the moment the ball is passed to him or her than the last defender apart from the goalkeeper.

On Frame: at the goal.

On the Front Foot: a team that has the momentum.

One of Our Own: when a player on a team originally comes from somewhere in that area, he or she is hailed as "one of our own."

One-Two: a passing move in which Player 1 passes the football to Player 2, who immediately passes it back to Player 1.

Open Play: a team can score a goal one of three ways – off a set piece or a penalty – or during the normal run of play in the game, called open play.

Own Goal: a goal scored accidentally by a member of the defending team that counts in favor of the attacking team.

Open Up: when a game has been bogged down and then starts to flow, with lots of chances.

Pace: speed.

Park the Bus: a derisive term meaning a team is not even trying to score, they are just going for a scoreless draw or protecting a one-goal lead. It means that team has parked a bus in front of its own goal – brought all of its players back.

Passenger: someone who sits back while his/her teammates do all the work whilst contributing nothing themselves.

Penalty: a free shot at a goal from 12 yards awarded by the referee to a team after a foul has been committed in the penalty area.

Penalty Shoot-out: in a knock-out competition, a penalty shoot-out takes place if a match is a draw after full-time and extra-time. Five players from each team take a penalty each, and if the score is still level after that, one player from each team takes a penalty in turn, to decide who wins the match.

Physio: a trainer, in England.

Pipped: edged out, in England.

Pitch: the area where footballers play a match.

Premier League: top league in English football. Comprised of 20 teams.

Promotion: the concept of going up in leagues, either automatically by a top finish, or after winning a playoff competition.

Put Eleven Men Behind the Ball: referring to a team that defends with all its players and is not very interested in scoring goals. It is not a very exciting style of football to watch, but effective for lesser quality teams. (See: Park the Bus)

Qualify: to earn a place in a cup or club competition, or earn a place in the knockout rounds of those competitions.

Quality: similar to class, refers to skill.

Quick Off the Line: refers to a goalkeeper who is fast and makes quick decisions as to when to leave the goal to prevent an attacking player from reaching a pass or a cross.

Red Card: immediate expulsion from the game.

Relegation: the opposite of promotion. Teams in the bottom three spots in the table are going down to the next league.

Relegation Six-Pointer describes a game between two teams with similar league positions at the bottom of the table. A win is worth three points, but with the two teams so close, it feels like it is worth twice as much.

Result: score.

Run-In: the tail end of a team's regular season.

Safety: when a club is out of the relegation zone. For those clubs who do not have title aspirations, this can be equally important by the end of the season.

Scouser: slang for somebody from Liverpool.

Sent Off: received a red card.

Serie A: Italian premier league.

Service: same as delivery.

Set Piece: free kicks or corner kicks. Often a good opportunity to score a goal.

Shipped: allowed a goal.

Shite: a beautiful pronunciation for shit in the UK. Comes from the Scottish pronunciation. Heard quite often at matches and pubs, especially when the home side is not performing well.

Side: team.

Silverware: a trophy you get for winning something like the League or a Cup.

Skipper: the player who leads the team, also called the captain.

Small Matter: somewhat sarcastic, wry reference to big matches coming up on the schedule, especially derbies.

Sort it Out: another phrase often uttered at matches by supporters urging their team to get it together.

Space: getting into an open area. If a player is in space, he or she is currently unmarked.

Spot Kick: a penalty kick taken from the "spot," located 12 yards from the goal line, after the referee points to it to indicate a penalty.

Steward: an usher/security person at matches. Seen most commonly around the pitch toward the end of a match, as well as in the stands, especially in the section dividing home and away supporters.

Stoppage Time: also called injury time, added minutes at the end of the regular playing time at half-time or full-time. This time is entirely at the referee's discretion and is normally indicated on a big hand-held board held up by a fourth official on the sideline (touchline).

Strike: a shot on goal.

Substitute: a player who sits on the bench ready to replace another teammate on the pitch. Teams usually are allowed only three substitutes per match. When a player is substituted out, they cannot return to the match.

Suck the goal in: when the fans are so enthusiastic that they will their team to score.

Sweeper Keeper: a goalkeeper known for often playing off his or her line, like Germany's Manuel Neuer. These keepers are seen outside the penalty box and can somewhat be counted as the 11th field player because of their positioning – hence the reference to sweeper.

Switch Play: to change direction of play and pass the ball from one side of the pitch to the other.

Table: the league standings.

Technical Area: the area on the touchline where managers are supposed to stay during matches.

Three Points: the number of points earned for a win. A loss is zero points, and a tie is one point. When a team does not win, it is often said to have "dropped points."

Throw-in: a throw is taken from the sideline after the ball has gone out of play. This is the only time a player can handle the ball without committing a foul.

Tie: a multi-match meeting between clubs, most notably in cup settings. In the Champions League and Europa League, a tie is two matches, home and away, in the "knockout stages" leading up to the final. In the FA Cup, it's called a tie because, if the first game ends in a draw, there's a replay at the other team's stadium.

Tiki-taka: a style of play defined by the abundant use of short passes. Created by Barcelona and used by the Spanish national team during its 2008 and 2012 Euro and 2010 World Cup-winning runs.

Top Four: the top four teams in the Premier League get to play in the Champions League every year.

Total Football: a system of play, invented in Holland in the early 1970s, in which presumably every player other than the goalkeeper can play any of the other positions.

Touch: describes when a player handles a ball. Players are said to have a good touch or a poor touch, or a good first touch.

Touch line: the sidelines.

Transfer: the action taken whenever a player under contract moves between clubs. It refers to the transferring of a player's registration from one association football club to another.

Transfer Window: time during the year, at different periods, where players can be transferred from one club to another. There are two: summer and winter. The summer transfer window usually begins on June 10th, and will now last until 5 p.m. British Summer Time on the Thursday before the start of the season. The winter window usually opens on New Year's Day, and lasts until the end of January.

Treble: winning three titles in the same season. Last done in England in 1999 by Manchester United (League, FA Cup, Champions League).

Tube: London's rapid transit system. Vital for going to matches in and around the city, and just generally getting around.

Unlock: to open up a defense that, to that point, had been impenetrable.

Up top: at the front, meaning a team's forwards or strikers.

Volley: to kick a moving ball from the air before it hits the ground.

Wanker: a fool. Another term used in pubs to describe certain football personalities.

Wide: describes a form of play where wingers often get the ball and send numerous crosses in.

World-Class: a player who can play anywhere in the world.

Yellow Card: a warning; get two of them in one match and you get a red card and are sent off.

Yo-Yo Club: a club that is often promoted and relegated – also known as a ping pong club.

Appendix

English Stadiums by Capacity

1) Tottenham - Wembley Stadium (90,000)

2) Manchester United - Old Trafford (74,994)

3) West Ham United - London Stadium (60,000)

4) Arsenal - Emirates Stadium (59,867)

5) Manchester City - Etihad Stadium (55,017

6) Liverpool - Anfield (53,394)

7) Newcastle - St. James' Park (52,354)

8) Chelsea - Stamford Bridge (41,631)

9) Everton - Goodison Park (39,595)

10) Southampton - St. Mary's Stadium (32,384)

11) Cardiff City - Cardiff City Stadium (33,280)

12) Leicester City - King Power Stadium (32,273)

13) Wolverhampton Wanderers - Molineaux Stadium (31,700)

13) Brighton and Hove Albion - AmEx Stadium (30,666)

14) Fulham - Craven Cottage (25,700)

15) Crystal Palace - Selhurst Park (25,456)

16) Huddersfield Town - John Smith's Stadium (24,169)

17) Burnley - Turf Moor (21,994)

19) Watford - Vicarage Road (21,000)

20) Bournemouth - Vitality Stadium (11,360)

Premier League Attendance, 2017-18

	Total	Average
1) Manchester United	1,424,538	74,976
2) Tottenham Hotspur	1,291,103	67,953
3) Arsenal FC	1,127,133	59,323
4) West Ham United	1,080,808	56,885
5) Manchester City	1,022,434	53,812
6) Liverpool FC	1,007,931	53,049
7) Newcastle United	987,844	51,992
8) Chelsea FC	784,353	41,282
9) Everton FC	737,143	38,797
10) Leicester City	600,083	31,583
11) Southampton FC	585,084	30,794
12) Brighton & Hove Albion	577,701	30,405
13) Stoke City	556,317	29,280
14) Crystal Palace	476,189	25,063
15) West Bromwich Albion	465,878	24,520
16) Huddersfield Town	456,757	24,040
17) Burnley FC	393,080	20,688
18) Swansea City	391,830	20,623
19) Watford FC	384,388	20,231
20) AFC Bournemouth	202,154	10,640

First Division/Premier League Champions

1888–89	Preston North End
1889–90	Preston North End (2)
1890–91	Everton
1891–92	Sunderland
1892–93	Sunderland (2)
1893–94	Aston Villa
1894–95	Sunderland (3)
1895–96	Aston Villa (2)
1896–97	Aston Villa (3)
1897–98	Sheffield United
1898–99	Aston Villa (4)
1899–1900	Aston Villa (5)
1900–01	Liverpool
1901–02	Sunderland (4)
1902–03	The Wednesday
1903–04	The Wednesday(2)
1904–05	Newcastle United
1905–06	Liverpool (2)
1906–07	Newcastle United (2)
1907–08	Manchester United
1908–09	Newcastle United (3)
1909–10	Aston Villa (6)
1910–11	Manchester United (2)
1911–12	Blackburn Rovers
1912–13	Sunderland (5)
1913–14	Blackburn Rovers (2)
1914–15	Everton (2)
1915/16–1918/19	League suspended (WW1)

First Division/Premier League Champions

1919–20	West Bromwich Albion
1920–21	Burnley
1921–22	Liverpool (3)
1922–23	Liverpool (4)
1923–24	Huddersfield Town
1924–25	Huddersfield Town (2)
1925–26	Huddersfield Town (3)
1926–27	Newcastle United (4)
1927–28	Everton (3)
1928–29	The Wednesday (3)
1929–30	Sheffield Wednesday (4)
1930–31	Arsenal
1931–32	Everton (4)
1932–33	Arsenal (2)
1933–34	Arsenal (3)
1934–35	Arsenal (4)
1935–36	Sunderland (6)
1936–37	Manchester City
1937–38	Arsenal (5)
1938–39	Everton (5)
1939/40–1945/46	League suspended (WW2)
1946–47	Liverpool (5)
1947–48	Arsenal (6)
1948–49	Portsmouth
1949–50	Portsmouth (2)
1950–51	Tottenham Hotspur
1951–52	Manchester United (3)
1952–53	Arsenal (7)

First Division/Premier League Champions

1953–54	Wolverhampton Wanderers
1954–55	Chelsea
1955–56	Manchester United (4)
1956–57	Manchester United (5)
1957–58	Wolverhampton Wanderers(2)
1958–59	Wolverhampton Wanderers(3)
1959–60	Burnley (2)
1960–61	Tottenham Hotspur (2)
1961–62	Ipswich Town
1962–63	Everton (6)
1963–64	Liverpool (6)
1964–65	Manchester United (6)
1965–66	Liverpool (7)
1966–67	Manchester United (7)
1967–68	Manchester City (2)
1968–69	Leeds United
1969–70	Everton (7)
1970–71	Arsenal (8)
1971–72	Derby County
1972–73	Liverpool(8)
1973–74	Leeds United (2)
1974–75	Derby County (2)
1975–76	Liverpool(9)
1976–77	Liverpool(10)
1977–78	Nottingham Forest
1978–79	Liverpool (11)
1979–80	Liverpool (12)
1980–81	Aston Villa (7)

First Division/Premier League Champions

1981–82	Liverpool(13)
1982–83	Liverpool(14)
1983–84	Liverpool (15)
1984–85	Everton (8)
1985–86	Liverpool (16)
1986–87	Everton (9)
1987–88	Liverpool (17)
1988–89	Arsenal (9)
1989–90	Liverpool (18)
1990–91	Arsenal (10)
1991–92	Leeds United (3)
1992–93	Manchester United (8)
1993–94	Manchester United (9)
1994–95	Blackburn Rovers (3)
1995–96	Manchester United(10)
1996–97	Manchester United (11)
1997–98	Arsenal (11)
1998–99	Manchester United(12)
1999–2000	Manchester United (13)
2000–01	Manchester United (14)
2001–02	Arsenal (12)
2002–03	Manchester United (15)
2003–04	Arsenal(13)
2004–05	Chelsea(2)
2005–06	Chelsea (3)
2006–07	Manchester United (16)
2007–08	Manchester United(17)
2008–09	Manchester United(18)

First Division/Premier League Champions

2009–10	Chelsea (4)
2010–11	Manchester United (19)
2011–12	Manchester City (3)
2012–13	Manchester United (20)
2013–14	Manchester City (4)
2014–15	Chelsea (5)
2015–16	Leicester City
2016–17	Chelsea (6)
2017-18	Manchester City (5)

FA Cup Champions

1872	Wanderers
1873	Wanderers (2)
1874	Oxford University
1875	Royal Engineers
1876	Wanderers (3)
1877	Wanderers (4)
1878	Wanderers (5)
1879	Old Etonians
1880	Clapham Rovers
1881	Old Carthusians
1882	Old Etonians (2)
1883	Blackburn Olympic
1884	Blackburn Rovers
1885	Blackburn Rovers (2)
1886	Blackburn Rovers (3)
1887	Aston Villa
1888	West Bromwich Albion
1889	Preston North End
1890	Blackburn Rovers (4)
1891	Blackburn Rovers (5)
1892	West Bromwich Albion (2)
1893	Wolverhampton Wanderers
1894	Notts County
1895	Aston Villa (2)
1896	Sheffield Wednesday
1897	Aston Villa (3)
1898	Nottingham Forest
1899	Sheffield United

FA Cup Champions

1900	Bury
1901	Tottenham Hotspur
1902	Sheffield United (2)
1903	Bury (2)
1904	Manchester City
1905	Aston Villa (4)
1906	Everton
1907	Sheffield Wednesday (2)
1908	Wolverhampton Wanderers (2)
1909	Manchester United
1910	Newcastle United
1911	Bradford City
1912	Barnsley
1913	Aston Villa (5)
1914	Burnley
1915	Sheffield United (3)
1920	Aston Villa (6)
1921	Tottenham Hotspur (2)
1922	Huddersfield Town
1923	Bolton Wanderers
1924	Newcastle United (2)
1925	Sheffield United (4)
1926	Bolton Wanderers (2)
1927	Cardiff City
1928	Blackburn Rovers (6)
1929	Bolton Wanderers (3)
1930	Arsenal
1931	West Bromwich Albion

FA Cup Champions

1932	Newcastle United (3)
1933	Everton (2)
1934	Manchester City (2)
1935	Sheffield Wednesday (3)
1936	Arsenal (2)
1937	Sunderland
1938	Preston North End (2)
1939	Portsmouth
1946	Derby County
1947	Charlton Athletic
1948	Manchester United (2)
1949	Wolverhampton Wanderers (3)
1950	Arsenal (3)
1951	Newcastle United (4)
1952	Newcastle United (5)
1953	Blackpool
1954	West Bromwich Albion (4)
1955	Newcastle United (6)
1956	Manchester City (3)
1957	Aston Villa (7)
1958	Bolton Wanderers (4)
1959	Nottingham Forest (2)
1960	Wolverhampton Wanderers (4)
1961	Tottenham Hotspur (3)
1962	Tottenham Hotspur (4)
1963	Manchester United (3)
1964	West Ham United
1965	Liverpool

FA Cup Champions

1966	Everton (3)
1967	Tottenham Hotspur (5)
1968	West Bromwich Albion (5)
1969	Manchester City (4)
1970	Chelsea
1971	Arsenal (4)
1972	Leeds United
1973	Sunderland (2)
1974	Liverpool (2)
1975	West Ham United (2)
1976	Southampton
1977	Manchester United (4)
1978	Ipswich Town
1979	Arsenal (5)
1980	West Ham United (3)
1981	Tottenham Hotspur (6)
1982	Tottenham Hotspur (7)
1983	Manchester United (5)
1984	Everton (4)
1985	Manchester United (6)
1986	Liverpool (3)
1987	Coventry City
1988	Wimbledon
1989	Liverpool (4)
1990	Manchester United (7)
1991	Tottenham Hotspur (8)
1992	Liverpool (5)
1993	Arsenal (6)

FA Cup Champions

1994	Manchester United (8)
1995	Everton (5)
1996	Manchester United (9)
1997	Chelsea (2)
1998	Arsenal (7)
1999	Manchester United (10)
2000	Chelsea (3)
2001	Liverpool (6)
2002	Arsenal (8)
2003	Arsenal (9)
2004	Manchester United (11)
2005	Arsenal (10)
2006	Liverpool (7)
2007	Chelsea (4)
2008	Portsmouth (2)
2009	Chelsea (5)
2010	Chelsea (6)
2011	Manchester City (5)
2012	Chelsea (7)
2013	Wigan Athletic
2014	Arsenal (11)
2015	Arsenal (12)
2016	Manchester United (12)
2017	Arsenal (13)
2018	Chelsea (8)

League Cup Champions

1961	Aston Villa
1962	Norwich City
1963	Birmingham City
1964	Leicester City
1965	Chelsea
1966	West Bromwich Albion
1967	Queens Park Rangers
1968	Leeds United
1969	Swindon Town
1970	Manchester City
1971	Tottenham Hotspur
1972	Stoke City
1973	Tottenham Hotspur (2)
1974	Wolverhampton Wanderers
1975	Aston Villa (2)
1976	Manchester City (2)
1977	Aston Villa (3)
1978	Nottingham Forest
1979	Nottingham Forest (2)
1980	Wolverhampton Wanderers (2)
1981	Liverpool
1982	Liverpool (2)
1983	Liverpool (3)
1984	Liverpool (4)
1985	Norwich City (2)
1986	Oxford United
1987	Arsenal
1988	Luton Town
1989	Nottingham Forest (3)

League Cup Champions

1990	Nottingham Forest (4)
1991	Sheffield Wednesday
1992	Manchester United
1993	Arsenal (2)
1994	Aston Villa (4)
1995	Liverpool (5)
1996	Aston Villa (5)
1997	Leicester City (2)
1998	Chelsea (2)
1999	Tottenham Hotspur (3)
2000	Leicester City (3)
2001	Liverpool (6)
2002	Blackburn Rovers
2003	Liverpool (7)
2004	Middlesbrough
2005	Chelsea (3)
2006	Manchester United (2)
2007	Chelsea (4)
2008	Tottenham Hotspur (4)
2009	Manchester United (3)
2010	Manchester United (4)
2011	Birmingham City (2)
2012	Liverpool (8)
2013	Swansea City
2014	Manchester City (3)
2015	Chelsea (5)
2016	Manchester City (4)
2017	Manchester United (5)
2018	Manchester City (5)

European Cup/Champions League Winners

1955-56	Real Madrid
1956-57	Real Madrid (2)
1957-58	Real Madrid (3)
1958-59	Real Madrid (4)
1959-60	Real Madrid (5)
1960-61	Benfica
1961-62	Benfica (2)
1962-63	AC Milan
1963-64	Inter Milan
1964-65	Inter Milan (2)
1965-66	Real Madrid (6)
1966-67	Celtic
1967-68	Manchester United
1968-69	AC Milan (2)
1969-70	Feyenoord
1970-71	Ajax
1971-72	Ajax (2)
1972-73	Ajax (3)
1973-74	Bayern Munich
1974-75	Bayern Munich (2)
1975-76	Bayern Munich (3)
1976-77	Liverpool
1977-78	Liverpool (2)
1978-79	Nottingham Forest
1979-80	Nottingham Forest (2)
1980-81	Liverpool (3)
1981-82	Aston Villa
1982-83	Hamburg

European Cup/Champions League Winners

1983-84	Liverpool (4)
1984-85	Juventus
1985-86	Steaua Bucuresti
1986-87	Porto
1987-88	PSV Eindhoven
1988-89	AC Milan (3)
1989-90	AC Milan (4)
1990-91	Red Star Belgrade
1991-92	Barcelona
1992-93	Marseille
1993-94	AC Milan (5)
1994-95	Ajax (4)
1995-96	Juventus (2)
1996-97	Borussia Dortmund
1997-98	Real Madrid (7)
1998-99	Manchester United (2)
1999-00	Real Madrid (8)
2000-01	Bayern Munich (4)
2001-02	Real Madrid (9)
2002-03	AC Milan (6)
2003-04	Porto (2)
2004-05	Liverpool (5)
2005-06	Barcelona (2)
2006-07	AC Milan (7)
2007-08	Manchester United (3)
2008-09	Barcelona (3)
2009-10	Inter Milan (3)
2010-11	Barcelona (4)–

European Cup/Champions League Winners

2011-12	Chelsea
2012-13	Bayern Munich (5)
2013-14	Real Madrid (10)
2014-15	Barcelona (5)
2015-16	Real Madrid (11)
2016-17	Real Madrid (12)
2017-18	Real Madrid (13)

European Cup Winners Cup Winners

1960–61	Fiorentina
1961–62	Atlético Madrid
1962–63	Tottenham Hotspur
1963–64	Sporting CP
1964–65	West Ham United
1965–66	Borussia Dortmund
1966–67	Bayern Munich
1967–68	AC Milan
1968–69	Slovan Bratislava
1969–70	Manchester City
1970–71	Chelsea
1971–72	Rangers
1972–73	AC Milan (2)
1973–74	Magdeburg
1974–75	Dynamo Kyiv (2)
1975–76	Anderlecht
1976–77	Hamburg
1977–78	Anderlecht (2)
1978–79	Barcelona
1979–80	Valencia
1980–81	Dinamo Tbilisi
1981–82	Barcelona (2)
1982–83	Aberdeen
1983–84	Juventus
1984–85	Everton
1985–86	Dynamo Kyiv
1986–87	Ajax
1987–88	Mechelen

European Cup Winners Cup Winners

1988–89	Barcelona (3)
1989–90	Sampdoria
1990–91	Manchester United
1991–92	Werder Bremen
1992–93	Parma
1993–94	Arsenal
1994–95	Real Zaragoza
1995–96	Paris Saint-Germain
1996–97	Barcelona (4)
1997–98	Chelsea (2)
1998–99	Lazio

UEFA Cup/Europa League Winners

1972	Tottenham Hotspur
1973	Liverpool FC
1974	Feyenoord
1975	Borussia Mönchengladbach
1976	Liverpool FC (2)
1977	Juventus
1978	PSV Eindhoven
1979	Borussia Mönchengladbach (2)
1980	Eintracht Frankfurt
1981	Ipswich Town
1982	IFK Göteborg
1983	RSC Anderlecht
1984	Tottenham Hotspur (2)
1985	Real Madrid
1986	Real Madrid (2)
1987	IFK Göteborg (2)
1988	Bayer Leverkusen
1989	SSC Napoli
1990	Juventus (2)
1991	Inter
1992	AFC Ajax
1993	Juventus (3)
1994	Inter (2)
1995	Parma
1996	Bayern München
1997	FC Schalke 04
1998	Inter (3)
1999	Parma (2)

UEFA Cup/Europa League Winners

2000	Galatasaray
2001	Liverpool FC (3)
2002	Feyenoord (2)
2003	FC Porto
2004	Valencia CF
2005	CSKA Moskva
2006	Sevilla FC
2007	Sevilla FC (2)
2008	Zenit St. Petersburg
2009	Shakhtar Donetsk
2010	Atlético Madrid
2011	FC Porto (2)
2012	Atlético Madrid (2)
2013	Chelsea FC
2014	Sevilla FC (3)
2015	Sevilla FC (4)
2016	Sevilla FC (5)
2017	Manchester United
2018	Atlético Madrid (3)

Source Lists

Promotion and Relegation: Changing the Way Americans Think About Sports

Books:

Exall, K. (2008). Who Killed English Football?: An Analysis of the State of English Football (2nd ed.). Bloomington, IN: AuthorHouse.

Online Articles:

Ames, N. (2017, May 14). Forest Green stun Tranmere to claim league place for first time. *The Guardian.* Retrieved August 27, 2017, from https://www.theguardian.com/football/2017/may/14/tranmere-rovers-forest-green-national-league-play-off-final

Associated Press. (2017, May 29). Huddersfield Town wins soccer's richest game, promotion to Premier League. *Chicago Tribune.* Retrieved August 21, 2017, from http://www.chicagotribune.com/sports/soccer/ct-huddersfield-town-premier-league-20170529-story.html

Baxter, K. (2016, May 14). There are millions of reasons to want a promotion and avoid relegation in the English Premier League. *Los Angeles Times.* Retrieved August 23, 2017, from http://www.latimes.com/sports/soccer/la-sp-soccer-baxter-20160515-story.html

Belam, M. (2017, April 24). So you've been relegated from League Two. What happens next? *The Guardian.* Retrieved August 26, 2017, from https://www.theguardian.com/football/2017/apr/24/so-youve-been-relegated-from-league-two-what-happens-next

Curley, J., & Roeder, O. (2014, November 14). The Long Migration of English Football. *Five Thirty Eight.* Retrieved August 30, 2017, from https://fivethirtyeight.com/features/the-long-migration-of-english-football/

Gerald, P. (2017, April 14). A Guide to the Leagues and Cups of English Football. *An American's Guide to English Soccer.* Retrieved August 30, 2017, from http://englishsoccerguide.com/guide-leagues-cups-english-football/

Hall, J. (2017, March 2). Is the Football League due a TV rights revolution? Why Derby County are leading the cross-divisional rebellion. *City A.M.*

Retrieved August 28, 2017, from http://www.cityam.com/260194/football-league-due-tv-rights-revolution-why-derby-county

Hunt, J. (2017, May 20). Steve Morison volleyed a late winner as Milllwall won promotion to the Championship with victory over Bradford in the League One play-off final. *BBC*. Retrieved August 24, 2017, from http://www.bbc.com/sport/football/39905619

Law, J. (2017, May 28). Mark Cullen and Brad Potts starred to help Blackpool return to League One at the first time of asking with victory over Exeter in the play-off final. *BBC*. Retrieved August 25, 2017, from http://www.bbc.com/sport/football/39989418

Newman, M. (2015, September 7). Labor Day an important MLB benchmark. *MLB*. Retrieved August 26, 2017, from http://m.mlb.com/news/article/147622354/a-brief-history-of-the-wild-card-era/

Rodrigues, A. (2017, August 1). Updated MLS Expansion Quest Power Rankings. *Soccer Nation*. Retrieved August 22, 2017, from https://www.soccernation.com/updated-mls-expansion-quest-power-rankings/

Rodrigues, J. (2012, February 2). Premier League football at 20: 1992, the start of a whole new ball game. *The Guardian*. Retrieved August 25, 2017, from https://www.theguardian.com/football/from-the-archive-blog/2012/feb/02/20-years-premier-league-football-1992

Rose, G. (2012, May 13). How Manchester City won the Premier League title. *BBC*. Retrieved August 24, 2017, from http://www.bbc.com/sport/football/17853469

Taylor, L. (2017, May 15). What next for Championship-bound Hull, Middlesbrough and Sunderland? *The Guardian*. Retrieved August 28, 2017, from https://www.theguardian.com/football/blog/2017/may/15/hull-sunderland-middlesbrough-relegation-premier-league-championship

Vickers, A. (2017, March 27). Premier League relegation parachute payments 'could be cut', so what's the current situation? *Gazette Live*. Retrieved August 26, 2017, from http://www.gazettelive.co.uk/sport/football/football-news/premier-league-relegation-parachute-payments-12802639

Ward, J. (2009, December 29). The Founding Clubs of the English Football League: Where Are They Now? *Bleacher Report*. Retrieved September 1, 2017, from http://bleacherreport.com/articles/98145-the-founding-clubs-of-the-english-football-league-where-are-they-now

125 years of the Football League and the top flight – which team comes top? (n.d.). *The Guardian*. Retrieved August 26, 2017, from https://www.theguardian.com/football/datablog/2013/apr/17/football-league-125-years

Websites:

Geey, D. (2015, July 30). *Premier League Parachute Payments Explained. Daniel Geey*. Retrieved August 29, 2017, from http://www.danielgeey.com/premier-league-parachute-payments-explained/

Nair, R. (2017, July 18). EPL 2016/2017: How much prize money did each Premier League team win this season? Retrieved August 27, 2017, from https://www.sportskeeda.com/football/how-much-premier-league-club-earn-prize-money-epl-2016-17

Totalsportek2. (2017, June 6). *Premier League Prize Money 2017*. Retrieved August 28, 2017, from http://www.totalsportek.com/money/premier-league-prize-money/

Championship 2016/17 Table. (n.d.). Retrieved July 21, 2017, from http://www.skysports.com/championship-table/2016

League One 2016/17 Table. (n.d.). Retrieved July 21, 2017, from http://www.skysports.com/league-1-table/2016

League Two 2016/17 Table. (n.d.). Retrieved July 21, 2017, from http://www.skysports.com/league-2-table/2016

National League 2016/17 Table. (n.d.). Retrieved July 21, 2017, from http://www.skysports.com/football/forest-grn-vs-dag-red/table/371747

Premier League 2016/17 Table. (n.d.). Retrieved July 21, 2017, from http://www.skysports.com/premier-league-table/2016

The Football League 1888-2013. (n.d.). Retrieved August 23, 2017, from http://www.fl125.co.uk/about

The History of the FA. (n.d.). Retrieved September 1, 2017, from http://www.thefa.com/about-football-association/what-we-do/history

Wild Card Golden Nuggets. (n.d.). Retrieved August 28, 2017, from http://www.profootballhof.com/news/history-of-the-wild-card/

A Basic Guide to England and Europe's "Other" Trophies

Online Articles:

Bass, J. (2015, May 30). Most FA Cup wins all-time: Arsenal wears the crown. *Fansided.* Retrieved September 11, 2017, from https://fansided.com/2015/05/30/most-fa-cup-wins-all-time-arsenal/

Early, C. (2017, April 25). May 31, 1985: English football teams banned from Europe after Heysel Stadium deaths. *BT.* Retrieved September 16, 2017, from http://home.bt.com/news/on-this-day/may-31-1985-english-football-teams-banned-from-europe-after-heysel-stadium-deaths-11363984048674

Harris, C. (2017, June 6). Real Madrid-Juventus Champions League final totalled 3 million viewers on FOX and FOX Deportes. *World Soccer Talk.* Retrieved September 16, 2017, from http://worldsoccertalk.com/2017/06/06/real-madrid-juventus-champions-league-final-totalled-3-million-viewers-fox-fox-deportes/

Hope, C. (2015, January 2). Sunderland FA Cup final heroes Jim Montgomery, Dick Malone and Micky Horswill relive famous 1973 victory over Leeds United ahead of third-round clash. *Daily Mail Online.* Retrieved September 16, 2017, from http://www.dailymail.co.uk/sport/football/article-2894818/Sunderland-FA-Cup-final-heroes-Jim-Montgomery-Dick-Malone-Micky-Horswill-relive-famous-1973-victory-Leeds-United.html

Kraidelman, M. (2015, June 5). The Super Bowl Is No Match For The UEFA Champions League. *Vocative.* Retrieved September 16, 2017, from http://www.vocativ.com/198079/the-super-bowl-is-no-match-for-the-uefa-champions-league/

Murray, S. (2008, November 12). Why the League Cup still has its place in English football. *The Guardian.* Retrieved August 8, 2017, from https://www.theguardian.com/football/blog/2008/nov/12/carlingcup

Murray, S. (2015, June 3). A bried history of the Champions League - and why it's so hard to win two in a row. *The Guardian.* Retrieved August 8, 2017, from https://www.theguardian.com/football/2015/jun/03/champions-league-brief-history-barcelona-juventus

Murray, S. (2017, May 27). Arsenal 2-1 Chelsea: 2017 FA Cup final – as it happened. *The Guardian.* Retrieved September 16, 2017, from https://www.theguardian.com/football/live/2017/may/27/arsenal-v-chelsea-2017-fa-cup-final-live

Richardson, A. (2017, February 6). Flowers of Manchester: Munich Air Disaster: Manchester United lost eight players, including Tommy Taylor, Roger Byrne and Buncan Edwards, in tragic plane crash 59 years ago today. *The Sun.* Retrieved September 16, 2017, from https://www.thesun.co.uk/sport/football/2788868/munich-air-disaster-manchester-united-lost-eight-players-including-tommy-taylor-roger-byrne-and-duncan-edwards-in-tragic-plane-crash-59-years-ago-today/

Taylor, D. (2015, October 10). Brian Clough and the miracle of Nottingham Forest. *The Guardian.* Retrieved September 16, 2017, from https://www.theguardian.com/football/2015/oct/10/brian-clough-miracle-nottingham-forest-european-champions-film-jose-mourinho

Telegraph Sport. (2016, November 4). EFL Cup to be known as Carabao Cup after sponsorship deal with Thai energy drink. *The Telegraph.* Retrieved August 8, 2017, from http://www.telegraph.co.uk/football/2016/11/04/efl-trophy-to-be-known-as-carabao-cup-after-sponsorship-deal-wit/

Ziegler, M. (2017, June 8). Champions League: Champions League final audience lower than US. *The Times.* Retrieved September 16, 2017, from https://www.thetimes.co.uk/article/champions-league-final-audience-lower-than-us-hvl975363

Is there a future for the FA Cup's little brother? (1998, March 26). *BBC.* Retrieved August 8, 2017, from http://news.bbc.co.uk/1/hi/sport/football/68671.stm

Why the League Cup? (2012, September 29). *Sportstar.* Retrieved August 8, 2017, from http://www.sportstaronnet.com/tss3539/stories/20120929505904800.htm

Websites:

Barber, D. (2016, November 2). *The History of the FA Cup.* Retrieved August 8, 2017, from http://www.thefa.com/news/2016/nov/02/history-of-the-fa-cup

Jenifer. (2017, March 20). *FA Cup 2017-18 Schedule (Qualifying & Proper Stage).* Retrieved August 8, 2017, from http://sportsmaza.com/football/fa-cup-schedule/

Champions League 2017-18 Qualifying Rounds Teams Explained. (2017, June 12). *Goal.* Retrieved August 8, 2017, from http://www.goal.com/en/news/champions-league-2017-18-qualifying-rounds-teams-explained/7z4j7mutx8vw1jh72zuxfyjnm

Competition History. (n.d.) Retrieved August 8, 2017, from https://www.efl.com/clubs-and-competitions/carabao-cup/about-the-carabao-cup/league-cup-competition-history/

European qualification for UEFA competitions explained. (n.d.). Retrieved August 8, 2017, from https://www.premierleague.com/european-qualification-explained

FA Cup memories: Radford's Hereford. (2015, January 13). *BBC.* Retrieved September 16, 2017, from http://www.bbc.com/sport/football/30267370

Football's top club competition. (n.d.). *UEFA.* Retrieved August 8, 2017, from http://www.uefa.com/uefachampionsleague/history/background/index.html

From Fairs Cup via UEFA Cup to UEFA Europa League. (n.d.). Retrieved August 8, 2017, from http://www.uefa.com/uefaeuropaleague/history/index.html

How do teams qualify for the FA Cup? (2016, April 21). Retrieved August 8, 2017, from https://sports.ladbrokes.com/sports-central/in-the-know/how-do-teams-qualify-for-the-fa-cup/

The greatest League Cup upset ever? (2013, March 3). *BBC.* Retrieved September 16, 2017, from http://www.bbc.com/sport/football/21423401

UEFA Cup. (n.d.). Retrieved August 8, 2017, from http://www.footballhistory.org/tournament/uefa-cup.html

Wembley's First Ever Match. (2013, April 26). Retrieved September 16, 2017, from http://www.wembleystadium.com/Press/Press-Releases/2013/4/The-First-Ever-Match-At-Wembley.aspx

2016/17 Champions League revenue distribution. (2016, August, 25). *UEFA.* Retrieved September 16, 2017, from http://www.uefa.com/uefachampionsleague/news/newsid=2398575.html

Arsenal

Articles:

Lawrence, A. (2017, May 25). It was Arsenal's day in 2002 – but it has mostly been Chelsea's ever since. *The Guardian.*

Taylor, D. (2017, February 18). Arsenal's 'Wenger Out' crowd should look at Manchester United's labours. *The Guardian.*

Taylor, D. (2017, May 27). Aaron Ramsey fires Arsenal to FA Cup final win over 10-man Chelsea. *The Guardian.*

Wilson, P. (2017, May 28). 'No one gave Arsenal a chance, and we responded,' says Arsene Wenger. *The Guardian.*

Books:

Lawrence, A. (2015). *Invincible: Inside Arsenal's Unbeaten 2003-2004 Season.*[Kindle version]. Retrieved from Amazon.com

Online Articles:

Cross, J. (2018, August 24). Unai Emery already addressing Arsenal's main problems – but it's a long road to the top, insists Alan Smith. *The Mirror.* Retrieved October 15, 2018, from https://www.mirror.co.uk/sport/football/news/unai-emery-already-addressing-arsenals-13130935

Fifield, D. (2018, October 7). Alexandre Lacazette keeps up fine form as stylish Arsenal sweep Fulham aside. *The Guardian.* Retrieved October 14, 2018, from https://www.theguardian.com/football/2018/oct/07/fulham-arsenal-premier-league-match-report

Hytner, D. (2018, November 3). Alexandre Lacazette's glorious goal earns Arsenal a point again Liverpool. *The Guardian.* Retrieved November 4, 2018, from https://www.theguardian.com/football/2018/nov/03/arsenal-liverpool-premier-league-match-report

Hytner, D. (2018, October 5). Unai Emrey's quiet revolution at Arsenal reaping early rewards. *The Guardian.* Retrieved October 10, 2018, from https://www.theguardian.com/football/2018/oct/05/unai-emery-arsenal-quiet-revolution-premier-league?CMP=Share_iOSApp_Other

Hytner, D. (2018, May 23). Unai Emrey says he wants to make Arsenal 'the best team in the world'. *The Guardian*. Retrieved October 13, 2018, from https://www.theguardian.com/football/2018/may/23/arsenal-appoint-unai-emery-manager

Johnson, S. (2018, May 15). End of Season Review: Arsenal's Report Card From the 2017/18 Campaign. *90Min*. Retrieved October 12, 2018, from https://www.90min.com/posts/6060832-end-of-season-review-arsenal-s-report-card-from-the-2017-18-campaign

Lawrence, A. (2018, September 20). Arsenal's Pierre-Emerick Aubameyang at the double against Vorskla Poltava. *The Guardian*. Retrieved October 15, 2018, from https://www.theguardian.com/football/2018/sep/20/arsenal-vorskla-europea-league-match-report

Lawrence, A. (2018, August 12). New manager but same old script for Arsenal as Unai Emrey enters stage. *The Guardian*. Retrieved October 13, 2018, from https://www.theguardian.com/football/2018/aug/12/new-manager-but-same-old-script-for-arsenal-as-unai-emery-enters-stage

Martin, A. (2017, April 29). Tottenham vs arsenal: The 10 greatest north London derbies ever played at White Hart Lane. *Daily Mail Online*. Retrieved September 18, 2017, from http://www.dailymail.co.uk/sport/football/article-4455866/Tottenham-v-Arsenal-10-best-north-London-derbies.html

Ogden, M. (2016, November 4). Arsenal vs Tottenham: North London derby lacks history of others but there are none more significant this season. *The Independent*. Retrieved September 19, 2017, from http://www.independent.co.uk/sport/football/premier-league/arsenal-vs-tottenham-north-london-derby-history-liverpool-manchester-united-city-a7397281.html

Ronay, B. (2018, November 4). Lucas Torreira, the Mighty Insect, embodies Arsenal's new grit. *The Guardian*. Retrieved October 12, 2018, from https://www.theguardian.com/football/blog/2018/nov/04/lucas-torreira-arsenal-new-grit-under-unai-emery-liverpool

Taylor, L. (2018, September 15). Arsenal's Mesut Özil leaves Ciaran Clark and Newcastle too much to do. *The Guardian*. Retrieved October 14, 2018, from https://www.theguardian.com/football/2018/sep/15/newcastle-arsenal-premier-league-report

Arsenal 2017/18 Premier League season review. (2018, May 14). *Sky Sports*. Retrieved October 10, 2018, from, https://www.skysports.com/football/news/11095/11371039/arsenal-201718-premier-league-season-review

Arsenal: Lucas Torreira agrees deal & Matteo Guendouzi set for medical. (2018, July 10). *BBC.* Retrieved October 16, 2018, from https://www.bbc.com/sport/football/44764063

Programmes:

Arsenal v. Vorskla Portava. (2018, September 20). *Official Matchday Programme.*

Websites:

Newman, D. (2015, February 15). A Brief History of The North London Derby: Arsenal and Tottenham. *Soccer Politics.* Retrieved September 19, 2017, from https://sites.duke.edu/wcwp/2015/02/15/a-brief-history-of-the-north-london-derby-arsenal-and-tottenham/

Club moves to Emirates Stadium. (2017, May 10). Retrieved September 20, 2017, from https://www.arsenal.com/history/the-wenger-years/club-moves-to-emirates-stadium

History: Dial Square to north London. (2017, 10 May). Retrieved September 19, 2017, from https://www.arsenal.com/history/laying-the-foundations/laying-the-foundations-overview

History: Goalscorers. (2017, 1 June). Retrieved September 19, 2017, from https://www.arsenal.com/history/club-records/goalscoring-records

History: Graham's Glory Years. (2017, 10 May). Retrieved September 19, 2017, from https://www.arsenal.com/history/grahams-glory-years/graham-s-glory-years-overview

History: Herbert Chapman - The great innovator. (2017, 10 May). Retrieved September 19, 2017, from https://www.arsenal.com/history/herbert-chapman/herbert-chapman-overview

History: The Seventies. (2017, 10 May). Retrieved September 19, 2017, from https://www.arsenal.com/history/the-seventies/the-seventies-overview

10 Things You Need To Know About Stan Kronke. (n.d.). Retrieved August 4, 2017, from https://www.shortlist.com/entertainment/10-things-you-need-to-know-about-stan-kroenke/98435

Bournemouth

Articles:

Fifield, D. (2015, April 28). Eddie Howe writes new chapter for Bournemouth – now for the legacy. *The Guardian*.

Fisher, B. (2016, December 9). AFC Bournemouth begin search for new stadium site for 2020-21 season. *The Guardian*.

Latchem, T. (2015, April 29). Now you have heard of Bournemouth and we diehard fans really do care. *The Guardian*.

Press Association. (2016, March 18). Eddie Howe hopes expansion plans mean Bournemouth can stop turning fans away at the Vitality Stadium gate. *Daily Mail*.

Steinberg, J. (2016, December 5). Bournemouth happy in the middle lane and travelling in the right direction. *The Guardian*.

Welch, J. (2002, January 6). 8 January 1984: Bournemouth 2 Man Utd 0. *The Guardian*.

Online Articles:

Barnish, A. (2018, May 15). End of Season Review: Bournemouth's Report Card From the 2017/18 Campaign. *90Min*. Retrieved September 20, 2018, from https://www.90min.com/posts/6060815-end-of-season-review-bournemouth-s-report-card-from-the-2017-18-campaign

Farrell, S. (2017, April 26). Accounts Reveal Bournemouth's Premier League Windfall. *Insider Media*. Retrieved July 25, 2017, from https://www.insidermedia.com/insider/southwest/accounts-reveal-afc-bournemouths-premier-league-windfall

Fifield, D. (2018, October 1). Bournemouth's Junior Stanislas keeps cool to make Crystal Palace pay penalty. *The Guardian*. Retrieved October 4, 2018, from https://www.theguardian.com/football/2018/oct/01/bournemouth-crystal-palace-premier-league-match-report

Keith, F. (2016, December 9). Bournemouth to build new stadium after Vitality Stadium expansion ruled out. *Squawka.com*. Retrieved July 23, 2017, from http://www.squawka.com/news/bournemouth-to-build-new-stadium-after-vitality-stadium-expansion-ruled-out/848465#z3B9Tj2lPePKs5JA.97

Mitchener, M. (2009, April 26). Fletcher relishes Cherries escape act. *BBC*. Retrieved July 23, 2017, from http://news.bbc.co.uk/sport1/hi/football/teams/b/bournemouth/8019135.stm

Molyneux-Carter, J. Harry Redknapp. (n.d.). *ESPN FC*. Retrieved September 22, 2017, from http://www.espnfc.com/manager/16/harry-redknapp

Nash, K. (2010, June 30). Twenty years on from crash tragedy, Cherries MD Brian Tiler is remembered. *Bournemouth Echo*. Retrieved September 22, 2017, from http://www.bournemouthecho.co.uk/news/8246917.Twenty_years_on_from _crash_tragedy__Cherries_MD_Brian_Tiler_is_remembered/

Payne, N. (2015, October 30). AFC Bournemouth: What should we call the derby between Cherries and Southampton? *Bournemouth Echo*. Retrieved September 23, 2017, from http://www.bournemouthecho. co.uk/sport/13926409.AFC_Bournemouth_What_should_we_call_the_derb y_between_Cherries _and_Southampton_/

Prince-Wright, J. The New Forest Derby: Just 30 miles apart, Southampton and Bournemouth have lived in different parts of the football universe for years. Until they meet on Sunday, that is. (n.d.). *NBC Sports*. Retrieved September 23, 2017, from http://sportsworld.nbcsports.com/southampton-bournemouth-new-forest-derby/

Stuart, J. (2018, October 19). 'No limits': how Bournemouth's managerial duo worked their magic. *The Guardian*. Retrieved October 20, 2018, from https://www.theguardian.com/football/2018/oct/19/jason-tindall-bournemouth-assistant-manager-eddie-howe-burnley

Wadley, I. (2011, Janaury 11). Cherries: Rumor after rumor and the viral blog. *The Bournemouth Echo*. Retrieved October 10, 2018, from https://www.bournemouthecho.co.uk/news/8781878.Cherries__Rumour_aft er_rumour_and_the_viral_blog/

Wilson, P. (2015, December 11). 'Manchester United didn't fancy it': Bournemouth's FA Cup shock recalled. *The Guardian*. Retrieved September 22, 2017, from https://www.theguardian.com/football/2015/dec/11/bournemouth-manchester-united-fa-cup-1984

8 January 1984: Bournemouth 2 Man Utd 0. (2002, January 6). *The Guardian*. Retrieved September 22, 2017, from https://www.theguardian.com/observer/osm/story/0,,626795,00.html

Administration: How it works. (2002, October 21). *BBC*. Retrieved October 10, 2018, from http://news.bbc.co.uk/sport2/hi/football/2336289.stm

AFC Bournemouth v Crystal Palace: Match Preview. (2018, September 27). *Premier League.* Retrieved October 14, 2018, from https://www.premierleague.com/news/860665

Bournemouth 2017/18 Premier League season review. (2018, May 13). *Sky Sports.* Retrieved September 23, 2018, from https://www.skysports.com/football/news/11743/11367607/bournemouth-201718-premier-league-season-review

Bournemouth to start League Two with 17-point deduction. (2008, August, 8). *Daily Mail Online.* Retrieved October 14, 2018, from https://www.dailymail.co.uk/sport/football/article-1042684/Bournemouth-start-League-Two-17-point-deduction.html

Programmes:

Bournemouth v. Crystal Palace. (2018, October 1). *Official Matchday Programme, Issue 4.*

Websites:

Han. *The Beautiful History Of Club Crests, Club Colours & Nicknames: Bournemouth AFC.* (n.d.). Retrieved September 22, 2017, from https://thebeautifulhistory.wordpress.com/clubs/bournemouth-afc/

Rann, C. (2016, February 26). The not a derby derby: How do Saints and Bournemouth Really Feels About Each Other? *George Weah's Cousin.* Retrieved September 23, 2017, from http://georgeweahscousin.com/tag/new-forest-derby/

History of English Football: AFC Bournemouth. (n.d.). Retrieved July 23, 2017, from http://european-football-statistics.co.uk/attnclub/bour.htm

Brighton

Articles:

Fifield, D. (2017, April 17). Brighton seal promotion after win over Wigan and Huddersfield draw at Derby. *The Guardian*.

Fifield, D. (2017, April 17). Promotion to Premier League is our reward, says Brighton's Chris Hughton. *The Guardian*.

Fifield, D. (2017, April, 18). I wasn't playing too much at Leicester and it was time to go, says Knockaert. *The Guardian*.

McRae, D. (2017, April 28). Chris Hughton: I have a thirst for knowledge. I won't always be a manager. *The Guardian*.

Miller, N. (2017, April 18). Brighton's long march ends in Chris Hughton's completion of a job well done. *The Guardian*.

Wood, G. (1996, April 29). How have Brighton gone from this… to this? *The Independent*.

Online Articles:

Aarons, E. (2018, October 5). Brighton's Glenn Murray fires winner to end West Ham's resurgence. *The Guardian*. Retrieved October 24, 2018, from https://www.theguardian.com/football/2018/oct/05/brighton-west-ham-premier-league-match-report

Bailey, S. (2018, November 7). Former Brighton defender says Lewis Dunk is an inspiration for Sussex footballers. *Brighton & Hove Independent*. Retrieved November 7, 2018, from https://www.brightonandhoveindependent.co.uk/sport/football/albion/former-brighton-defender-says-lewis-dunk-is-an-inspiration-for-sussex-footballers-1-8695977

Burnton, S. (2014, September 23). Which two rivals have the world's closest derby record? *The Guardian*. Retrieved September 19, 2017, from https://www.theguardian.com/football/2014/sep/24/the-knowledge-crystal-palace-brighton-closest-derby

Cleeves, K. (2017, April 29). Hughton's Mixed Emotions. *Brighton And Hove Albion*. Retrieved September 19, 2017, from https://www.brightonandhovealbion.com/news/2017/april/hughtons-mixed-emotions/#EgzTfMSETYBbOvQ1.99

Colla, C. (2018, October 6). Official - Brighton sign DUNK and DUFFY on new long-terms. *Transfer Market Web*. Retrieved October 8, 2018, from http://www.transfermarketweb.com/?action=read&idsel=195749

Cove, B. (2013, May 10). Brighton vs Crystal Palace: The Unlikely Rivalry That Sparked A War. *Sabotage Times*. Retrieved September 19, 2017, from https://sabotagetimes.com/football/brighton-and-crystal-palace-the-unlikely-rivalry-that-sparked-a-war

Drury, S. (2018, May 15). End of Season Review: Brighton's Report Card From the 2017/18 Campaign. *90Min*. Retrieved October 24, 2018, from https://www.90min.com/posts/6060887-end-of-season-review-brighton-s-report-card-from-the-2017-18-campaign

Fifield, D. (2013, May 20). Brighton apologise to Crystal Palace over excrement in dressing room. *The Guardian*. Retrieved September 19, 2017, from https://www.theguardian.com/football/2013/may/20/brighton-excrement-crystal-palace

Hilsu, J. (2018, October 27). Report: Albion 1 Wolves 0. *Brighton and Hove Albion*. Retrieved November 3, 2018, from https://www.brightonandhovealbion.com/matches/fixtures/first-team/2018192/october/brighton-and-hove-albion-vs-wolverhampton-wanderers-on-27-oct-18/

Hytner, D. (2018, January 8). Glenn Murray leaves it late as Brighton knock Crystal Palace out of FA Cup. *The Guardian*. Retrieved October 24, 2018, from https://www.theguardian.com/football/2018/jan/08/brighton-hove-albion-crystal-palace-fa-cup-third-round-match-report

Macaskill, S. (2009, May 20). Brighton's future secured by £80m cash injection by multi-millionaire Tony Bloom. *The Telegraph*. Retrieved September 20, 2017, from http://www.telegraph.co.uk/sport/football/teams/brighton-hove-albion/5357550/Brightons-future-secured-by-80m-cash-injection-by-multi-millionaire-Tony-Bloom.html

PA Sport. (2017, January 31). Brighton sign Glenn Murray on permanent deal from Bournemouth. *ESPN*. Retrieved October 10, 1028, from http://www.espn.co.uk/soccer/soccer-transfers/story/3050297/brighton-sign-glenn-murray-on-permanent-deal-from-bournemouth

Pye, S. (2017, May 25). When Brighton last played in the top flight – and the FA Cup final – 34 years ago. *The Guardian*. Retrieved September 20, 2017, from https://www.theguardian.com/football/that-1980s-sports-blog/2017/may/25/brighton-top-flight-fa-cup-final

Ridgway, T. (2010, June 22). Brighton's American Express Community Stadium unveiled. *The Argus*. Retrieved September 20, 2017, from http://www.theargus.co.uk/news/8231146.Brighton_s_American_Express_Community_Stadium_unveiled/

Site Staff. (2017, January 12). All Time Leading Goalscorers - 51 To 74. *Vital Football: news and fans community*. Retrieved September 20, 2017, from http://www.bha.vitalfootball.co.uk/article.asp?a=576585

Smee, G. (2017, April 17). Brighton & Hove Albion 2 - 1 Wigan Athletic. *BBC*. Retrieved October 10, 2018, from https://www.bbc.com/sport/football/39549523

Stone, J. (2014, July 20). 40 years on. how falling out with Clough helped Peter Taylor reinvent Brighton and Hove Albion forever. *Made of Stone: The personal blog of Jem Stone*. Retrieved September 20, 2017, from https://jemstone.wordpress.com/2014/07/20/40-years-on-how-falling-out-with-clough-helped-peter-taylor-reinvent-brighton-and-hove-albion-forever/

Brighton Amex stadium wins best new venue award. (2012, May 16). *BBC*. Retrieved September 20, 2017, from http://www.bbc.com/news/uk-england-sussex-18084063

Brighton 2017/18 Premier League season review. (2018, May 14). *Sky Sports*. Retrieved September 22, 2018, from https://www.skysports.com/football/news/11741/11370829/brighton-201718-premier-league-season-review

Dunk and Duffy get new five-year Brighton deals. (2018, October 5). *Scoresway*. Retrieved October 5, 2018, from http://www.scoresway.com/?sport=golf&page=news&view=article&news_id=1061662

Shane Duffy: New Brighton deal rewards Republic of Ireland man's persistence. (2018, October 11). *BBC*. Retrieved October 24, from https://www.bbc.com/sport/football/45826689

Programmes:

Brighton and Hove Albion v. West Ham United. (2018, October 5). *Official Matchday Programme*.

428

Websites:

Carder, T. *Brighton & Hove Albion: History.* (n.d.). Retrieved September 20, 2017, from https://www.brightonandhovealbion.com/club-info/history/

Club News. (2014, April 17). *Zamora Named Brighton's Best. Brighton & Hove Albion.* Retrieved September 20, 2017, from https://www.brightonandhovealbion.com/news/2014/april/zamora-named-brightons-best/

Dudding, T. (2008, November 28). *Club Signs Stadium Contract.* Retrieved September 20, 2017, from https://web.archive.org/web/20100904173126/http://www.seagulls.co.uk/pa ge/Stadium/0%2C%2C10433~1469754%2C00.html

Outside Write. *Palace v. Brighton: The Enduring M23 Derby.* (n.d.). Retrieved September 20, 2017, from http://outsidewrite.co.uk/palace-v-brighton-enduring-m23-derby/

Chris Hughton Manager Coaching Staff. (n.d.). Retrieved October 24, 2018, from https://www.brightonandhovealbion.com/teams/first-team/coaching-staff2/chris-hughton/

Falmer stadium. (n.d.). Retrieved September 20, 2017, from https://web.archive.org/web/20100209025559/http://www.sussex.ac.uk/fal merstadium/timeline.php

Glenn Murray. (2018). Retrieved October 14, 2018, from http://terracechants.me.uk/player/chants/Glenn+Murray

The England DNA is the playing and coaching philosophy of the England teams. (n.d.). Retrieved October 24, 2018, from https://community.thefa.com/england_dna/

Withdean's Greatest XI. (n.d.). Retrieved September 20, 2017, from http://www.wearebrighton.com/features/withdean-greatest-11.html

Videos:

Brighton 0-2 Crystal Palace - Championship Play-Off Semi-Final - 13th May 2013 [Video file]. (2014, May 13). Retrieved from https://www.youtube.com/watch?v=zSRvtkQC4Yw

Burnley

Articles:

Ponting, I. (1996, January 22). Obituary: Harry Potts. *The Independent.*

Books:

Thomas, D. (2014). *Who Says Football Doesn't Do Fairytales: How Burnley Defied the Odds to Join the Elite.* Durrington: Pitch Publishing.

Online Articles:

Burt, J. Premier League doctors call for 'concussion bins' in proposal to match rugby's head injury protocols. (2018, June 13). *The Telegraph.* Retrieved October 24, 2018, from https://www.telegraph.co.uk/football/2018/06/13/premier-league-doctors-call-concussion-bins-proposal-match-rugbys/

Garner, S. (2009, October 17). East Lancashire derby: Welcome to hell. *The Independent.* Retrieved September 18, 2017, from http://www.independent.co.uk/sport/football/premier-league/east-lancashire-derby-welcome-to-hell-1804815.html

Geldard, S. (2009, November 25). Turf Moor facelift back on for Burnley. *Lancashire Telegraph.* Retrieved September 20, 2017, from http://www.lancashiretelegraph.co.uk/sport/football/burnley_fc/news/4758508.display/

Lianos, K. (2016, June 29). Which Premier League team has the oldest stadium? Where does your club's ground rank? *Daily Star.* Retrieved September 20, 2017, from https://www.dailystar.co.uk/sport/football/526270/Premier-League-team-oldest-stadium-West-Ham-new-ground-rank

Marshall, T. (2018, May 17). Revealed: How much money Burnley made from 2017/18 Premier League season. *Lancashire Telegraph.* Retrieved October 24, 2018, from https://www.lancashiretelegraph.co.uk/sport/16232702.revealed-how-much-money-burnley-made-from-201718-premier-league-season/

Marshall, T. (2014, June 27). Turf moor redevelopment plans revealed. *Lancashire Telegraph.* Retrieved September 20, 2017, from http://www.lancashiretelegraph.co.uk/news/11304337.Turf_moor_redevelopment_plans_revealed/

Mitten, A. (2015, October 25). The sporting read: Blackburn-Burnley rivalry - enmity that runs deeper than simple geography. *The National.* Retrieved September 18, 2017, from https://www.thenational.ae/sport/the-sporting-read-blackburn-burnley-rivalry-enmity-that-runs-deeper-than-simple-geography-1.55382

Spratt, B. Dyche: Burnley can't use Europa League results. (2018, August 19). *Goal.* Retrieved October 24, 2018, from http://www.goal.com/brasilglobaltour/en-ng/news/4055/mamain/2018/08/19/47147532/dyche-burnley-cant-use-europa-league-as-excuse-for-poor

Burnley FC plans Turf Moor redevelopment. (n.d.). *EN The Magazine for Entrepreneurs.* Retrieved September 20, 2017, from http://www.enforbusiness.com/news/burnley-fc-plans-turf-moor-redevelopment-20102900

Premier League side Burnley fifth in European profit league for 2015. (2017, January 13). *BBC.* Retrieved October 24, 2018, from https://www.bbc.com/sport/football/38605455

Ten Of UK's 12 'Most Struggling Cities' In North. (2016, February 26). *Sky News.* Retrieved July 23, 2017, July 23, 2017, from http://news.sky.com/story/ten-of-uks-12-most-struggling-cities-in-north-10186031

Programmes:

Bentley, D. (Ed.). (2018, September 6) Burnley v. Huddersfield Town. *Turf: Official Matchday Programme, Issue 7.*

Websites:

GOTP Editorial. (2013, August 9). Great Reputations: Burnley 1959-60 - a good year for claret. *GOTP: Game of the People.* Retrieved September 20, 2017, from https://gameofthepeople.com/2013/08/09/great-reputations-burnley-1959-60-a-good-year-for-claret/

Scholes, T. (2013, July 10). Champions Of England - Burnley FC 1920 To 1930. *Clarets Mad: Proud Supporters of Burnley FC.* Retrieved September 20, 2017, from http://www.clarets-mad.co.uk/feat/edx1/champions_of_england__burnley_fc_1920_to_1930_7 99701/index.shtml

Burnley FC History. (n.d.). Retrieved September 20, 2017, from https://www.burnleyfootballclub.com/club/history/

Burnley: Turf Moor. (2017). Retrieved September 20, 2017, from https://www.premierleague.com/clubs/43/Burnley/stadium

FA Concussion Guidelines If In Doubt Sit Them Out. (2018). Retrieved October 24, 2018 from http://www.thefa.com/get-involved/fa-concussion-guidelines-if-in-doubt-sit-them-out

The History of Turf Moor. (2007). Retrieved September 20, 2017, from http://www.claretsmuseum.com/turfmoor.html

Turf Moor Developments. (2016, June 20). Retrieved September 20, 2017, from https://www.burnleyfootballclub.com/news/2016/june/turf-moor-developments/

Who's the best all-time Burnley player? (2005, October 7). *BBC Lancashire.* Retrieved September 20, 2017, from http://www.bbc.co.uk/lancashire/content/articles/2005/10/07/lancashire_sport_burnley_best.shtml

Cardiff

Books:

Hayes, D. (2006). *The Who's Who of Cardiff City: 1899-2006.* Nottingham, UK: Breedon Books.

Online Articles:

Gholam, S. (2018, June 5). Neil Warnock wins record eighth promotion with Cardiff. *Sky Sports.* Retrieved October 4, 2018, from https://www.skysports.com/football/news/11688/11358416/neil-warnock-wins-record-eighth-promotion-with-cardiff

Hall, D. (2018, May 16). End of Season Review: Cardiff City's Report Card From the 2017/18 Campaign. *90Min.* Retrieved October 24, 2018, from https://www.90min.com/posts/6061809-end-of-season-review-cardiff-city-s-report-card-from-the-2017-18-campaign

James, S. (2013, November 1). Cardiff and Swansea make Premier League history but hatred continues. *The Guardian.* Retrieved October 24, 2018, from https://www.theguardian.com/football/2013/nov/01/cardiff-city-swansea-premier-league-hatred

Kemble, J. (2018, May 8). The big Cardiff City season review: We have our say on the best and worst of the Bluebirds' promotion campaign. *Inside Wales Sport.* Retrieved October 4, 2018, from http://www.insidewalessport.co.uk/cardiff-city-season-review/

Martin, P. (2016, October 14). Five facts about the Cardiff v Bristol City rivalry. *HITC.* Retrieved October 10, 2018, from https://www.hitc.com/en-gb/2016/10/13/five-facts-about-the-cardiff-v-bristol-city-rivalry/

Mitten, A. (2009, May 1). The bitter battle for Welsh supremacy: Swansea vs Cardiff. *FourFourTwo.* Retrieved October 24, 2018, https://www.fourfourtwo.com/us/features/bitter-battle-welsh-supremacy-swansea-vs-cardiff

Pearlman, M. (2018, October 5). Neil Warnock: Manager fears Cardiff City sack. *BBC.* Retrieved October 5, 2018, from https://www.bbc.com/sport/football/45756398

Phillips, T. (2014, August 11). Cardiff City 1-0 Real Madrid: What happened to the 1971 heroes who beat Spanish giants at Ninian Park? *Wales Online.* Retrieved October 12, 2018, from https://www.walesonline.co.uk/sport/football/football-news/cardiff-city-1-0-real-madrid-7596380

Scott, N. (2013, December 26). America, meet Vincent Tan, the worst owner in sports. *USA Today.* Retrieved October 10, 2018, from https://ftw.usatoday.com/2013/12/vincent-tan-cardiff-city-owner

Shepherd, R. (2013, March 21). 1964-1973 The Scoular Years. *Cardiff City FC.* Retrieved September 30, 2018, from https://www.cardiffcityfc.co.uk/news/2013/march/1964-1973-the-scoular-years/

Shepherd, R. (2013, March 21). 2000-2010 Ignition & Progression. *Cardiff City FC.* Retrieved September 30, 2018, from https://www.cardiffcityfc.co.uk/news/2013/march/2000-2010-ignition--progression/

Shepherd. R. (2013, March 19). 1920-1947 Great Days, Lows & Recovery. *Cardiff City FC.* Retrieved September 30, 2018, from https://www.cardiffcityfc.co.uk/news/2013/march/1920-1947-great-days-lows--recovery/

Steinberg, J. (2018, September 30). Sam Vokes nods rejuvenated Burnley to victory over toothless Cardiff. *The Guardian.* Retrieved October 2, 2018, from https://www.theguardian.com/football/live/2018/sep/30/cardiff-city-v-burnley-premier-league-live?page=with:block-5bb09c4ee4b025721fc87368#liveblog-navigation

Tucker, S. (2012, May 9). The obscure story of Cardiff City's blue kit and nickname. *Wales Online.* Retrieved October 10, 2018, from https://www.walesonline.co.uk/sport/football/football-news/obscure-story-cardiff-citys-blue-2030463

Wilson, P. (2018, October 17). Things already looking bleak for clubs near the Premier League basement. *The Guardian.* Retrieved October 17, 2018, from https://www.theguardian.com/football/blog/2018/oct/17/bleak-future-premier-league-basement-huddersfield-newcastle-cardiff-football

Fulham's first league defeat of 2018 confirmed Cardiff City's place in the Premier League, despite a 0-0 draw with Reading. (2018, May 6). *FourFourTwo.* Retrieved October 10, 2018, from https://www.fourfourtwo.com/news/championship-review-cardiff-promoted-bolton-leave-it-late-survive

The 20 fiercest rivalries in English football. (2018, April 7). *The Telegraph.* Retrieved October 10, 2018, from https://www.telegraph.co.uk/football/0/20-fiercest-rivalries-english-football/1-cardiff-city-v-swansea-city/

Top Welsh clubs could re-join Welsh Cup. (2011, April 20). *BBC.* Retrieved September 30, 2018, from https://www.bbc.com/sport/football/13150160

Websites:

Cardiff City FC. (2018). Retrieved October 4, 2018, from https://www.footballhistory.org/club/cardiff.html

Cardiff City Stadium. (2018). Retrieved October 24, 2018 https://www.footballgroundguide.com/leagues/england/premier-league/cardiff-city-stadium.html#arecord-and-average-attendance

Cardiff City Stadium. (n.d.). Retrieved October 24, 2018, from http://www.visitcardiff.com/seedo/cardiff-city-stadium/

History. (n.d.). Retrieved September 30, 2018, from https://www.cardiffcityfc.co.uk/club/history/

Welsh Cup Summary. (n.d.). Retrieved September 30, 2018, from http://fchd.info/cups/welshcupsummary.htm

Chelsea

Books:

Kuper, S., & Syzmanski, S. (2014). *Soccernomics: Why England Loses, Why Spain, Germany, and Brazil Win, and Why the U.S., Japan, Australia – and Even Iraq – Are Destined to Become the Kings of the World's Most Popular Sport.* New York: Nation Books.

Online Articles:

Fifield, D. Chelsea not at same level as Liverpool, says Maurizio Sarri. (2018, September 23). *The Guardian.* Retrieved October 24, 2018, from https://www.theguardian.com/football/2018/sep/23/maybe-in-one-year-we-will-be-at-the-same-level-as-liverpool-maurizio-sarri?CMP=Share_iOSApp_Other

Fifield, D. Chelsea rediscover energy and optimism under Maurizio Sarri. (2018, September 28). *The Guardian.* Retrieved October 24, 2018, from https://www.theguardian.com/football/2018/sep/28/chelsea-maurizio-sarri-energy-optimism-eden-hazard?CMP=Share_iOSApp_Other

Fifield, D. Chelsea's Maurizio Sarri humble before first encounter with José Mourinho. (2018, October 19). *The Guardian.* Retrieved October 24, 2018, from https://www.theguardian.com/football/2018/oct/19/chelsea-maurizio-sarri-jose-mourinho-manchester-united

Hickman, N. (2014, December 26). The day that changed football! Chelsea's non-British side of Boxing Day '99. *Express.* Retrieved July 15, 2017, from http://www.express.co.uk/sport/football/548650/Chelsea-s-non-British-starting-XI-Gianluca-Vialli-against-Southampton

Mannion, D. (2016, November 25). London derbies ranked on ferocity of rivalry, including Tottenham v Arsenal and West Ham v Chelsea. *Talk Sport.* Retrieved July 15, 2017, from https://talksport.com/football/london-derbies-ranked-ferocity-rivalry-including-tottenham-v-arsenal-and-west-ham-v-chelsea?p=1

Massarella, L. (2016, April 1). Best Chelsea players: the 11 greatest of all time. *Four Four Two.* Retrieved July 14, 2017, from https://www.fourfourtwo.com/features/best-chelsea-players-11-greatest-all-time

Press Association. (2017, January 11). Chelsea hope for 60,000 capacity Stamford Bridge development boost after formal planning application. *Mirror.* Retrieved July 15, 2017, from http://www.mirror.co.uk/sport/football/news/chelsea-hope-60000-capacity-stamford-9601423

Sharp, W. (2017, April 18). The transfer that defined an era: Ashley Cole's move from Arsenal to Chelsea. *These Football Times*. Retrieved July 13, 2017, from http://thesefootballtimes.co/2017/04/18/the-transfer-that-defined-an-era-ashley-coles-move-from-arsenal-to-chelsea/

Todd, O. (2017, May 2). Chelsea face tour-year exile from Stamford Bridge as new stadium move gets pushed to 2023. *The Daily Mail Online*. Retrieved July 14, 2017, from http://www.dailymail.co.uk/sport/football/article-4467172/Chelsea-face-FOUR-year-exile-Stamford-Bridge.html

Watts, J. (2017, March 24). Premier League: How long do managers stay at your club, on average. *Daily Star*. Retrieved July 18, 2017, from http://www.dailystar.co.uk/sport/football/599550/Premier-League-managers-stay-at-your-club-average-manager-tenure-sportgalleries

Wilson, J. (2012, April 25). Queens Park Rangers defender Anton Ferdinand will refuse to shake hands with Chelsea's John Terry. *The Telegraph*. Retrieved July 18, 2017, from http://www.telegraph.co.uk/sport/football/teams/chelsea/9227559/Queens-Park-Rangers-defender-Anton-Ferdinand-will-refuse-to-shake-hands-with-Chelseas-John-Terry.html

Lampard & the 20 greatest Chelsea players of all time. (n.d.). *Goal*. Retrieved July 11, 2017, from http://www.goal.com/en-gb/news/7182/galleries/2017/02/02/20140592/lampard-the-20-greatest-chelsea-players-of-all-time

Premier League has highest percentage of Foreign players – UEFA report. (January 12, 2017). *Sky Sports*. Retrieved July 15, 2017, from http://www.skysports.com/football/news/11661/10725849/premier-league-has-highest-percentage-of-foreign-players-8211-uefa-report

Russian businessman buys Chelsea. (2003, July 2). *BBC*. Retrieved July 16, 2017, from http://news.bbc.co.uk/2/hi/3036838.stm

The 10 biggest rivalries in London football. (2016, January 21). *The Telegraph*. Retrieved July 16, 2017, from http://www.telegraph.co.uk/football/2016/02/08/the-10-biggest-rivalries-in-london-football/arsenal-and-chelsea-players/

Programmes:

Anthill, D. (Ed.). (2018, October 4). Chelsea FC v. Vidi: Europa League Group L. *Official Matchday Program, 5*.

Chelsea v. Southampton. (2017, April, 25). *Official Matchday Programme.*

Websites:

Pasztor, D. (2016, March 1). Chelsea pay tribute to Peter Osgood, the King of Stamford Bridge. Retrieved July 17, 2017, from https://weaintgotnohistory.sbnation.com/2016/3/1/11137302/chelsea-pay-tribute-to-peter-osgood-the-king-of-stamford-bridge

Carefree: CFC Songs. (n.d.). Retrieved July 12, 2017, from https://www.fanchants.com/football-songs/chelsea-chants/carefree/

Chelsea players: Best 11 of all time. (n.d.). *The Telegraph.* Retrieved July 14, 2017, from http://www.telegraph.co.uk/sport/football/teams/chelsea/11282960/Chelsea-players-Best-11-of-all-time.html

History of Chelsea Football Club. (n.d.). Retrieved July 13, 2017, from http://www.soccermaniak.com/history-of-chelsea-football-club.html

London Football Stadiums [Map]. (n.d.). Retrieved from https://www.google.com/maps/d/viewer?mid=1dp9FAbQkO7Lmlj5-HXq6HEk-9hM&hl=en_US&ll=51.52479529494215%2C-0.12045200000000023&z=10

Original Wall of Stamford Bridge Stadium [Photograph]. (n.d.). Retrieved July 15, 2017, from https://www.tripadvisor.com/LocationPhotoDirectLink-g186338-d548817-i24733934-Chelsea_FC_Stadium_Tour_Museum-London_England.html

Premier League Player Stats. (n.d.). Retrieved July 12, 2017, from https://www.premierleague.com/stats/top/players/clean_sheet

Premier League teams ranked by stadium capacity in the 2017/2018 season. (n.d.). Retrieved July 16, 2017, from https://www.statista.com/statistics/384458/premier-league-stadium-capacity/

Premier League 2016/2017. (n.d.). Retrieved July 25, 2017, from http://www.worldfootball.net/attendance/eng-premier-league-2016-2017/1/

Pubs near Stamford Bridge. (n.d.). Retrieved July 14, 2017, from http://thechels.info/wiki/Pubs_near_Stamford_Bridge

Stadium History. (n.d.). Retrieved July 12, 2017, from http://www.chelseafc.com/the-club/history/style/stadium-history.html

The Birth of a Club. (n.d.). Retrieved July 11, 2017, from www.chelseafc.com/the-club/club-history/1900.html

The History of Stamford Bridge. (n.d.). Retrieved July 18, 2017, from http://www.stamford-bridge.com/bridge.htm

Crystal Palace

Online Articles:

Benge, J. (2016, November 19). Crystal Palace's American owners are here for the long term not a quick profit, says Alan Pardew. *Evening Standard.* Retrieved August 1, 2017, from http://www.standard.co.uk/sport/football/crystal-palaces-american-owners-are-here-for-the-long-term-not-a-quick-profit-says-alan-pardew-a3399731.html

Booker, J. (2016, September 16). Why do Crystal Palace fans sing Glad All Over and what are its lyrics. *Croydon Advertiser.* Retrieved August 4, 2017, from http://www.croydonadvertiser.co.uk/crystal-palace-fans-sing-glad-lyrics/story-29298166-detail/story.html

Burnton, S. (2011, September 27). How Brighton v Crystal Palace grew into an unlikely rivalry. *The Guardian.* Retrieved August 2, 2017, from https://www.theguardian.com/football/football-league-blog/2011/sep/27/brighton-crystal-palace-rivalry

Douglas, S. (2017, September 12). Crystal Palace hires Roy Hodgseon as manager after dumping Frank de Boer. *The Star.* Retrieved August 4, 2017, from https://www.thestar.com/sports/soccer/2017/09/12/crystal-palace-hires-roy-hodgson-as-manager-after-dumping-frank-de-boer.html

Fletcher, P. (2013, May 27). Veteran Kevin Phillips scored the only goal as Crystal Palace deservedly defeated Watford in tense Championship play-off final at Wembley. *BBC.* Retrieved August 8, 2017, from http://www.bbc.com/sport/football/22592831

Jones, M. (2018, September 20). Wilfried Zaha Talks Manchester United 'Hell', Was 'Depressed' at Old Trafford. *Bleacher Report.* Retrieved October 24, 2018 from https://bleacherreport.com/articles/2796814-wilfried-zaha-talks-manchester-united-hell-was-depressed-at-old-trafford

Lea, G. (2014, November 14). Ranking Crystal Palace's Top 5 Players of All Time. *Bleacher Report.* Retrieved August 7, 2017, from http://bleacherreport.com/articles/2267624-ranking-crystal-palaces-top-5-players-of-all-time

Mann, M. (2018, September 15). Huddersfield Town 0 -1 Crystal Palace. *BBC.* Retrieved October 24, 2018, from https://www.bbc.com/sport/football/45456655

McDermott, J. (2017, March 31). Kayle the Eagle: Who is Crystal Palace's mascot? *BBC*. Retrieved August 2, 2017, from http://www.bbc.com/news/uk-england-london-39257227

Ostlere, L. (2018, September 26). Crystal Palace to create major singing section at Selhurst Park in bid to restore raucous reputation. *Independent*. Retrieved October 24, 2018, from https://www.independent.co.uk/sport/football/premier-league/crystal-palace-singing-section-selhurst-park-holmesdale-stand-fanatics-ultras-a8556221.html

PA Sport. Wilf or without you - how Crystal Palace fare when Zaha is in the team. (2018, September). *Give Me Sport*. Retrieved October 24, 2018, from https://www.givemesport.com/1373145-wilf-or-without-you-how-crystal-palace-fare-when-zaha-is-in-the-team

Ranscombe, S. (2015, April 21). The Crystals: meet English football's only cheerleading squad. *The Telegraph*. Retrieved August 5, 2017, from http://www.telegraph.co.uk/men/the-filter/11549733/The-Crystals-meet-English-footballs-only-cheerleading-squad.html

Zdrojkowski, W. (2016, May 11). Crystal Palace's 10 greatest ever players but who do you think is the best? *Croydon Advertiser*. Retrieved August 3, 2017, from http://www.croydonadvertiser.co.uk/crystal-palace-s-10-greatest-players/story-29259240-detail/story.html

What does is mean when a football club goes into administration? (2013, March 29). *ITV*. Retrieved August 2, 2017, from http://www.itv.com/news/central/2013-03-29/what-does-it-mean-when-a-football-club-goes-into-administration/

11 Things You Probably Didn't Know About Selhurst Park. (n.d.). *Croydon Advertiser*. Retrieved August 1, 2017, from http://www.croydonadvertiser.co.uk/11-things-probably-didn-t-know-selhurst-park/story-29032981-detail/story.html

Websites:

Vajjha, A. (2014, August 30). How does it work when a European soccer player is "on loan" to another club? *Quora*. Retrieved August 6, 2017, from https://www.quora.com/How-does-it-work-when-a-European-soccer-player-is-on-loan-to-another-club

Back in the Day: April 19 – Crystal Palace Promoted to the Top Flight for the First Time. (n.d.). Retrieved August 2, 2017, from https://rednbluearmy.co.uk/articles/19-04-17-back-day-april-19th-crystal-palace-promoted-top-flight-first-time

Club History. (n.d.). Retrieved July 30, 2017, from www.cpfc.co.uk/club/club-history

Ground History. (2002, September 9). Retrieved August 6, 2017, from https://www.holmesdale.net/page.php?id=82&story=4158&p=2

Premier League Club Stats. (n.d.). Retrieved August 1, 2017, from https://www.premierleague.com/stats/top/clubs/wins?se=54

The Stadium Guide, Selhurst Park. (n.d.). Retrieved August 7, 2017, from http://www.stadiumguide.com/selhurstpark/

Wilf Wins Player of the Year. (2017, May 14). Retrieved August 1, 2017, from https://www.cpfc.co.uk/news/2017/may/wilf-wins-player-of-the-year/

1969 – 1984: Allison's & Venable's Eagles. (n.d.). Retrieved August 5, 2017, from https://www.cpfc.co.uk/club/club-history/1969-1984-allisons-eagles/

Everton

Books:

Carpenter, C. (2014). *Everton Quiz Book: 101 Fun and Interesting Questions to Test Your Knowledge of Everton Football Club.* [Kindle version]. Retrieved from amazon.com

Online Articles:

Austin, J. (2017, March 23). Everton to leave Goodison Park after Bramley Moore stadium move is confirmed. *The Independent.* Retrieved June 21, 2017, from http://www.independent.co.uk/sport/football/premier-league/everton-bramley-moore-new-stadium-goodison-park-liverpool-plans-confirmed-a7645381.html

Beesley, C. (2017, March 24). Everton's new Bramley Moore stadium – Answering the key questions. *Liverpool Echo.* Retrieved June 24, 2017, from http://www.liverpoolecho.co.uk/sport/football/football-news/evertons-new-bramley-moore-stadium-12791353

Guardian sport. (2018, September 17). Premier League: 10 talking points from the weekend's action. *The Guardian.* Retrieved September 17, 2018, from https://www.theguardian.com/football/blog/2018/sep/17/premier-league-10-talking-points-from-the-weekend-action

Hunter, A. (2018, October 26). Marco Silva urges Everton to show no fear against Manchester United. *The Guardian.* Retrieved October 27, 2018, from https://www.theguardian.com/football/2018/oct/26/marco-silva-manchester-united-everton

Hunter, A. (2018, September 16). Yarmolenko double against Everton helps West Ham to first league win. *The Guardian.* Retrieved September 16, 2018, from https://www.theguardian.com/football/2018/sep/16/everton-west-ham-united-premier-league-match-report

Hunter, A. (2018, September 14). Everton's Marco Silva unfazed by illegal approach investigation. *The Guardian.* Retrieved September 14, 2018, from https://www.theguardian.com/football/2018/sep/14/premier-league-investigate-everton-marco-silva

Hunter, A. (2017, March 23). Everton seek £300m to build stadium on Mersey site at Bramley Moore dock. *The Guardian.* Retrieved June 19, 2017, from https://www.theguardian.com/football/2017/mar/23/everton-waterfront-bramley-moore-dock-merseyside-stadium

Kirkbride, P. (2014, April 29). Dixie Dean statue on the move as Wall of Fame to be unveiled. *Liverpool Echo.* Retrieved June 17, 2017, from http://www.liverpoolecho.co.uk/sport/football/football-news/dixie-dean-statue-goodison-park-7045449

O'Keeffe, G. (2017, January 7). Goodison Park mural tells the story of Everton FC. *Daily Post.* Retrieved June 22, 2017, from http://www.dailypost.co.uk/sport/football/football-news/goodison-park-mural-tells-story-12419619

Prentice, D. (2013, May 7). Everton FC legend Dixie Dean scored 85 goals in a year – just like Lionel Messi and Gerd Muller. *Liverpool Echo.* Retrieved June 18, 2017, from http://www.liverpoolecho.co.uk/sport/football/football-news/everton-fc-legend-dixie-dean-3327234

Taylor. D. (2018, September 15). If tapper-uppers won't change their ways then penalty must be points. *The Guardian.* Retrieved September 15, 2018, from https://www.theguardian.com/football/blog/2018/sep/15/tapping-up-watford-everton-marco-silva

Wilson, P. (2018, September 27). Everton move helped me to become England's keeper, says Jordan Pickford. *The Guardian.* Retrieved September 27, 2018, from https://www.theguardian.com/football/2018/sep/27/everton-move-england-goalkeeper-jordan-pickford-sunderland

Wilson, P. (2018, September 22). Marco Silva can kickstart Everton reign by defying history at Arsenal. *The Guardian.* Retrieved September 22, 2018, from https://www.theguardian.com/football/blog/2018/sep/22/marco-silva-everton-arsenal-low-expectations

Websites:

Hughes, R. (2016, January 15). *Stanley Park: A Liverpool Treasure.* Retrieved June 18, 2017, from https://asenseofplace.com/2016/01/15/stanley-park-a-liverpool-treasure/

Wahl, M. (n.d.). *Everton FC.* Retrieved June 21, 2017, from http://www.footballhistory.org/club/everton.html

Dixie Dean. (n.d.). Retrieved June 22, 2017, from http://www.evertonfc.com/players/d/dd/dixie-dean

Everton, Goodison Park. (n.d.). Retrieved June 20, 2017, from https://www.premierleague.com/clubs/7/Everton/stadium

History of Goodison Park. (n.d.). Retrieved June 24, 2017, from http://www.evertonfc.com/content/history/history-of-goodison-park

Honours and Records. (n.d.). Retrieved June 20, 2017, from http://www.evertonfc.com/content/history/honours-and-records

How Everton Came To Move. (n.d.). Retrieved June 19, 2017, from http://www.evertonfc.com/news/2017/01/25/how-everton-came-to-move

Our Former Homes. (n.d.). Retrieved June 23, 2017, from http://www.evertonfc.com/content/history/history-of-goodison-park/the-grounds-of-everton

Season in the Top Flight of English Football by Clubs 1888-89 to 2016-17. (n.d.). Retrieved June 18, 2017, from http://www.myfootballfacts.com/SEASONS-IN-TOP-FLIGHT----1888-89-to-2009-10.html

The Stadium Guide: Goodison Park. (n.d.). Retrieved June 20, 2017, from http://www.stadiumguide.com/goodison/

12 facts and figures about the 227th Merseyside derby. (2016, December 19). Retrieved June 19, 2017, from http://www.liverpoolfc.com/news/first-team/247254-12-facts-and-figures-about-the-227th-merseyside-derby

Fulham

Online Articles:

Abbott, G. (2018, August 1). 2018/19 - Fulham Season Preview. *The Sports Geek*. Retrieved October 24, 2018, from https://www.thesportsgeek.com/blog/2018-19-fulham-season-preview-3623/

Hilditch, N. (2018, May 16). End of Season Review: Fulham's Report Card From the 2017/18 Campaign. *90Min*. Retrieved October 2, 2018, from https://www.90min.com/posts/6061849-end-of-season-review-fulham-s-report-card-from-the-2017-18-campaign

Keehner, S. (2018, July 19). The Special Relationship Between Fulham and American Players. *These Football Times*. Retrieved September 22, 2018, from https://thesefootballtimes.co/2018/07/19/the-special-relationship-between-fulham-and-american-players/

Memon,T. (n.d.). 5 biggest London derbies. *Sports Keeda*. Retrieved October 4, 2018, from https://www.sportskeeda.com/football/5-biggest-london-derbies

Ponting, I. (2005, October 20). Jonny Haynes. *The Independent*. Retrieved October 14, 2018, from https://www.independent.co.uk/news/obituaries/johnny-haynes-320776.html

Robinson, B. (2018, June 8). End of Season Review 2017/18. *Fulham Focus*. Retrieved October 2, 2018, from http://fulhamfocus.com/end-of-season-review-2017-18

Shread, J. (2018, July 31). Aleksandar Mitrovic joins Fulham from Newcastle on five-year deal. *Sky Sport*. Retrieved September 23, 2018, from https://www.skysports.com/football/news/11681/11454605/aleksandar-mitrovic-joins-fulham-from-newcastle-on-five-year-deal

Smyth, R. (2018, September 22). The impressive Aleksandar Mitrovic's equalizer earned Fulham a point after they were battered in the first half by Watford. *The Guardian*. Retrieved September 22, 2018, from

Sounders FC Communications. (2018, August 29). Clint Dempsey announces retirement from professional soccer. *Sounders FC*. Retrieved September 22, 2018, from https://www.soundersfc.com/post/2018/08/29/clint-dempsey-announces-retirement-professional-soccer

Programmes:

Fulham v. Watford. (2018, September 22). *Official Matchday Programme, Issue 4.*

Websites:

50 Moments That Made Fulham. (2013, July 1). Retrieved September 28, 2018, from http://www.fulhamfc.com/news/2013/july/01/moments-that-made-ffc

Fulhamerica: U.S. Players who have passed through Craven Cottage. (2017, May 6). Retrieved September 24, 2018, from https://www.ussoccer.com/stories/2017/05/06/12/05/20170506-feat-mnt-gallery-fulhamerica-usmnt-players-at-fulham

Fulham FC. (2018). Retrieved October 2, 2018, from https://www.footballhistory.org/club/fulham.html

McBride's. (n.d.). Retrieved September 23, 2018, from http://www.fulhamfc.com/hospitality/packages/mcbrides

Huddersfield

Articles:

Doyle, P. (2017, June 30). David Wagner sticks with Huddersfield Town for Premier League adventure. *The Guardian.*

Hunter, A. (2015, December 6). Huddersfield's David Wagner: I've known Jurgen Klopp longer than I've known my wife. *The Guardian.*

Jolly, R. (2017, January 24). Huddersfield Town's Aaron Mooy: From A-League footballer to Championship star to possible Manchester City regular. *The National.*

Press Association. (2017, June 23). Loyal Huddersfield fans can watch home Premier League games for £5.26. *The Guardian.*

Slater, M. (2017, May 11). Deloitte estimates Premier League promotion for clubs without parachute payments is worth at least 170million pounds. *Daily Mail.*

Taylor, L. (2017, February 16). Championship's Yorkshire revival gives football its northern soul back. *The Guardian.*

Williams, A. (2017, May 29). Huddersfield Town promoted to Premier League: David Wagner 'in fairy tale.' *BBC.*

Online Articles:

Atkinson, N. (2015, December 17). How does John Smith's Stadium compare to the new breed of sports grounds? *The Huddersfield Daily Examiner.* Retrieved October 8, 2017, from http://www.examiner.co.uk/news/west-yorkshire-news/how-john-smiths-stadium-compare-10615587

Beedle, M. (2016, September 6). Leeds United v Huddersfield Town: Four of United's best West Torkshire derby wins. *Yorkshire Evening Post.* Retrieved October 8, 2017, from http://www.yorkshireeveningpost.co.uk/sport/football/leeds-united/leeds-united-v-huddersfield-town-four-of-united-s-best-west-yorkshire-derby-wins-1-8108317

Benson, R. (2017, June 12). Huddersfield Town's John Smith's Stadium set for EA Sports FIFA debut. *The Huddersfield Daily Examiner.* Retrieved October 8, 2017, from http://www.examiner.co.uk/sport/football/news/huddersfield-towns-john-smiths-stadium-13173436

Booth, M. (2015, February 5). Owner-chairman Dean Hoyle has pumped £37.2m into Huddersfield Town over the last six years. *The Huddersfield Daily Examiner*. Retrieved July 17, 2017, from http://www.examiner.co.uk/sport/football/news/owner-chairman-dean-hoyle-pumped-372m-8580536

Dubas-Fisher, D. (2016, September 7). Huddersfield Town v Leeds United: The West Yorkshire derby in numbers. *The Huddersfield Daily Examiner*. Retrieved October 8, 2017, from http://www.examiner.co.uk/sport/football/news/huddersfield-town-v-leeds-united-11855894

Kent, D. (2015, May 28). Hull's regulation from Premier League highlights sad decline for Yorkshire clubs. *Daily Mail*. Retrieved October 24, 2018, from https://www.dailymail.co.uk/sport/football/article-3101017/Hull-s-relegation-Premier-League-highlights-sad-decline-Yorkshire-clubs.html

Perraudin, F. (2018, July 2). Why are so many of England's World Cup footballers from Yorkshire? *The Guardian*. Retrieved October 24, 2018, from https://www.theguardian.com/uk-news/2018/jul/02/why-are-so-many-of-england-world-cup-footballers-from-yorkshire

Prentice, D. (2017, May 30). Huddersfield Town promoted to the Premier League - All you need to know about the Terriers. *The Liverpool Echo*. Retrieved September 23, 2017, from http://www.liverpoolecho.co.uk/sport/football/football-news/who-what--huddersfield-town-13109959

Shaw, M. (2017, May 31). Behind the scenes at the John Smith's Stadium as they prepare to host Premier League football. *The Huddersfield Daily Examiner*. Retrieved October 8, 2017, from http://www.examiner.co.uk/news/behind-scenes-john-smiths-stadium-13114516

Welton, B. (2016, November 6). Bill Shankly - a case of 'what might have been' during the icon's time at Huddersfield Town. *The Huddersfield Daily Examiner*. Retrieved September 23, 2017, from http://www.examiner.co.uk/sport/football/news/bill-shankly-case-what-might-12134125

Wilson, P. (2018, September 29). Harry Kane scores double for Tottenham as Huddersfield stay bottom. *The Guardian*. Retrieved October 24, 2018, from https://www.theguardian.com/football/2018/sep/29/huddersfield-town-tottenham-hotspur-premier-league-match-report/

Fan ejected for unfurling Turkish flag during West Yorkshire derby. (2017, February 5). *ITV News*. Retrieved October 8, 2017, from http://www.itv.com/news/calendar/2017-02-05/fan-ejected-for-unfurling-turkey-flag-during-west-yorkshire-derby/

Holmes awarded £250,000. (2004, February 23). *BBC*. Retrieved October 8, 2017, from http://news.bbc.co.uk/sport2/hi/football/3514673.stm

Programmes:

Tomlinson, A. (Ed.). (2018, September 29) Huddersfield Town v. Tottenham Hotspur. *The Terrier: Official Matchday Programme*.

Websites:

Han. *The Beautiful History Of Club Crests, Club Colours & Nicknames: Huddersfield Town* (n.d.). Retrieved September 23, 2017, from https://thebeautifulhistory.wordpress.com/clubs/huddersfield-town/

Championship 2016/2017 - Attendance - home matches. (n.d.). Retrieved October 8, 2017, from http://www.worldfootball.net/attendance/eng-championship-2016-2017/1/

Huddersfield Town v Bradford City Head-to-Head Record. (n.d.). Retrieved October 8, 2017, from http://stats.football.co.uk/head_to_head/huddersfield_town/vs/bradford_city/index.shtml

John Smiths Stadium: Stadium History. (n.d.). Retrieved October 8, 2017, from http://www.johnsmithsstadium.com/stadium-history

Thrice Champions: The All Stars vs the No Marks. (n.d.). Retrieved September 23, 2017, from http://www.thricechampions.co.uk/all-stars/

Leicester

Online Articles:

Burns, J. F. (2015, March 26). Richard III Gets a Kingly Burial, on Second Try. *New York Times*. Retrieved July 20, 2017, from https://www.nytimes.com/2015/03/27/world/europe/king-richard-iii-burial-leicester.html?mcubz=0

Dodd, V. & Steinberg, J. (2018, October 28). Helicopter believed to be carrying Leicester City owner crashes after game. *The Guardian*. Retrieved October 28 2018, from https://www.theguardian.com/football/2018/oct/27/leicester-city-owners-helicopter-crash-car-park

Ebearryman. (2016, May 8). Why Andrea Bocelli singing at Leicester was one of the most beautiful things I've ever seen. *Dream Team*. Retrieved July 23, 2017, from https://www.dreamteamfc.com/c/archives/news-gossip/155222/andrea-bocelli-singing-leicester-one-beautiful-things-ive-ever-seen/

Ellis-Petersen, H. (2018, October 29). Thai sporting and political leaders pay tribute to Leicester City owner. *The Guardian*. Retrieved October 30, 2018, from https://www.theguardian.com/football/2018/oct/29/thai-sporting-and-political-leaders-pay-tribute-to-leicester-city-owner-vichai-srivaddhanaprabha

Halford, J. (2016, April 5). Leicester City's all-time best XI… featuring five Premier League winners. *Sky Sports*. Retrieved July 26, 2017, from http://www.skysports.com/football/news/11712/10263734/leicester-citys-all-time-best-xi-featuring-five-players-from-title-winning-season

James, S. (2018, October 28). Vichai Srivaddhanaprabha: the quiet man behind a sporting fairytale. *The Guardian*. Retrieved October 29, 2018, from https://www.theguardian.com/football/2018/oct/28/vichai-srivaddhanaprabha-quiet-man-delivered-dream

James, S. (2017, October 17). Craig Shakespeare sacked by Leicester City after four months in charge. *The Guardian*. Retrieved September 24, 2018, from https://www.theguardian.com/football/2017/oct/17/craig-shakespeare-sacked-leicester-city-manager

Lawless, J. (2018, November 3). Leicester City Players Wear Special Shirts In Honour Of Vichai Srivaddhanaprabha. *Sport Bible*. Retrieved, November 3, 2018, from http://www.sportbible.com/football/news-take-a-bow-leicester-wear-special-shirts-in-honour-of-vichai-srivaddhanapraba-20181103

Markazi, A. (2016, April 15). 10 things to know about Leicester City – and the city of Leicester. *ESPC FC*. Retrieved July 23, 2017, from http://www.espnfc.com/leicester-city/story/2848610/10-things-to-know-about-leicester-city

Mason, P. (2018, October 29,). Vichai Srivaddhanaprabha obituary. *The Guardian*. Retrieved October 29, 2018, from https://www.theguardian.com/football/2018/oct/29/vichai-srivaddhanaprabha-obiutary

Mewis, J. (2016, May 8). Andrea Bocelli sings spine-tingling Nessum Dorma as Leicester City celebrate title success in style. *Mirror*. Retrieved July 30, 2017, from http://www.mirror.co.uk/sport/football/news/andrea-bocelli-sings-spine-tingling-7919688

Pawley, L. (2018, May 12). End of Season Review: Leicester City's Report Card From the 2017/18 Campaign. *90Min*. Retrieved September 19, 2018, from https://www.90min.com/posts/6057990-end-of-season-review-leicester-city-s-report-card-from-the-2017-18-campaign

Simmons, B. (n.d.). Rules for being a true fan. *ESPN*. Retrieved July 25, 2017, from http://www.espn.com/espn/page2/story?page=simmons/020227

Williams, M. (2018, October 29). Leicester hero Riyad Mahrez points to sky in poignant moment after Man City goal. *Daily Star*. Retrieved October 29, 2018, from https://www.dailystar.co.uk/sport/football/739425/Leicester-helicopter-crash-Riyad-Mahrez-Manchester-City-Tottenham-Vichai-Srivaddhanaprabha

As Wayne Rooney breaks Sir Bobby Charlton's Man Utd haul, who is your Premier League club's all-time leading goalscorer? (2017, January 23). *The Telegraph*. Retrieved July 25, 2017, from http://www.telegraph.co.uk/football/0/every-premier-league-clubs-all-time-leading-goalscorer/leicester-city-arthur-chandler-1923-1935/

Claude Puel: Leicester City appoint ex-Southampton manager. (2017, October 25). *BBC*. Retrieved September 28, 2018, from https://www.bbc.com/sport/football/41746701

Gary Lineker. (2017, November 7). *Leicester Mercury*. Retrieved July 29, 2017, from http://www.leicestermercury.co.uk/all-about/gary-lineker

Leicester City players fly to owner's funeral in Thailand. (2018, November 3). *BBC*. Retrieved November 3, 2018, from https://www.bbc.com/news/uk-england-leicestershire-46082866

Leicester 2017/18 Premier League season review. (2018, May 13). *Sky Sports*. Retrieved September 21, 2018, from https://www.skysports.com/football/news/11712/11371124/leicester-201718-premier-league-season-review

Websites:

Alam, R. (n.d.). *From Rags to Riches: The Inspiring Story of Jamie Vardy*. Retrieved July 22, 2017, from https://sites.duke.edu/wcwp/capturing-the-game/players/from-rags-to-riches-the-inspiring-story-of-jamie-vardy/

Bates, T. (2007, May 31). *Sir Gordon Banks*. Retrieved July 26, 2017, from http://www.aboutderbyshire.co.uk/cms/people/sir-gordon-banks.shtml

Winner, A. (n.d.). *The Soccer Talisman*. Retrieved July 25, 2017, from http://www.soccer-training-info.com/the_talisman.asp

About the Centre. (n.d.). Retrieved on July 25, 2017, from https://kriii.com/about-the-centre/

History. (n.d.). Retrieved July 30, 2017, from https://www.lcfc.com/club/history

King Power Stadium: Leicester City FC. (n.d.). Retrieved July 23, 2017, from http://www.football-stadiums.co.uk/grounds/england/king-power-stadium/

King Power Stadium. (2015, October 19). Retrieved July 29, 2017, from http://footballtripper.com/king-power-stadium-leicester-city/

Leicester City football club: record v Coventry City. (n.d.). Retrieved July 27, 2017, from https://www.11v11.com/teams/leicester-city/tab/opposingTeams/opposition/Coventry%20City/

Leicester City football club: record v Derby County. (n.d.). Retrieved July 28, 2017, from https://www.11v11.com/teams/leicester-city/tab/opposingTeams/opposition/Derby%20County/

Leicester City football club: record v Nottingham Forest. (n.d.). Retrieved July 24, 2017, from https://www.11v11.com/teams/leicester-city/tab/opposingTeams/opposition/Nottingham%20Forest/

Leicester City: May 2009. (n.d.). *Sky Sports*. Retrieved July 24, 2017, from http://www.skysports.com/leicester-city-results/2008-09

Leicester City: May 2014. (n.d.). *Sky Sports*. Retrieved July 24, 2017, from http://www.skysports.com/leicester-city-results/2013-14

Leicester City: May 2016. (n.d.). *Sky Sports*. Retrieved July 24, 2017, from http://www.skysports.com/leicester-city-results/2015-16

Peter Shilton – England – Biography of his International goalkeeping career for England. The final years. (n.d.). Retrieved July 24, 2017, from http://www.sporting-heroes.net/football/england/peter-shilton-9704/biography-of-his-international-goalkeeping-career-for-england-the-final-years_a19270/

Premier League Player Stats. (n.d.). Retrieved on July 30, 2017, from https://www.premierleague.com/stats/top/players/clean_sheet?po=GOALK EEPER

Steve Walsh – Leicester City FC – League appearances for The Foxes. (n.d.). Retrieved July 28, 2017, from http://www.sporting-heroes.net/football/leicester-city-fc/steve-walsh-10624/league-appearances-for-the-foxes_a18851/

Radio:

Wright, I. (2018, October 30). *BBC Radio 5 Live Sport*. [Live radio broadcast]. Salford, UK: BBC North.

Other:

kschmeichel1. (2018). [Twitter feed]. Retrieved from https://twitter.com/kschmeichel1?lang=en

Liverpool

Online Articles:

Burrows, B. (2017, June 27). Liverpool to face no punishment from Premier League over Virgil van Dijk 'tapping up' controversy. *Independent*. Retrieved September 24, 2018, from https://www.independent.co.uk/sport/football/transfers/liverpool-virgil-van-dijk-transfer-premier-league-punishment-a7810036.html

Cooper, L. (2017, May 24). 72,000 Liverpool FC Fans Singing 'You Will Never Walk Alone' In Sydney Is As Amazing As It Sounds. *Huffington Post*. Retrieved July 7, 2017, from http://www.huffingtonpost.com.au/2017/05/24/80-000-liverpool-fc-fans-singing-you-will-never-walk-alone-in_a_22106870/

Dawson, A. (2017, May 22). This is how much prize money each Premier League club won in the most lucrative season ever. *Business Insider*. Retrieved July 7, 2017, from http://uk.businessinsider.com/total-prize-money-each-premier-league-club-won-in-lucrative-season-2017-5/#5-manchester-united-1436-million-finished-6th-16

Doré, L. (2018, May 26). How 'Allez, Allez, Allez' became the soundtrack to Liverpool's incredible Champions League run. *I news*. Retrieved October 24, 2018, from https://inews.co.uk/sport/football/champions-league/allez-allez-allez-liverpool-song-lyrics-why/

Durkan, J. (2018, May 13). End of Season Review: Liverpool's Report Card From the 2017/18 Campaign. *90Min*. Retrieved October 4, 2018, from https://www.90min.com/posts/6059247-end-of-season-review-liverpool-s-report-card-from-the-2017-18-campaign

Edwards, L. (2018, October 3). Manchester City reassured by police there will be no repeat of team bus attack in Liverpool. *The Telegraph*. Retrieved October 3, 2018, from https://www.telegraph.co.uk/football/2018/10/03/manchester-city-reassured-police-will-no-repeat-team-bus-attack/

Hunter, A. (2018, October 8). Gabriel Jesus unhappy he was not allowed take Manchester City penalty. *The Guardian*. Retrieved October 8, 2018, from https://www.theguardian.com/football/2018/oct/08/gabriel-jesus-unhappy-manchester-city-penalty-liverpool-riyad-mahrez

Lynch, D. (2018, November 4). 'Ridiculous' level of Premier League rivals mean Liverpool must not drop points, warns Joe Gomez. *Evening Standard*.

Retrieved October 8, 2018, from
https://www.standard.co.uk/sport/football/ridiculous-level-of-premier-league-rivals-means-liverpool-must-not-drop-points-warns-joe-gomez-a3980296.html

McKenna, C. (2018, October 8). Pep Guardiola apologizes to Gabriel Jesus after Riyad Mahrez penalty miss vs Liverpool. *Express*. Retrieved October 8, 2018, from
https://www.express.co.uk/sport/football/1028200/Mahrez-penalty-Jesus-Guardiola-Klopp-Liverpool-Man-City-Premier-League

Press Association. (2018, January 1). Virgil van Dijk completes £75m Liverpool move: 'I can't do anything about the price'. *The Guardian*. Retrieved October 4, 2018, from
https://www.theguardian.com/football/2018/jan/01/virgil-van-dijk-describes-liverpool-as-perfect-match-after-completing-75m-world-record-transfer

Sandomir, R. (2015, August 10). NBC Retains Rights to Premier League in Six-Year Deal. *The New York Times*. Retrieved July 7, 2017, from
https://www.nytimes.com/2015/08/11/sports/soccer/nbc-retains-rights-to-premier-league-in-six-year-deal.html

Shaw, S. (2018, May 15). Salah's Kop song gets official James seal of approval. *Liverpool FC*. Retrieved October 4, 2018, from
https://www.liverpoolfc.com/news/features/303025-liverpool-fc-tim-booth-mohamed-salah-song

Sky Sports News. (2018, July 20). Liverpool sign Alisson from Roma in record deal for a goalkeeper. *Sky Sports*. Retrieved September 24, 2018, from https://www.skysports.com/football/news/11669/11441825/liverpool-sign-alisson-from-roma-in-record-deal-for-a-goalkeeper

Liverpool v Man City: Why is Jurgen Klopp Pep Guardiola's 'Kryptonite'? (2018, October 5). *BBC*. Retrieved October 5, 2018, from
https://www.bbc.com/sport/football/45602473

Liverpool 2017/18 Premier League season review. (2018, May 13). *Sky Sports*. Retrieved October 6, 2018, from
https://www.skysports.com/football/news/11669/11371507/liverpool-201718-premier-league-season-review

Manchester City have not beaten Liverpool at Anfield in the Premier League since 2003. (2018, January 11). Sky *Sports*. Retrieved October 4, 2018, from
https://www.skysports.com/football/news/11095/11202126/manchester-city-have-not-beaten-liverpool-at-anfield-in-the-premier-league-since-2003

Websites:

Bill Shankly. (n.d.). Retrieved September 19, 2017, from
http://www.liverpoolfc.com/history/heroes/bill-shankly

LFC Honours. (n.d.). Retrieved September 19, 2017, from
http://www.liverpoolfc.com/history/honours

Timeline. (n.d.). Retrieved
from http://www.liverpoolfc.com/history/timeline

Manchester City

Articles:

Doyle, P. (2017, April 23). Imperial age of Manchester City yet to dawn despite Pep Guardiola's arrival. *The Guardian.*

Wilson, P. (2017, April 22). Pep Guardiola knows Manchester City fortunes must translate to trophies. *The Guardian.*

Online Articles:

Armitt, J. (2016, September 17). How Old Trafford and the Etihad Stadium became world-famous sporting arenas and helped make Manchester. *Manchester Evening News.* Retrieved September 25, 2017, from http://www.manchestereveningnews.co.uk/news/nostalgia/old-trafford-etihad-stadium-history-11895567

Brennan, S. (2018, October 2). Why Man City fans boo UEFA Champions League anthem. *Manchester Evening New.* Retrieved September 22, 2018, from https://www.manchestereveningnews.co.uk/sport/football/football-news/why-city-fans-boo-uefa-13674961

Brennan, S. (2013, January 10). Porto hit with fine for racist Manchester City abuse. *Manchester Evening News.* Retrieved September 22, 2018, from https://www.manchestereveningnews.co.uk/sport/football/football-news/porto-hit-with-fine-for-racist-manchester-686046

Carradice, P. (2012, December 13). Billy Meredith: football superstar. *BBC.* Retrieved September 25, 2017, from http://www.bbc.co.uk/blogs/wales/entries/5c1f57b7-167c-362f-aa30-59310d24fdc3

Conn, D. (2012, May 14). Sportblog: Manchester City's next task is to strike Champions League gold. *The Guardian.* Retrieved August 31, 2017, from https://www.theguardian.com/football/blog/2012/may/14/manchester-city-champions-league

Conn, D. (2013, July 30). Abu Dhabi accused of 'using Manchester City to launder image'. *The Guardian.* Retrieved August 31, 2017, from https://www.theguardian.com/football/2013/jul/30/manchester-city-human-rights-accusations

Gibson, O. (2014, May 16). Manchester City accept £49m fine and transfer cap from Uefa over FFP. *The Guardian.* Retrieved September 28, 2018, from https://www.theguardian.com/football/2014/may/16/manchester-city-fine-transfer-cap-uefa-ffp

Gorst, P. (2018, June 19). The knee injury history of Nabil Fekir that might have help up Liverpool transfer. *Liverpool Echo.* Retrieved October 12, 2018, from https://www.liverpoolecho.co.uk/sport/football/transfer-news/liverpool-target-fekir-injury-history-14764186

Imbo, W. (2018, May 17). End of Season Review: Newcastle United's Report Card From the 2017/18 Campaign. *90Min.* Retrieved October 4, 2018, from https://www.90min.com/posts/6063123-end-of-season-review-newcastle-united-s-report-card-from-the-2017-18-campaign

Lynch, D. (2014, November 4). Man City fans planning pre-match UEFA protest. *Manchester Evening News.* Retrieved October 3, from https://www.manchestereveningnews.co.uk/sport/football/footbalmanl-news/-city-fans-planning-pre-match-8042418

Manchester Evening News. (2012, April 11). Manchester City late-start fine from UEFA more than Porto's racism penalty. *Manchester Evening News.* Retrieved September 28, 2018, from https://www.manchestereveningnews.co.uk/sport/football/football-news/manchester-city-late-start-fine-from-uefa-686540

Robson, J. (2014, July 10). City greats: Frank Swift. *Manchester Evening News.* Retrieved October 12, 2017, from http://www.manchestereveningnews.co.uk/sport/football/football-news/manchester-city-greats-frank-swift-7417158

Smith, J. (2018, May 13). Manchester City smash 11 Premier League records in title-winning season. *ESPN.* Retrieved October 13, from http://www.espn.com/soccer/club/manchester-city/382/blog/post/3333011/can-man-city-smash-the-premier-league-points-and-goals-records

Steinberg, J. (2018, September 19). Manchester City made an aweful start to their Champions League campaign as they suffered a shock defeat at home to Lyon in Group F. *The Guardian.* Retrieved October 5, 2018, from https://www.theguardian.com/football/live/2018/sep/19/manchester-city-v-lyon-champions-league-live

Wilson, S. (2011, January 13). How Manchester City won the stadium lottery. *The Telegraph.* Retrieved October 12, 2017, from http://www.telegraph.co.uk/sport/football/teams/manchester-city/8257210/How-Manchester-City-won-the-stadium-lottery.html

Manchester City 2017/18 Premier League season review. (2018, May 14). *Sky Sports.* Retrieved September 1, 2018, from https://www.skysports.com/football/news/11679/11370933/manchester-city-201718-premier-league-season-review

Websites:

boswell. (2011, July 29). *Manchester City v Gornik European Cup Winners Cup Final 1969/70*. Retrieved September 25, 2017, from http://www.citytilidie.com/latest/gornik-european-cup-winners-cup-final-196970/

boswell. (2011, August 29). *Leicester City v Manchester City FA Cup Final 1968/69*. Retrieved September 25, 2017, from http://www.citytilidie.com/latest/leicester-fa-cup-final-196869/

Burns, S. (2017, February 26). Memory Lane: The heroic story of former City striker Fred Tilson. *Inside Manchester City*. Retrieved September 25, 2017, from http://www.insidemcfc.com/the-heroic-story-of-former-manchester-city-striker-fred-tilson/

Citizen Jay. (2016, April 23). *Billy Meredith and the 1904 FA Cup*. Retrieved September 25, 2017, from https://bitterandblue.sbnation.com/2016/4/23/11493780/billy-meredith-and-the-1904-fa-cup

MPHenson. (2016, February 22). *#CITYATWEMBLEY Famous Wins: 1934 FA Cup Final*. Retrieved September 25, 2017, from https://www.mancity.com/news/first-team/first-team-news/2016/february/city-at-wembley-7-famous-wins-1934-fa-cup-final

Tales of Your City. (n.d.). Retrieved September 25, 2017, from https://www.mancity.com/Fans%20and%20Community/Club/Club%20History

Video:

The Guardian. (2017, May 16). *Pep Guardiola: Barcelona and Bayern Munich would have sacked me* [Video file]. Retrieved from https://www.theguardian.com/football/video/2017/may/16/pep-guardiola-barcelona-bayern-munich-would-have-sacked-manchester-city-video

Manchester United

Books:

Kuper, S., & Syzmanski, S. (2014). *Soccernomics: Why England Loses, Why Spain, Germany, and Brazil Win, and Why the U.S., Japan, Australia – and Even Iraq – Are Destined to Become the Kings of the World's Most Popular Sport.* New York: Nation Books.

White, J. (2009). *Manchester United: The Biography.* U.K.: Little, Brown.

Online Articles:

Aarons, E. (2016, August 9). Paul Pogba: Manchester United confirm record £93.2m signing on five-year deal. *The Guardian.* Retrieved August 12, 2017, from https://www.theguardian.com/football/2016/aug/09/manchester-united-sign-paul-pogba-93-million-juventus

Badenhausen, K. (2017, July 12). Full List: the World's 50 Most Valuable Sports Teams 2017. *Forbes.* Retrieved July 16, 2017, from https://www.forbes.com/sites/kurtbadenhausen/2017/07/12/full-list-the-worlds-50-most-valuable-sports-teams-2017/#7d2481c64a05

Bates, A. (2017, July 20). Manchester derby classics: Best of Man Utd v Man City at Old Trafford. *Sky Sports.* Retrieved August 14, 2017, from http://www.skysports.com/football/news/11661/10951440/manchester-derby-classics-best-of-man-utd-v-man-city-at-old-trafford

Borden, S. (2018, November 5). Jose Mourinho's Last Stand. *ESPN.* Retrieved November 5, 2018, from http://www.espn.com/espn/feature/story/_/id/25145480/jose-mourinho-last-stand

Bunyan, N. (2010, September 15). Nobby Stiles weeps over 1966 World Cup medal sale. *The Telegraph.* Retrieved August 13, 2017, from http://www.telegraph.co.uk/sport/football/news/8002155/Nobby-Stiles-weeps-over-1966-World-Cup-medal-sale.html

Conn, D. (2018, October 4). Manchester United have been owned by the Glazers for 13 years. No wonder they're struggling. *The Guardian.* Retrieved October 4, 2018, from https://www.theguardian.com/football/2018/oct/04/glazers-manchester-united

Jackson, J. (2018, October 19). José Mourinho denies Manchester United attack only after falling behind. *The Guardian*. Retrieved October 24, 2018, from https://www.theguardian.com/football/2018/oct/19/jose-mourinho-manchester-united-chelsea-gloat

Jackson, J. (2018, October 6). Manchester United back José Mourinho and have no plans to remove manager. *The Guardian*. Retrieved October 6, 2018, from https://www.theguardian.com/football/2018/oct/06/jose-mourinho-manchester-united-board-back-manager

Jackson, J. (2018, September 26). José Mourinho clashed with Paul Pogba over timing of Instagram post. *The Guardian*. Retrieved September 26, 2018, from https://www.theguardian.com/football/2018/sep/26/manchester-united-back-jose-mourinho-paul-pogba-power-struggle-vice-captaincy-football

Jackson, J. (2018, September 25). José Mourinho says Paul Pogba wil never captain Manchester United again. *The Guardian*. Retrieved September 26, 2018, from https://www.theguardian.com/football/2018/sep/25/jose-mourinho-paul-pogba-never-captain-manchester-united

Jackson, J. (2018, September 25). Manchester United earn record revenues but still have debt of £487m. *The Guardian*. Retrieved September 26, 2018, from https://www.theguardian.com/football/2018/sep/25/manchester-united-record-revenues-debt-financial-results-football

Ogden, M., & Percy, J. (2015, November 25). Best Manchester United players ever, the top 50. *The Telegraph*. Retrieved August 10, 2017, from http://www.telegraph.co.uk/sport/football/teams/manchester-united/11491116/Best-Manchester-United-players-ever-the-top-50.html

Press Association. (2018, September 22). Sir Alex Ferguson receives emotion ovation on return to Old Trafford. *The Guardian*. Retrieved September 24, 2018 from https://www.theguardian.com/football/2018/sep/22/alex-ferguson-manchester-united-old-trafford

Ronay, B. (2018, October 2). Alexis Sanchez embodies drift at a ghost ship of a sporting giant. *The Guardian*. Retrieved October 2, 2018, from https://www.theguardian.com/football/2018/oct/02/alexis-sanchez-embodies-drift-ghost-ship-sporting-giant

Steinberg, J. (2018, September 30). Quipping Paul Pogba underlines rift with Mourinho after West Ham defeat. *The Guardian.* Retrieved September 30, 2018, from https://www.theguardian.com/football/2018/sep/30/paul-pogba-rift-jose-mourinho-west-ham-defeat

Wilson J. (2018, October 3). Manchester United are a mess - a team without a pattern or a plan. *The Guardian.* Retrieved October 3, 2018, from https://www.theguardian.com/football/2018/oct/03/manchester-united-jose-mourinho-no-plan-attack-moyes-van-gaal

Wilson, P. (2018, October 6). José Mouinho complains he is being blamed for 'the rain and Brexit' *The Guardian.* Retrieved October 6, 2018, from https://www.theguardian.com/football/2018/oct/06/jose-mourinho-complains-he-is-being-blamed-for-the-rain-and-brexit

Wilson, P. (2018, October 2). 'I don't need to know what Paul Scholes said,' says José Mourinho. *The Guardian.* Retrieved October 2, 2018, from https://www.theguardian.com/football/2018/oct/02/jose-mourinho-happy-manchester-united-improvement-valencia-champions-league

Wilson, P. (2018, October 2). Manchester United show little sign of improvement in draw with Valencia. *The Guardian.* Retrieved October 2, 2018, from https://www.theguardian.com/football/2018/oct/02/manchester-united-valencia-champions-league-match-report

Wilson, P. (2018, October 1). José Mourinho cuts chipper figure as crunch Valencia visit looms. *The Guardian.* Retrieved October 1, 2018, from https://www.theguardian.com/football/2018/oct/01/jose-mourinho-manchester-united-valencia-champions-league

Wilson, P. (2018, October 1). José Mourinho: some Manchester United players care more than others. *The Guardian.* Retrieved October 1, 2018, from https://www.theguardian.com/football/2018/oct/01/jose-mourinho-manchester-united-players-care-more-than-others-valencia-champions-league

Wilson, P. (2018, September 27). Why is no one at Manchester United stopping this unedifying spectacle? *The Guardian.* Retrieved September 28, 2018, from https://www.theguardian.com/football/blog/2018/sep/27/manchester-united-jose-mourinho-paul-pogba-alex-ferguson

Wahl, G. (n.d.). Once in a Blue Moon: An Oral History of the Premier League's Most Dramatic Finish Ever. *Sports Illustrated*. Retrieved August 14, 2017, from https://www.si.com/longform/manchester-city-2012-epl-title-final-day-oral-history/index.html

Sir Alex Ferguson's Best Quotes. (2013, May 8). *The Guardian*. Retrieved July 15, 2017, from https://www.theguardian.com/football/2013/may/08/sir-alex-ferguson-best-quotes

Websites:

Dhar, D. (2017, March 8). *Know your club – Why Manchester United are called the 'Red Devils'*. Retrieved August 16, 2017, from https://www.sportskeeda.com/football/know-your-club-why-manchester-united-are-called-the-red-devils

Froggatt, M. (2016, February 5). *Fans to Hold Annual Munich Memorial*. Retrieved August 15, 2017, from http://www.manutd.com/en/Fanzone/News-And-Blogs/2016/Feb/Fans-to-hold-annual-memorial-service-for-Munich-Air-Disaster.aspx

Marshall, A. (2016, March 22). *Sir Bobby Charlton: Old Trafford and Me*. Retrieved August 17, 2017, from http://www.manutd.com/en/Home/History/Thank-You-Sir-Bobby-Charlton/Thank-You-Sir-Bobby-News-And-Features/2016/Mar/interview-sir-bobby-charlton-old-trafford-and-me.aspx

McCarra, K. (2012, April 30). Vincent Kompany helps Manchester City grab title race control from United. *The Guardian*. Retrieved August 11, 2017, from https://www.theguardian.com/football/2012/apr/30/manchester-city-united-premier-league

Menon, A. (2017, March 8). *Did Denis Law really score "the goal relegated Manchester United"*. Retrieved August 16, 2017, from https://www.sportskeeda.com/football/did-denis-law-score-goal-relegated-manchester-united

Legends. (n.d.). Retrieved August 12, 2017, from http://www.manutd.com/en/History/Legends.aspx?sortOrder=appearances

Manchester United Become Fifth Major Team to Win All Three Major European Trophies. (2017, May 24). Retrieved July 19, 2017, from http://www.goal.com/en/news/166/europa-league/2017/05/24/35811932/manchester-united-become-fifth-team-to-win-all-three-major

Manchester United football club: record v Liverpool. (n.d.). Retrieved August 12, 2017, from https://www.11v11.com/teams/manchester-united/tab/opposingTeams/opposition/Liverpool/

The Old Trafford Story: 1910 – 1930. (n.d.). Retrieved August 11, 2017, from http://www.manutd.com/en/History/The-Old-Trafford-Story/The-Old-Trafford-Story/2014/Oct/The-Old-Trafford-Story-1910-1930.aspx

United History: 1878 to 1909. (n.d.). Retrieved August 10, 2017, from http://www.manutd.com/en/History/History-By-Decade/History-By-Decade/2014/Oct/manchester-united-history-1878-to-1909.aspx

United History: 1950 to 1959. (n.d.). Retrieved August 10, 2017, from http://www.manutd.com/en/History/History-By-Decade/History-By-Decade/2014/Oct/manchester-united-history-1950-to-1959.aspx

Victims of the 1958 Munich Air Disaster. (n.d.). Retrieved July 28, 2017, from http://www.thebusbybabes.com/victims/victims.htm

Why Man Utd & Liverpool rivalry runs deep. (2017, January 13). Retrieved August 10, 2017, from http://www.bbc.com/sport/football/37673147

Newcastle

Articles:

Taylor, L. (2017, April 25). Newcastle are back in the Premier League – what happens now depends on Mike Ashley. *The Guardian.*

Taylor, L. (2017, April 27). Rafael Benitez to have talks with Mike Ashley before extending Newcastle stay. *The Guardian.*

Books:

Cassidy, D. (2010, December 14). *Newcastle United: The Day the Promises Had to Stop.* Stroud, UK: Amberley Publishing.

Clarke, G. (2006, October 1). *Newcastle United: Fifty Years of Hurt.* Edinburgh: Mainstream Publishing Company Limited.

Online Articles:

Aarons, E. (2018, September 22). Mike Ashley booed by Newcastle fans as Crytal Palace fluff chances for victory. *The Guardian.* Retrieved September 22, 2018, from https://www.theguardian.com/football/2018/sep/22/crystal-palace-newcastle-premier-league-match-report

Corless, L. (2018, October 3). How Man City owner nearly bought a different Premier League club. *Manchester Evening News.* Retrieved October 3, 2018, from https://www.manchestereveningnews.co.uk/sport/football/football-news/man-city-sheikh-mansour-newcastle-15234596

Cox, D. (2016, July 4). Eric Burdon: Being a Newcastle United ballboy helped me get over a fear of crowds. *Chronicle Live.* Retrieved September 10, 2018, from https://www.chroniclelive.co.uk/whats-on/music-nightlife-news/eric-burdon-being-newcastle-united-11561755

Douglas, M. (2018, September 11). Why 'banned Kevin Keegan went to St James Park in disguise: First explosive revelations from new book. *Chronicle Live.* Retrieved September 15, 2018, from https://www.chroniclelive.co.uk/sport/football/football-news/banned-kevin-keegan-went-st-15137124

Edwards, L. (2014, December 20). Newcastle vs Sunderland: Why is the Tyne-Wear derby such a big deal? *The Telegraph.* Retrieved October 13,

2017, from http://www.telegraph.co.uk/sport/football/teams/newcastle-united/11306241/Newcastle-vs-Sunderland-Why-is-the-Tyne-Wear-derby-such-a-big-deal.html

Graham, H. (2017, April 14). Listen to Newcastle United's new version of The Blaydon Races - what do you think? *Chronicle Live*. Retrieved September 24, 2018, from https://www.chroniclelive.co.uk/news/north-east-news/listen-newcastle-uniteds-new-version-12895994

Guardian sport. (2018, September 17). Premier League: 10 talking points from the weekend's action. *The Guardian*. Retrieved September 17, 2018, from https://www.theguardian.com/football/blog/2018/sep/17/premier-league-10-talking-points-from-the-weekend-action

Guardian writers. (2018, September 30). Premier League: 10 talking points from the weekend's action. *The Guardian*. Retrieved October 1, 2018, from https://www.theguardian.com/football/blog/2018/oct/01/premier-league-10-talking-points-from-the-weekend-action-david-luiz-henderson-liverpool-chelsea

Hope, C. (2016, March 18). Newcastle vs Sunderland is more than local rivalry… this Tyne-Wear derby is the biggest in years with Premier League riches at stake. *Daily Mail*. Retrieved October 13, 2017, from http://www.dailymail.co.uk/sport/football/article-3499331/Newcastle-vs-Sunderland-local-rivalry-Tyne-Wear-derby-biggest-years-Premier-League-riches-stake.html

Imbo, W. (2018, May 17). End of Season Review: Newcastle United's Report Card From the 2017/18 Campaign. 90Min. Retrieved October 10, 2018, from https://www.90min.com/posts/6063123-end-of-season-review-newcastle-united-s-report-card-from-the-2017-18-campaign

McCarthy, A. (2017, May). Newcastle United fans stun Sunderland by flying banner over the Stadium of Light. *Give Me Sport*. Retrieved October 13, 2017, from http://www.givemesport.com/1052675-newcastle-united-fans-stun-sunderland-by-flying-banner-over-the-stadium-of-light

Meyers, B. (2018, September 16). Newcastle Boss Rafael Benitez Reveals Why Captain Jamaal Lescelles Had to be Subbed in Arsenal Loss. *90Min*. Retrieved September 12, 2018, from https://www.90min.com/posts/6172245-newcastle-boss-rafael-benitez-reveals-why-captain-jamaal-lascelles-had-to-be-subbed-in-arsenal-loss

Morton, D. (2018, October 24). It's Newcastle United's worst start to a season since 1898 - but what was the outcome back then? *Chronicle Live*. Retrieved October 27, 2018, from https://www.chroniclelive.co.uk/news/history/its-newcastle-uniteds-worst-start-15320874

Morton, D. (2016, March 16). Newcastle-Sunderland: 15 titanic Tyne-Wear derbies from across the decades. *Chronicle Live*. Retrieved October 13, 2017, from http://www.chroniclelive.co.uk/news/history/newcastle-sunderland-15-titanic-tyne-11050935

Stonehouse, R. (2005, October 22). A rivalry with roots in kings and coal. *The Guardian*. Retrieved October 13, 2017, from https://www.theguardian.com/football/2005/oct/23/newsstory.sport

Taylor, L. (2018, October 1). Dubravka calls for Newcastle players' meeting as winless start goes on. *The Guardian*. Retrieved October 1, 2018, from https://www.theguardian.com/football/2018/oct/01/dubravka-newcastle-players-meeting-winless-start?CMP=Share_iOSApp_Other

Taylor, L. (2018, September 21). The night Kevin Keegan sneaked back into Newcastle in a flat cap and overcoat. *The Guardian*. Retrieved September 21, 2018 from https://www.theguardian.com/football/2018/sep/21/the-night-kevin-keegan-sneaked-back-into-newcastle-in-a-flat-cap-and-overcoat

Taylor, L. (2018, July 20). Newcastle transfer impasse goes on as Benítez and Ashley play waiting game. *The Guardian*. Retrieved September 5, 2018, from https://www.theguardian.com/football/2018/jul/20/newcastle-impasse-benitez-ashley-waiting-game-signings

Taylor, L. (2017, August 25). Trouble on Tyne: Benítez and Ashley reach boiling point again at Newcastle. *The Guardian*. Retrieved September 4, 2018, from https://www.theguardian.com/football/blog/2017/aug/25/newcastle-united-rafael-benitez-mike-ashley-signings

Westby, M. (2016, March 20). Newcastle v Sunderland: How the Black Cats have dominated the past six Tyne-Wear derbies. *Sky Sports*. Retrieved October 13, 2017, from http://www.skysports.com/football/news/11662/10206068/newcastle-v-sunderland-how-the-black-cats-have-dominated-the-past-six-tyne-wear-derbies

Newcastle 2017/18 Premier League season review. (2018, May 13). *Sky Sports*. Retrieved September 22, 2018, from https://www.skysports.com/football/news/11678/11371201/newcastle-201718-premier-league-season-review

Programmes:

Newcastle v. Arsenal. (2018, September 15). *Official Matchday Programme, Issue 4.*

Websites:

History of our home: The story of St. James' Park. (n.d.). Retrieved October 13, 2017, from https://www.nufc.co.uk/club/history/history-of-our-home

Sunderland football club: record v Newcastle United. (n.d.). Retrieved October 13, 2017, from https://www.11v11.com/teams/sunderland/tab/opposingTeams/opposition/Newcastle%20United/

The post-war years: 1945 - 1969. (n.d.). Retrieved September 28, 2017, from https://www.nufc.co.uk/club/history/eras/the-post-war-years/

Southampton

Online Articles:

Cooper, T. (2012, February 14). Harry Redknapp's Top 10 Moments in Management. *Bleacher Report*. Retrieved October 11, 2017, from http://bleacherreport.com/articles/1063923

Culley, J. (2017, February 23). The sad story of Bobby Stokes, Southampton's forgotten Cup final hero. *The Independent*. Retrieved October 10, 2017, from http://www.independent.co.uk/sport/football/fa-league-cups/efl-cup-final-southampton-bobby-stokes-a7596371.html

Fay, S. (2017, April 2). Southampton FC: A club ruined by transfers. *Isportsweb*. Retrieved October 10, 2017, from http://www.isportsweb.com/2017/04/02/southampton-fc-club-ruined-transfers/

Fifield, D. (2018, September 17). Brighton peg back Southampton thanks to Glenn Murray's last-gasp penalty. *The Guardian*. Retrieved October 24, 2018, from https://www.theguardian.com/football/2018/sep/17/southampton-brighton-premier-league-match-report

Hughes, J. (2017, May 17). Ralph Krueger: Southampton do not have to sell their best players any more. *SB Nation*. Retrieved October 10, 2017, from https://stmarysmusings.sbnation.com/2017/5/17/15651812/ralph-krueger-southampton-sell-best-players-summer-transfer-talk-van-dijk-liverpool-chelsea

Hytner, D. (2017, February 25). Lawrie McMenemy: 'Southampton didn't have a cat in hell's chance'. *The Guardian*. Retrieved October 10, 2017, from https://www.theguardian.com/football/2017/feb/25/lawrie-mcmenemy-southampton-manchester-united-1976-fa-cup-final

Ley, J. (2001, November 25). Saints lift curse of St Mary's. *The Telegraph*. Retrieved October 11, 2017, from http://www.telegraph.co.uk/sport/football/teams/charlton-athletic/3017536/Saints-lift-curse-of-St-Marys.html

McCarthy, S. (2018, September 15). Southampton v Brighton: A 'derby' fans don't care about. *Brighton and Hove Independent*. Retrieved October 24, 2018, from https://www.brightonandhoveindependent.co.uk/sport/football/albion/southampton-v-brighton-a-derby-fans-don-t-care-about-scott-mccarthy-1-8634188

Sackley, N. (2010, February 9). Southampton v Portmouth: A history of rivalry. *BBC*. Retrieved October 11, 2017, from http://news.bbc.co.uk/local/hampshire/hi/people_and_places/history/newsid _8493000/8493003.stm

Wilson, J. (2017, January 24). Lawrie McMenemy: Southampton winning a cup 40 years on will create a memory that will never fade. *The Telegraph*. Retrieved October 11, 2017, from http://www.telegraph.co.uk/football/2017/01/24/lawrie-mcmenemy-southampton-winning-cup-40-years-will-create/

Pierre-Emile Hojbjerg is sent off as Southampton are beaten 2-1 by Leicester at St Mary's. (2018, August 25). *Daily Echo*. Retrieved October 24, 2018, from https://www.dailyecho.co.uk/sport/16599434.pierre-emile-hojbjerg-is-sent-off-as-southampton-are-beaten-2-1-by-leicester-at-st-marys/

Websites:

SFC Media. (2017, June 23). *Saints make history with LED floodlighting*. Retrieved October 11, 2017, from https://southamptonfc.com/news/2014-06-23/saints-make-history-with-led-floodlighting

Saints History. (n.d.). Retrieved October 10, 2017, from https://southamptonfc.com/saints-history/brief-history/2010-present

Southampton FC. (n.d.). Retrieved October 10, 2017, from http://www.footballhistory.org/club/southampton.html

Tottenham

Books:

Cloake, M., & Fisher, A. (2016). *A People's History of Tottenham Hotspur Football Club: How Spurs Fans Shaped the Identity of One of the World's Most Famous Clubs*. Sussex, UK.: Pitch Publishing.

Welch, J. (2015). *The Biography of Tottenham Hotspur*. Surrey, UK.: Vision Sports Publishing.

Online Articles:

Brown, L. (2017, May 15). Tottenham new stadium: Now White Hart Lane is over – here's what Spurs fans have to look forward to. *The Independent*. Retrieved July 18, 2017, from http://www.independent.co.uk/sport/football/premier-league/tottenham-new-stadium-pictures-video-when-will-it-open-cost-a7736456.html

Burt, H. (2018, May 17). End of Season Review: Tottenham Hotspur's Report Card From the 2017/18 Campaign. *90Min*. Retrieved September 10, 2018, from https://www.90min.com/posts/6062834-end-of-season-review-tottenham-hotspur-s-report-card-from-the-2017-18-campaign

Cloake, M. (2017, May 13). White Hart Lane has seen Diego Maradona and Johan Cruyff, but after 118 years Tottenham have outgrown it. *The Independent*. Retrieved July 21, 2017, from https://www.independent.co.uk/sport/football/premier-league/tottenham-hotspur-spurs-white-hart-lane-farewell-goodbye-diego-maradon-johan-cruyff-a7733846.html

Corless, L. (2017, April 8). Harry Kane returns from injury in Tottenham's win over Watford to boost Spurs' title chances. *Mirror*. Retrieved July 18, 2017, from http://www.mirror.co.uk/sport/football/news/harry-kane-named-tottenham-bench-10183026

Evans, G. (2018, October 29). Eagles-Jaguars Game at Wembley Messed Up the Field for Premier League Match. *Complex*. Retrieved October 26, 2018, from https://www.complex.com/sports/2018/10/nfl-game-at-wembley-messed-up-field-for-premier-league-match

Flint, A. (2015, December 29). 10 years later, did the Big Dig deliver? *The Boston Globe*. Retrieved September 22, 2018, from https://www.bostonglobe.com/magazine/2015/12/29/years-later-did-big-dig-deliver/tSb8PIMS4QJUETsMpA7SpI/story.html

Hughes, S. (2001, February 16). The crestfallen cockerels. *The Telegraph.* Retrieved July 20, 2017, from http://www.telegraph.co.uk/sport/football/teams/tottenham-hotspur/2998982/The-crestfallen-cockerels.html

Innes, R., & Jones, M. (2017, October 2). Revealed: When Harry Kane could break Alan Shearer's record as the Premier League's all-time top goalscorer. *Mirror.* Retrieved October 15, 2017, from http://www.mirror.co.uk/sport/row-zed/harry-kane-premier-league-record-10484052

Johnson, J & Wallace, S. (2018, September 20). Workers on Spurs' new White Hart Lane stadium 'off their heads on cocaine' during construction. *The Telegraph.* Retrieved September 20, 2018, from https://www.telegraph.co.uk/football/2018/09/20/spurs-stadium-workers-heads-cocaine-alcohol-construction/

Menno, D. (2017, June 20). Tottenham Hotspur will not be permitted to alter the pitch size at Wembley. *SB Nation.* Retrieved July 20, 2017, from https://cartilagefreecaptain.sbnation.com/2017/6/20/15837414/tottenham-hotspur-news-wembley-stadium-pitch-size-alteration-white-hart-lane-denied

Parry, R., & Richman, G. (2017, May 12). 118 pictures to celebrate Tottenham's 118 years at White Hart Lane. *The Standard.* Retrieved July 21, 2017, from https://www.standard.co.uk/sport/football/118-pictures-to-celebrate-tottenham-s-118-years-at-white-hart-lane-a3537081.html

Pitt-Brooke, J. (2017, May 12). The ten best games in Tottenham's history at White Hart Lane, from Gornik Zbraze to beating Arsenal. *The Independent.* Retrieved July 21, 2017, from http://www.independent.co.uk/sport/football/premier-league/tottenham-hotspur-10-best-games-in-the-history-of-white-hart-lane-farewell-a7732801.html

Quarrell, D. (2017, April 8). What is St. Totteringham's Day? When is it? How did it start? Will Tottenham finish above Arsenal? *Eurosport.* Retrieved July 18, 2017, from http://www.eurosport.com/football/premier-league/2016-2017/what-is-st-totteringham-s-day-when-is-it-how-did-it-start-will-tottenham-finish-above-arsenal_sto6122619/story.shtml

Reed, A. (2018, August 15). Why a new soccer stadium in England is disrupting the Premier League… and the NFL. *CNBC.* Retrieved September 10, 2018, from https://www.cnbc.com/2018/08/15/tottenham-hotspur-stadium-is-disrupting-the-premier-league-and-the-nfl.html

Taylor, D. (2018, October 3). Lionel Messi's masterclass gives Barcelona win over Tottenham. *The Guardian.* Retrieved September 19, 2018, from https://www.theguardian.com/football/2018/oct/03/tottenham-hotspur-barcelona-champions-league-match-report

Walker Robers, J. (2018, March, 8). Tottenham 1-2 Juventus (Agg:3-4):Gonzalo Higuain and Paulo Dybala stun Spurs at Wembley. *Sky Sports.* Retrieved September 20, 2018, from https://www.skysports.com/football/tottenham-vs-juventus/386496

Wainwright, O. (2017, June 15). Stadiums of the future: a revolution for the fan experience in sport. *The Guardian.* Retrieved July 18, 2017, from https://www.theguardian.com/sport/2017/jun/15/stadiums-future-holograms-drones-fan-experience?CMP=share_btn_tw

Wilson, J. (2018, November 11). Tottenham will continue to play 'home' games at Wembley this season but will cap attendances to 51,000. *The Telegraph.* Retrieved November 11, 2018, from https://www.telegraph.co.uk/football/2018/11/11/tottenham-will-continue-play-home-games-wembley-season-will/

Wilson, J. (2017, February 28). Special report: Jimmy Greaves pays tribute to Cristiano Rinaldo as Portuguese closes in on his magical mark. *The Telegraph.* Retrieved July 20, 2017, from http://www.telegraph.co.uk/football/2017/02/28/cristiano-ronaldo-can-match-magical-mark-set-jimmy-greaves/

Winters, M. (2018, August 9). Tottemham have failed to sign any new palyers this summer... making them the first Premier League club to add no new faces since the transfer window was first introduced. *Daily Mail Online.* Retrieved September 23, 2018, from https://www.dailymail.co.uk/sport/football/article-6044005/Tottenham-club-sign-no-one-transfer-window-used.html

Programmes:

Tottenham Hotspur v. Watford. (2017, April 8). *Official Matchday Programme.*

Websites:

Club Honours. (n.d.). Retrieved July 18, 2017, from http://m.tottenhamhotspur.com/history/honours/

England Football Online: Harry Kane Profile. (n.d.). Retrieved July 18, 2017, from http://www.englandfootballonline.com/TeamPlyrsBios/PlayersK/BioKaneHE.html

It Was 50 Years Ago Today – Our Historic Win in Europe... (2013, May 15). Retrieved July 20, 2017, from http://www.tottenhamhotspur.com/news/it-was-50-years-ago-today-our-historic-win-in-europe-150513/

Kinnear, Robertson, England and Mullery: 1967 FA Cup Heroes on Playing Chelsea at Wembley. (2017 April 19). Retrieved July 20, 2017, from http://www.tottenhamhotspur.com/news/club/history/joe-kinnear-mike-england-jimmy-robertson-1967-spurs-fa-cup-chelsea-190417/

NFL, Tottenham Hotspur ink 10-year stadium partnership. (2015, July 7). Retrieved July 18, 2017, from http://www.nfl.com/news/story/0ap3000000500560/article/nfl-tottenham-hotspur-ink-10year-stadium-partnership

The Bill Nicholson Years – Glory, Glory – 1960-74. (2014, October 25). Retrieved July 20, 2017, from http://www.tottenhamhotspur.com/news/bill-years-part-three-251014/

Tottenham Hotspur football club: record v Arsenal. (n.d.). Retrieved July 20, 2017, from https://www.11v11.com/teams/tottenham-hotspur/tab/opposingTeams/opposition/Arsenal/
History of White Hart Lane. (n.d.). Retrieved July 21, 2017, from http://www.tottenhamhotspur.com/the-stadium/history/

Tottenham new stadium capacity increases to 61559. (2017, May 5). *Sporting Life.* Retrieved July 18, 2017, from https://www.sportinglife.com/football/news/tottenham-capacity-to-increase/63544

Wembley Stadium Stats and Facts. (n.d.). Retrieved July 20, 2017, from http://www.wembleystadium.com/Press/Presspack/Stats-and-Facts

1961-Spurs' double year. (2001, May 10). *BBC.* Retrieved July 20, 2017, from http://news.bbc.co.uk/sport2/hi/football/fa_cup/1321969.stm

Watford

Online Articles:

Balague, G. (2018, September 14). Just like the Mourinho of old: How Garcia is working wonders at Watford. *Goal*. Retrieved October 24, 2018, from https://www.goal.com/en-ie/news/just-like-the-mourinho-of-old-how-gracia-is-working-wonders/176hs8qjtr1um1fqkdth0x3lqv

Burnton, S. (2017, January 12). Graham Taylor: a man of great achievements and small kindnesses. *The Guardian*. Retrieved August 22, 2017, from https://www.theguardian.com/football/blog/2017/jan/12/graham-taylor-watford-rescued-paul-mcgrath-aston-villa

Burt, J. (2018, September 13). Javi Gracia's secret to Watford's success: yoga, handshakes and £100 fines for being a minute late. *The Telegraph*. Retrieved September 13, 2018, from https://www.telegraph.co.uk/football/2018/09/13/watfords-secrets-success-yoga-firm-discipline/

Glendenning, B. (2013, May 27). Crystal Palace v Watford - as it happened. *The Guardian*. Retrieved September 13, 2018, from https://www.theguardian.com/football/2013/may/27/crystal-palace-watford-live-championship-play-off-final

Lawrence, A. (2018, September 15). Manchester United end Watford's streak thanks to Chris Smalling's swivel. *The Guardian*. Retrieved September 15, 2018, from https://www.theguardian.com/football/2018/sep/15/watford-manchester-united-premier-league-match-report

Logan, G. (2018, September 20). Meeting the real Troy Deeney - what is Watford striker like when the cameras stop? *BBC*. Retrieved September 20, 2018, from https://www.bbc.com/sport/football/45583138

O'Mara, O. (2015, August 14). Is the Watford-Luton Town Rivalry Still Alive? *The Last Word on Sports*. Retrieved August 21, 2017, from http://lastwordonsports.com/2015/08/14/watford-luton-town-rivalry-still-alive/

Press Association. (2016, December 27). Harry the Hornet was 'out of order' - Allardyce wants action against Mascot. *The* Guardian. Retrieved September 14, from https://www.theguardian.com/football/2016/dec/27/sam-allardyce-watford-mascot-harry-hornet-out-of-order

Price, O. (2006, July 1). 'Elton and I were almost like brothers': Graham Taylor on his football firsts and lasts. *The Guardian*. Retrieved August 22, 2017, from https://www.theguardian.com/football/2006/jul/02/1

Telegraph Sport. (2018, September 13). Everton face potential points deduction over Marco Silva 'tapping up' when he was at Watford. *The Telegraph*. Retrieved September 13, 2018, from https://www.telegraph.co.uk/football/2018/09/13/everton-face-potential-points-deduction-marco-silva-tapping/

Telegraph Sport. (2018, September 7). Watford's Javi Gracia named Premier League manager of the month for August. *The Telegraph*. Retrieved September 9, 2018, from https://www.telegraph.co.uk/football/2018/09/07/watfords-javi-gracia-named-premier-league-manager-month-august/

Graham Taylor funeral: Crowds gather for England boss. (2017, February 1). *BBC*. Retrieved August 22, 2017, from http://www.bbc.com/news/uk-england-beds-bucks-herts-38826311

Roy Hodgson hits out at Watford mascot Harry the Hornet over 'disgraceful' Zaha taunt. (2018, August 25). *Sky News*. Retrieved September 13, 2018, from https://news.sky.com/story/roy-hodgson-hits-out-at-watford-mascot-harry-the-hornet-over-disgraceful-zaha-taunt-11481395

Watford: All change for Harry the Hornet. (2018, September 13). *Watford Observer*. Retrieved September 13, 2018, from https://www.watfordobserver.co.uk/sport/16859543.watford-all-change-for-harry-the-hornet/

Programme:

Watford v. West Brom. (2017, April 4). *The Hornet, Official Matchday Programme*.

Websites:

Chandler, M. (2016, March 4). *Cult Heroes and Club Icons: The Legend of Luther Blissett*. Retrieved August 22, 2017, from https://www.thescore.com/news/974168

Harmer, A. (2016, April 2). *Greatest Player in Every Premier League Team's History*. Retrieved August 21, 2017, from http://www.thesportster.com/soccer/greatest-player-in-every-premier-league-teams-history/

Keith, J. (n.d.). *The Day Elton John Suffered An Attack of Anfield Nerves.* Retrieved August 22, 2017, from http://www.lfchistory.net/Articles/Article/3836

Slade, M. (n.d.). *Sir Elton John Stand Photo.* Retrieved August 22, 2017, from https://www.flickr.com/photos/127691193@N02/29235443696/

Video:

Jack M. (2015, April 26). *What a Day. What a team. Our team. Our day. Watford FC* [Video file]. Retrieved from https://www.youtube.com/watch?v=PHCtxfJm6Bk

West Ham

Articles:

Gibson, O. (2016, April 14). West Ham's Olympic Stadium contract: club to pay £2.5m per season in rent. *The Guardian.*

Hill, D. (2015, September 5). Blitz film: Myths, realities and how London took it. *The Guardian.*

Hytner, D. (2016, April 8). Arsene Wenger: West Ham have 'won the lottery' with Olympic Stadium. *The Guardian.*

Jewsbury, M. (2010, September 4). The Blitz: Survivors' Stories. *The Independent.*

Laville, S. (2002, April 1). Cockneys pay tribute to their beacon in the Blitz. *The Telegraph.*

The Gentle Author. (2012, June 26). There's more to cockney culture than being born in earshot of Bow Bells. *The Guardian.*

Online Articles:

Brown, O. (2009, August 28). West Ham v millwall: a history of how the rivalry started. *The Telegraph.* Retrieved September 19, 2017, from http://www.telegraph.co.uk/sport/football/teams/west-ham/6105500/West-Ham-v-Millwall-a-history-of-how-the-rivalry-started.html

Clough, M. (2018, August 1). West Ham building a team to watch after tumultuous move to London Stadium. *The Athletic.* Retrieved September 22, 2018, from https://theathletic.com/455296/2018/08/01/west-ham-building-a-team-to-watch-after-tumultuous-move-to-london-stadium/

Cooper, T. (2016, November 15). West Ham's New Stadium Experience is a Taste of What is Ahead for Tottenham. *The Bleacher Report.* Retrieved September 19, 2017, from http://bleacherreport.com/articles/2675917-west-hams-new-stadium-experiences-are-a-taste-of-what-is-ahead-for-tottenham

Daily Mail Reporter. (2009, August 26). 'Bring your bats… but don't bring your kids': Thugs planned West Ham v Millwall rampage on internet chatrooms. *Daily Mail.* Retrieved September 19, 2017, from http://www.dailymail.co.uk/news/article-1209028/Man-stabbed-West-Ham-Millwall-fans-brawl-outside-stadium.html

Fifield, D. (2018, September 24). West Ham need to secure Declan Rice's signature, says Pablo Zabaleta. *The Guardian.* Retrieved September 24, 2018, from https://www.theguardian.com/football/2018/sep/24/west-ham-need-secure-declan-rice-says-pablo-zabaleta

Fifield, D. (2018, September 23). Andriy Yarmolenko's horror miss leaves West Ham and Chelsea at impasse. *The Guardian.* Retrieved September 23, 2018, from https://www.theguardian.com/football/2018/sep/23/west-ham-united-chelsea-premier-league-match-report

James, S. (2018, October 26). Interview: Lukasz Fabianski: 'I needed to build myself up again almost from scratch'. *The Guardian.* Retrieved October 26, 2018, from https://www.theguardian.com/football/2018/oct/26/lukasz-fabianski-west-ham-most-saves-europe-arsenal-interview

Steinberg, J. (2018, September 26). Grady Diangana's debut doubles crowns West Ham's 8-0 rout of Macclesfield. *The Guardian.* Retrieved September 27, from https://www.theguardian.com/football/2018/sep/26/west-ham-macclesfield-carabao-cup-match-report

Steinberg, J. (2018, September 26). West Ham complain to TalkSport over Danny Murphy remarks on Declan Rice. *The Guardian.* Retrieved September 27, 2018, from https://www.theguardian.com/football/2018/sep/26/west-ham-complain-talksport-danny-murphy-declan-rice-agent-contract-football

Steinberg, J. (2018, September 22). Marko Arnautovic: 'I love Slaven Bilic but I let him down a little bit'. *The Guardian.* Retrieved September 24, 2018, from https://www.theguardian.com/football/2018/sep/22/marko-arnautovic-slaven-bilic-west-ham-david-moyes

Steinberg, J. (2018, September 15). Manuel Pellegrini ploughs on as anxiety grows at pointless West Ham. *The Guardian.* Retrieved September 15, 2018, from https://www.theguardian.com/football/blog/2018/sep/15/manuel-pellegrini-ploughs-on-at-anxious-west-ham

Steinberg, J. (2018, September 14). West Ham manager Manuel Pellegrini denies being angry over leaked teams. *The Guardian.* Retrieved September 15, from https://www.theguardian.com/football/2018/sep/14/west-ham-manuel-pellegrini

Wilson, P. (2018, September 9). Manuel Pellegrini must convince West Ham he's not yesterday's man. *The Guardian.* Retrieved September 9, 2018, from https://www.theguardian.com/football/blog/2018/sep/09/manuel-pellegrini-must-convince-west-ham-hes-not-yesterdays-man

The 10 biggest rivalries in London football. (2016, January 21). *The Telegraph*. Retrieved September 19, 2017, from http://www.telegraph.co.uk/football/2016/02/08/the-10-biggest-rivalries-in-london-football/millwall-and-west-ham-fans/

Programmes:

Pritchard, R. (Ed.). (2018, September 23) West Ham United v. Chelsea. *Official Matchday Programme, Issue 3*.

Websites:

Club History: 80s. (2017, August 27). Retrieved September 22, 2017, from https://www.whufc.com/club/history/club-history/1980/80s

Ranked! The 30 Most Hated Ever Teams in British Football: 30-21. (2017, April 12). *Four Four Two*. Retrieved September 22, 2017, from https://www.fourfourtwo.com/features/ranked-30-most-hated-ever-teams-british-football-30-21

Videos:

1usainBOLT. (2009, August 27). *West Ham Millwall fighting 2009* [Video file]. Retrieved from https://www.youtube.com/watch?v=lFQV1djN8eg

Wolverhampton

Online Articles:

Ste. (2011, October 13). Wolves Fans On The Black Country Derby. *Daisy Cutter*. Retrieved October 24, 2018, from http://www.thedaisycutter.co.uk/2011/10/wolves-fans-on-the-black-country-derby/

Mayhem as derby fans clash. (2007, Jan 29). *Express & Star*. Retrieved October 24, 2018, from https://www.expressandstar.com/sport/2007/01/29/mayhem-as-derby-fans-clash/

Wolves 0-3 West Brom. (2007, Jan 28). *BBC*. Retrieved October 24, 2018, from http://news.bbc.co.uk/sport2/hi/football/fa_cup/6282191.stm

Programmes:

Ridgeway, M. (Ed.). (2018, September 25) Wolves v. Leicester City: Carabao Cup. *Official Matchday Programme, Issue 4.*

Other:

Wolves Museum. (2018) Wolverhampton, UK: Molineux Stadium.